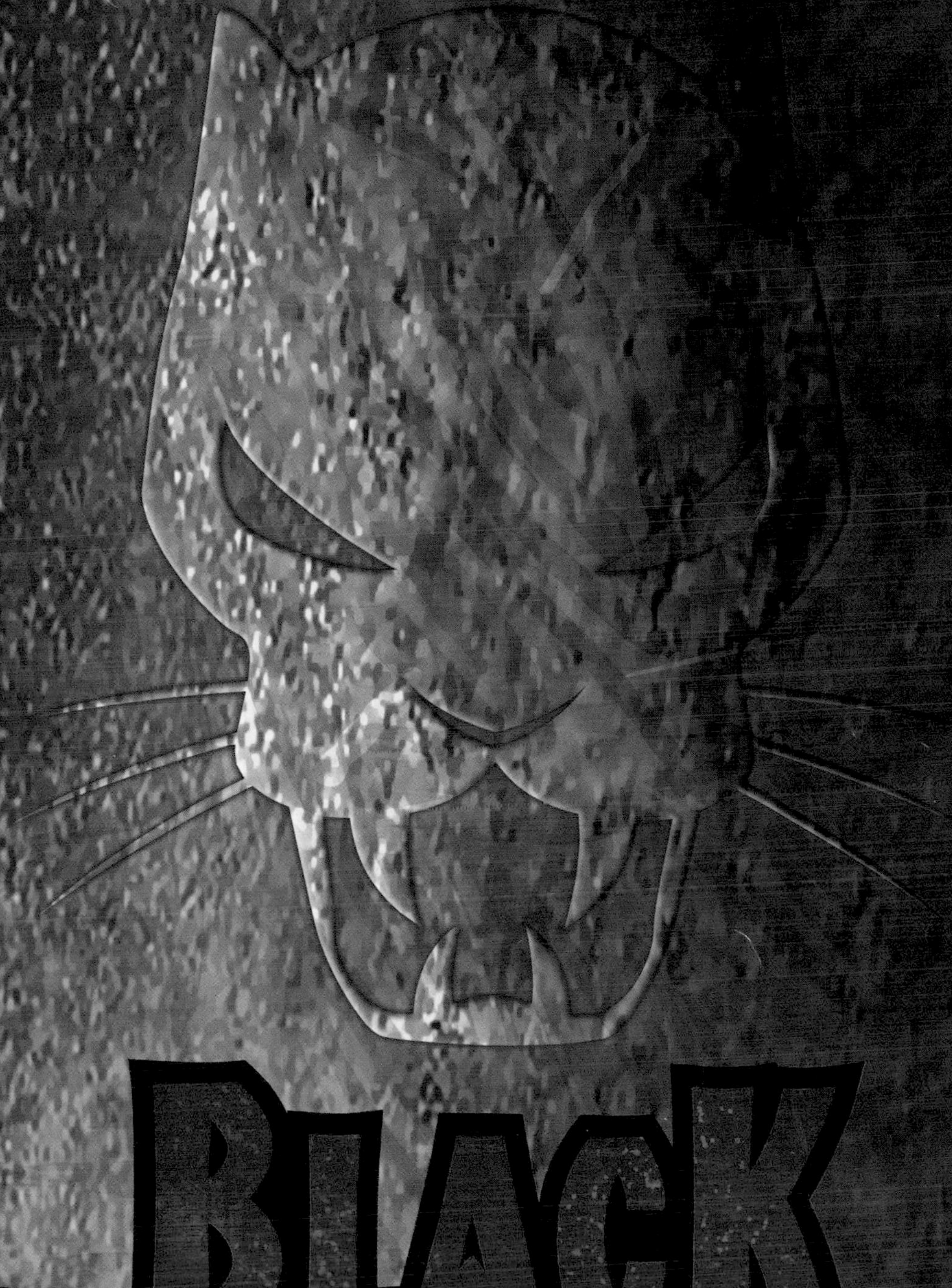

BLACK PANTHER

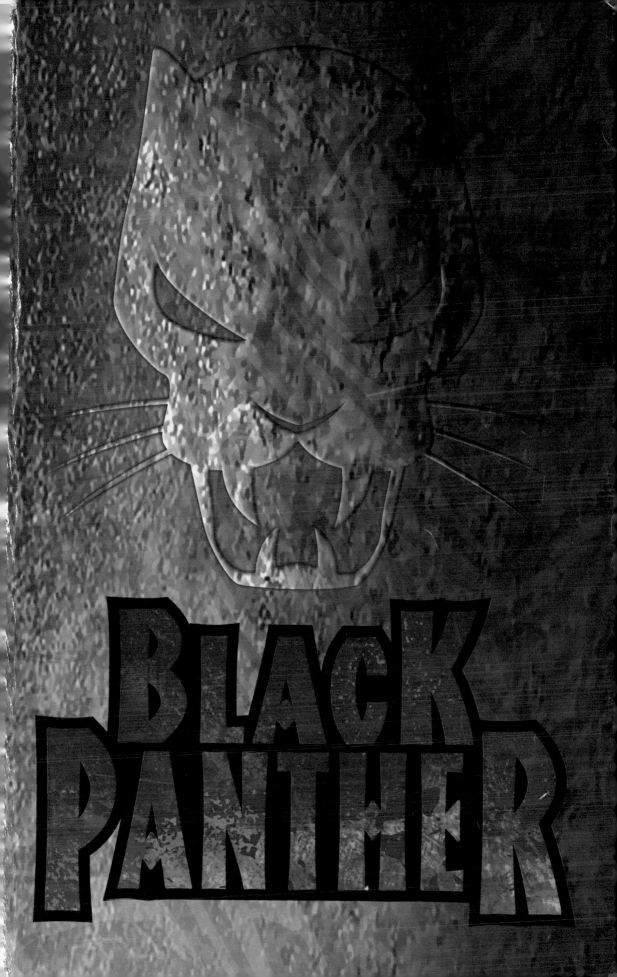

WRITER: **REGINALD HUDLIN**

PENCILER: **JOHN ROMITA JR.**

INKER: **KLAUS JANSON**

COLORS: **DEAN WHITE**

LETTERS: **VC's RANDY GENTILE & CHRIS ELIOPOULOS**

COVER ARTISTS: **JOHN ROMITA JR., ESAD RIBIC, FRANK CHO, JOHN CASSADAY, TERRY DODSON & KAARE ANDREWS**

ASSISTANT EDITOR: **CORY SEDLMEIER**
EDITOR: **AXEL ALONSO**

COLLECTION EDITOR: **JENNIFER GRÜNWALD**
ASSISTANT EDITOR: **MICHAEL SHORT**
SENIOR EDITOR, SPECIAL PROJECTS: **JEFF YOUNGQUIST**
DIRECTOR OF SALES: **DAVID GABRIEL**
PRODUCTION: **JERRY KALINOWSKI**
BOOK DESIGNER: **JEOF VITA**
CREATIVE DIRECTOR: **TOM MARVELLI**

EDITOR-IN-CHIEF: **JOE QUESADA**
PUBLISHER: **DAN BUCKLEY**

WHO IS THE
BLACK PANTHER

BLACK PANTHER: WHO IS THE BLACK PANTHER. Contains material originally published in magazine form as BLACK PANTHER #1-6. First printing 2005. ISBN# 0-7851-1748-2. Published by MARVEL COMICS, a division of MARVEL ENTERTAINMENT GROUP, INC. OFFICE OF PUBLICATION: 417 5th Avenue, New York, NY 10016. Copyright © 2005 Marvel Characters, Inc. All rights reserved. $21.99 per copy in the U.S. and $35.25 in Canada (GST #R127032852); Canadian Agreement #40668537. All characters featured in this issue and the distinctive names and likenesses thereof, and all related indicia are trademarks of Marvel Characters, Inc. No similarity between any of the names, characters, persons, and/or institutions in this magazine with those of any living or dead person or institution is intended, and any such similarity which may exist is purely coincidental. **Printed In Canada.** AVI ARAD, Chief Creative Officer; ALAN FINE, President & CEO Of Toy Biz and Marvel Publishing; DAVID BOGART, VP of Editorial Operations; DAN CARR, Director of Production; ELAINE CALLENDER, Director of Manufacturing; JUSTIN F. GABRIE, Managing Editor; STAN LEE, Chairman Emeritus. For information regarding advertising in Marvel Comics or on Marvel.com, please contact Joe Maimone, Advertising Director, at jmaimone@marvel.com or 212-576-8534.

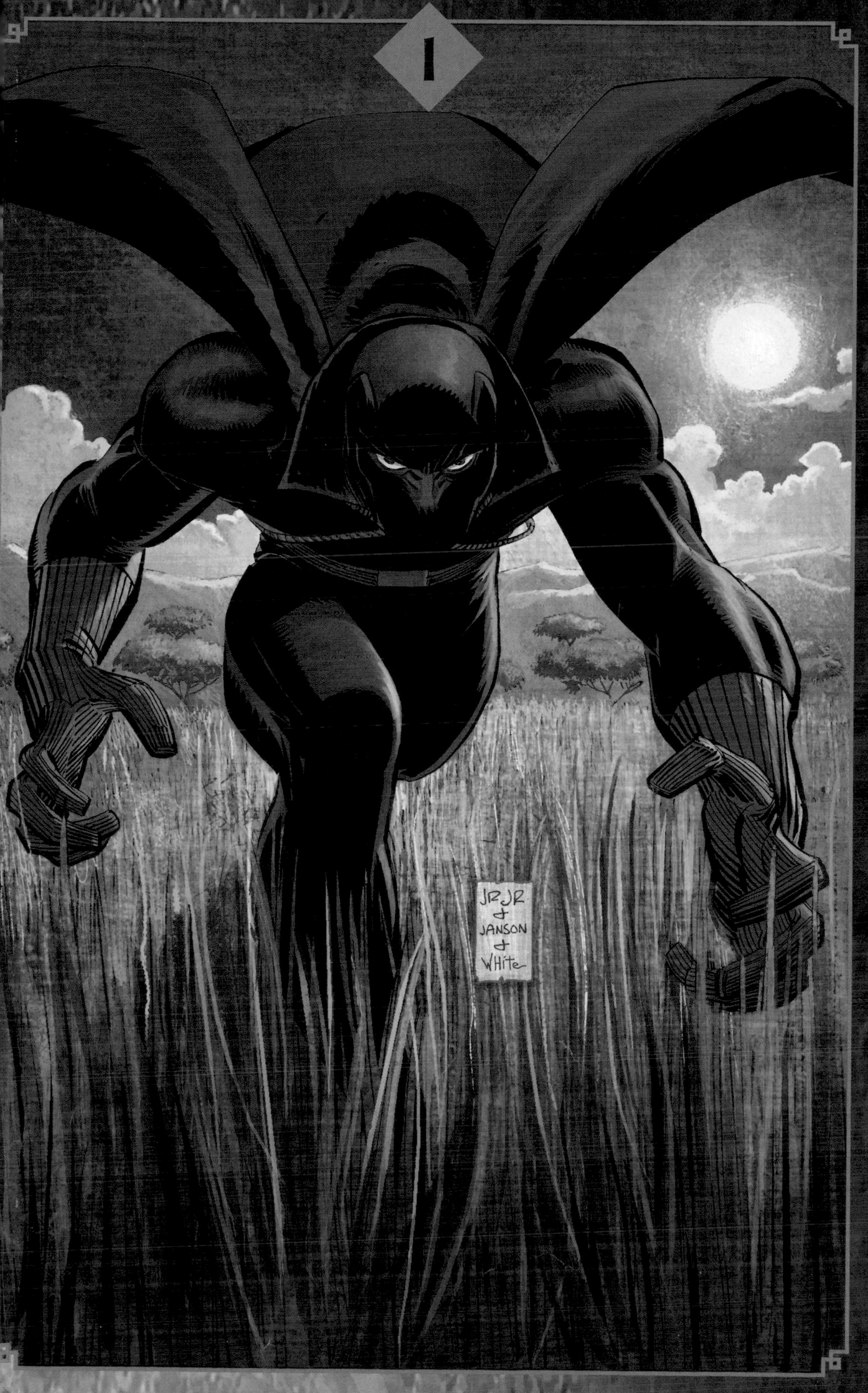
1
JRJR
&
JANSON
&
WHITE

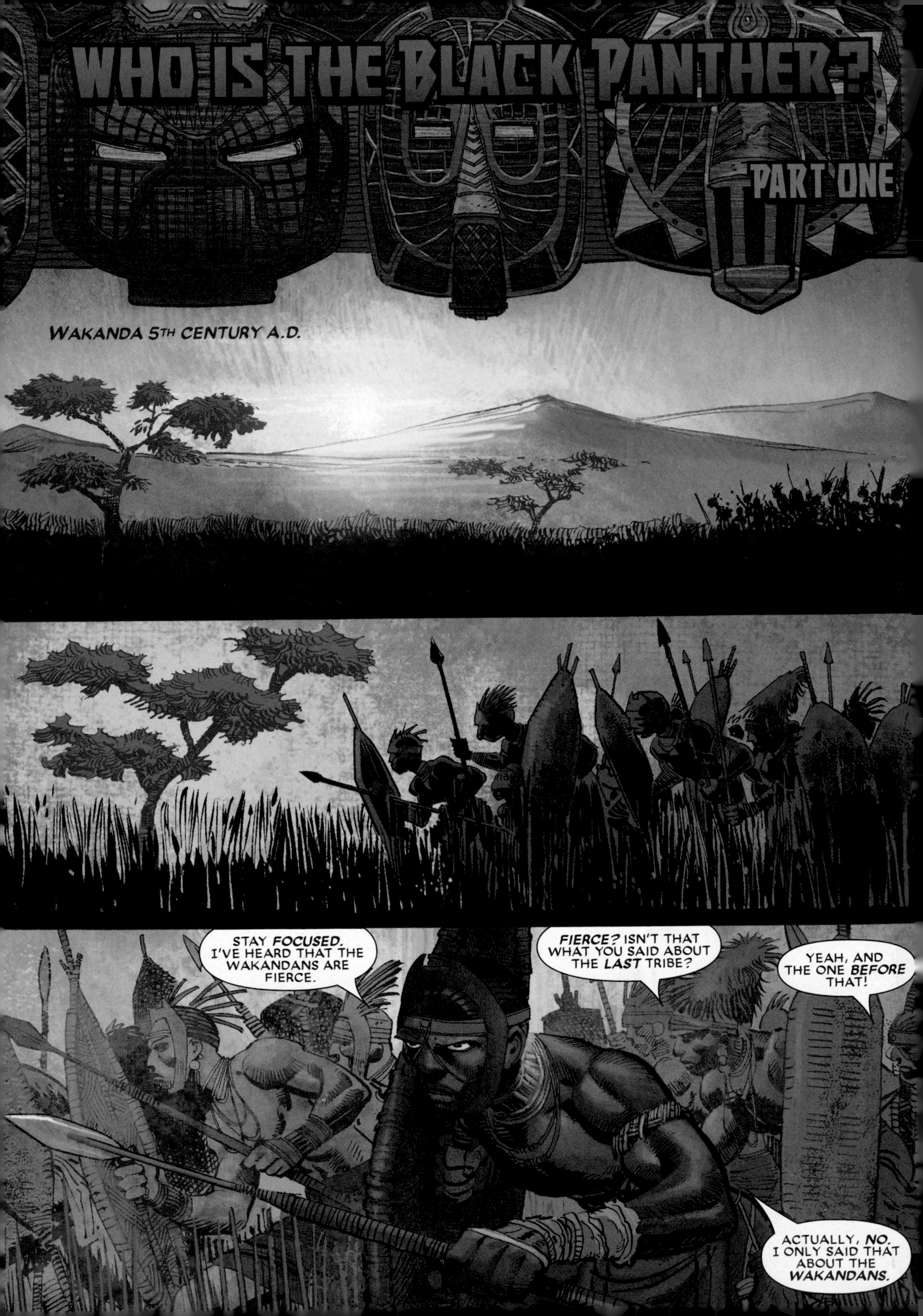
WHO IS THE BLACK PANTHER?
PART ONE
WAKANDA 5TH CENTURY A.D.
STAY FOCUSED. I'VE HEARD THAT THE WAKANDANS ARE FIERCE.
FIERCE? ISN'T THAT WHAT YOU SAID ABOUT THE LAST TRIBE?
YEAH, AND THE ONE BEFORE THAT!
ACTUALLY, NO. I ONLY SAID THAT ABOUT THE WAKANDANS.

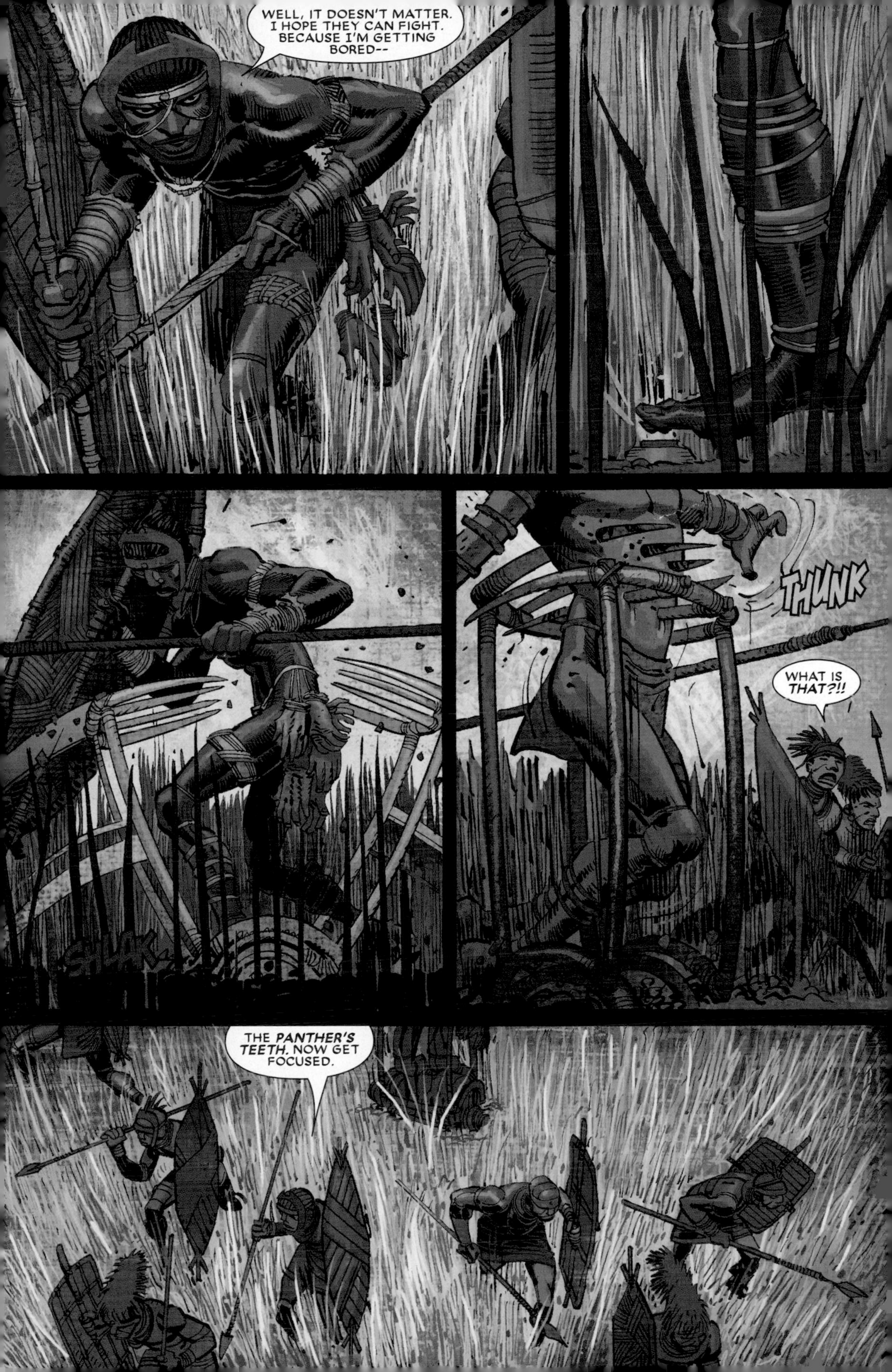
WELL, IT DOESN'T MATTER. I HOPE THEY CAN FIGHT. BECAUSE I'M GETTING BORED--
THUNK
WHAT IS *THAT?!!*
THE *PANTHER'S TEETH.* NOW GET FOCUSED.

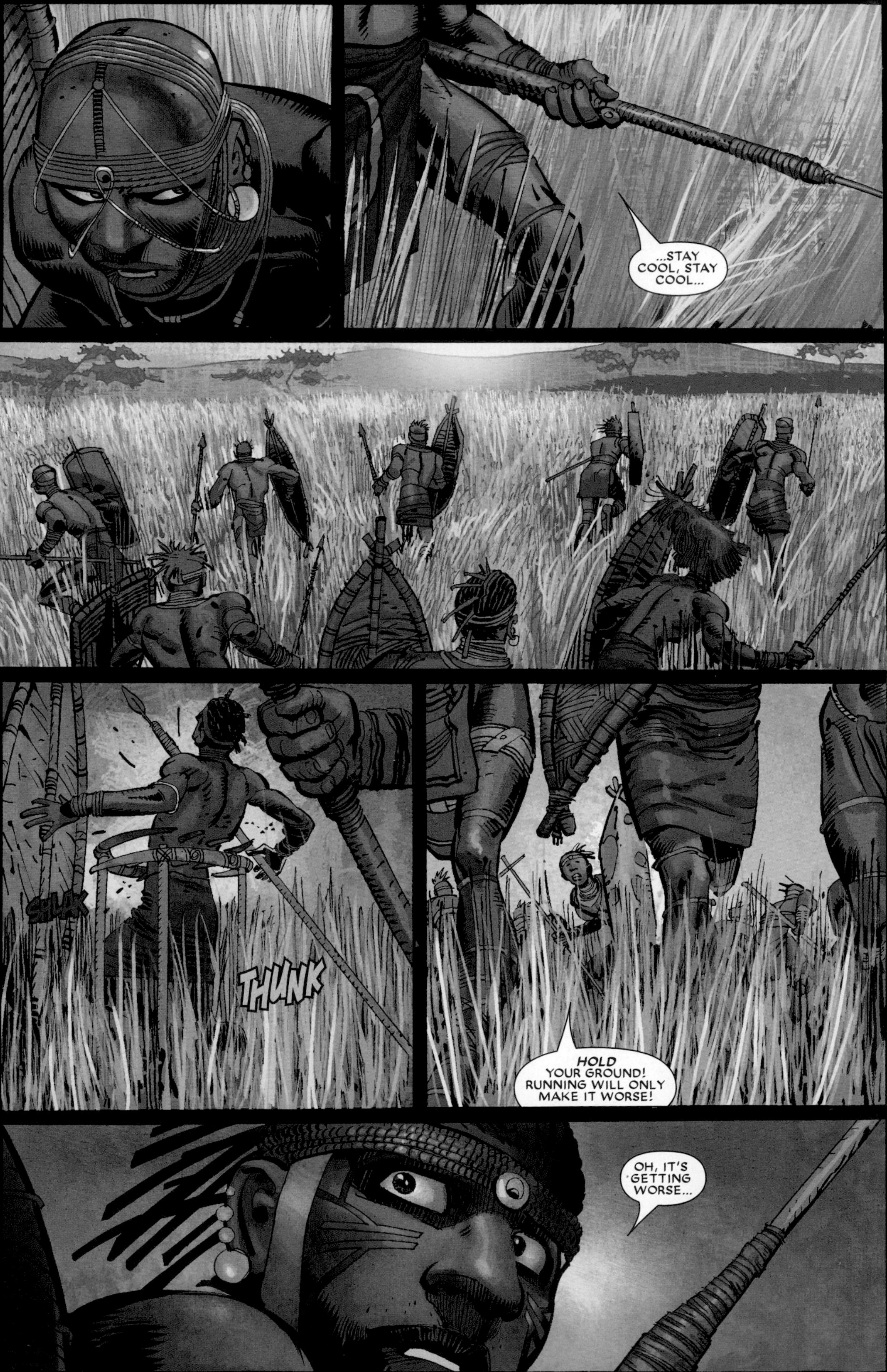
...STAY COOL, STAY COOL...
THUNK
HOLD YOUR GROUND! RUNNING WILL ONLY MAKE IT WORSE!
OH, IT'S GETTING WORSE...

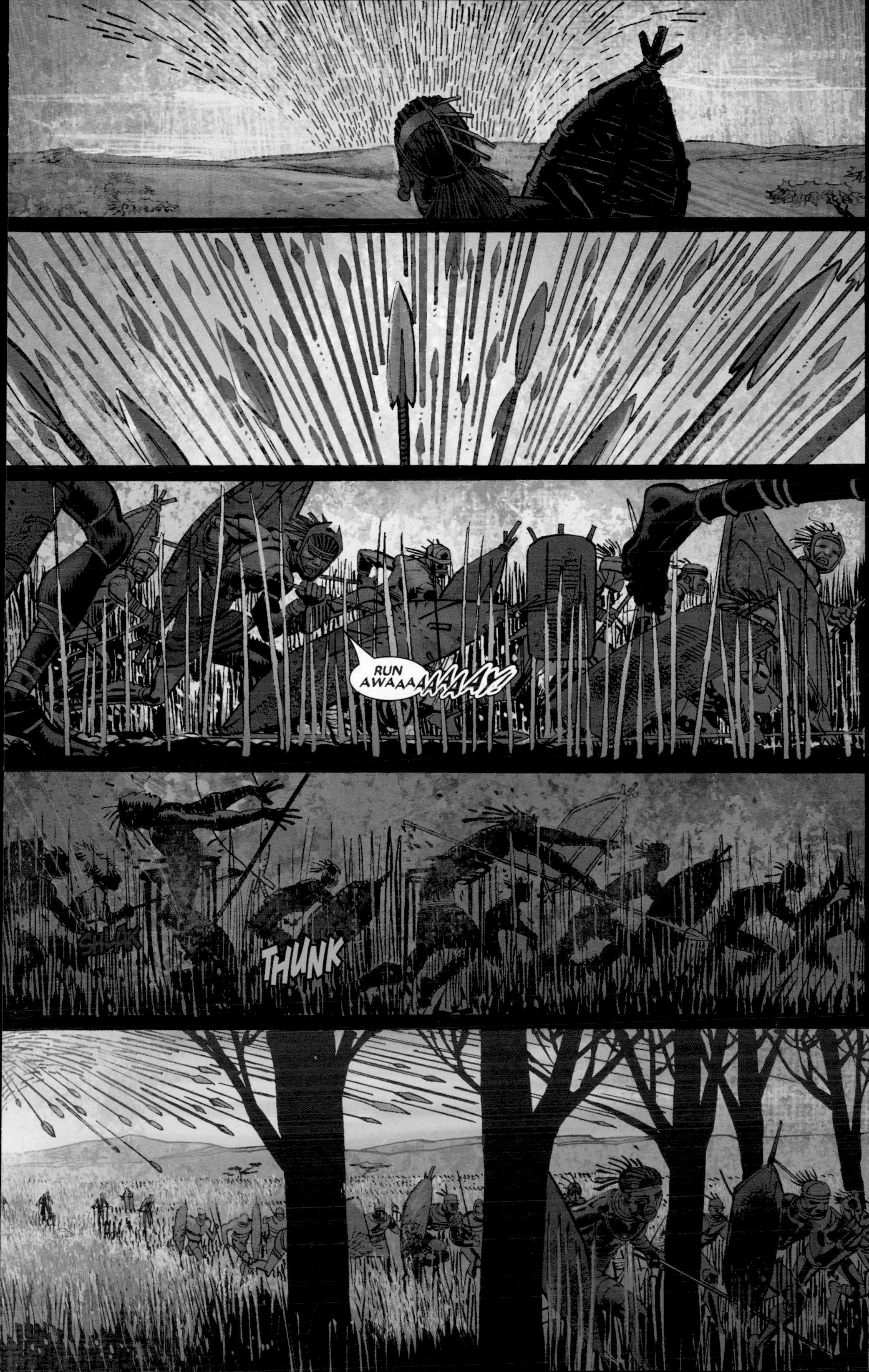
RUN AWAAAAAAAAY!
THUNK

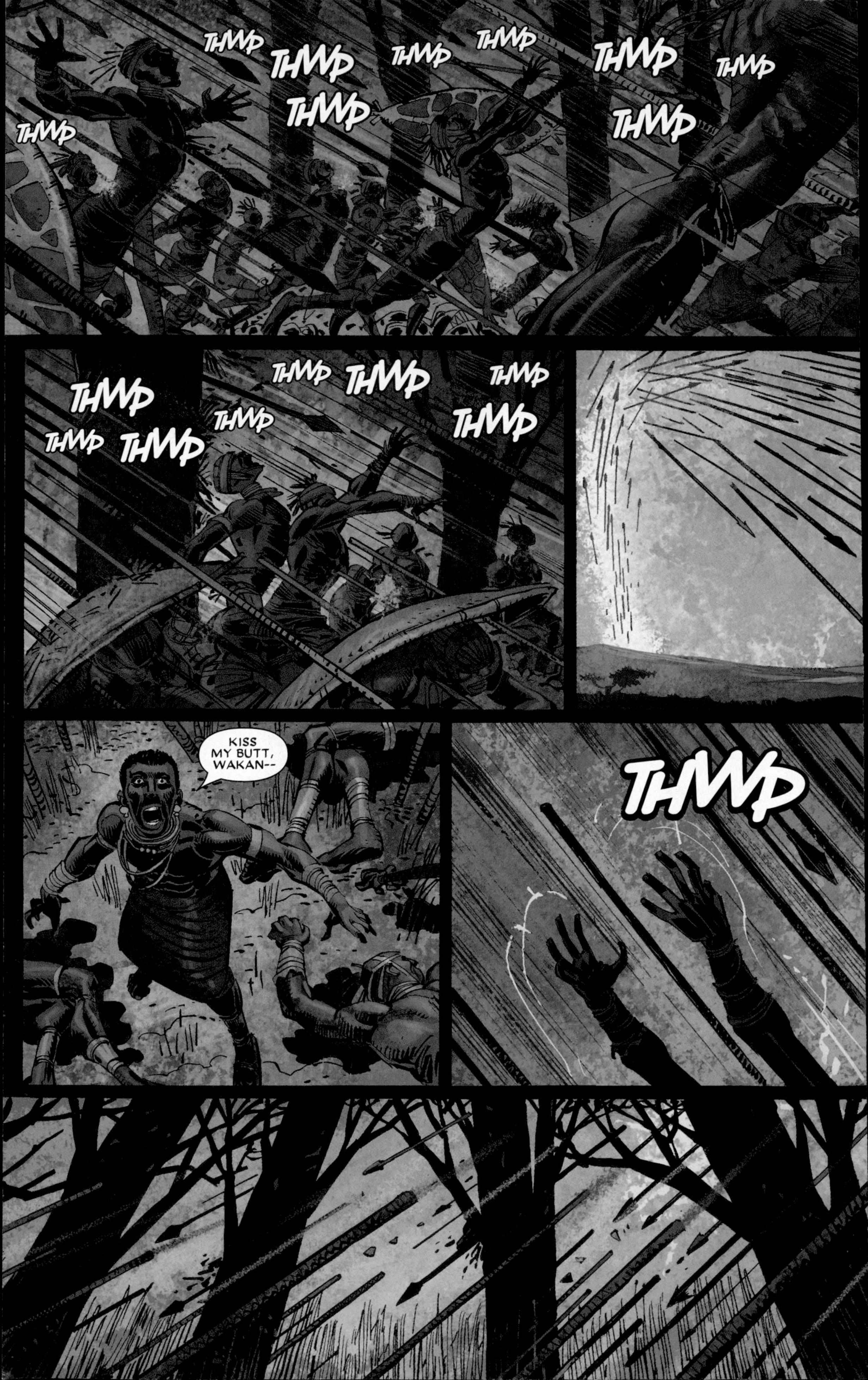
THWP
THWP
THWP
THWP
THWP
THWP
THWP
THWP
THWP
THWP
THWP
THWP
THWP
THWP
THWP
THWP
THWP
KISS MY BUTT, WAKAN--
THWP

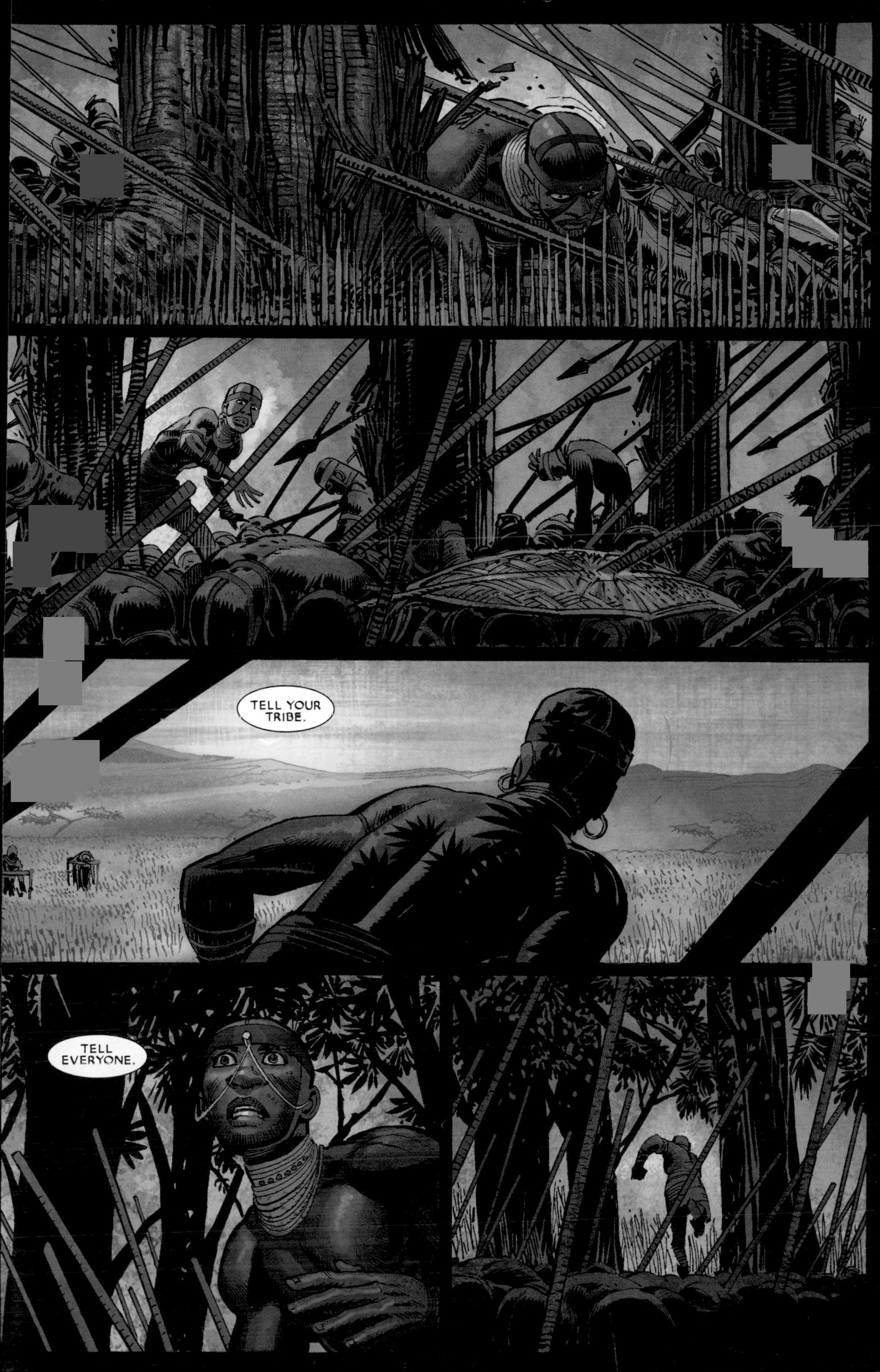
TELL YOUR TRIBE.
TELL EVERYONE.

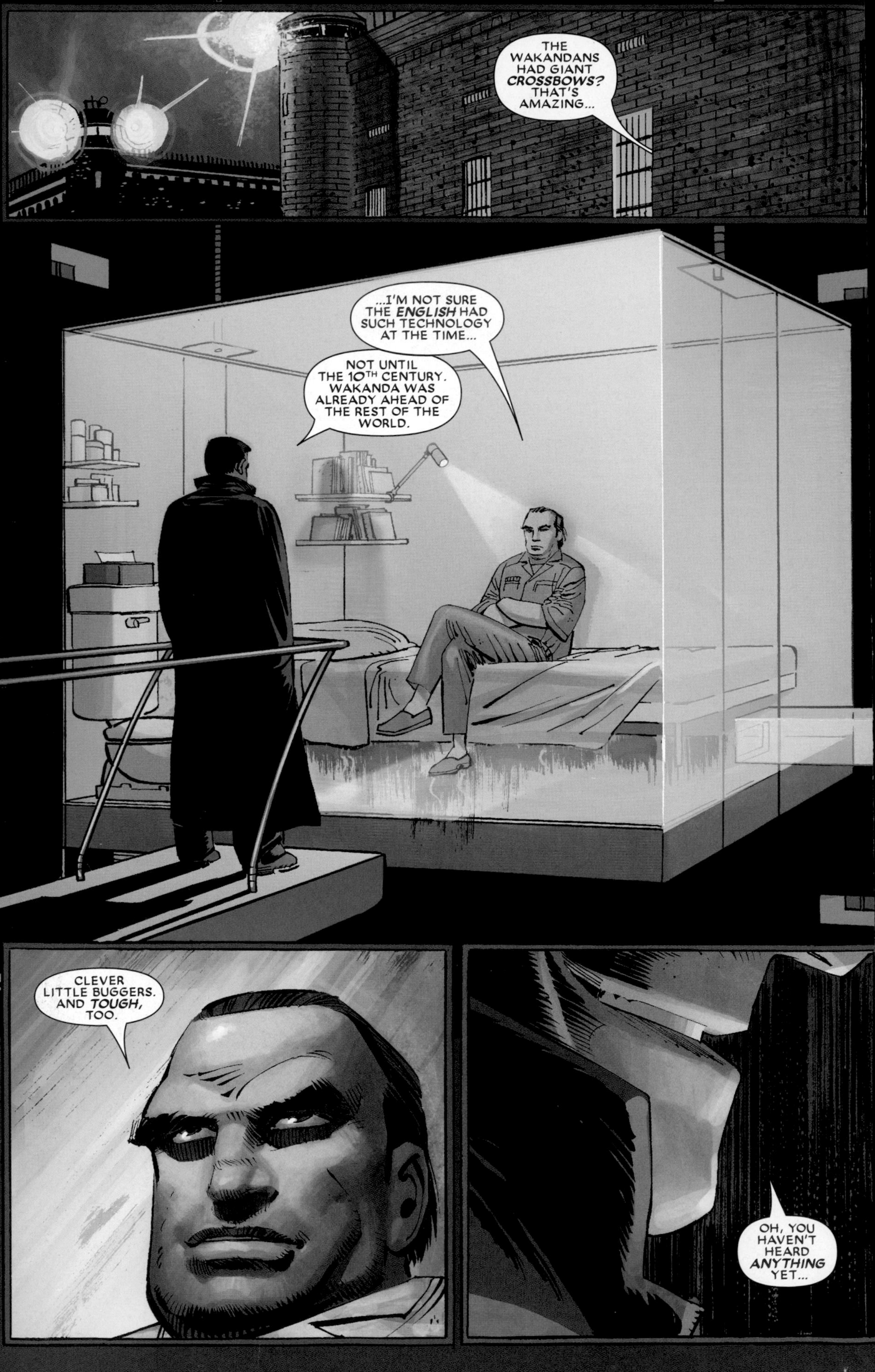
THE WAKANDANS HAD GIANT *CROSSBOWS?* THAT'S AMAZING...
...I'M NOT SURE THE *ENGLISH* HAD SUCH TECHNOLOGY AT THE TIME...
NOT UNTIL THE 10TH CENTURY. WAKANDA WAS ALREADY AHEAD OF THE REST OF THE WORLD.
CLEVER LITTLE BUGGERS. AND *TOUGH,* TOO.
OH, YOU HAVEN'T HEARD *ANYTHING* YET...

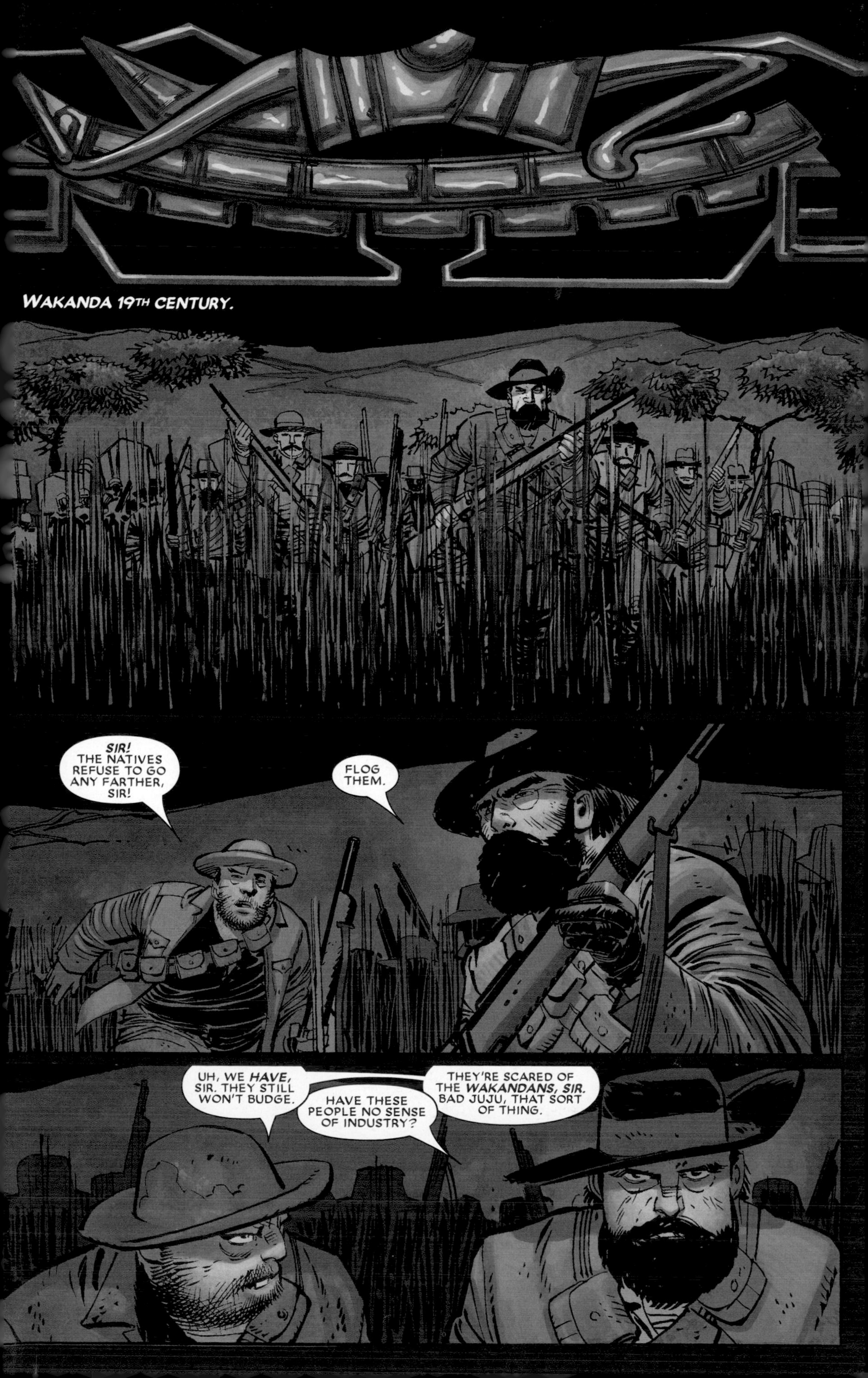
WAKANDA 19TH CENTURY.
SIR! THE NATIVES REFUSE TO GO ANY FARTHER, SIR!
FLOG THEM.
UH, WE HAVE, SIR. THEY STILL WON'T BUDGE.
HAVE THESE PEOPLE NO SENSE OF INDUSTRY?
THEY'RE SCARED OF THE WAKANDANS, SIR. BAD JUJU, THAT SORT OF THING.

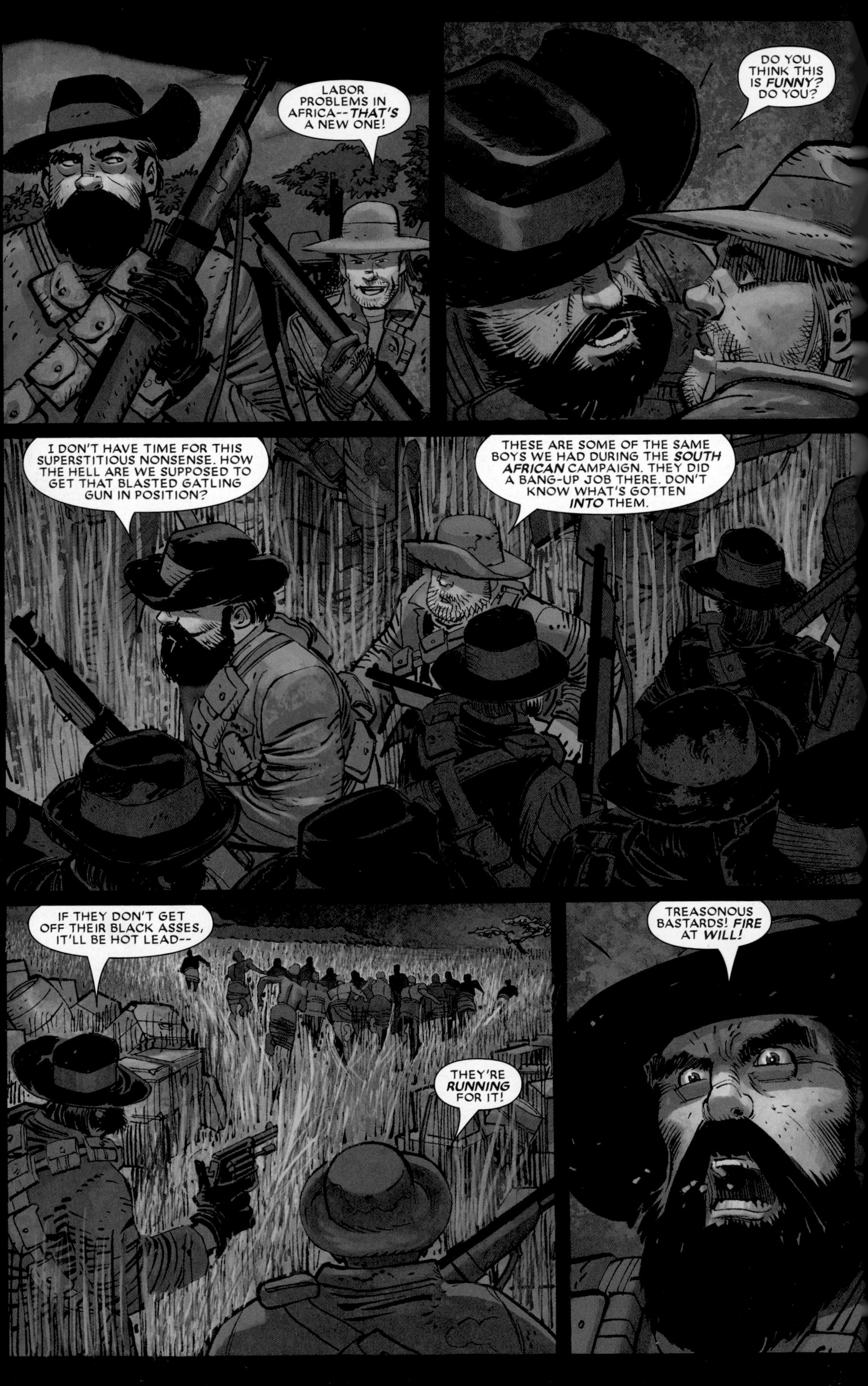
LABOR PROBLEMS IN AFRICA--THAT'S A NEW ONE!
DO YOU THINK THIS IS FUNNY? DO YOU?
I DON'T HAVE TIME FOR THIS SUPERSTITIOUS NONSENSE. HOW THE HELL ARE WE SUPPOSED TO GET THAT BLASTED GATLING GUN IN POSITION?
THESE ARE SOME OF THE SAME BOYS WE HAD DURING THE SOUTH AFRICAN CAMPAIGN. THEY DID A BANG-UP JOB THERE. DON'T KNOW WHAT'S GOTTEN INTO THEM.
IF THEY DON'T GET OFF THEIR BLACK ASSES, IT'LL BE HOT LEAD--
THEY'RE RUNNING FOR IT!
TREASONOUS BASTARDS! FIRE AT WILL!

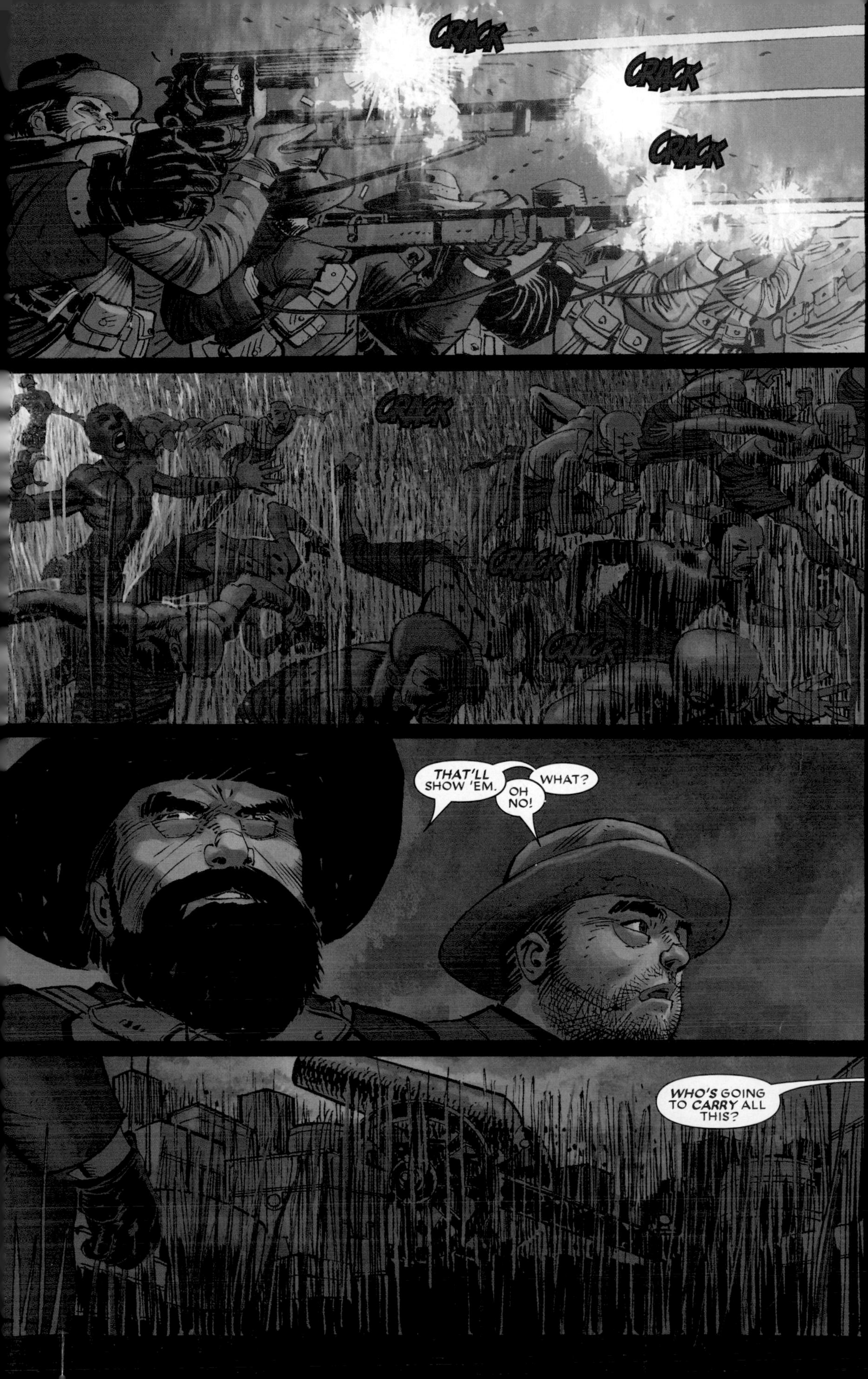
CRACK
CRACK
CRACK
CRACK
CRACK
CRACK
THAT'LL SHOW 'EM.
WHAT?
OH NO!
WHO'S GOING TO CARRY ALL THIS?

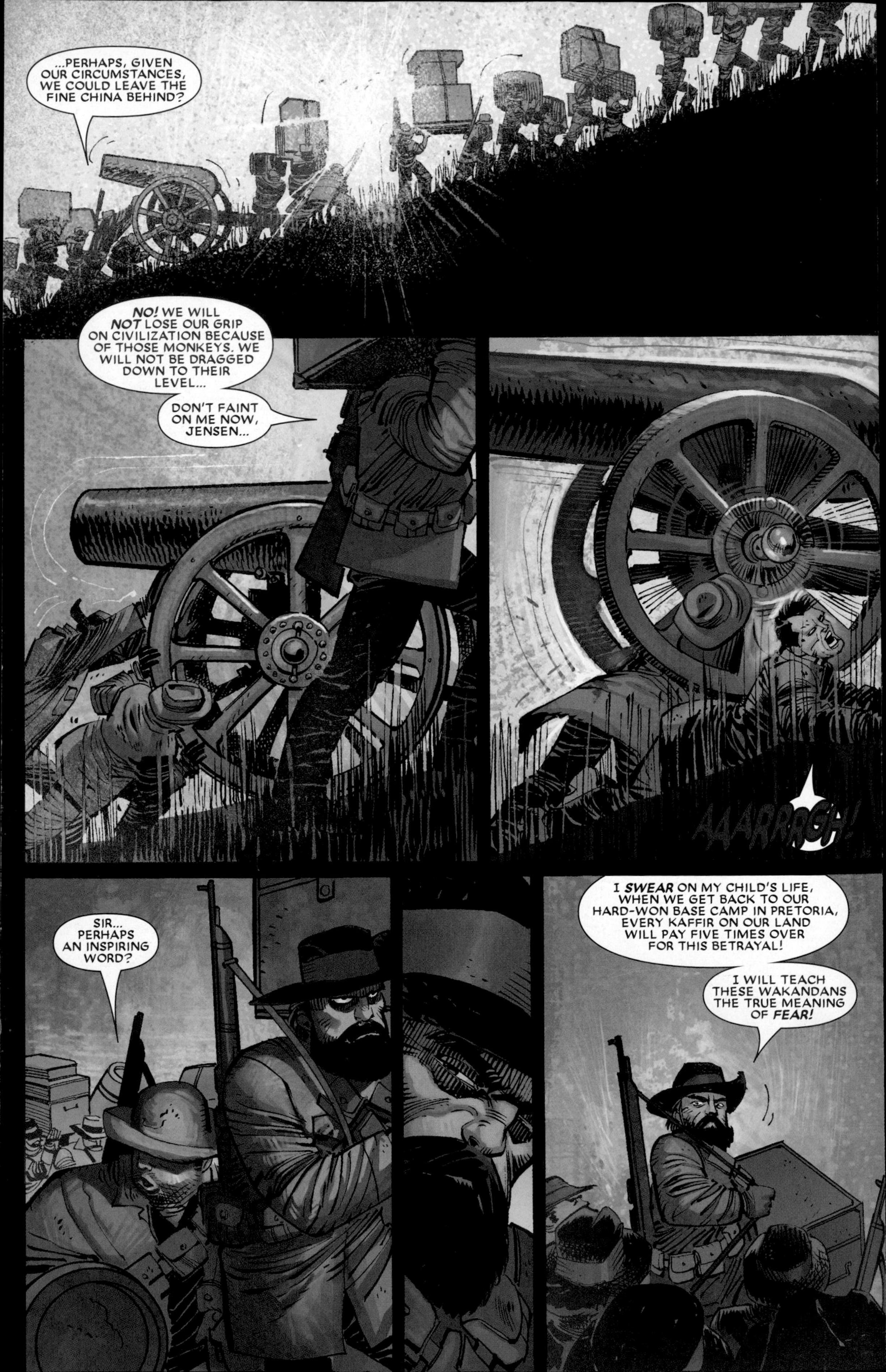

...PERHAPS, GIVEN OUR CIRCUMSTANCES, WE COULD LEAVE THE FINE CHINA BEHIND?
NO! WE WILL NOT LOSE OUR GRIP ON CIVILIZATION BECAUSE OF THOSE MONKEYS. WE WILL NOT BE DRAGGED DOWN TO THEIR LEVEL...
DON'T FAINT ON ME NOW, JENSEN...
AAARRRGH!
SIR... PERHAPS AN INSPIRING WORD?
I SWEAR ON MY CHILD'S LIFE, WHEN WE GET BACK TO OUR HARD-WON BASE CAMP IN PRETORIA, EVERY KAFFIR ON OUR LAND WILL PAY FIVE TIMES OVER FOR THIS BETRAYAL!
I WILL TEACH THESE WAKANDANS THE TRUE MEANING OF FEAR!

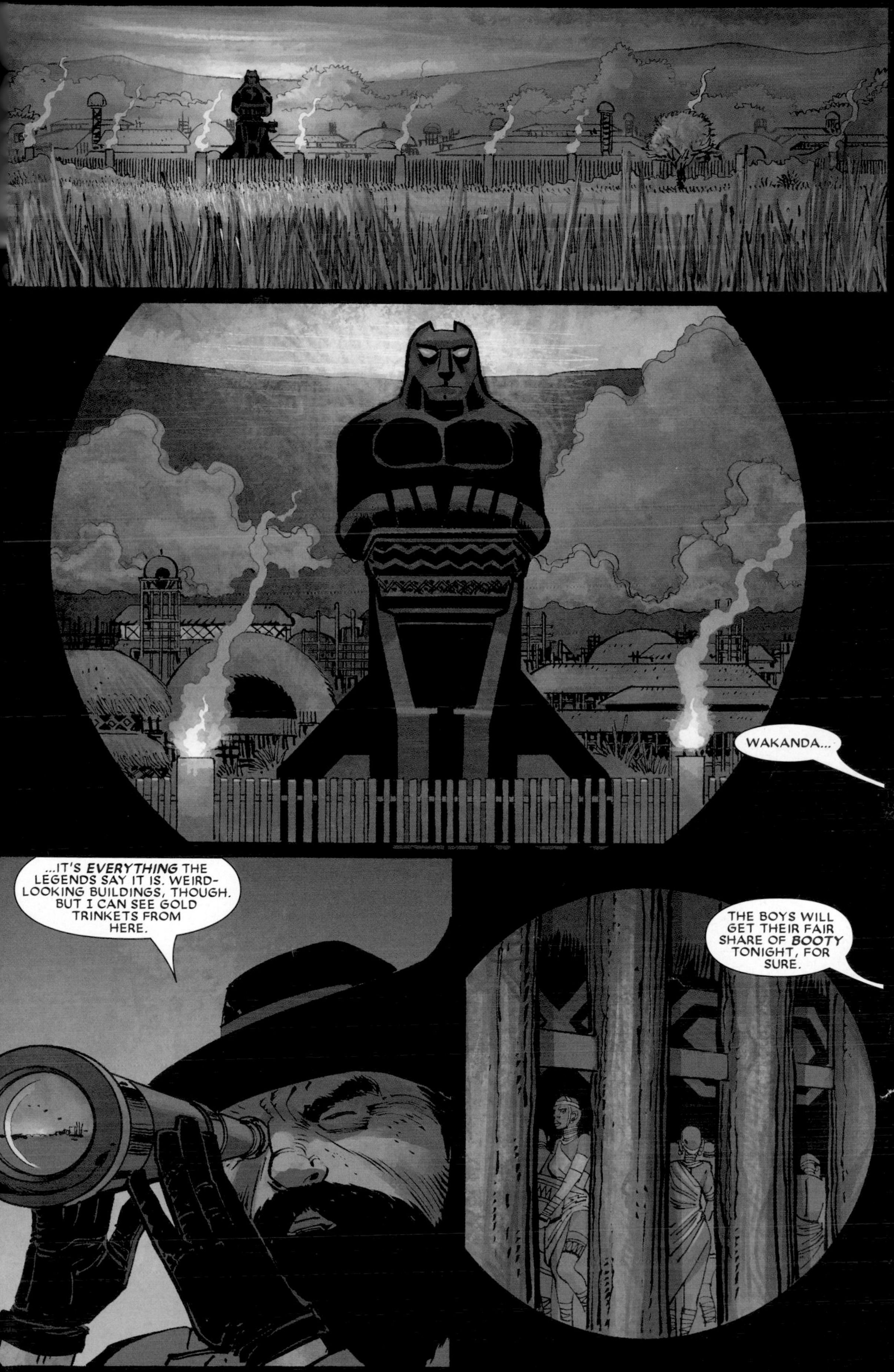
WAKANDA...
...IT'S EVERYTHING THE LEGENDS SAY IT IS. WEIRD-LOOKING BUILDINGS, THOUGH. BUT I CAN SEE GOLD TRINKETS FROM HERE.
THE BOYS WILL GET THEIR FAIR SHARE OF BOOTY TONIGHT, FOR SURE.

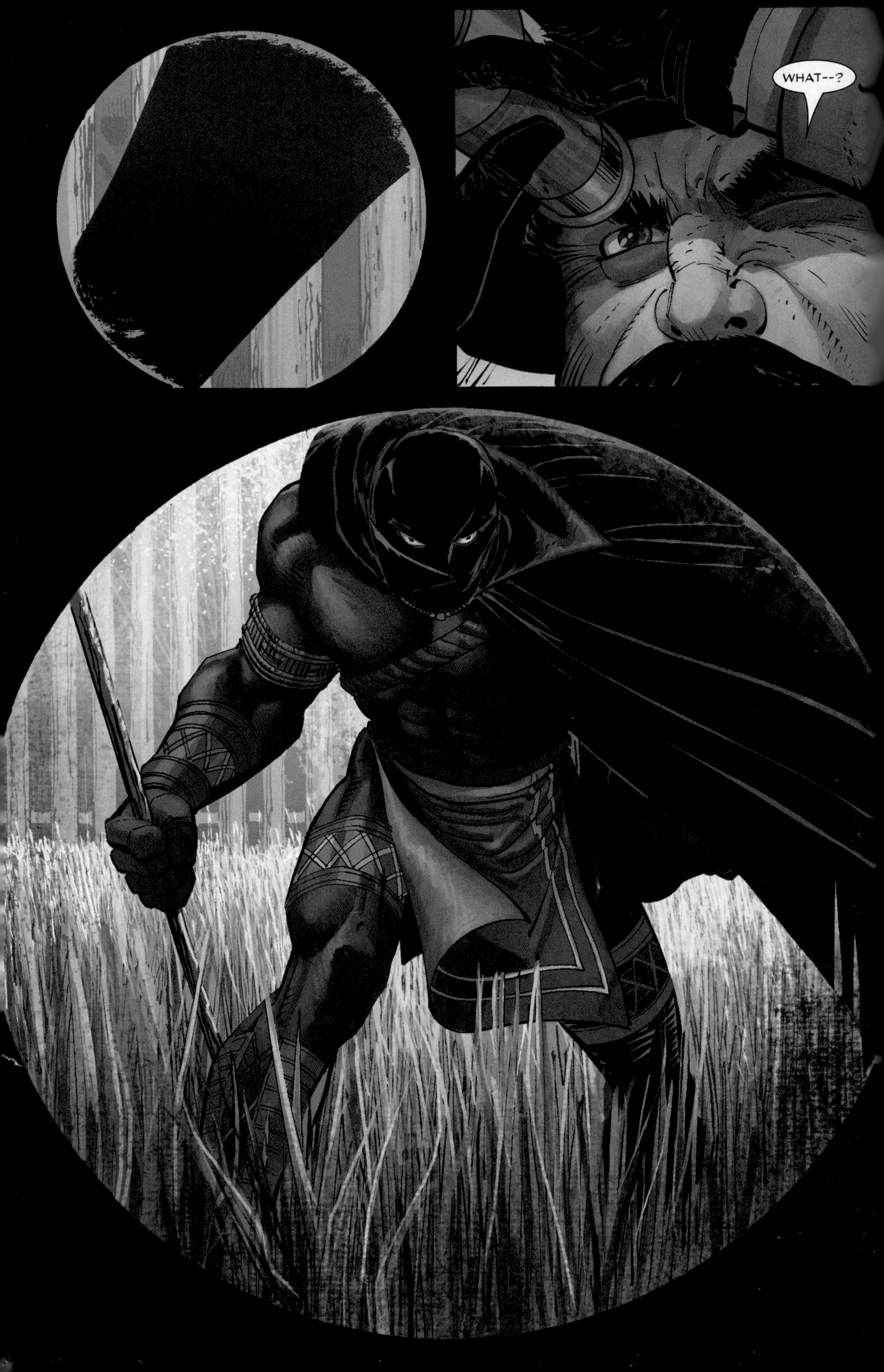
WHAT--?

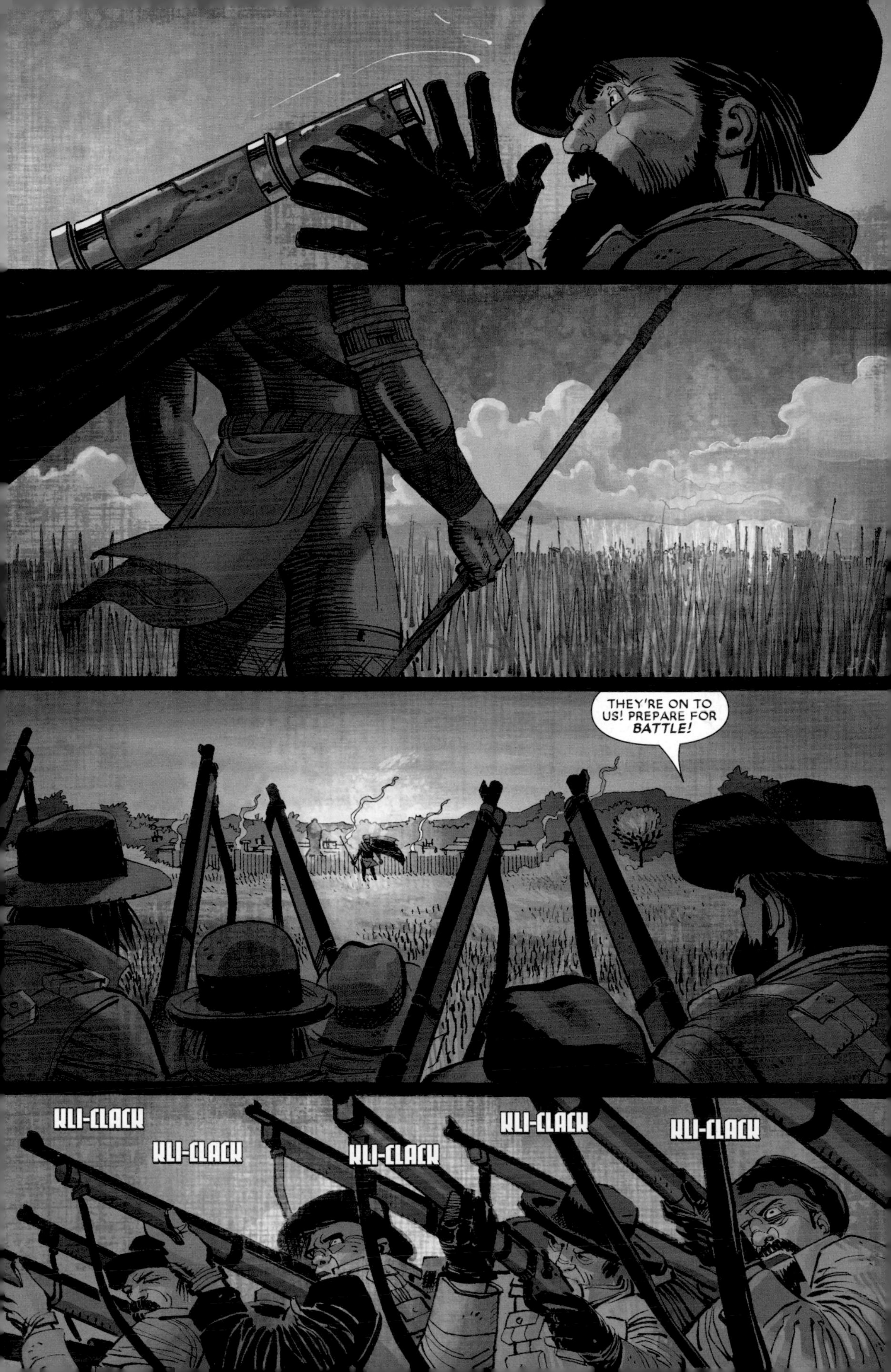
THEY'RE ON TO US! PREPARE FOR *BATTLE!*
KLI-CLACK
KLI-CLACK
KLI-CLACK
KLI-CLACK
KLI-CLACK

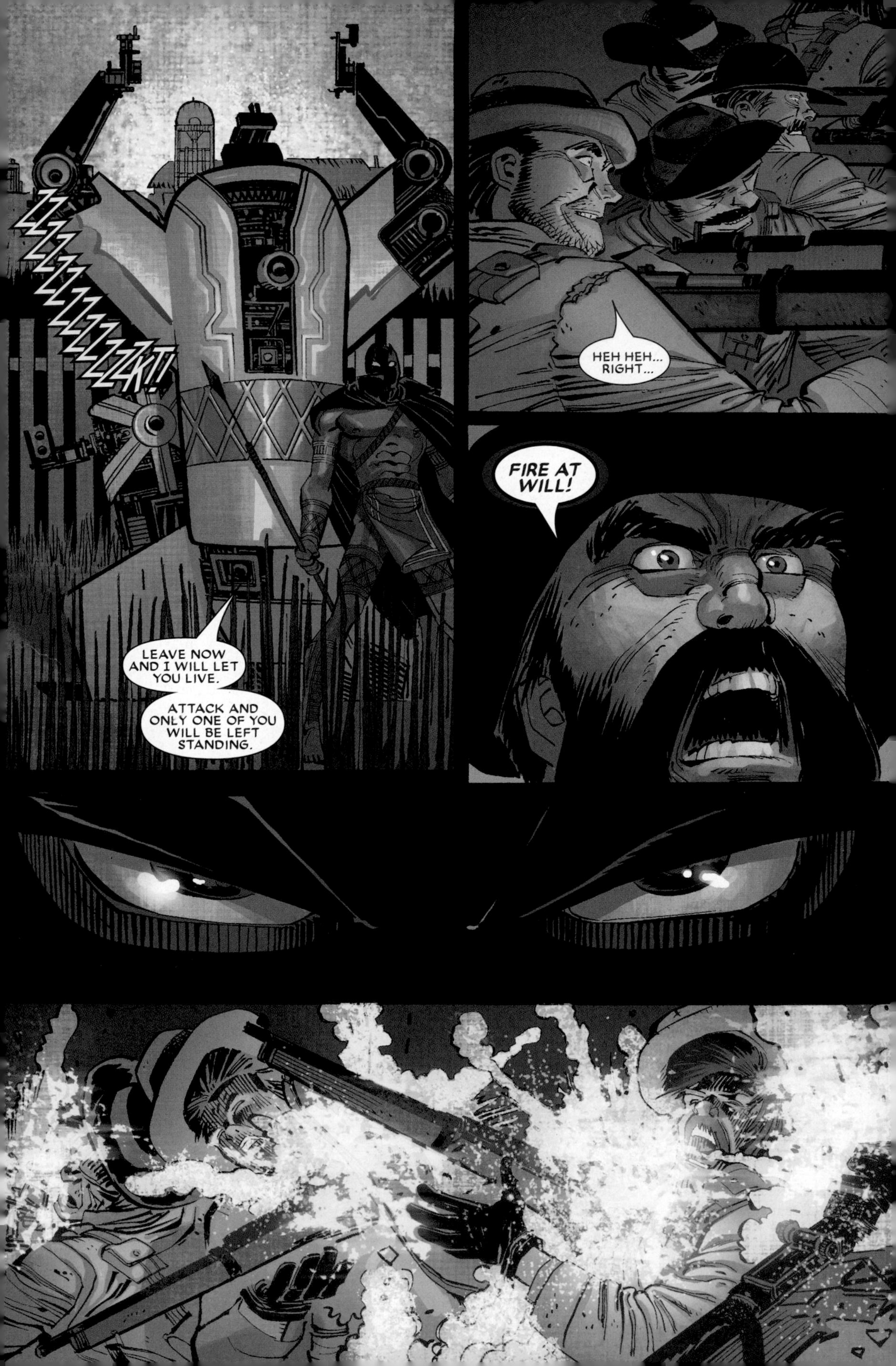
ZZZZZZZZZZZKT!!
LEAVE NOW AND I WILL LET YOU LIVE.
ATTACK AND ONLY ONE OF YOU WILL BE LEFT STANDING.
HEH HEH... RIGHT...
FIRE AT WILL!

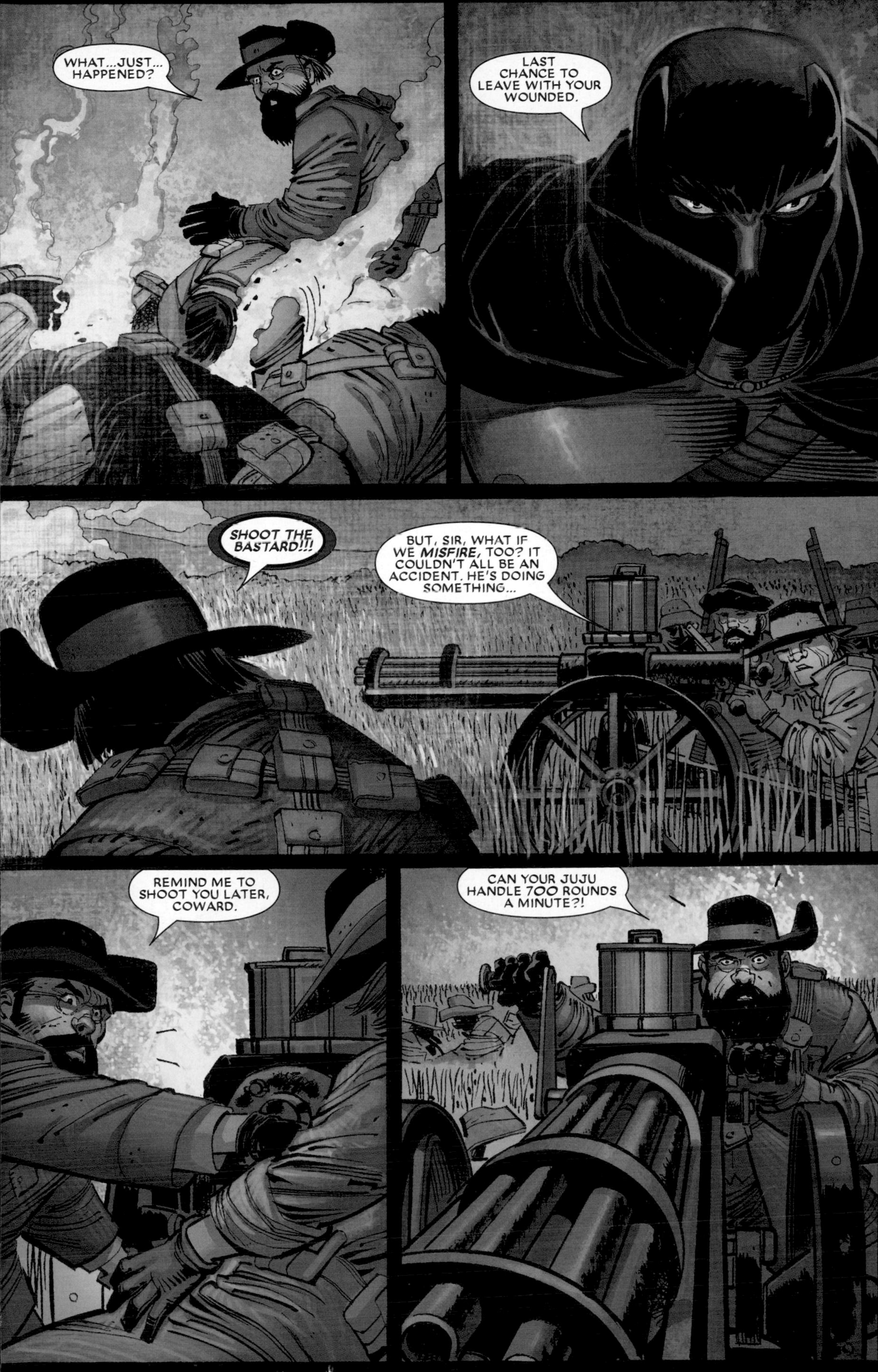
WHAT...JUST... HAPPENED?
LAST CHANCE TO LEAVE WITH YOUR WOUNDED.
SHOOT THE BASTARD!!!
BUT, SIR, WHAT IF WE MISFIRE, TOO? IT COULDN'T ALL BE AN ACCIDENT. HE'S DOING SOMETHING...
REMIND ME TO SHOOT YOU LATER, COWARD.
CAN YOUR JUJU HANDLE 700 ROUNDS A MINUTE?!

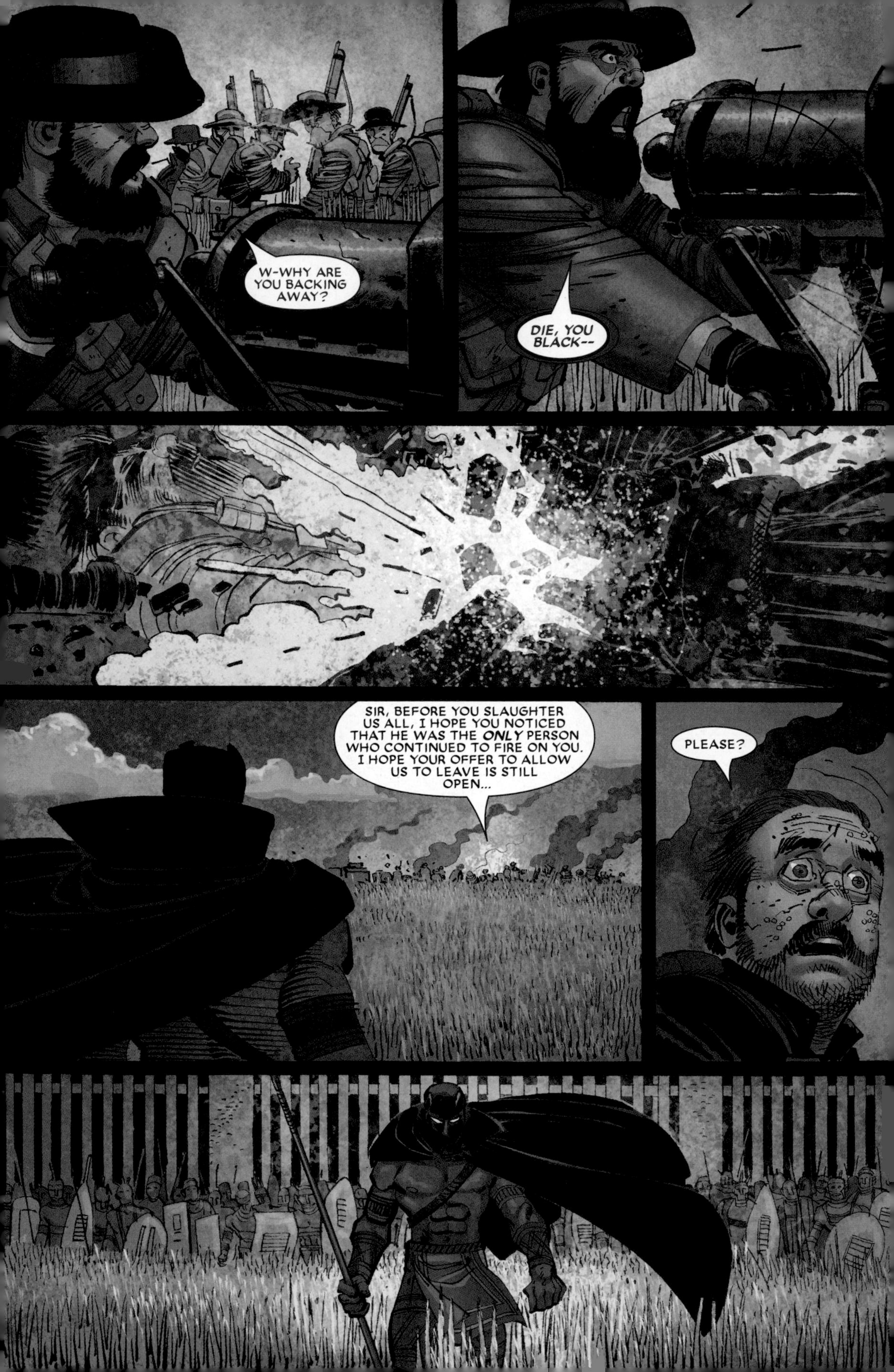
W-WHY ARE YOU BACKING AWAY?
DIE, YOU BLACK--
SIR, BEFORE YOU SLAUGHTER US ALL, I HOPE YOU NOTICED THAT HE WAS THE ONLY PERSON WHO CONTINUED TO FIRE ON YOU. I HOPE YOUR OFFER TO ALLOW US TO LEAVE IS STILL OPEN...
PLEASE?

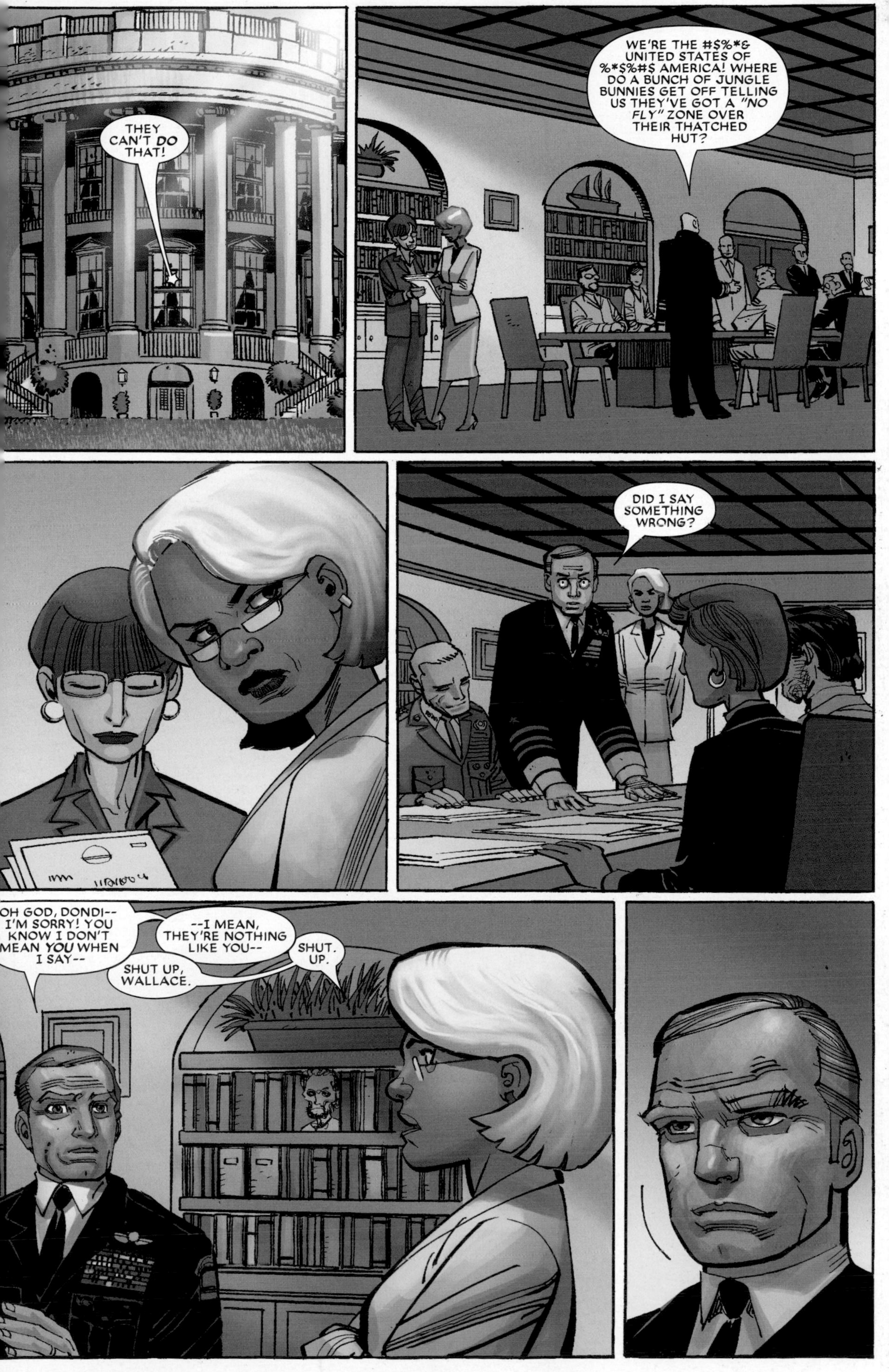
THEY CAN'T DO THAT!
WE'RE THE #$%*& UNITED STATES OF %*$%#$ AMERICA! WHERE DO A BUNCH OF JUNGLE BUNNIES GET OFF TELLING US THEY'VE GOT A "NO FLY" ZONE OVER THEIR THATCHED HUT?
DID I SAY SOMETHING WRONG?
OH GOD, DONDI-- I'M SORRY! YOU KNOW I DON'T MEAN YOU WHEN I SAY--
--I MEAN, THEY'RE NOTHING LIKE YOU--
SHUT UP, WALLACE.
SHUT. UP.

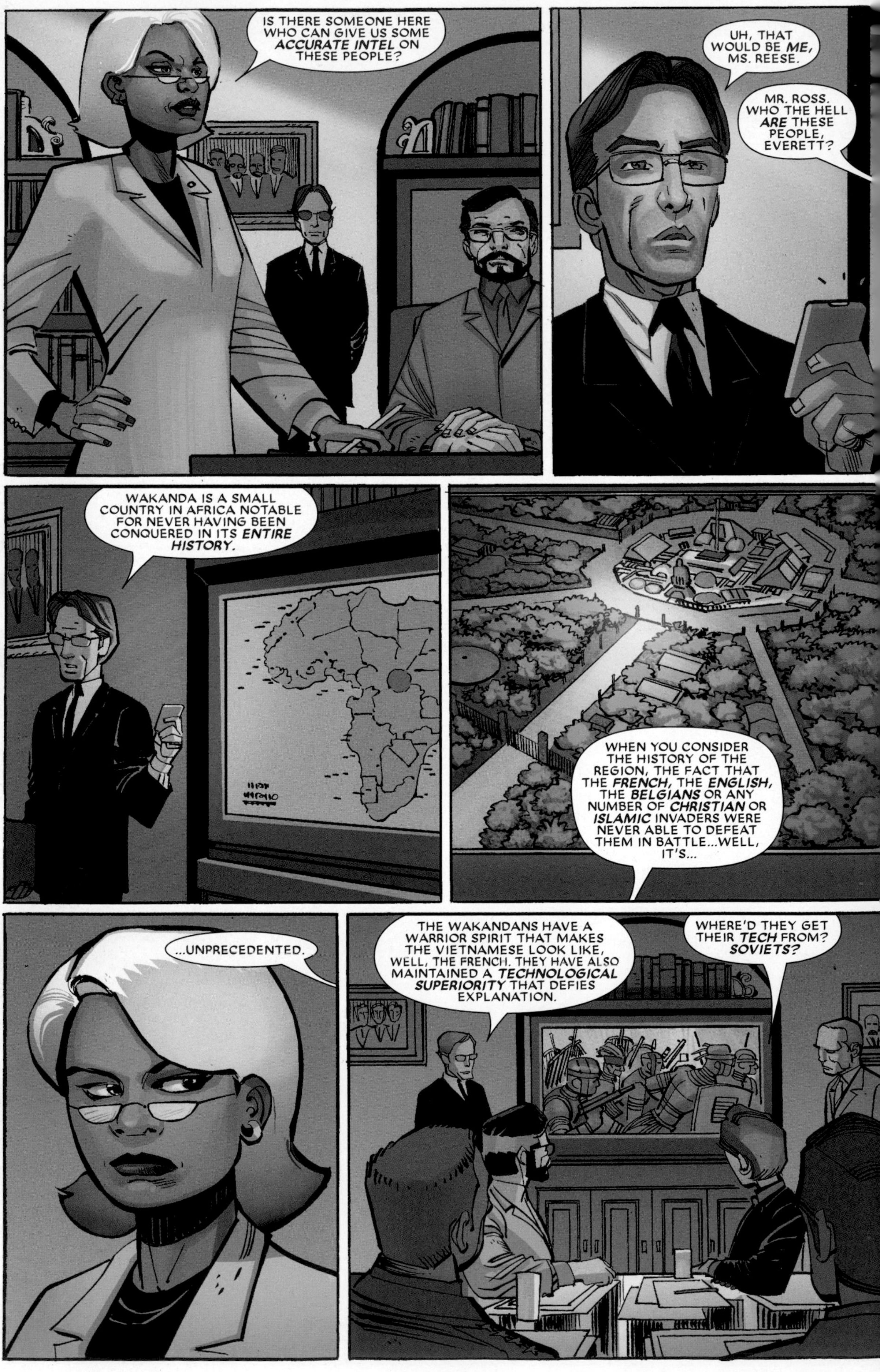
IS THERE SOMEONE HERE WHO CAN GIVE US SOME ACCURATE INTEL ON THESE PEOPLE?
UH, THAT WOULD BE ME, MS. REESE.
MR. ROSS. WHO THE HELL ARE THESE PEOPLE, EVERETT?
WAKANDA IS A SMALL COUNTRY IN AFRICA NOTABLE FOR NEVER HAVING BEEN CONQUERED IN ITS ENTIRE HISTORY.
WHEN YOU CONSIDER THE HISTORY OF THE REGION, THE FACT THAT THE FRENCH, THE ENGLISH, THE BELGIANS OR ANY NUMBER OF CHRISTIAN OR ISLAMIC INVADERS WERE NEVER ABLE TO DEFEAT THEM IN BATTLE...WELL, IT'S...
...UNPRECEDENTED.
THE WAKANDANS HAVE A WARRIOR SPIRIT THAT MAKES THE VIETNAMESE LOOK LIKE, WELL, THE FRENCH. THEY HAVE ALSO MAINTAINED A TECHNOLOGICAL SUPERIORITY THAT DEFIES EXPLANATION.
WHERE'D THEY GET THEIR TECH FROM? SOVIETS?

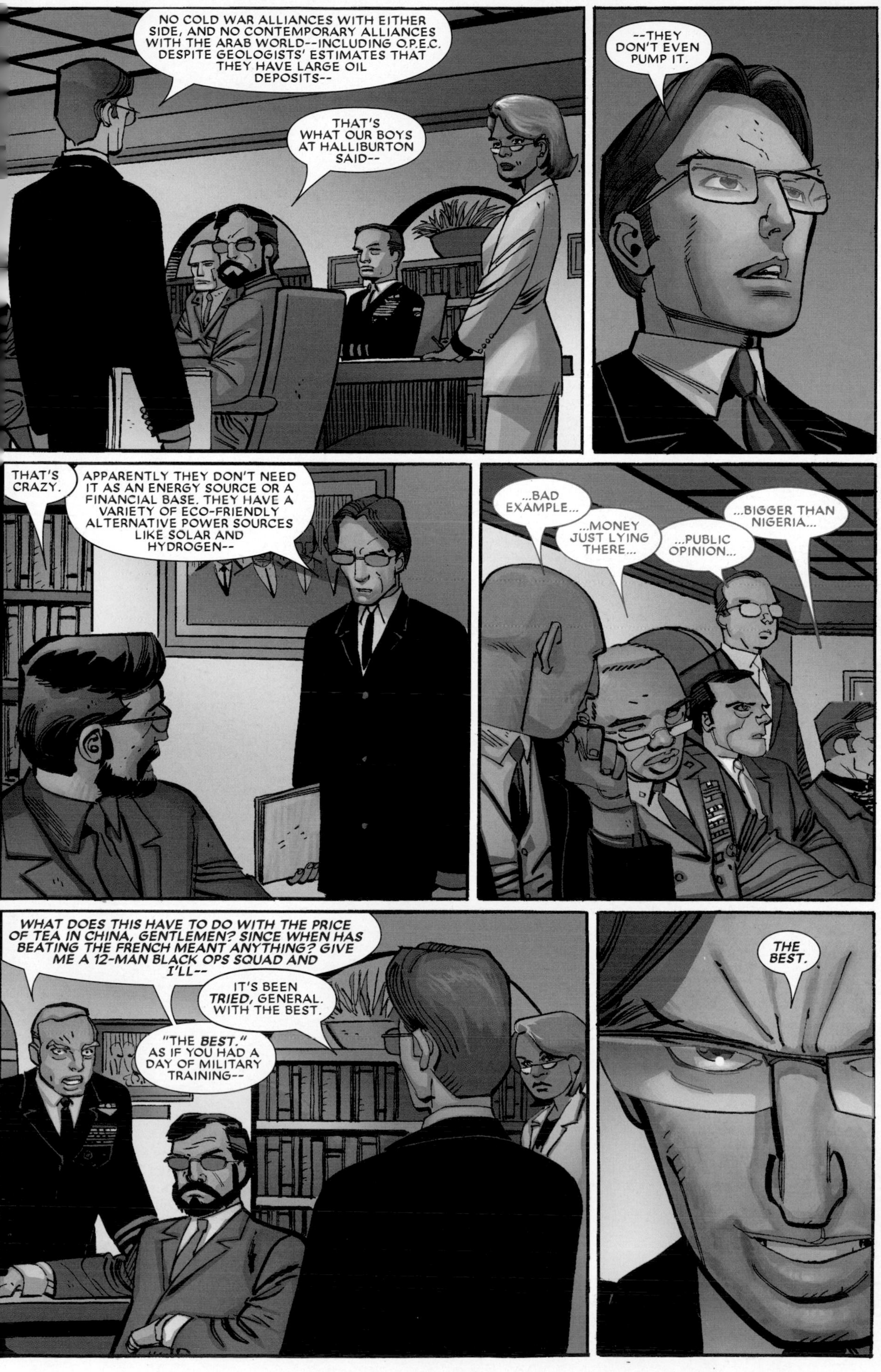
NO COLD WAR ALLIANCES WITH EITHER SIDE, AND NO CONTEMPORARY ALLIANCES WITH THE ARAB WORLD--INCLUDING O.P.E.C. DESPITE GEOLOGISTS' ESTIMATES THAT THEY HAVE LARGE OIL DEPOSITS--
THAT'S WHAT OUR BOYS AT HALLIBURTON SAID--
--THEY DON'T EVEN PUMP IT.
THAT'S CRAZY.
APPARENTLY THEY DON'T NEED IT AS AN ENERGY SOURCE OR A FINANCIAL BASE. THEY HAVE A VARIETY OF ECO-FRIENDLY ALTERNATIVE POWER SOURCES LIKE SOLAR AND HYDROGEN--
...BAD EXAMPLE...
...MONEY JUST LYING THERE...
...PUBLIC OPINION...
...BIGGER THAN NIGERIA...
WHAT DOES THIS HAVE TO DO WITH THE PRICE OF TEA IN CHINA, GENTLEMEN? SINCE WHEN HAS BEATING THE FRENCH MEANT ANYTHING? GIVE ME A 12-MAN BLACK OPS SQUAD AND I'LL--
IT'S BEEN TRIED, GENERAL. WITH THE BEST.
"THE BEST." AS IF YOU HAD A DAY OF MILITARY TRAINING--
THE BEST.

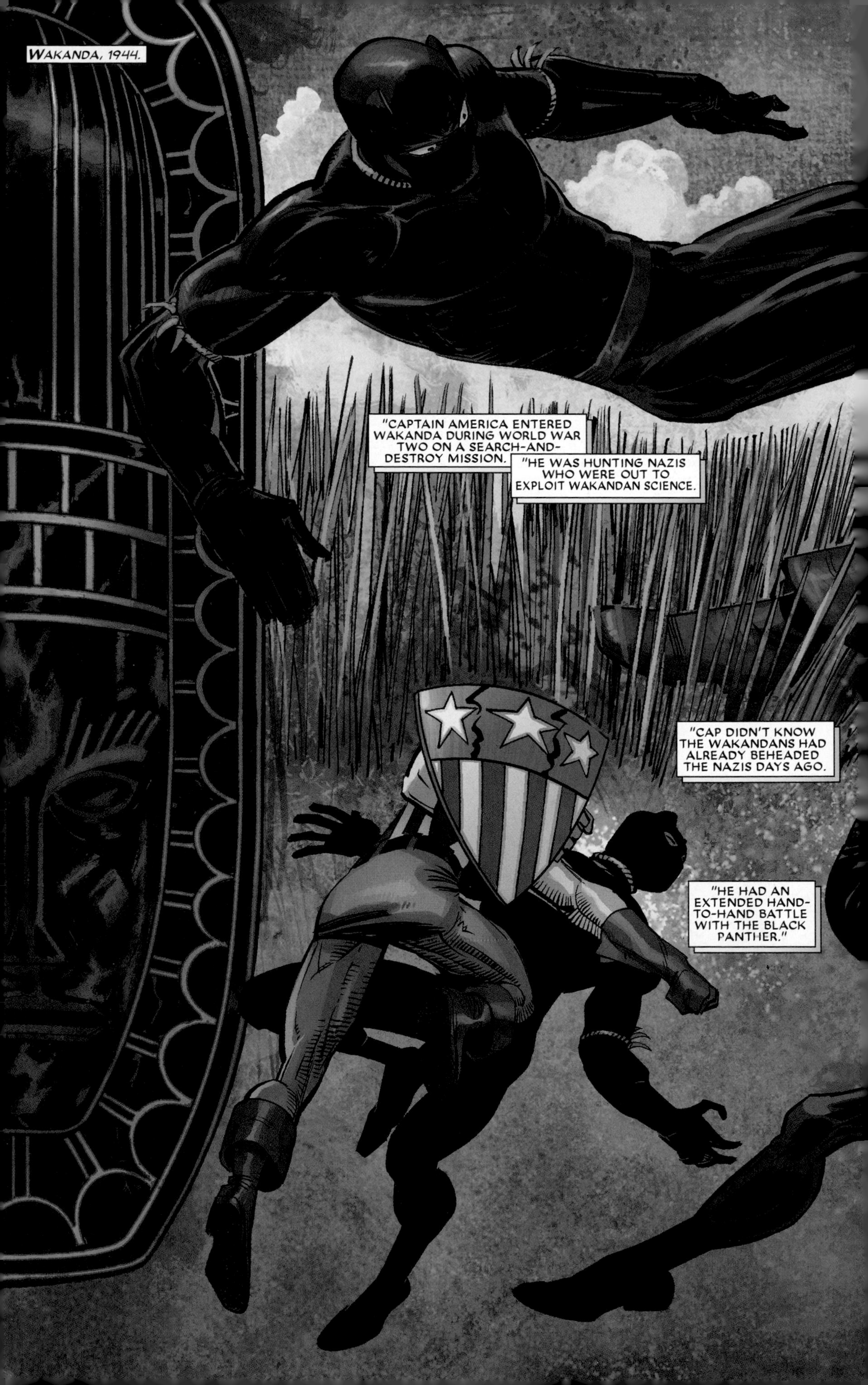
WAKANDA, 1944.
"CAPTAIN AMERICA ENTERED WAKANDA DURING WORLD WAR TWO ON A SEARCH-AND-DESTROY MISSION.
"HE WAS HUNTING NAZIS WHO WERE OUT TO EXPLOIT WAKANDAN SCIENCE.
"CAP DIDN'T KNOW THE WAKANDANS HAD ALREADY BEHEADED THE NAZIS DAYS AGO.
"HE HAD AN EXTENDED HAND-TO-HAND BATTLE WITH THE BLACK PANTHER."

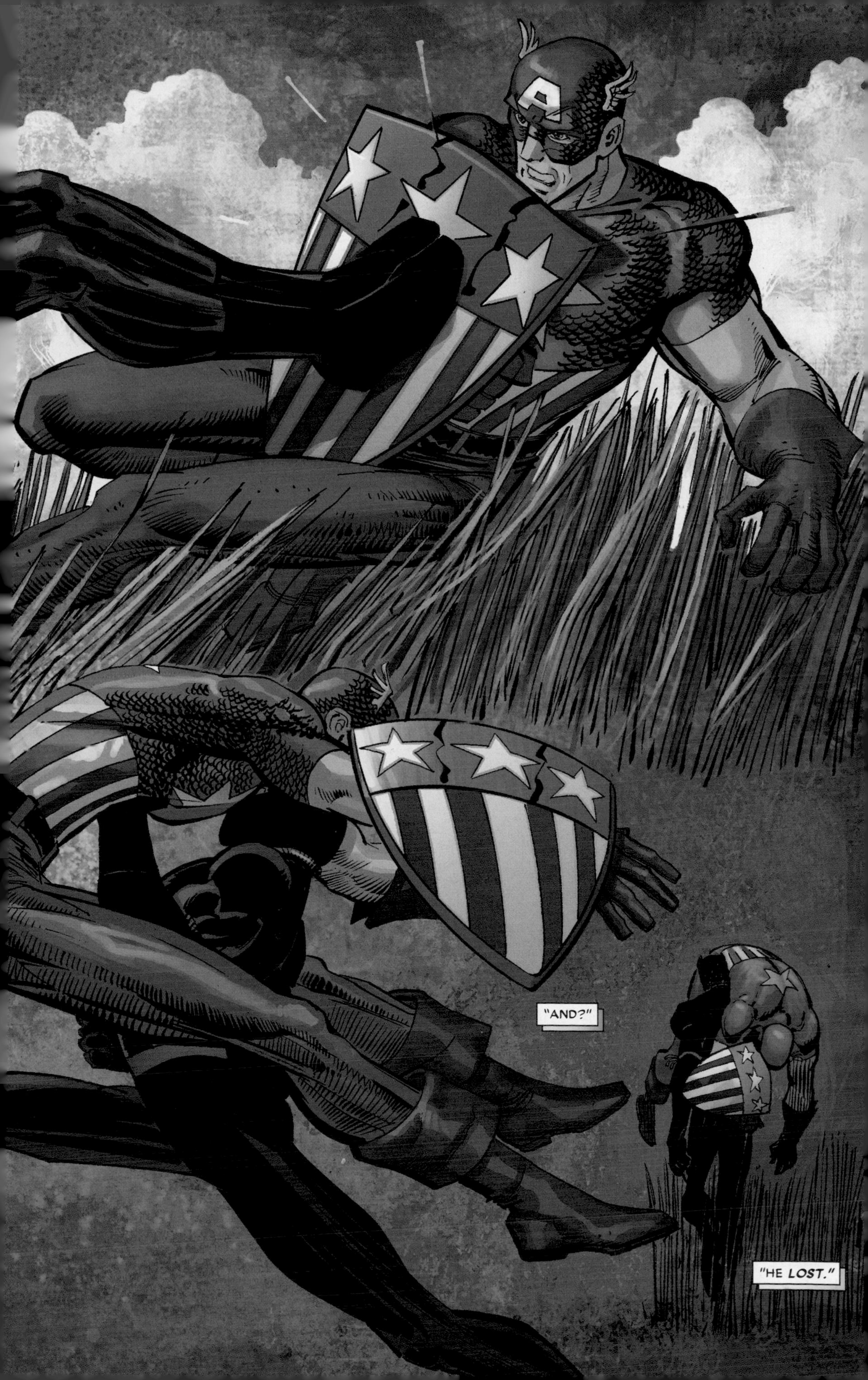
"AND?"
"HE LOST."

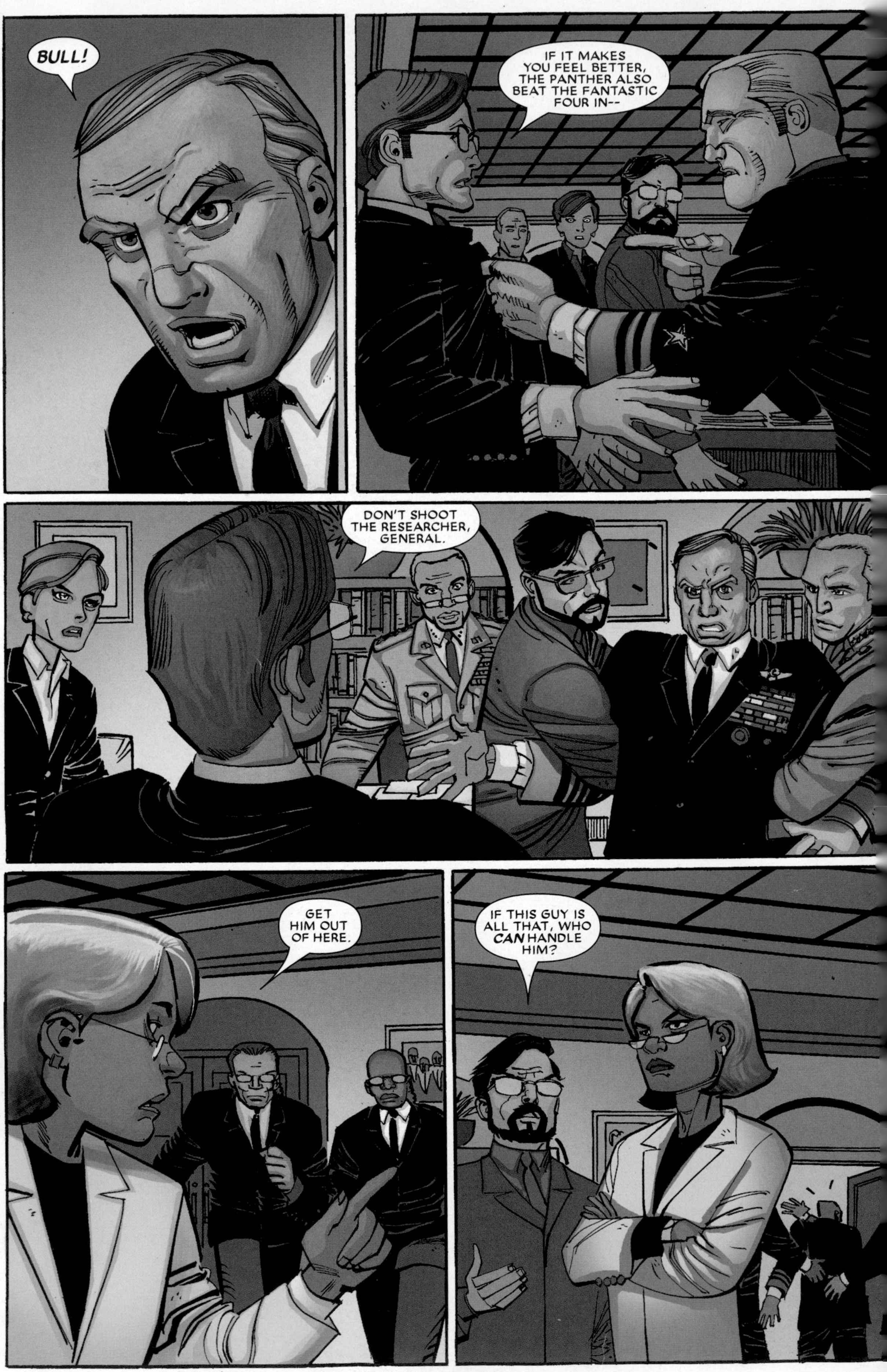
BULL!
IF IT MAKES YOU FEEL BETTER, THE PANTHER ALSO BEAT THE FANTASTIC FOUR IN--
DON'T SHOOT THE RESEARCHER, GENERAL.
GET HIM OUT OF HERE.
IF THIS GUY IS ALL THAT, WHO *CAN* HANDLE HIM?

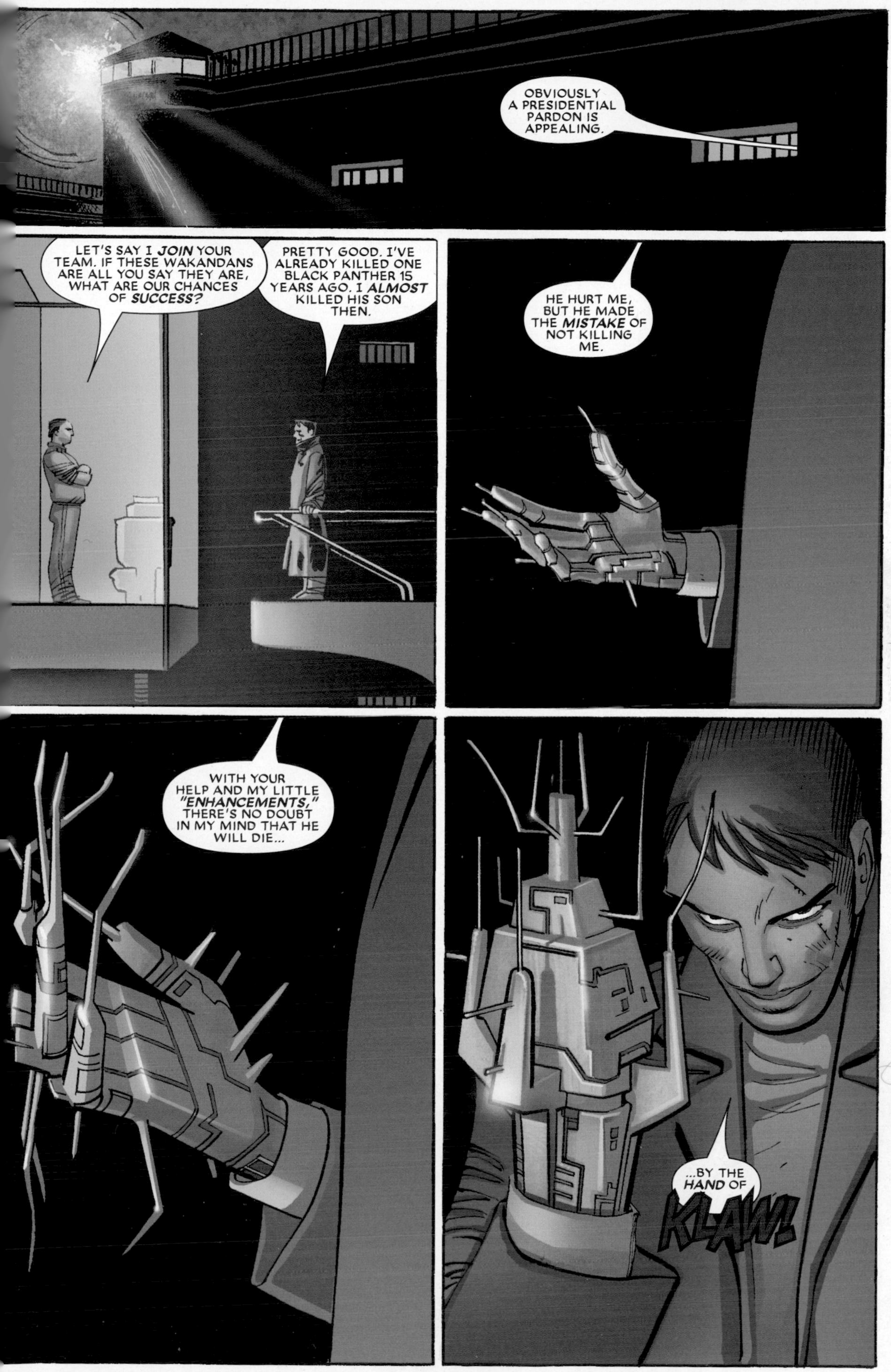
OBVIOUSLY A PRESIDENTIAL PARDON IS APPEALING.
LET'S SAY I *JOIN* YOUR TEAM. IF THESE WAKANDANS ARE ALL YOU SAY THEY ARE, WHAT ARE OUR CHANCES OF *SUCCESS?*
PRETTY GOOD. I'VE ALREADY KILLED ONE BLACK PANTHER 15 YEARS AGO. I *ALMOST* KILLED HIS SON THEN.
HE HURT ME, BUT HE MADE THE *MISTAKE* OF NOT KILLING ME.
WITH YOUR HELP AND MY LITTLE *"ENHANCEMENTS,"* THERE'S NO DOUBT IN MY MIND THAT HE WILL DIE...
...BY THE *HAND* OF
KLAW!

2

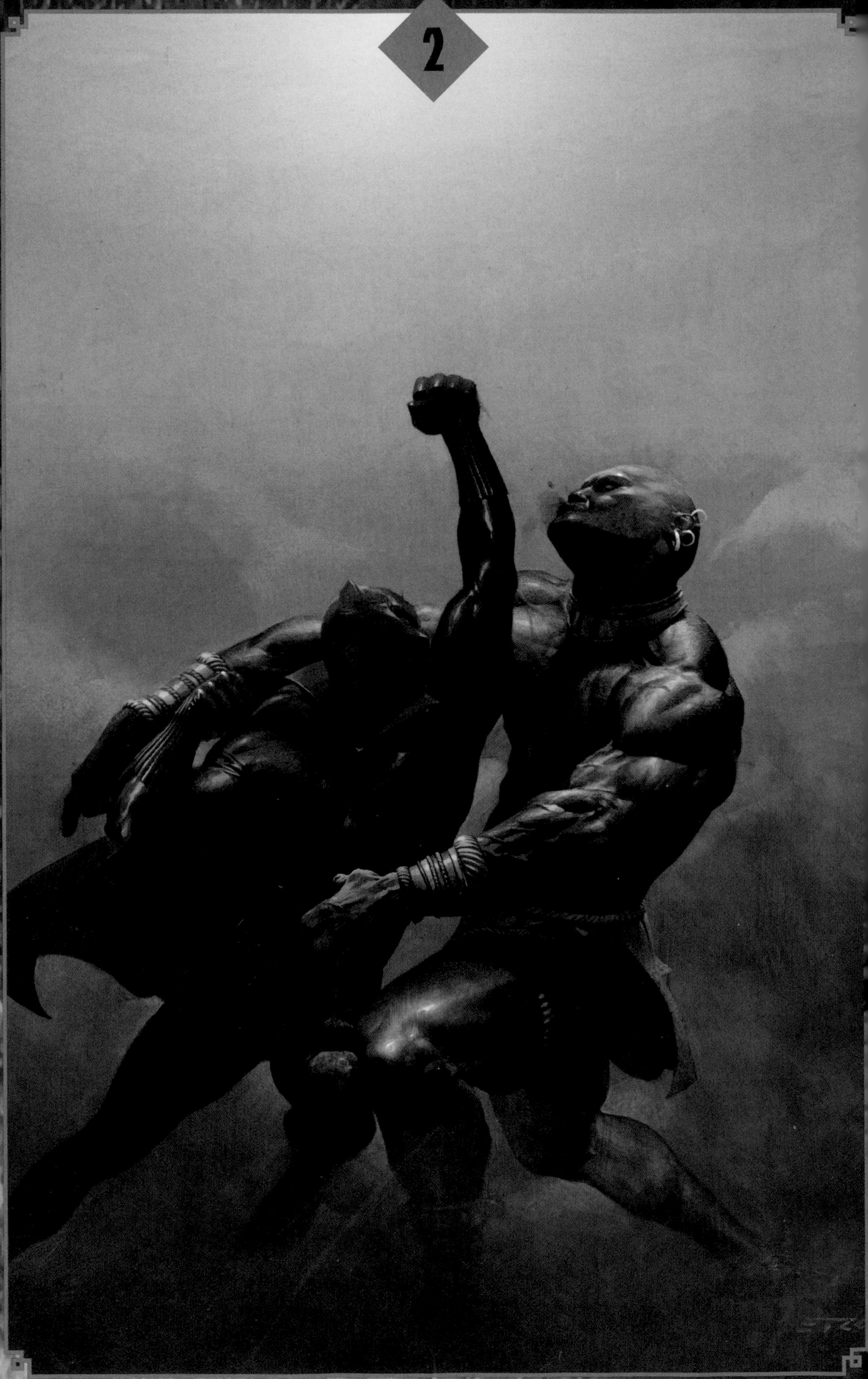

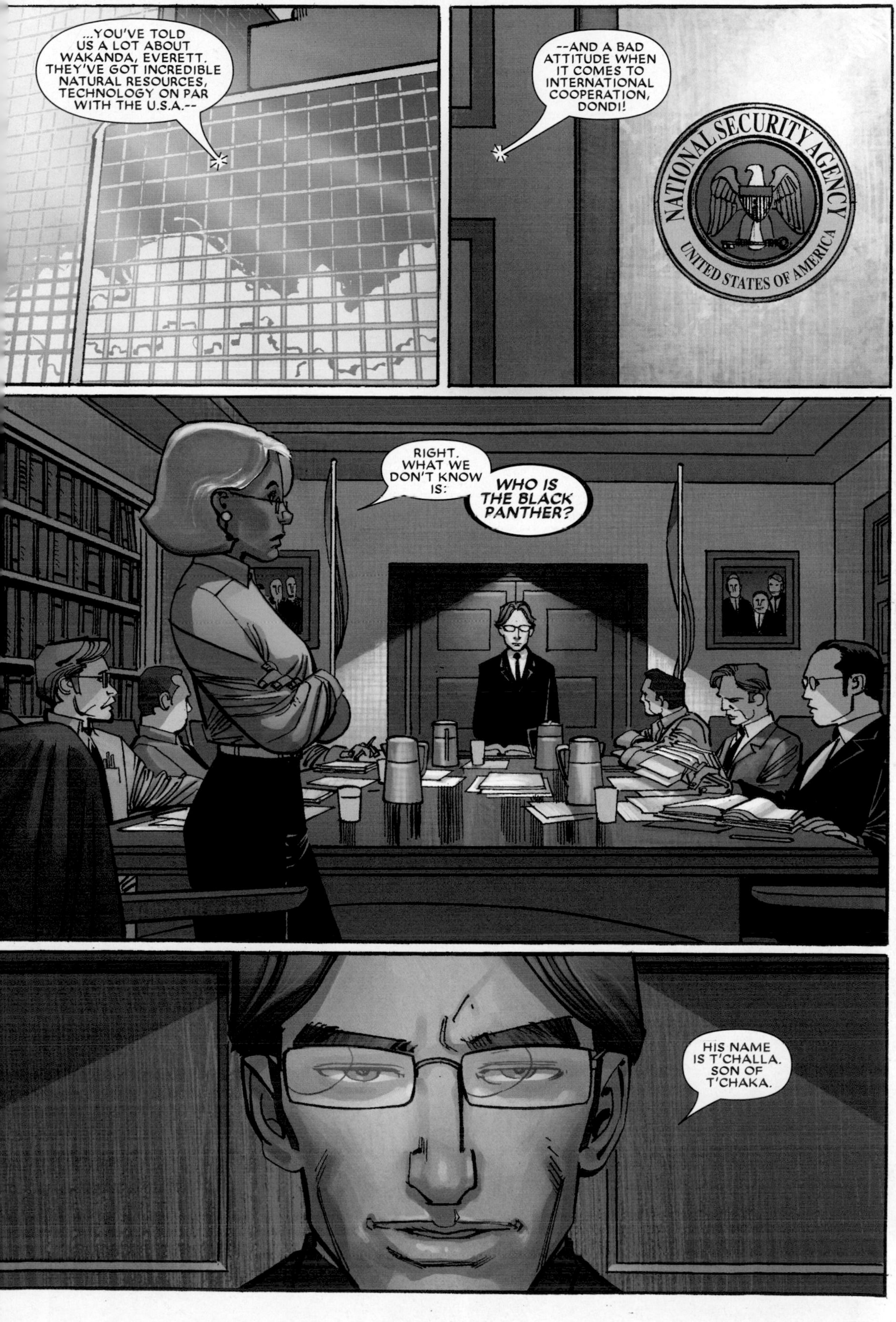
...YOU'VE TOLD US A LOT ABOUT WAKANDA, EVERETT. THEY'VE GOT INCREDIBLE NATURAL RESOURCES, TECHNOLOGY ON PAR WITH THE U.S.A.--
--AND A BAD ATTITUDE WHEN IT COMES TO INTERNATIONAL COOPERATION, DONDI!
NATIONAL SECURITY AGENCY
UNITED STATES OF AMERICA
RIGHT. WHAT WE DON'T KNOW IS:
WHO IS THE BLACK PANTHER?
HIS NAME IS T'CHALLA. SON OF T'CHAKA.

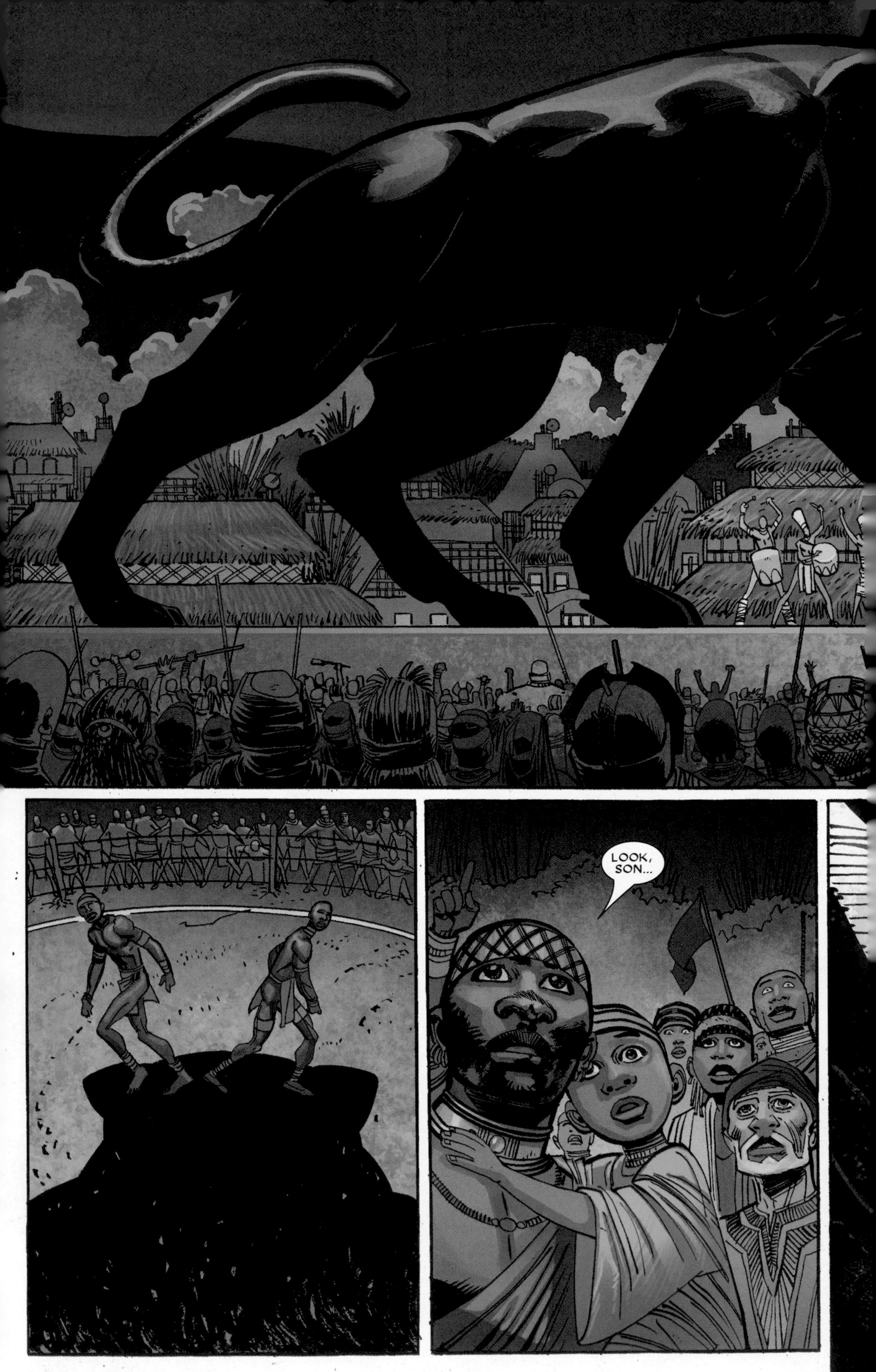
LOOK, SON...

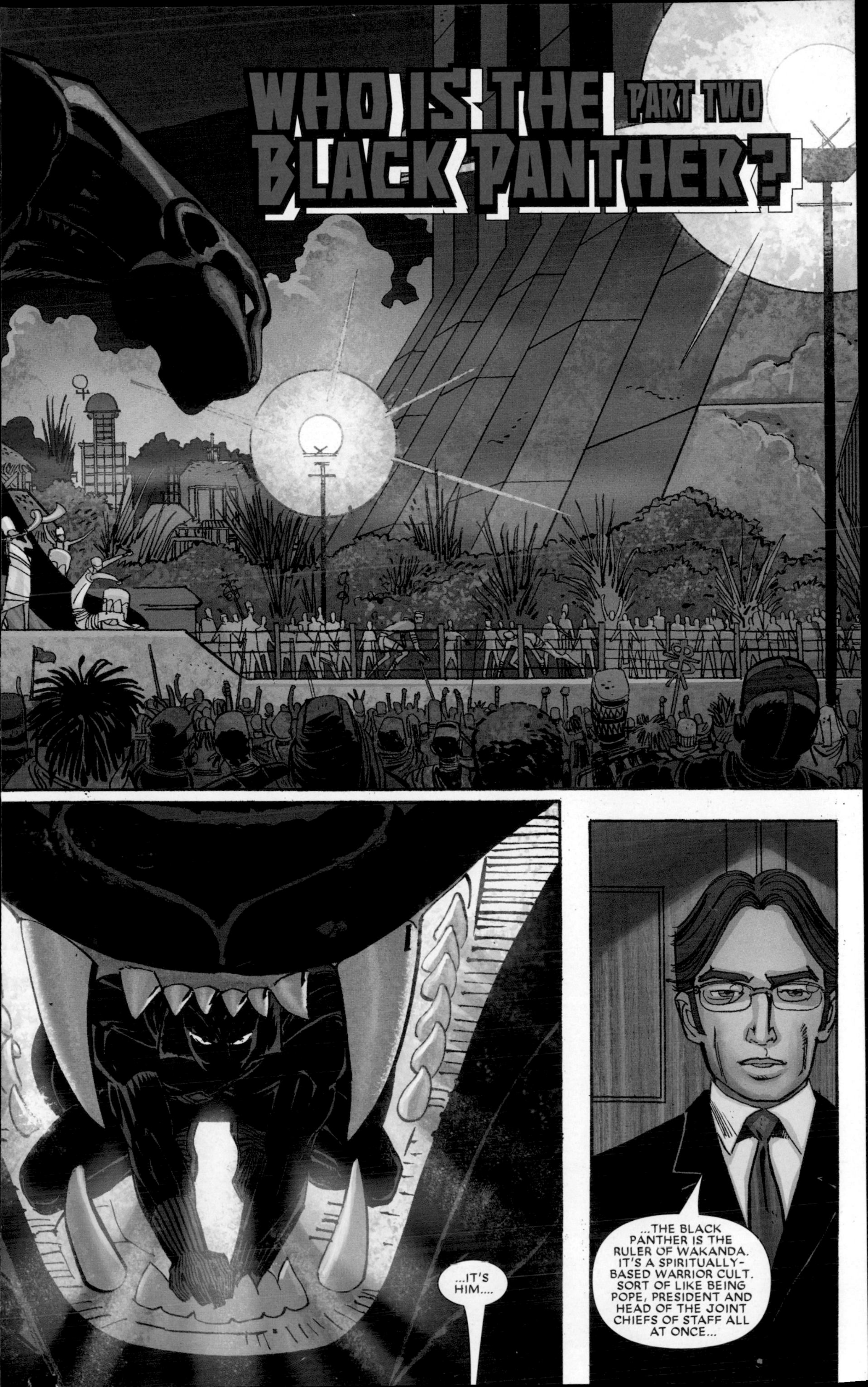
WHO IS THE BLACK PANTHER?
PART TWO
...IT'S HIM....
...THE BLACK PANTHER IS THE RULER OF WAKANDA. IT'S A SPIRITUALLY-BASED WARRIOR CULT. SORT OF LIKE BEING POPE, PRESIDENT AND HEAD OF THE JOINT CHIEFS OF STAFF ALL AT ONCE...

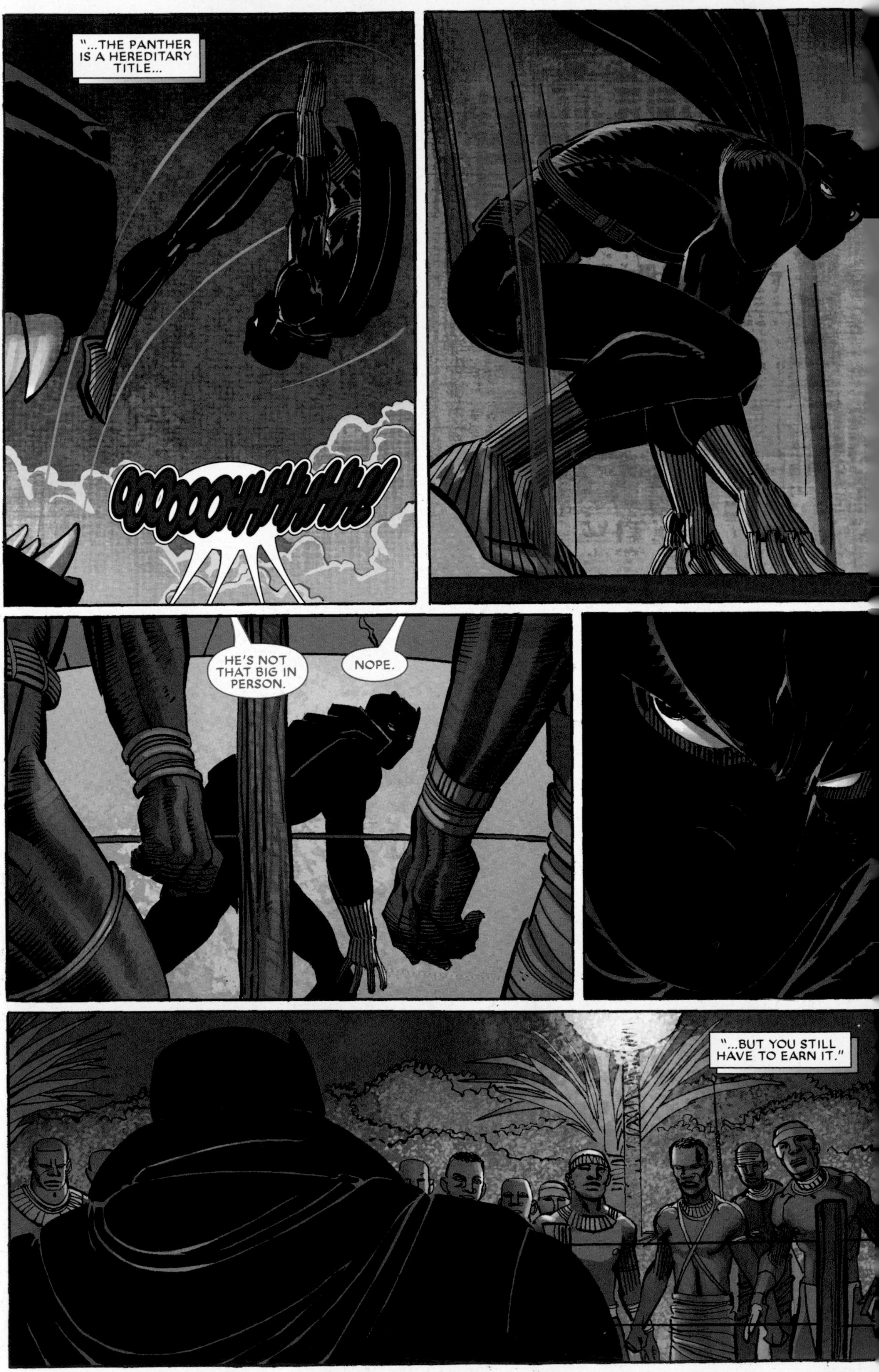
"...THE PANTHER IS A HEREDITARY TITLE...
OOOOOOOHHHHHHH!
HE'S NOT THAT BIG IN PERSON.
NOPE.
"...BUT YOU STILL HAVE TO EARN IT."

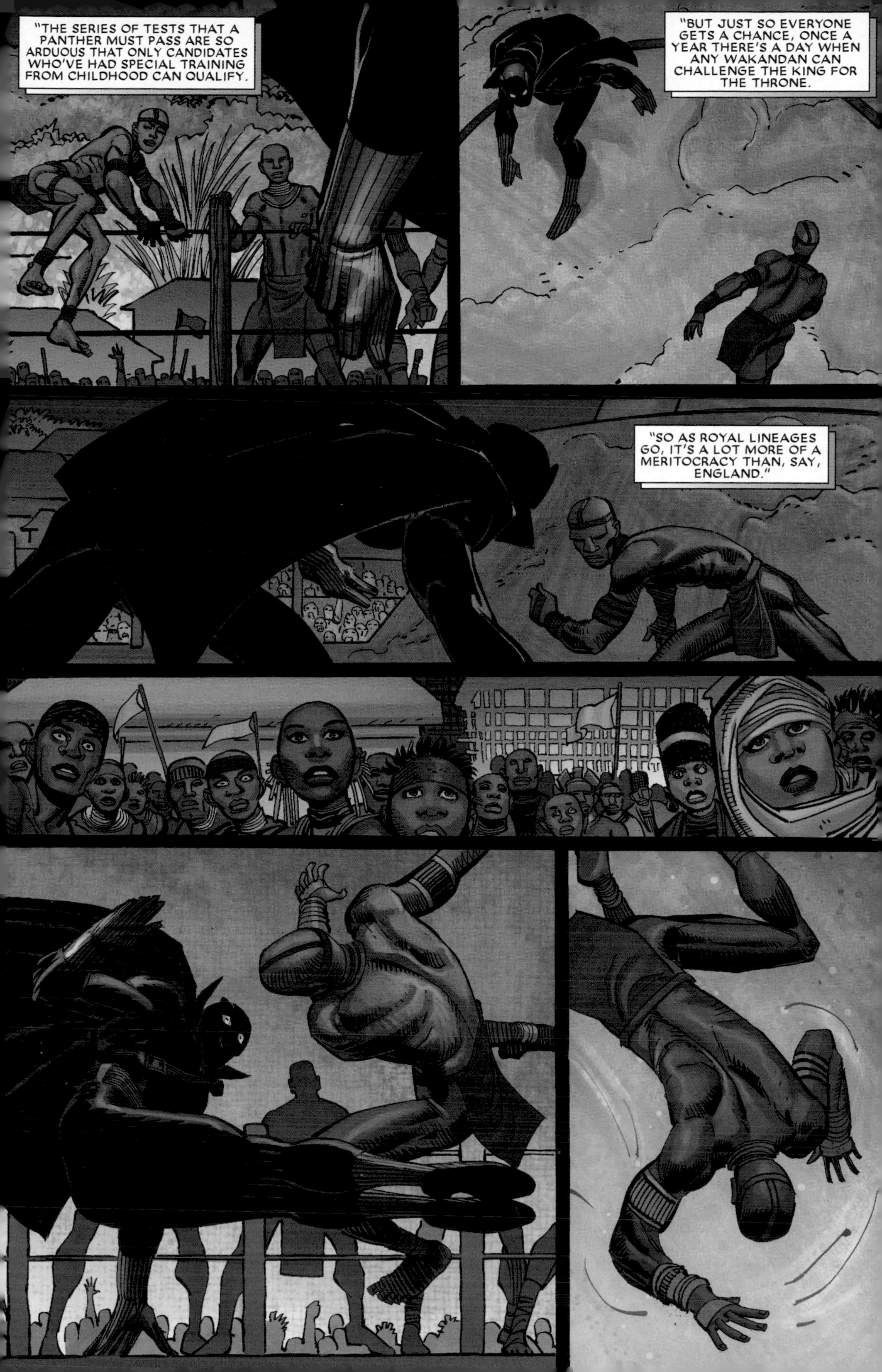
"THE SERIES OF TESTS THAT A PANTHER MUST PASS ARE SO ARDUOUS THAT ONLY CANDIDATES WHO'VE HAD SPECIAL TRAINING FROM CHILDHOOD CAN QUALIFY.
"BUT JUST SO EVERYONE GETS A CHANCE, ONCE A YEAR THERE'S A DAY WHEN ANY WAKANDAN CAN CHALLENGE THE KING FOR THE THRONE.
"SO AS ROYAL LINEAGES GO, IT'S A LOT MORE OF A MERITOCRACY THAN, SAY, ENGLAND."

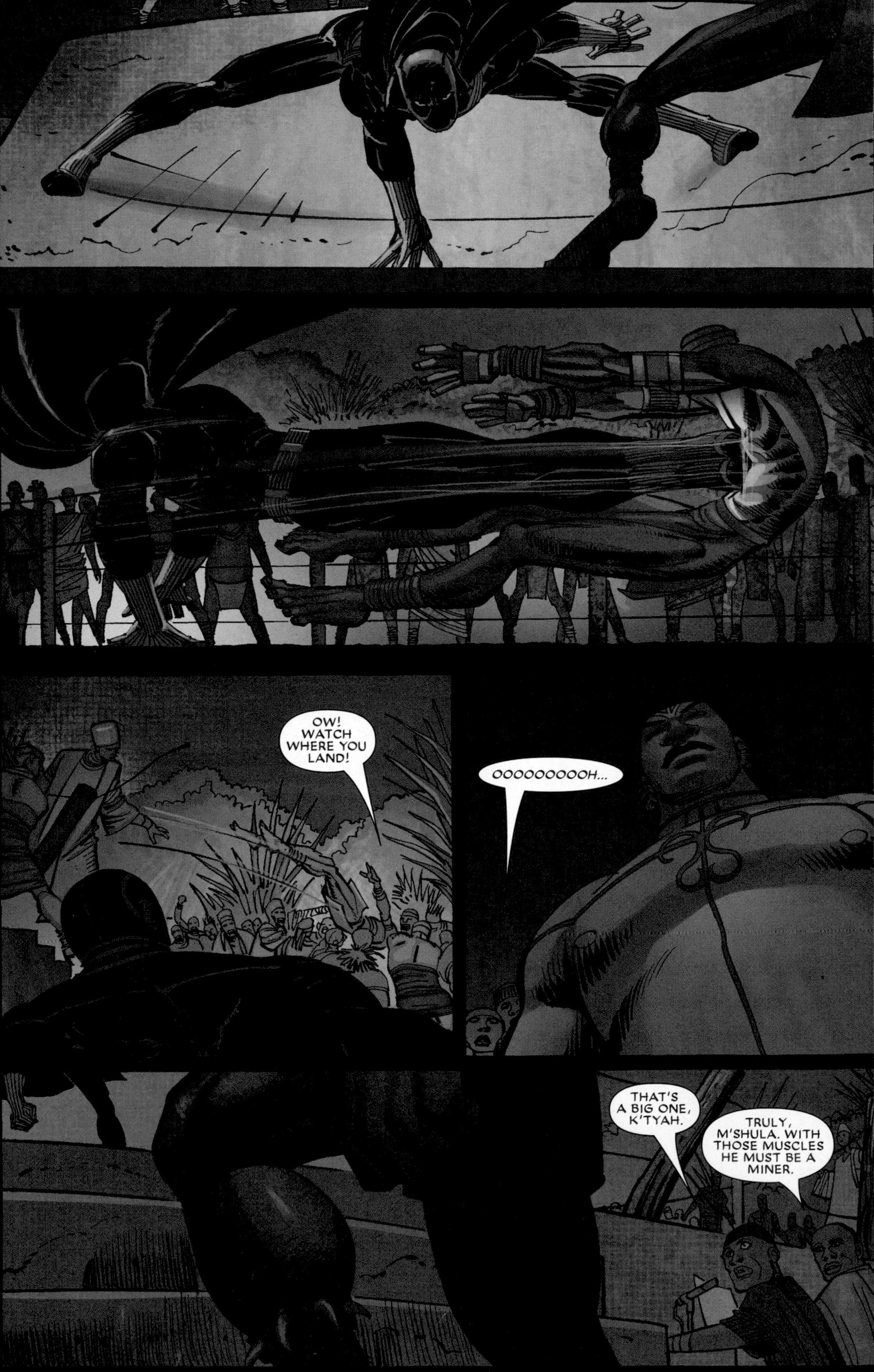
OW! WATCH WHERE YOU LAND!
OOOOOOOOOH...
THAT'S A BIG ONE, K'TYAH.
TRULY, M'SHULA. WITH THOSE MUSCLES HE MUST BE A MINER.

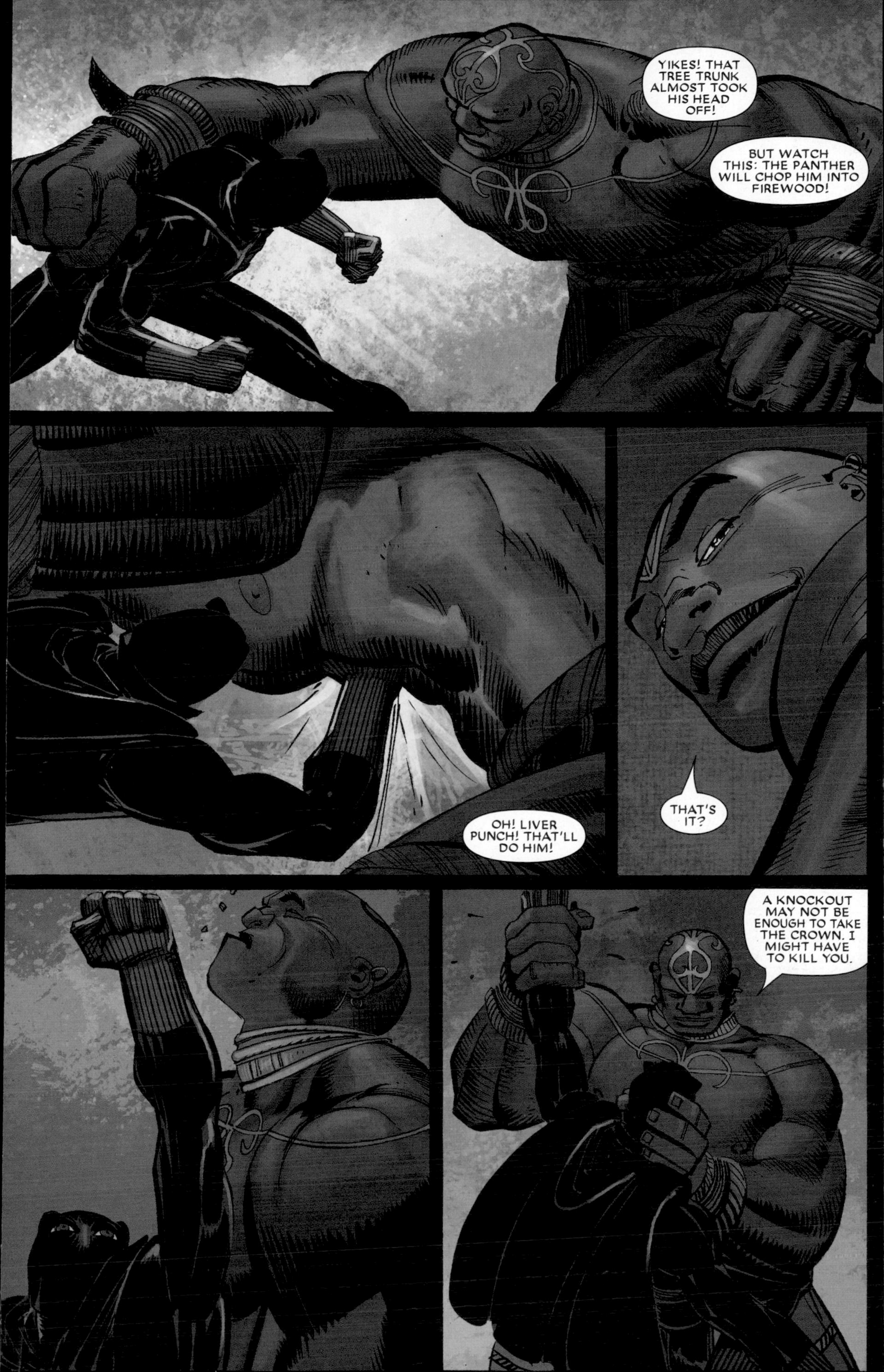
YIKES! THAT TREE TRUNK ALMOST TOOK HIS HEAD OFF!
BUT WATCH THIS: THE PANTHER WILL CHOP HIM INTO FIREWOOD!
OH! LIVER PUNCH! THAT'LL DO HIM!
THAT'S IT?
A KNOCKOUT MAY NOT BE ENOUGH TO TAKE THE CROWN. I MIGHT HAVE TO KILL YOU.

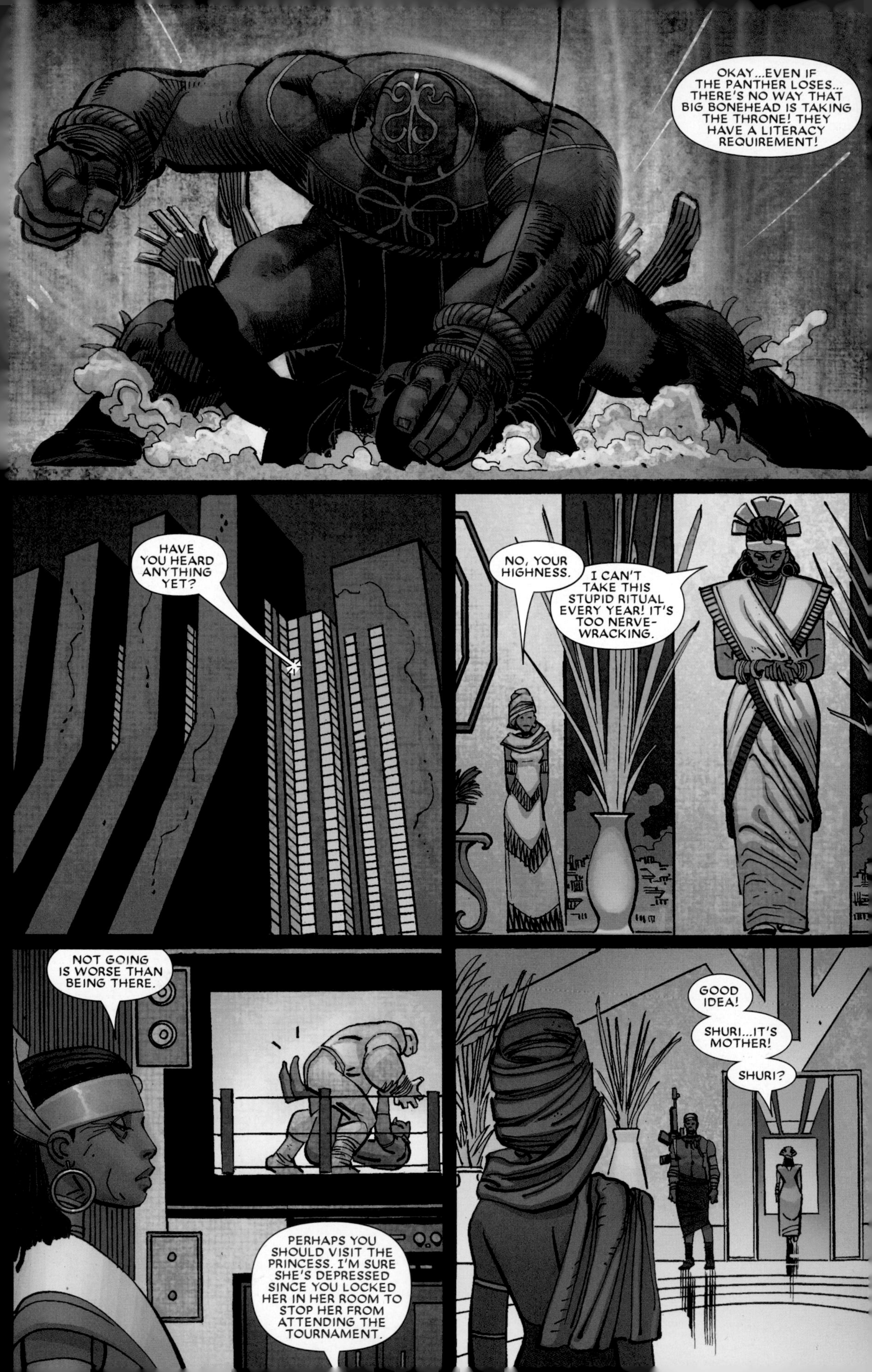
OKAY...EVEN IF THE PANTHER LOSES... THERE'S NO WAY THAT BIG BONEHEAD IS TAKING THE THRONE! THEY HAVE A LITERACY REQUIREMENT!
HAVE YOU HEARD ANYTHING YET?
NO, YOUR HIGHNESS.
I CAN'T TAKE THIS STUPID RITUAL EVERY YEAR! IT'S TOO NERVE-WRACKING.
NOT GOING IS WORSE THAN BEING THERE.
PERHAPS YOU SHOULD VISIT THE PRINCESS. I'M SURE SHE'S DEPRESSED SINCE YOU LOCKED HER IN HER ROOM TO STOP HER FROM ATTENDING THE TOURNAMENT.
GOOD IDEA!
SHURI...IT'S MOTHER!
SHURI?

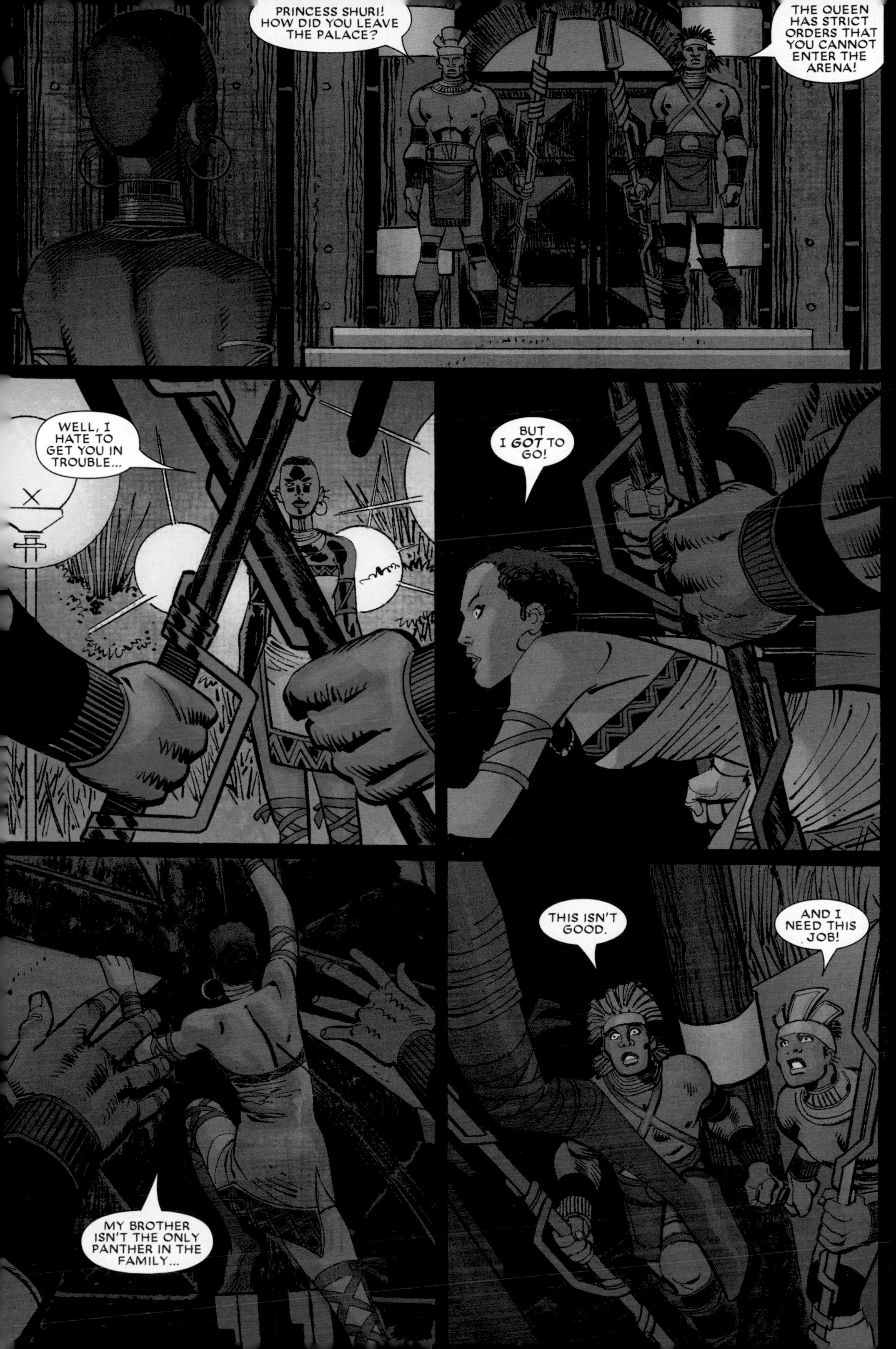
PRINCESS SHURI! HOW DID YOU LEAVE THE PALACE?
THE QUEEN HAS STRICT ORDERS THAT YOU CANNOT ENTER THE ARENA!
WELL, I HATE TO GET YOU IN TROUBLE...
BUT I GOT TO GO!
MY BROTHER ISN'T THE ONLY PANTHER IN THE FAMILY...
THIS ISN'T GOOD.
AND I NEED THIS JOB!

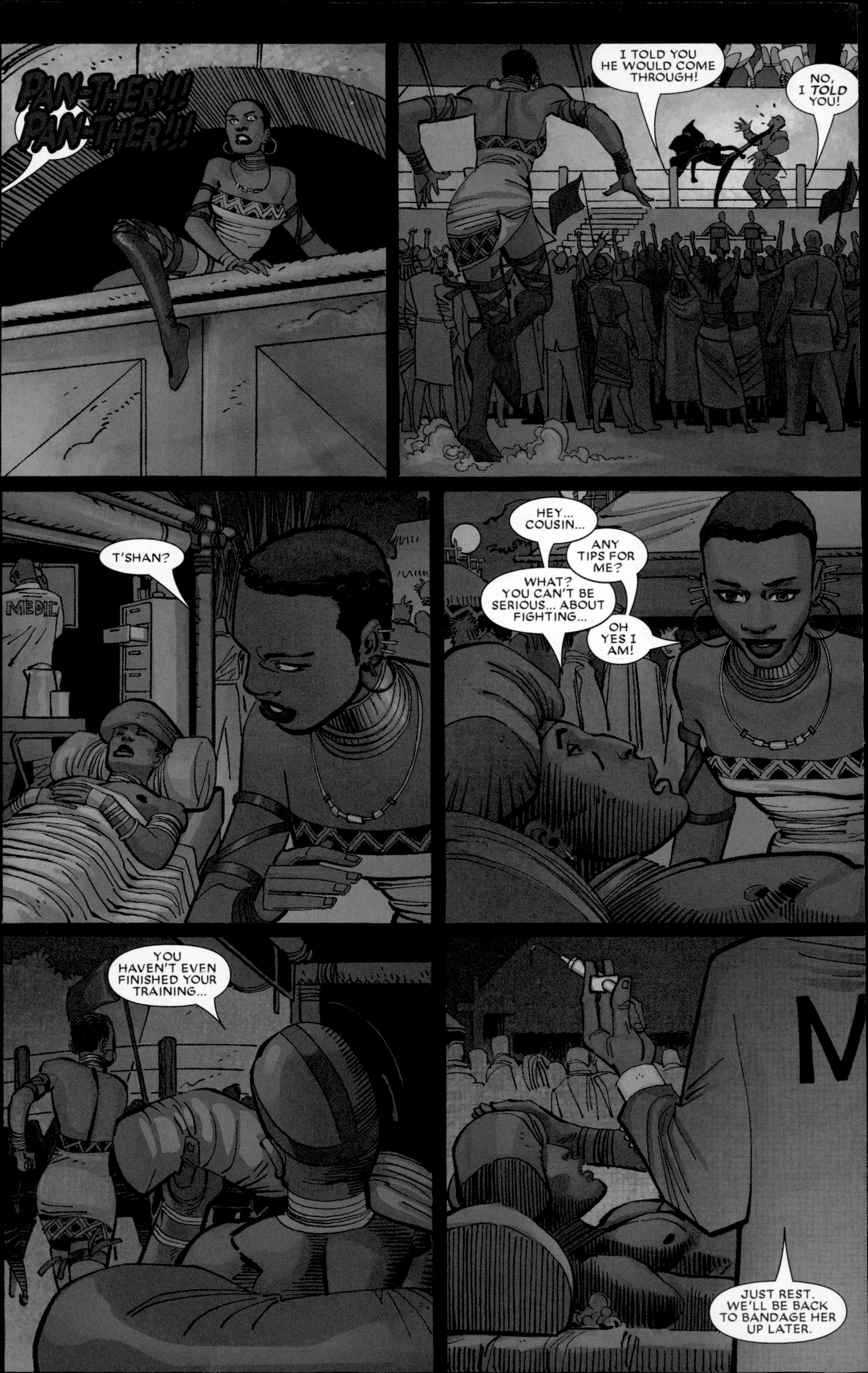
PAN-THER!!!
PAN-THER!!!
I TOLD YOU HE WOULD COME THROUGH!
NO, I TOLD YOU!
T'SHAN?
MEDIC
HEY... COUSIN...
ANY TIPS FOR ME?
WHAT? YOU CAN'T BE SERIOUS... ABOUT FIGHTING...
OH YES I AM!
YOU HAVEN'T EVEN FINISHED YOUR TRAINING...
JUST REST. WE'LL BE BACK TO BANDAGE HER UP LATER.

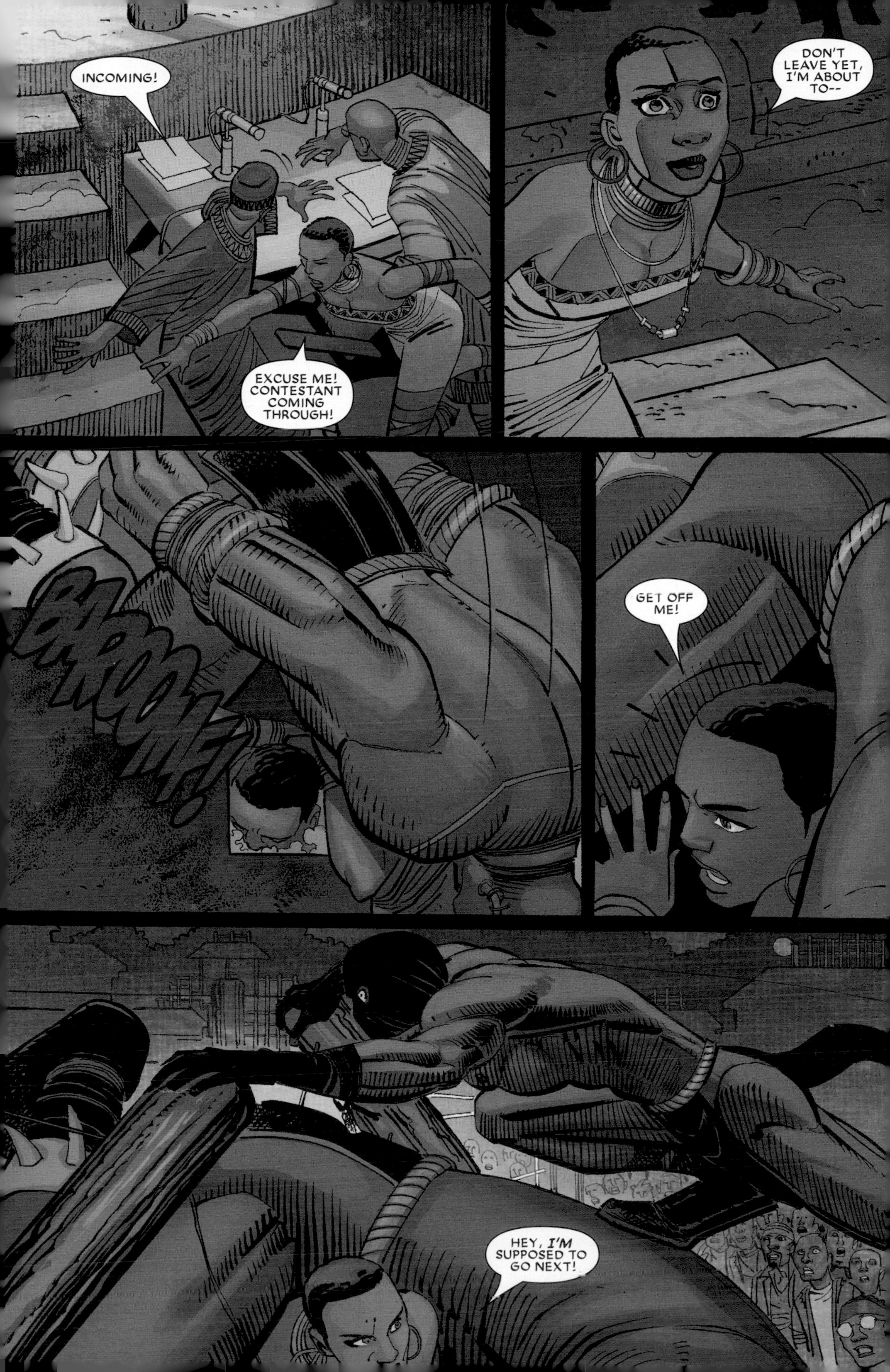
INCOMING!
EXCUSE ME! CONTESTANT COMING THROUGH!
DON'T LEAVE YET, I'M ABOUT TO--
GET OFF ME!
HEY, *I'M* SUPPOSED TO GO NEXT!

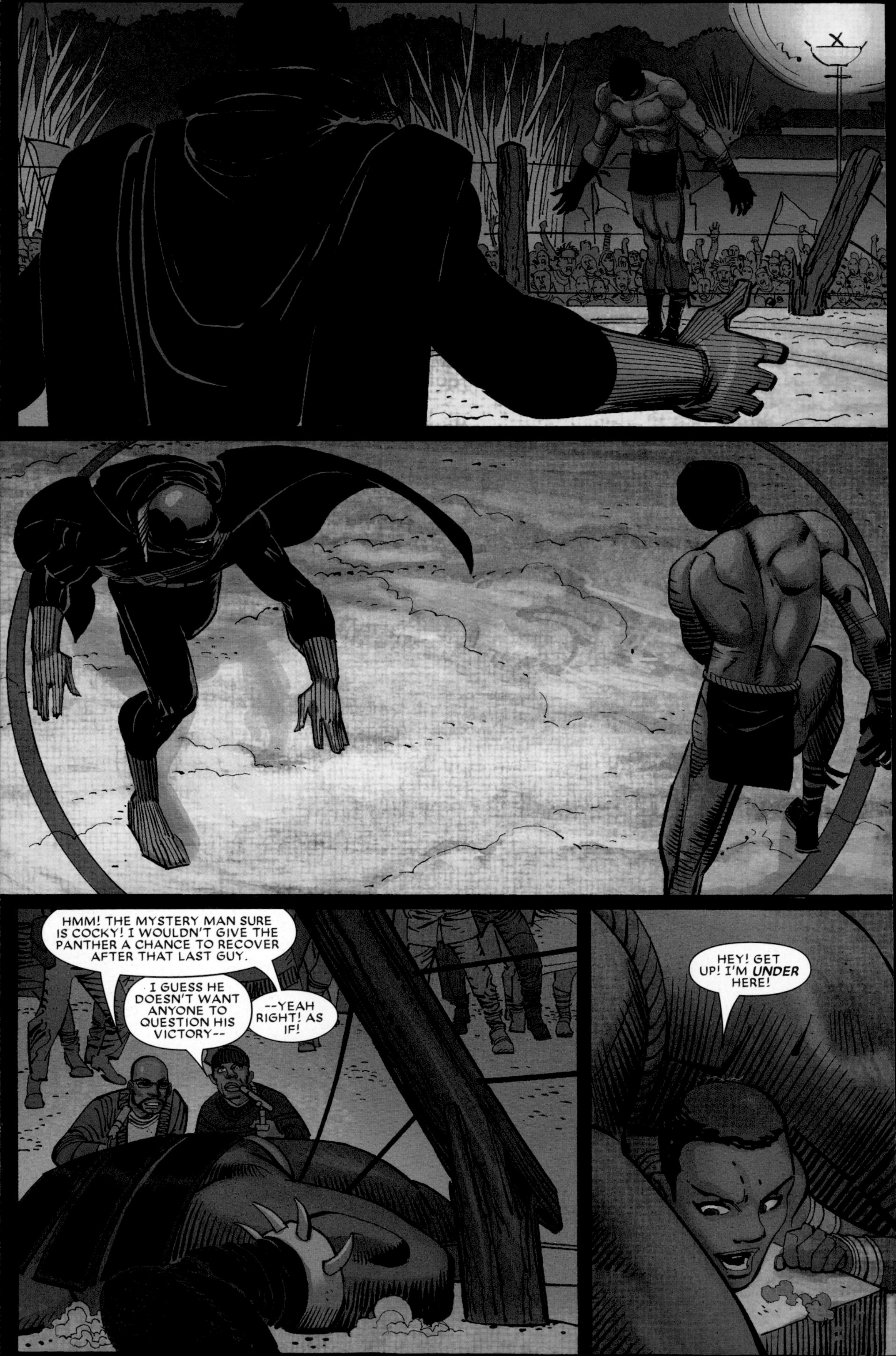
HMM! THE MYSTERY MAN SURE IS COCKY! I WOULDN'T GIVE THE PANTHER A CHANCE TO RECOVER AFTER THAT LAST GUY.
I GUESS HE DOESN'T WANT ANYONE TO QUESTION HIS VICTORY--
--YEAH RIGHT! AS IF!
HEY! GET UP! I'M ***UNDER*** HERE!

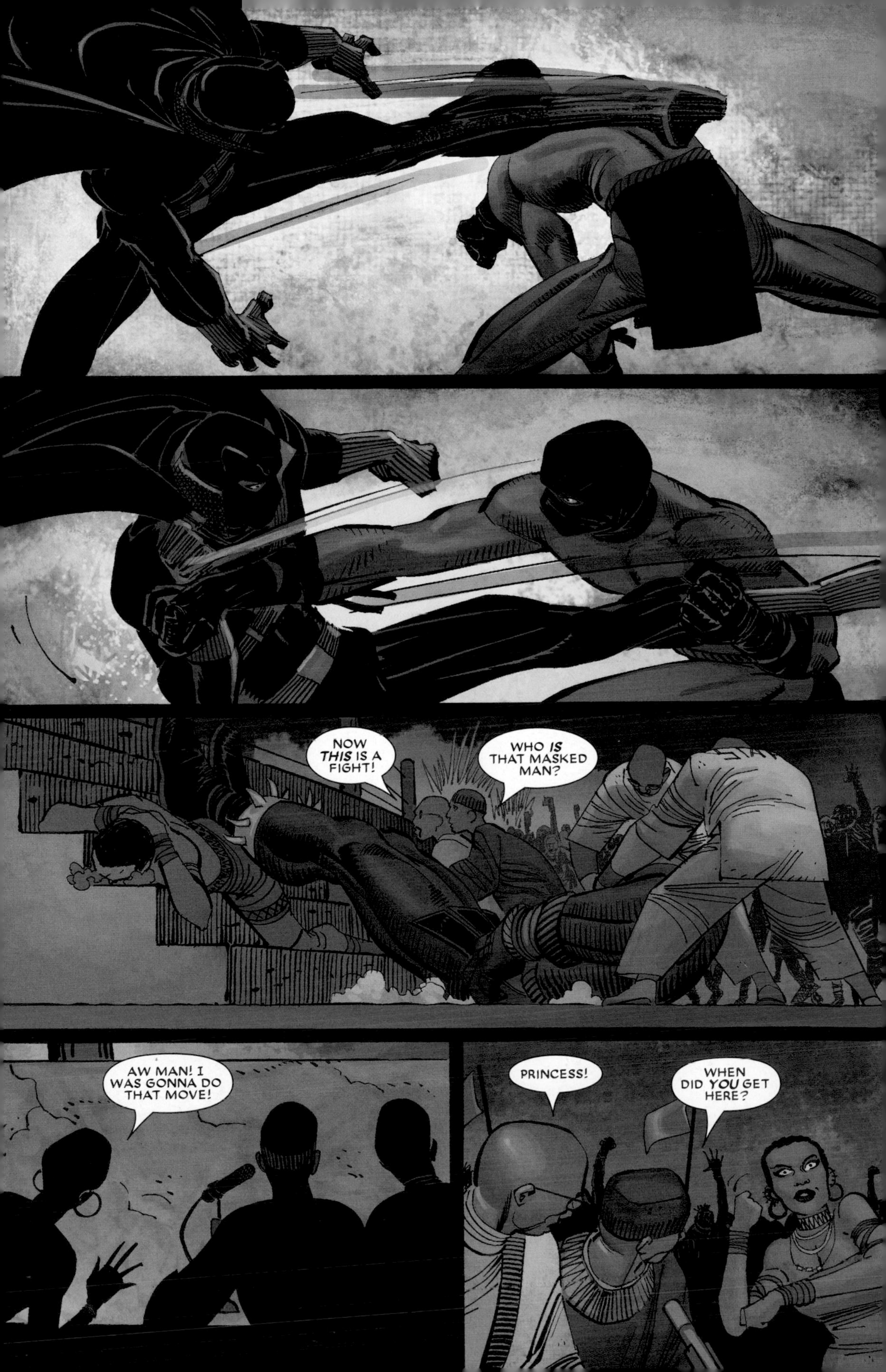
NOW THIS IS A FIGHT!
WHO IS THAT MASKED MAN?
AW MAN! I WAS GONNA DO THAT MOVE!
PRINCESS!
WHEN DID YOU GET HERE?

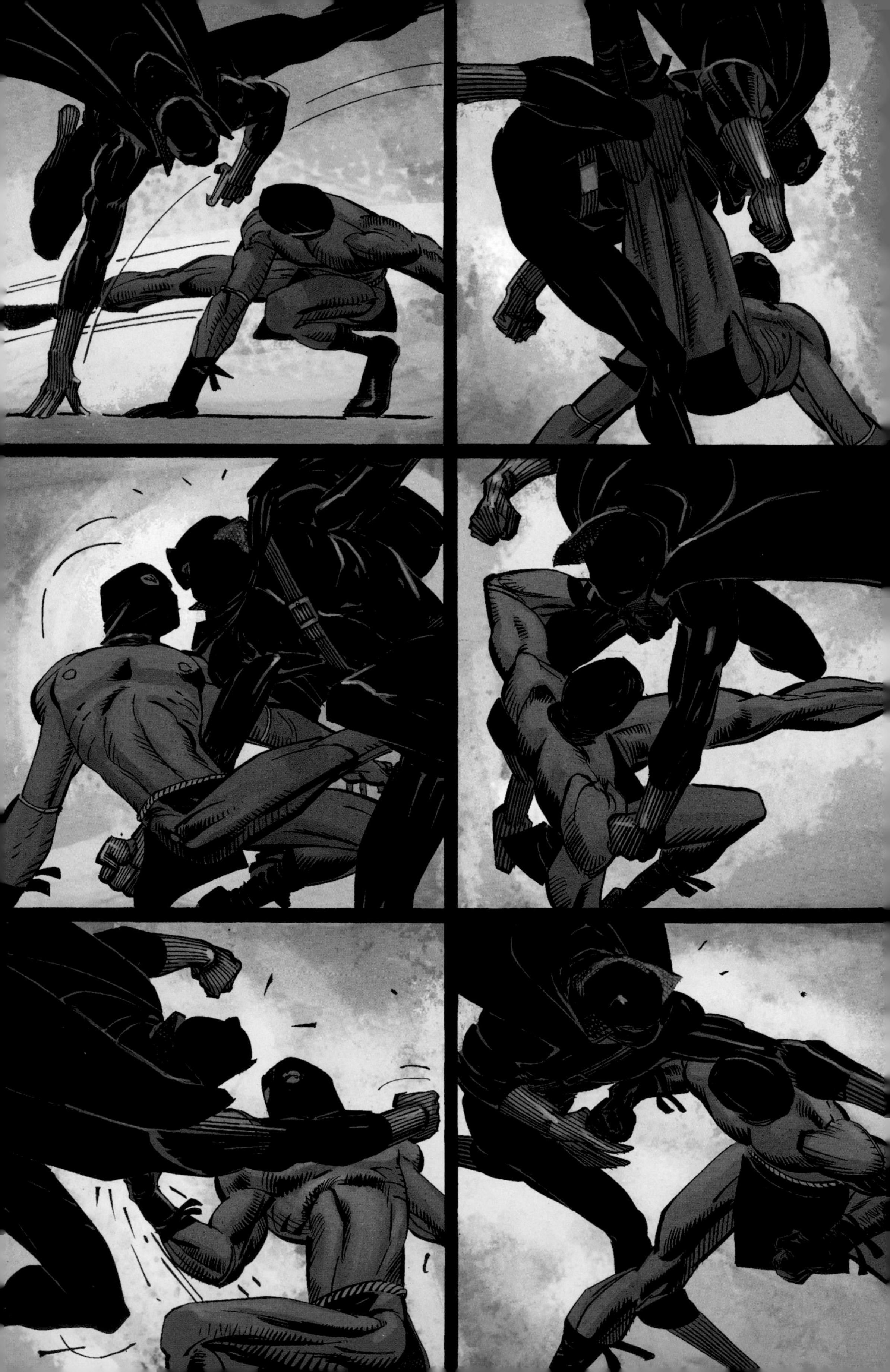

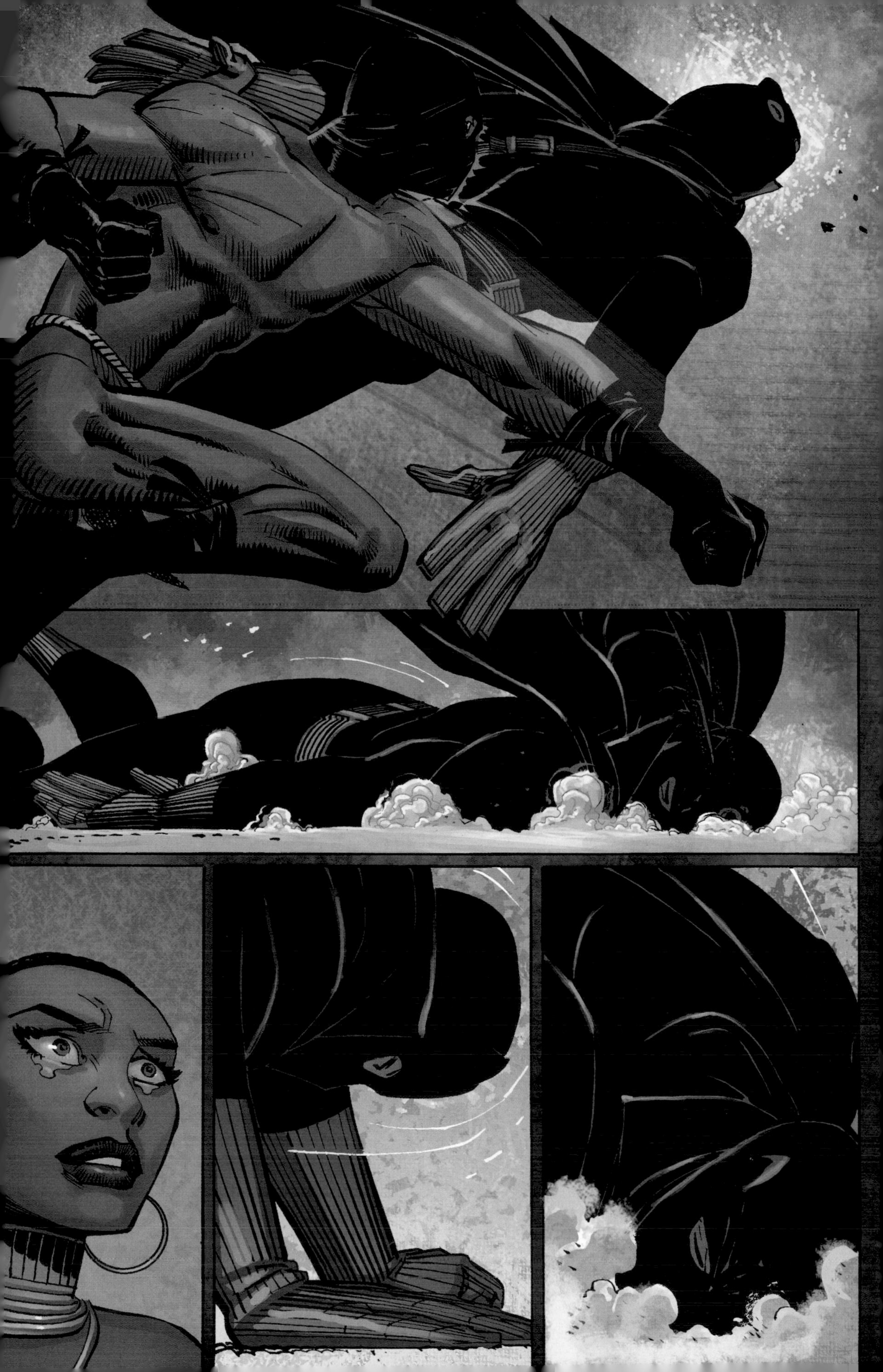

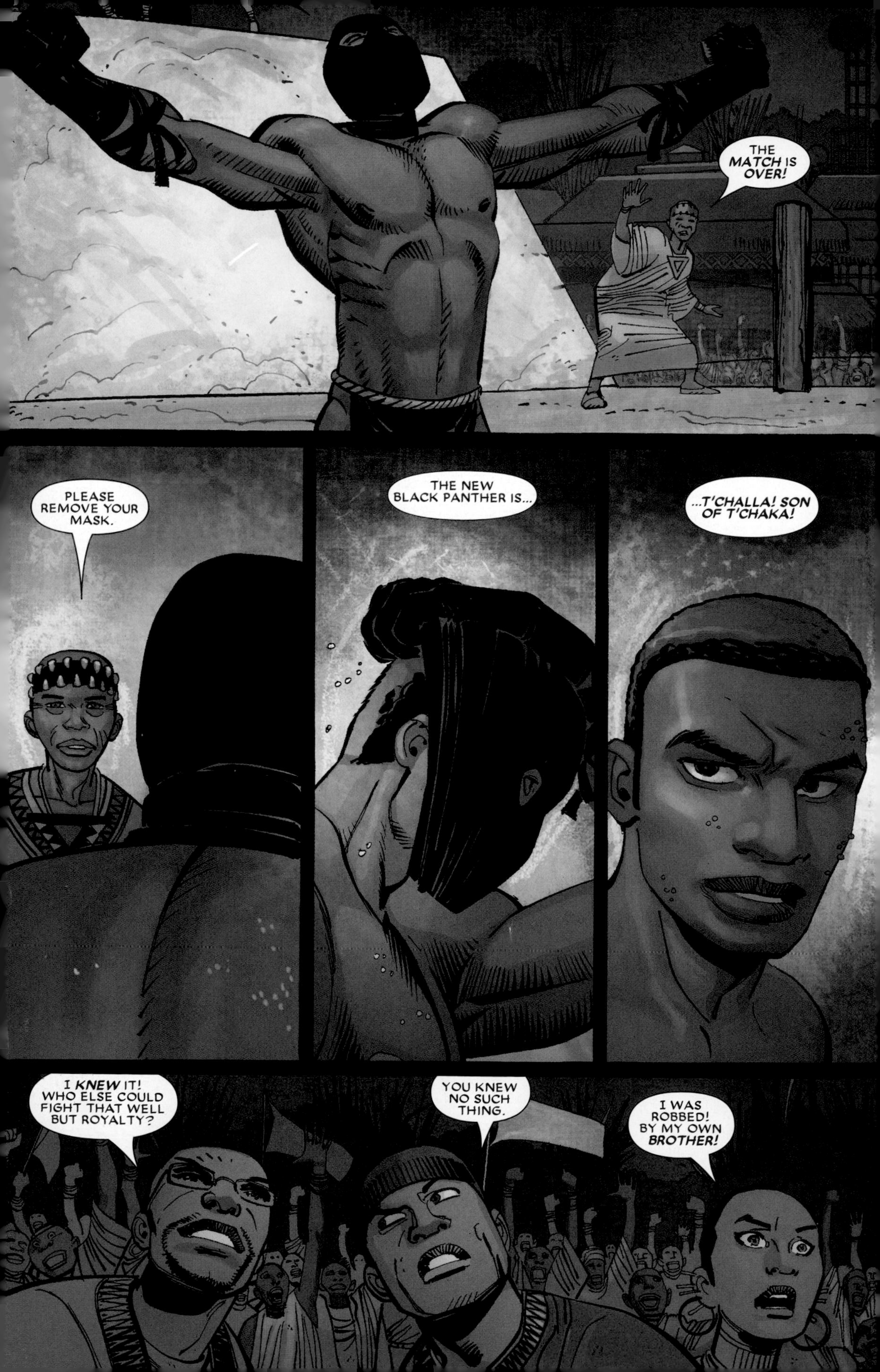
THE MATCH IS OVER!
PLEASE REMOVE YOUR MASK.
THE NEW BLACK PANTHER IS...
...T'CHALLA! SON OF T'CHAKA!
I KNEW IT! WHO ELSE COULD FIGHT THAT WELL BUT ROYALTY?
YOU KNEW NO SUCH THING.
I WAS ROBBED! BY MY OWN BROTHER!

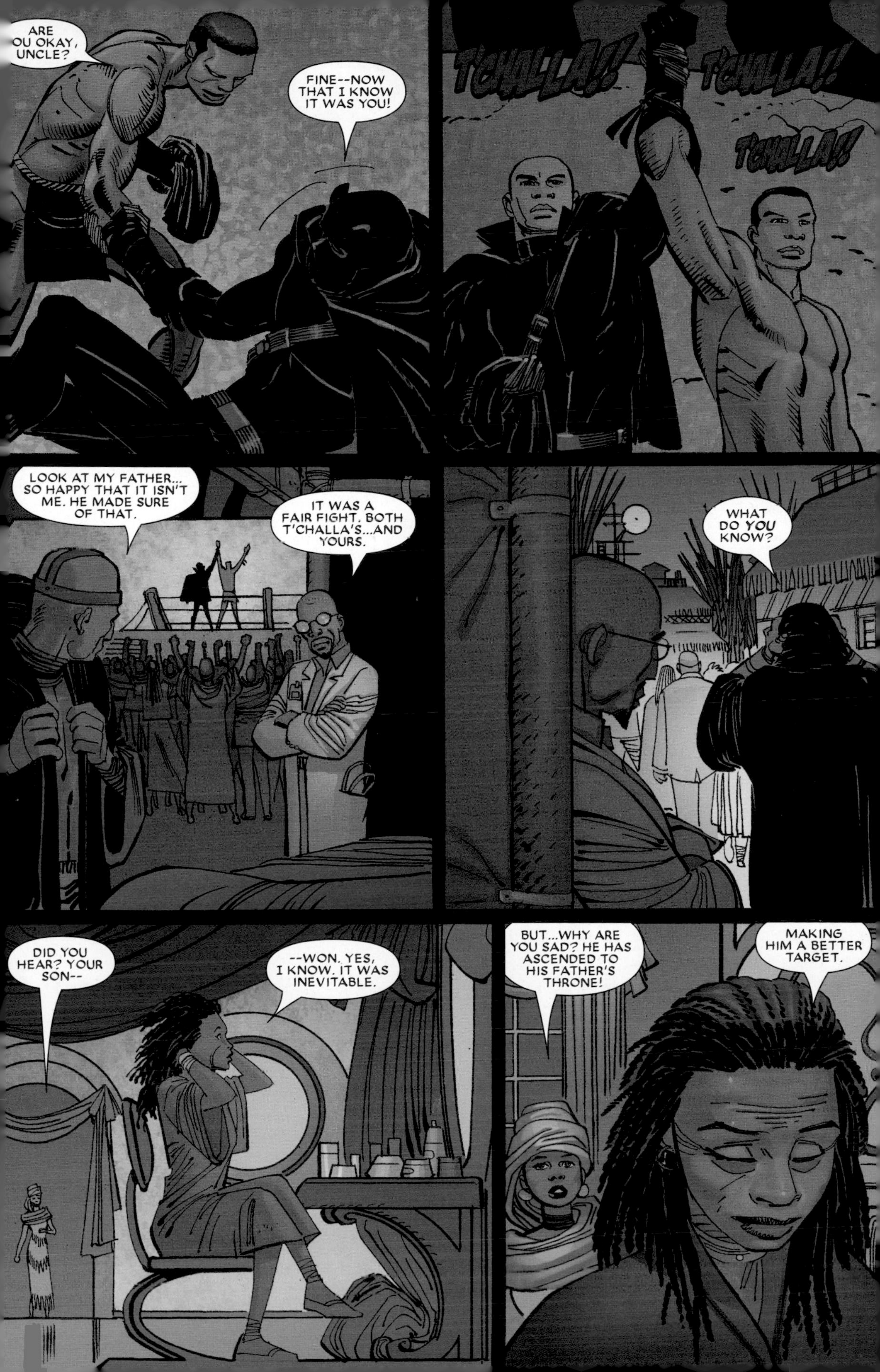
ARE OU OKAY, UNCLE?
FINE--NOW THAT I KNOW IT WAS YOU!
T'CHALLA!!
T'CHALLA!
T'CHALLA!!
LOOK AT MY FATHER... SO HAPPY THAT IT ISN'T ME. HE MADE SURE OF THAT.
IT WAS A FAIR FIGHT. BOTH T'CHALLA'S...AND YOURS.
WHAT DO YOU KNOW?
DID YOU HEAR? YOUR SON--
--WON. YES, I KNOW. IT WAS INEVITABLE.
BUT...WHY ARE YOU SAD? HE HAS ASCENDED TO HIS FATHER'S THRONE!
MAKING HIM A BETTER TARGET.

...SO WHAT WE'VE GOT HERE IS A HIGHLY MILITARISTIC CULTURE WITH NO TIES TO THE UNITED STATES....

THEY'RE A ROGUE STATE!

BEFORE YOU GO ADDING THEM TO THE "AXIS OF EVIL," I SHOULD POINT OUT THAT THEY HAVE NEVER INVADED ANYONE. THE ONLY TIME THEY'VE TAKEN HOSTILE ACTION IS DEFENDING THEIR OWN BORDERS.

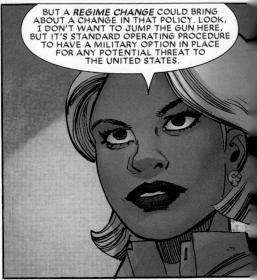

BUT A REGIME CHANGE COULD BRING ABOUT A CHANGE IN THAT POLICY. LOOK, I DON'T WANT TO JUMP THE GUN HERE, BUT IT'S STANDARD OPERATING PROCEDURE TO HAVE A MILITARY OPTION IN PLACE FOR ANY POTENTIAL THREAT TO THE UNITED STATES.

I CERTAINLY DON'T WANT TO SPEAK IN THE PLACE OF THE RECENTLY DEPARTED GENERAL, BUT WITH OUR MILITARY FORCES STRETCHED ALL OVER THE MIDDLE EAST, DO WE EVEN HAVE THE RESOURCES--?

YOU'RE RIGHT, MR. ROSS, THAT IS NOT YOUR AREA OF EXPERTISE. YOU JUST KEEP PROVIDING ACCURATE INFORMATION.

BESIDES, THIS CONFLICT WOULD NOT BE APPROPRIATE FOR CONVENTIONAL FORCES. THIS IS A JOB FOR SPECIAL FORCES.

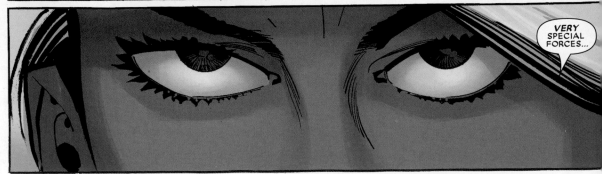

VERY SPECIAL FORCES...

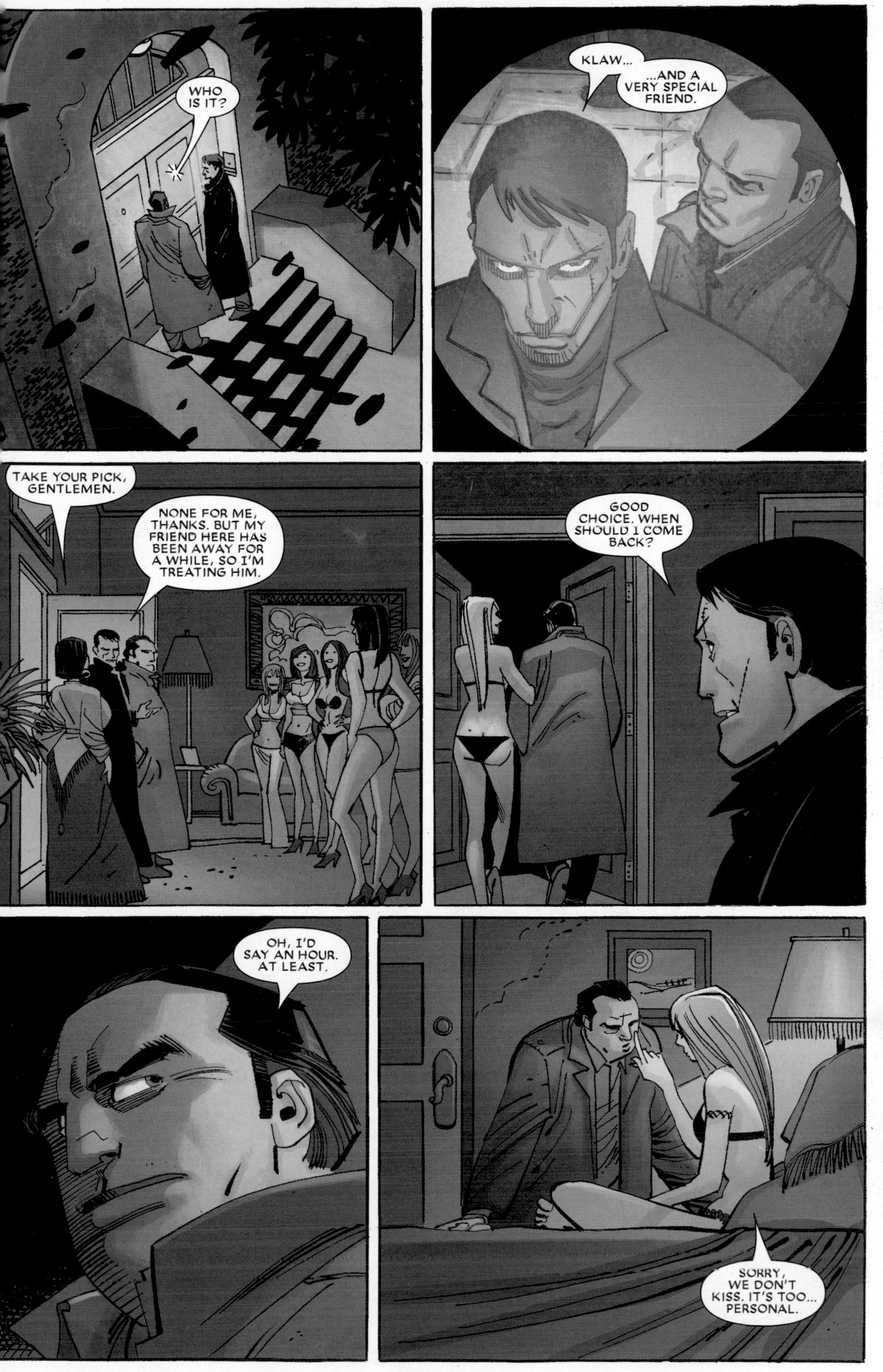
WHO IS IT?
KLAW...
...AND A VERY SPECIAL FRIEND.
TAKE YOUR PICK, GENTLEMEN.
NONE FOR ME, THANKS. BUT MY FRIEND HERE HAS BEEN AWAY FOR A WHILE, SO I'M TREATING HIM.
GOOD CHOICE. WHEN SHOULD I COME BACK?
OH, I'D SAY AN HOUR. AT LEAST.
SORRY, WE DON'T KISS. IT'S TOO... PERSONAL.

I UNDERSTAND. DOES THIS MAKE IT WORTH YOUR WHILE?

NO, I'M SORRY--

HOW ABOUT NOW? IT'S JUST ONE KISS.

OKAY... JUST ONE.

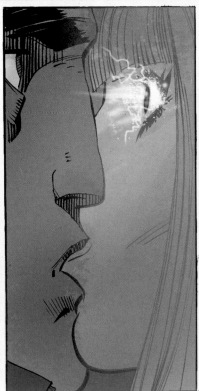

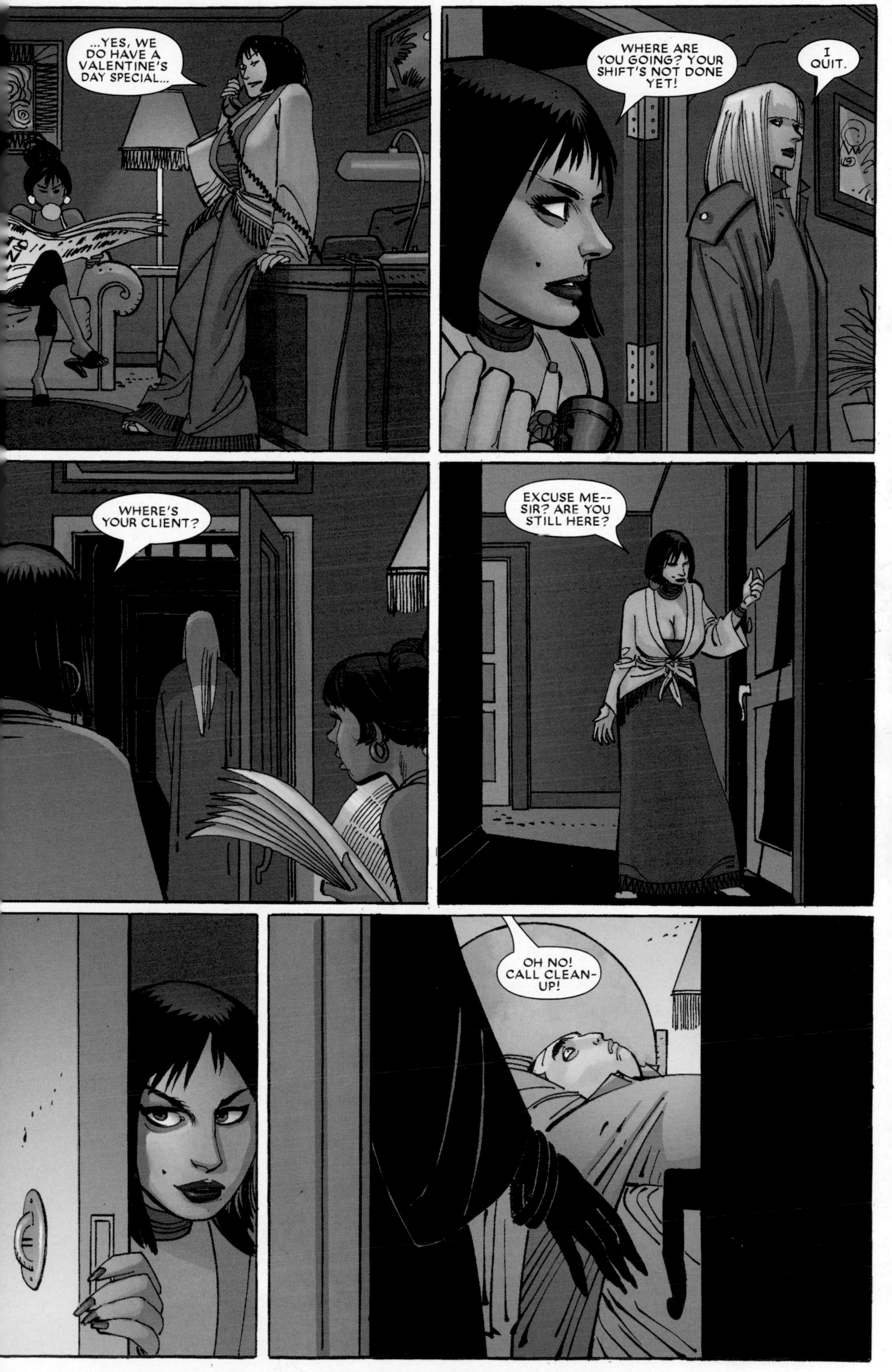
...YES, WE DO HAVE A VALENTINE'S DAY SPECIAL...
WHERE ARE YOU GOING? YOUR SHIFT'S NOT DONE YET!
I QUIT.
WHERE'S YOUR CLIENT?
EXCUSE ME-- SIR? ARE YOU STILL HERE?
OH NO! CALL CLEAN-UP!

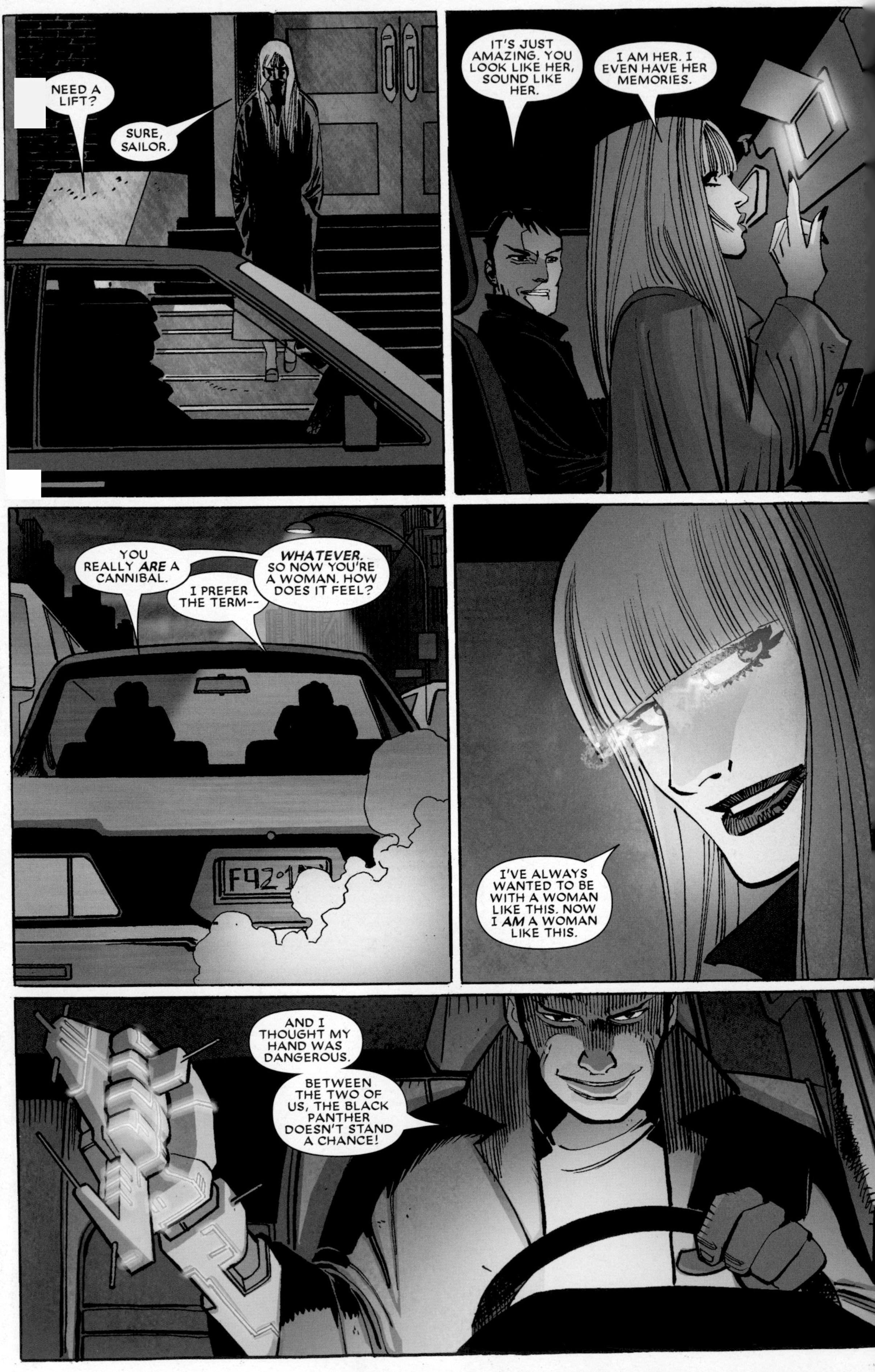
NEED A LIFT?
SURE, SAILOR.
IT'S JUST AMAZING. YOU LOOK LIKE HER, SOUND LIKE HER.
I AM HER. I EVEN HAVE HER MEMORIES.
YOU REALLY ARE A CANNIBAL.
I PREFER THE TERM--
WHATEVER. SO NOW YOU'RE A WOMAN. HOW DOES IT FEEL?
I'VE ALWAYS WANTED TO BE WITH A WOMAN LIKE THIS. NOW I AM A WOMAN LIKE THIS.
AND I THOUGHT MY HAND WAS DANGEROUS.
BETWEEN THE TWO OF US, THE BLACK PANTHER DOESN'T STAND A CHANCE!

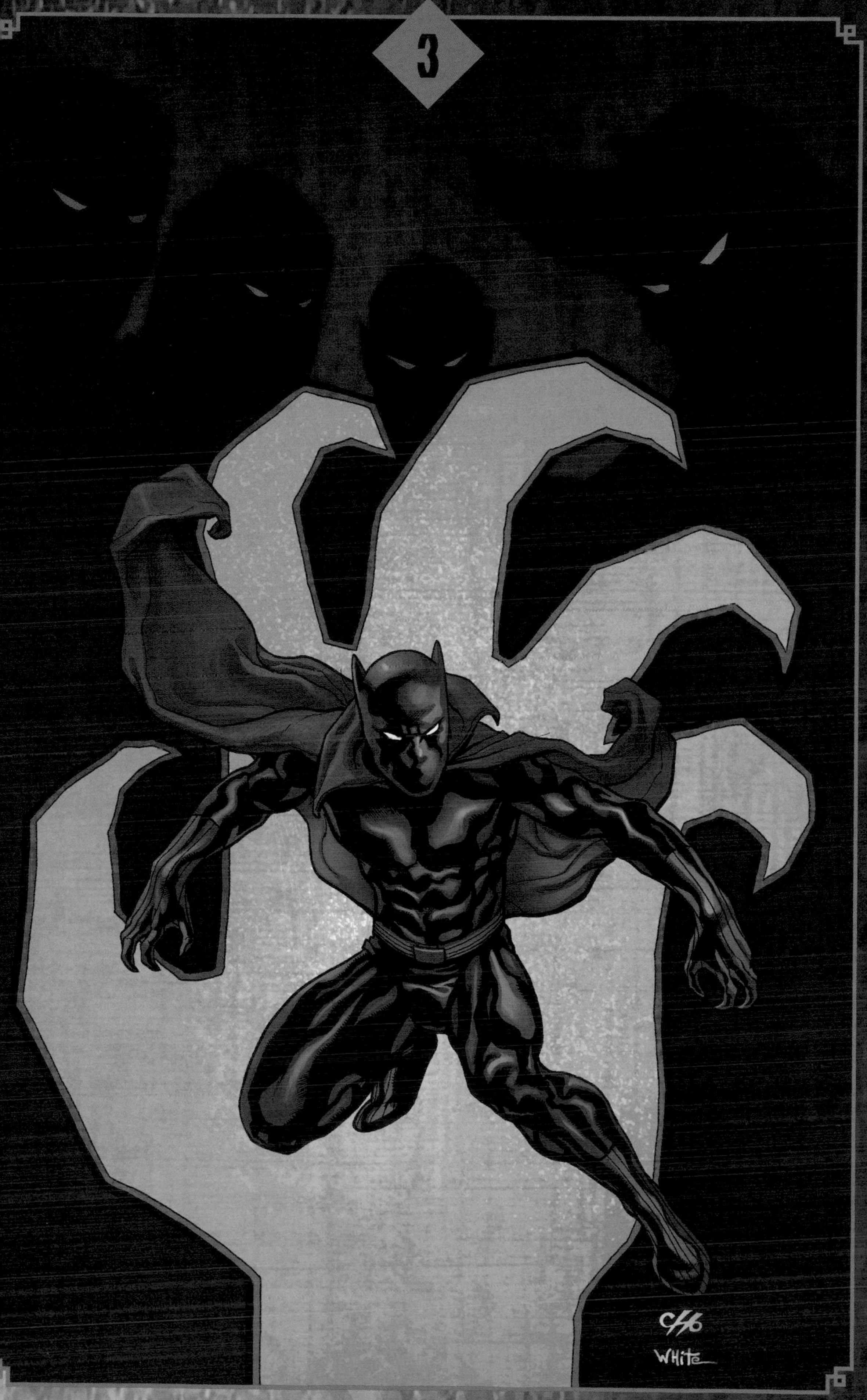
3
CHO
WHITE

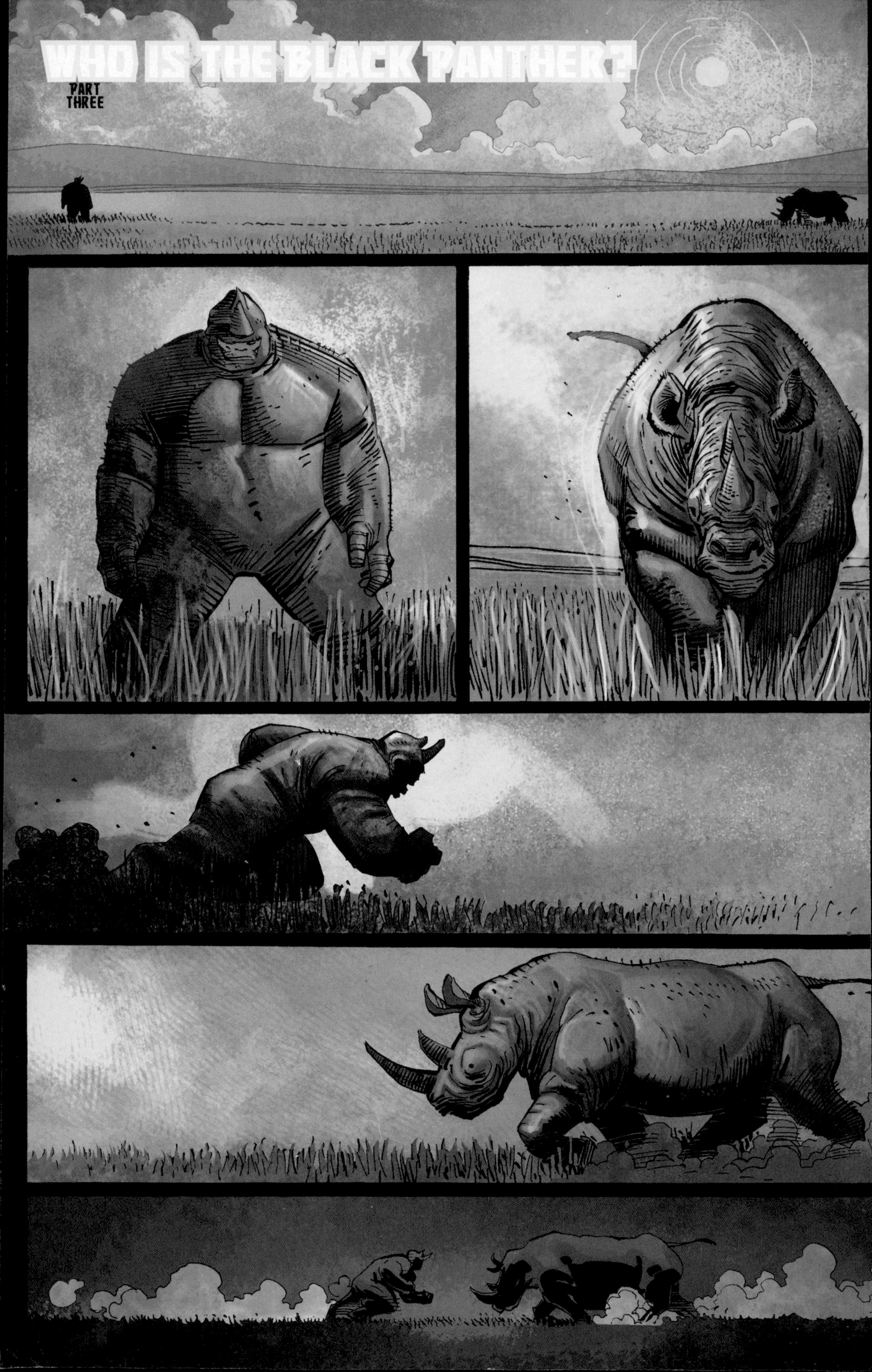
WHO IS THE BLACK PANTHER?
PART THREE

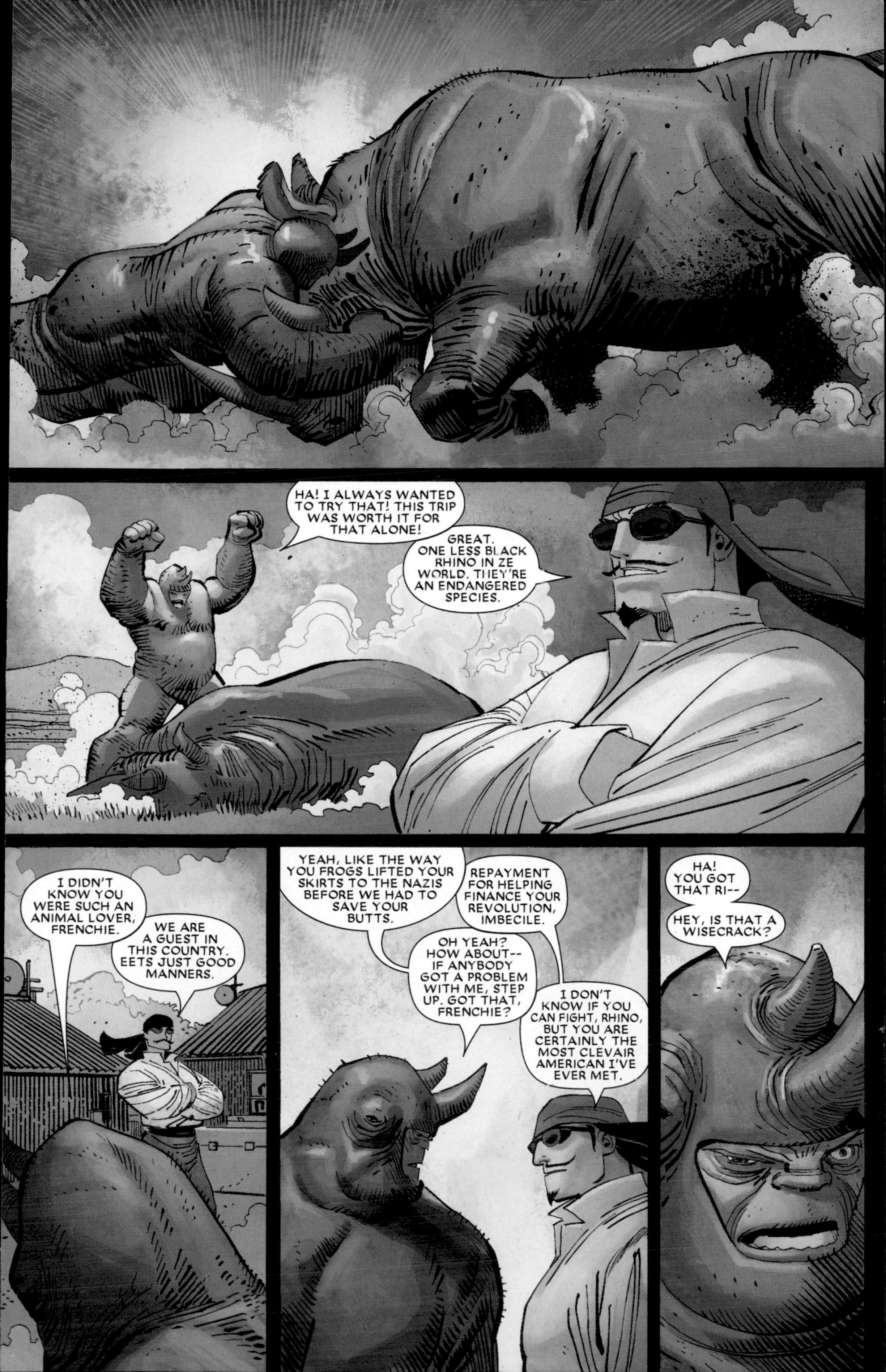
HA! I ALWAYS WANTED TO TRY THAT! THIS TRIP WAS WORTH IT FOR THAT ALONE!
GREAT. ONE LESS BLACK RHINO IN ZE WORLD. THEY'RE AN ENDANGERED SPECIES.
I DIDN'T KNOW YOU WERE SUCH AN ANIMAL LOVER, FRENCHIE.
WE ARE A GUEST IN THIS COUNTRY. EETS JUST GOOD MANNERS.
YEAH, LIKE THE WAY YOU FROGS LIFTED YOUR SKIRTS TO THE NAZIS BEFORE WE HAD TO SAVE YOUR BUTTS.
REPAYMENT FOR HELPING FINANCE YOUR REVOLUTION, IMBECILE.
OH YEAH? HOW ABOUT-- IF ANYBODY GOT A PROBLEM WITH ME, STEP UP. GOT THAT, FRENCHIE?
I DON'T KNOW IF YOU CAN FIGHT, RHINO, BUT YOU ARE CERTAINLY THE MOST CLEVAIR AMERICAN I'VE EVER MET.
HA! YOU GOT THAT RI--
HEY, IS THAT A WISECRACK?

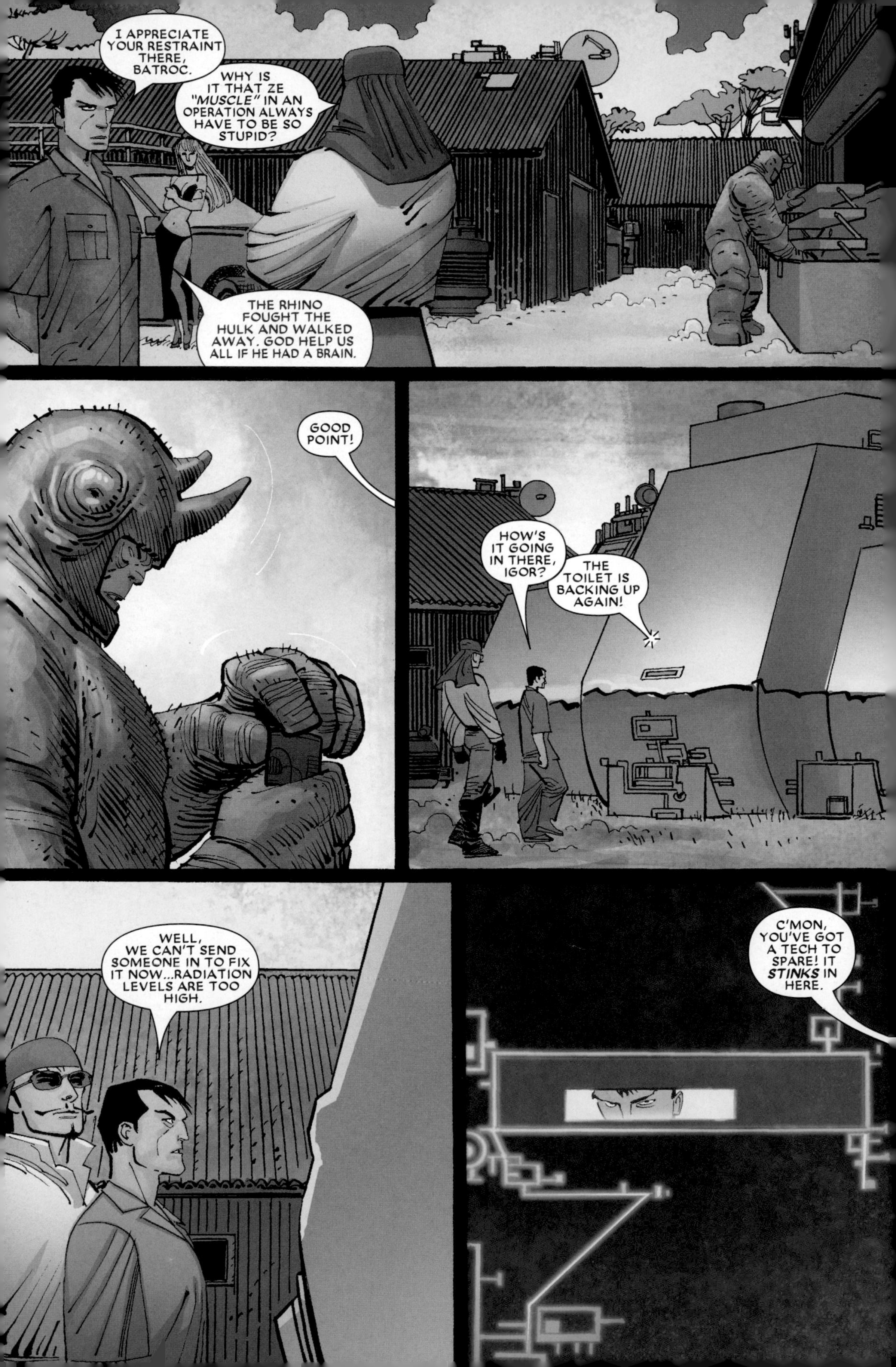
I APPRECIATE YOUR RESTRAINT THERE, BATROC.
WHY IS IT THAT ZE "MUSCLE" IN AN OPERATION ALWAYS HAVE TO BE SO STUPID?
THE RHINO FOUGHT THE HULK AND WALKED AWAY. GOD HELP US ALL IF HE HAD A BRAIN.
GOOD POINT!
HOW'S IT GOING IN THERE, IGOR?
THE TOILET IS BACKING UP AGAIN!
WELL, WE CAN'T SEND SOMEONE IN TO FIX IT NOW...RADIATION LEVELS ARE TOO HIGH.
C'MON, YOU'VE GOT A TECH TO SPARE! IT STINKS IN HERE.

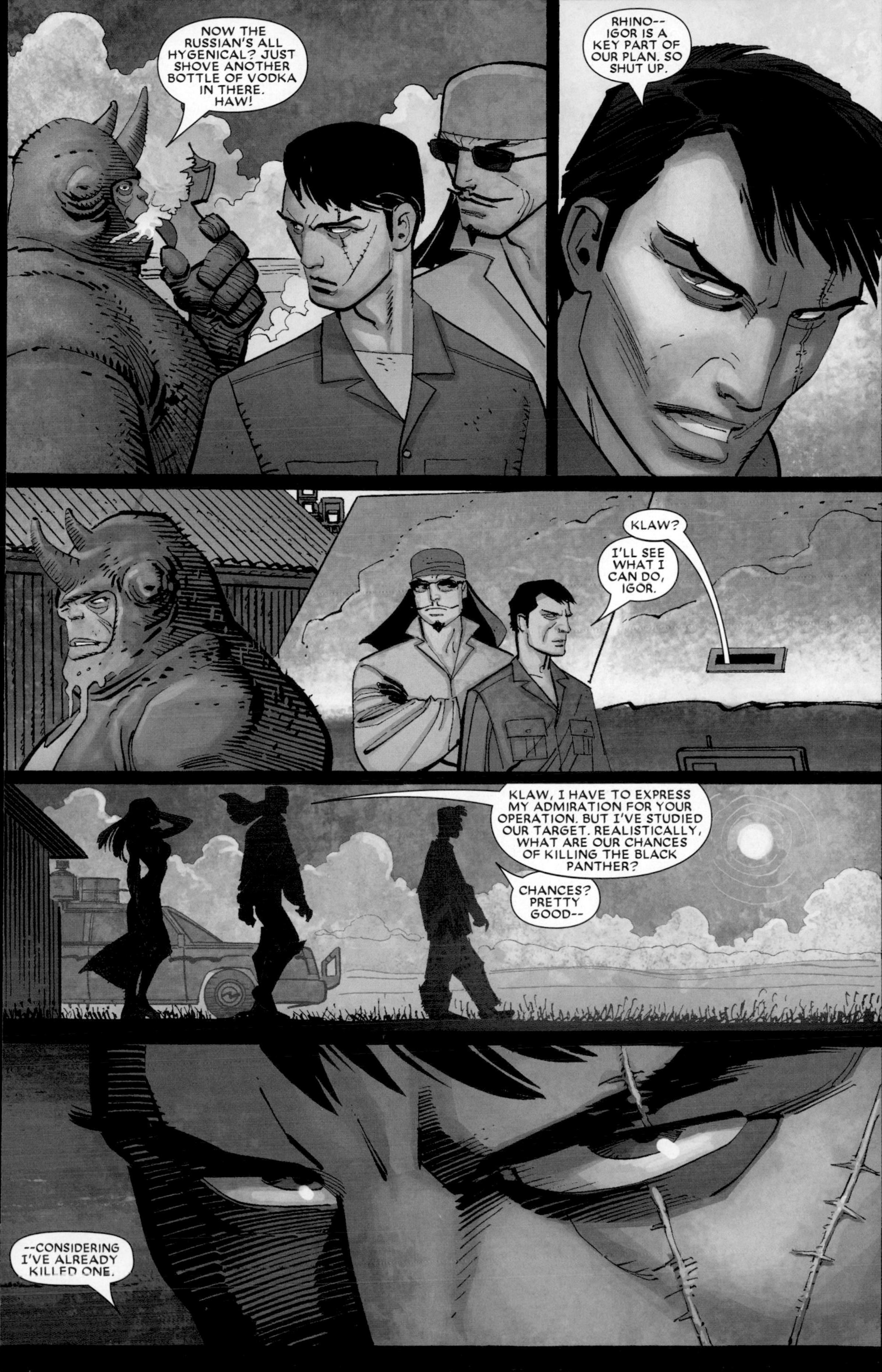
NOW THE RUSSIAN'S ALL HYGENICAL? JUST SHOVE ANOTHER BOTTLE OF VODKA IN THERE. HAW!
RHINO-- IGOR IS A KEY PART OF OUR PLAN. SO SHUT UP.
KLAW?
I'LL SEE WHAT I CAN DO, IGOR.
KLAW, I HAVE TO EXPRESS MY ADMIRATION FOR YOUR OPERATION. BUT I'VE STUDIED OUR TARGET. REALISTICALLY, WHAT ARE OUR CHANCES OF KILLING THE BLACK PANTHER?
CHANCES? PRETTY GOOD--
--CONSIDERING I'VE ALREADY KILLED ONE.

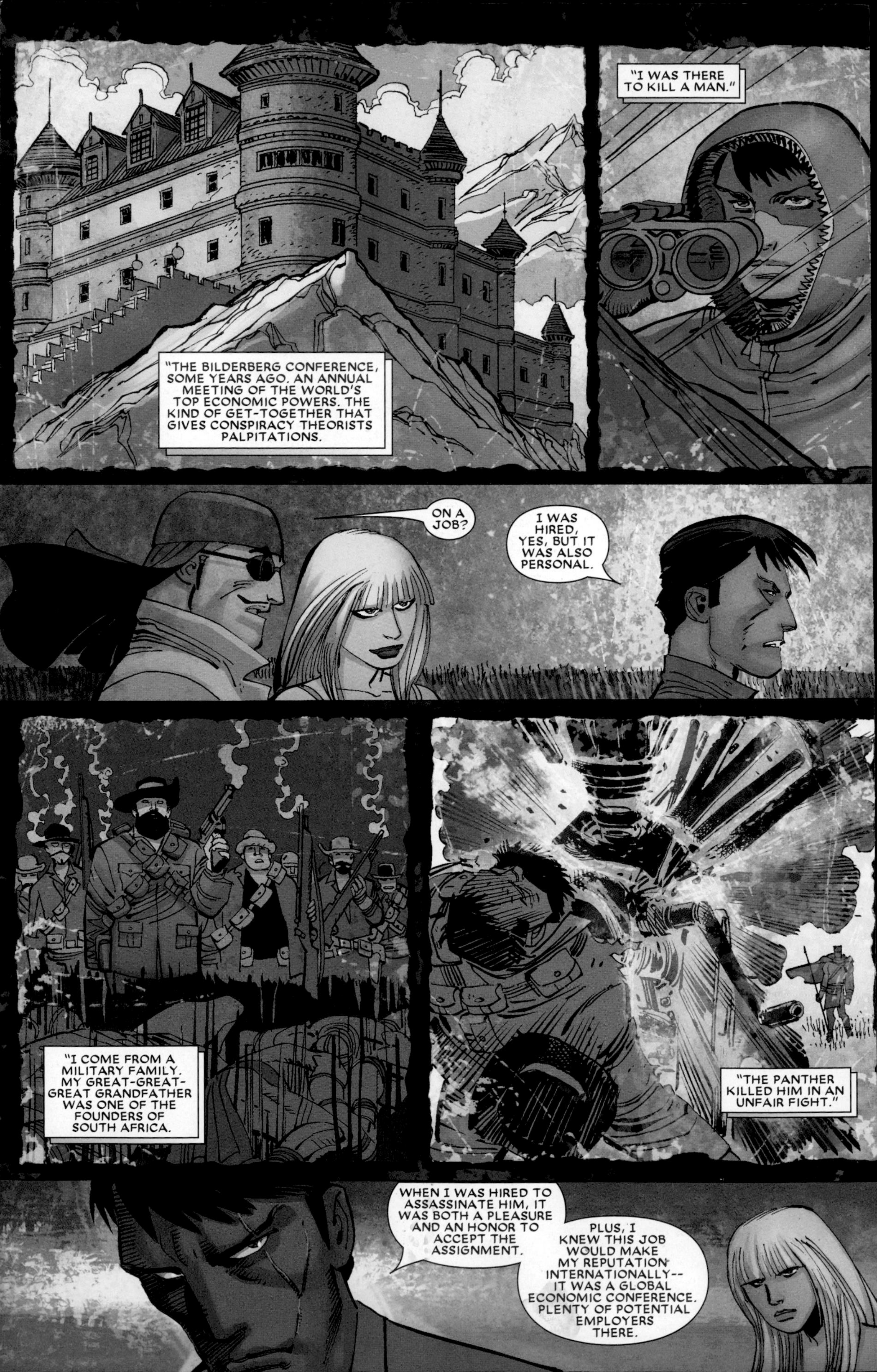
"THE BILDERBERG CONFERENCE, SOME YEARS AGO. AN ANNUAL MEETING OF THE WORLD'S TOP ECONOMIC POWERS. THE KIND OF GET-TOGETHER THAT GIVES CONSPIRACY THEORISTS PALPITATIONS.
"I WAS THERE TO KILL A MAN."
ON A JOB?
I WAS HIRED, YES, BUT IT WAS ALSO PERSONAL.
"I COME FROM A MILITARY FAMILY. MY GREAT-GREAT-GREAT GRANDFATHER WAS ONE OF THE FOUNDERS OF SOUTH AFRICA.
"THE PANTHER KILLED HIM IN AN UNFAIR FIGHT."
WHEN I WAS HIRED TO ASSASSINATE HIM, IT WAS BOTH A PLEASURE AND AN HONOR TO ACCEPT THE ASSIGNMENT.
PLUS, I KNEW THIS JOB WOULD MAKE MY REPUTATION INTERNATIONALLY-- IT WAS A GLOBAL ECONOMIC CONFERENCE. PLENTY OF POTENTIAL EMPLOYERS THERE.

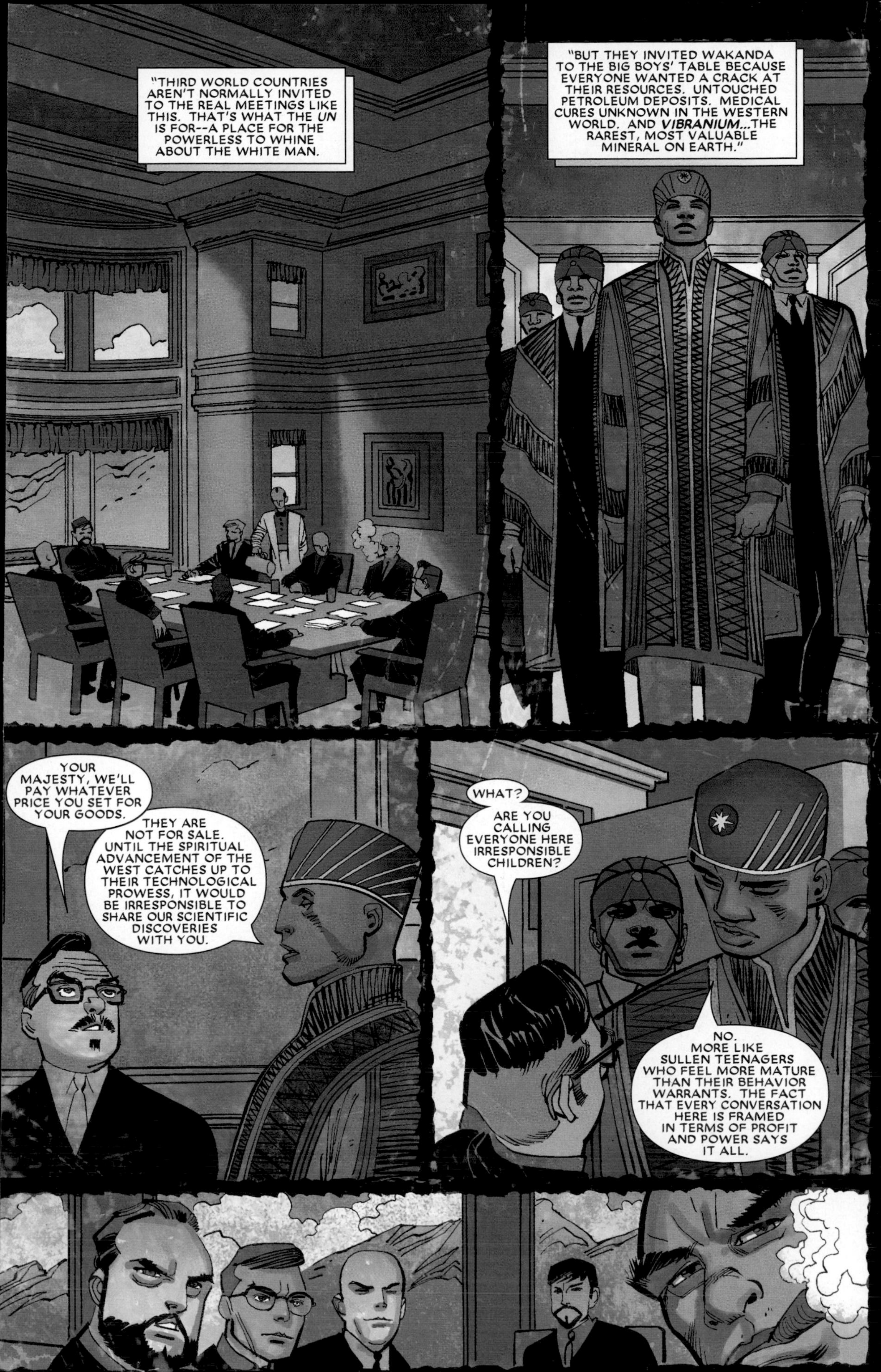
"THIRD WORLD COUNTRIES AREN'T NORMALLY INVITED TO THE REAL MEETINGS LIKE THIS. THAT'S WHAT THE *UN* IS FOR--A PLACE FOR THE POWERLESS TO WHINE ABOUT THE WHITE MAN.
"BUT THEY INVITED WAKANDA TO THE BIG BOYS' TABLE BECAUSE EVERYONE WANTED A CRACK AT THEIR RESOURCES. UNTOUCHED PETROLEUM DEPOSITS. MEDICAL CURES UNKNOWN IN THE WESTERN WORLD. AND ***VIBRANIUM...*** THE RAREST, MOST VALUABLE MINERAL ON EARTH."
YOUR MAJESTY, WE'LL PAY WHATEVER PRICE YOU SET FOR YOUR GOODS.
THEY ARE NOT FOR SALE. UNTIL THE SPIRITUAL ADVANCEMENT OF THE WEST CATCHES UP TO THEIR TECHNOLOGICAL PROWESS, IT WOULD BE IRRESPONSIBLE TO SHARE OUR SCIENTIFIC DISCOVERIES WITH YOU.
WHAT?
ARE YOU CALLING EVERYONE HERE IRRESPONSIBLE CHILDREN?
NO. MORE LIKE SULLEN TEENAGERS WHO FEEL MORE MATURE THAN THEIR BEHAVIOR WARRANTS. THE FACT THAT EVERY CONVERSATION HERE IS FRAMED IN TERMS OF PROFIT AND POWER SAYS IT ALL.

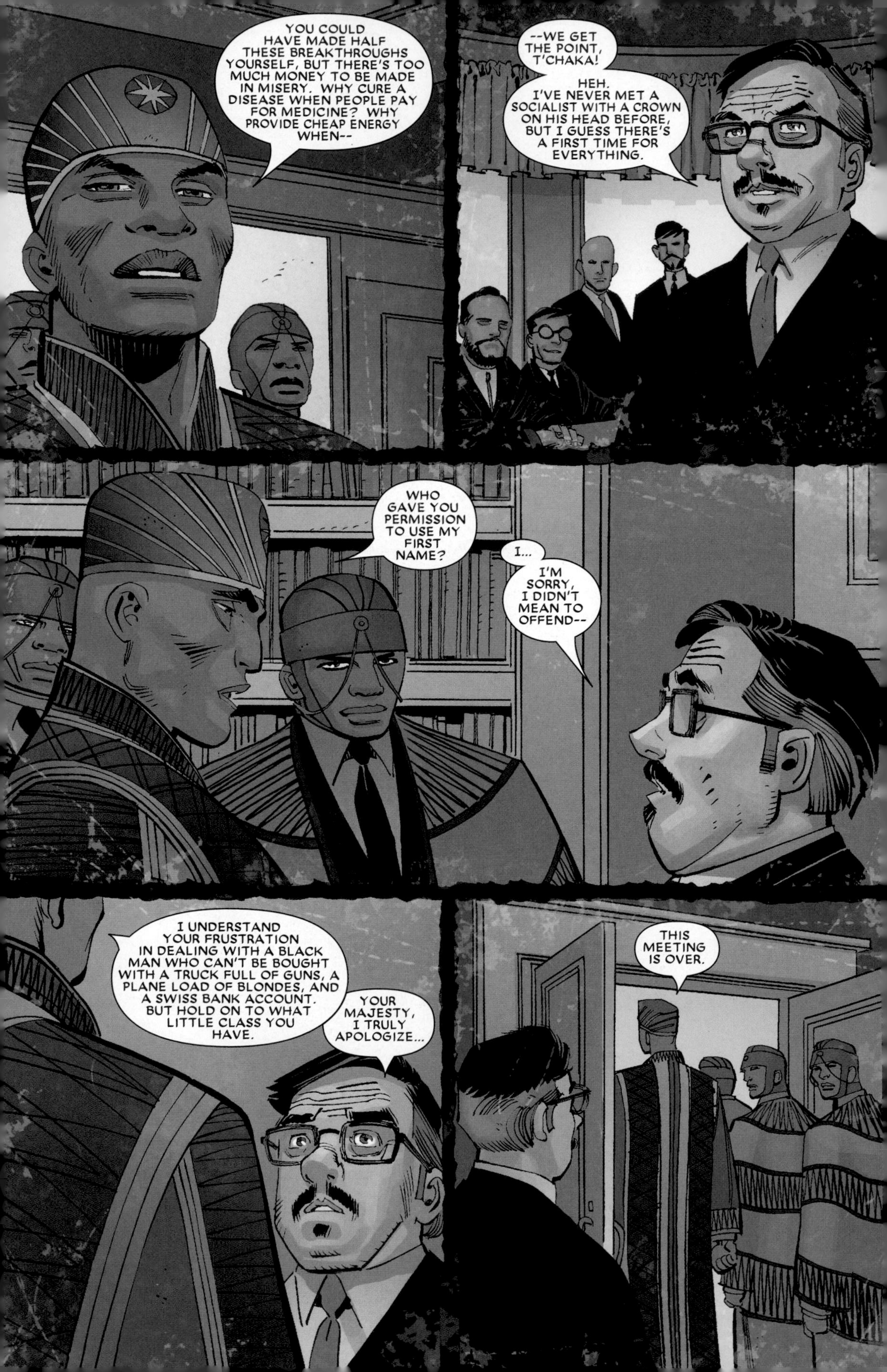
YOU COULD HAVE MADE HALF THESE BREAKTHROUGHS YOURSELF, BUT THERE'S TOO MUCH MONEY TO BE MADE IN MISERY. WHY CURE A DISEASE WHEN PEOPLE PAY FOR MEDICINE? WHY PROVIDE CHEAP ENERGY WHEN--
--WE GET THE POINT, T'CHAKA!
HEH. I'VE NEVER MET A SOCIALIST WITH A CROWN ON HIS HEAD BEFORE, BUT I GUESS THERE'S A FIRST TIME FOR EVERYTHING.
WHO GAVE YOU PERMISSION TO USE MY FIRST NAME?
I...
I'M SORRY, I DIDN'T MEAN TO OFFEND--
I UNDERSTAND YOUR FRUSTRATION IN DEALING WITH A BLACK MAN WHO CAN'T BE BOUGHT WITH A TRUCK FULL OF GUNS, A PLANE LOAD OF BLONDES, AND A SWISS BANK ACCOUNT. BUT HOLD ON TO WHAT LITTLE CLASS YOU HAVE.
YOUR MAJESTY, I TRULY APOLOGIZE...
THIS MEETING IS OVER.

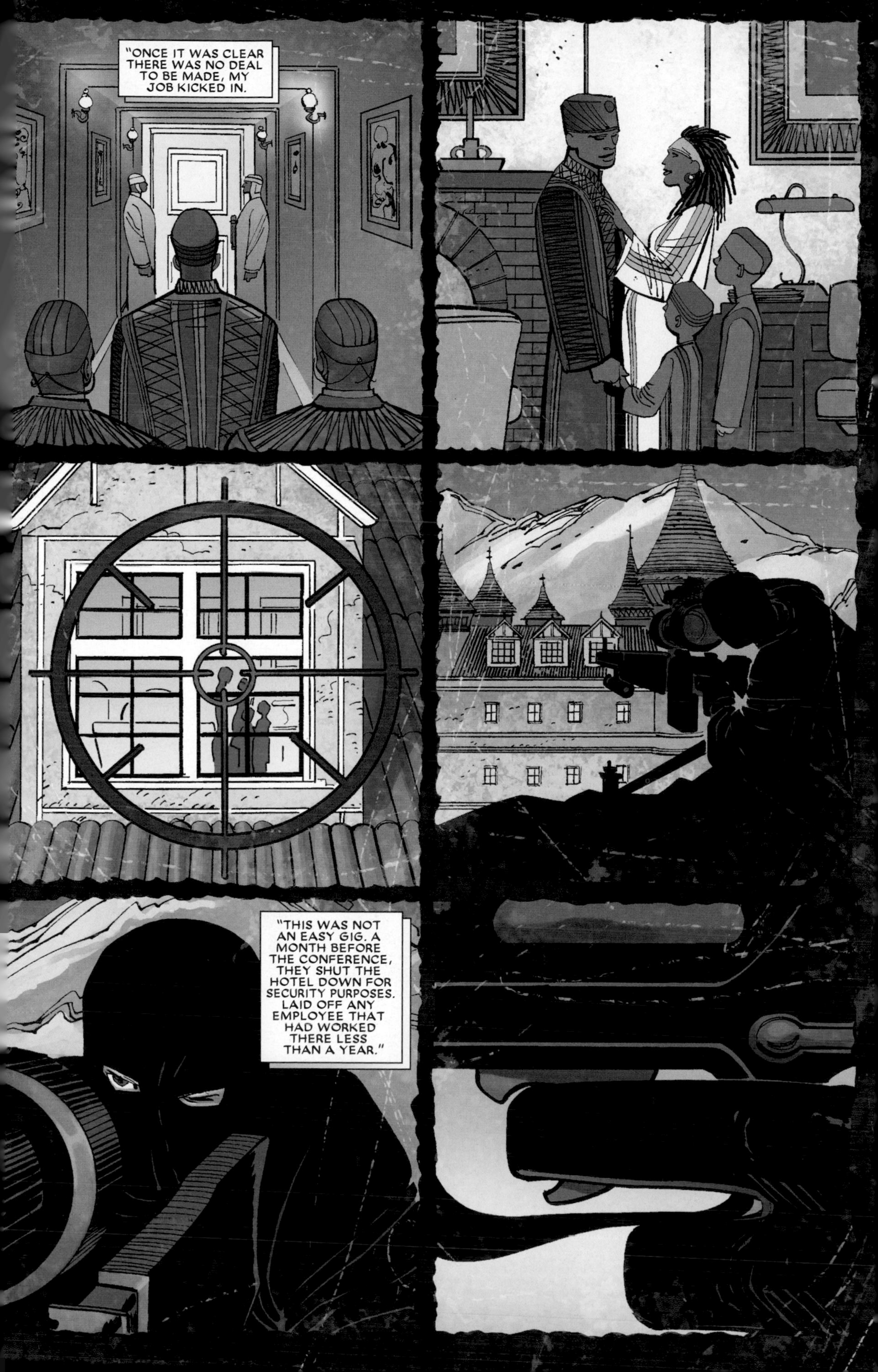
"ONCE IT WAS CLEAR THERE WAS NO DEAL TO BE MADE, MY JOB KICKED IN.
"THIS WAS NOT AN EASY GIG. A MONTH BEFORE THE CONFERENCE, THEY SHUT THE HOTEL DOWN FOR SECURITY PURPOSES. LAID OFF ANY EMPLOYEE THAT HAD WORKED THERE LESS THAN A YEAR."

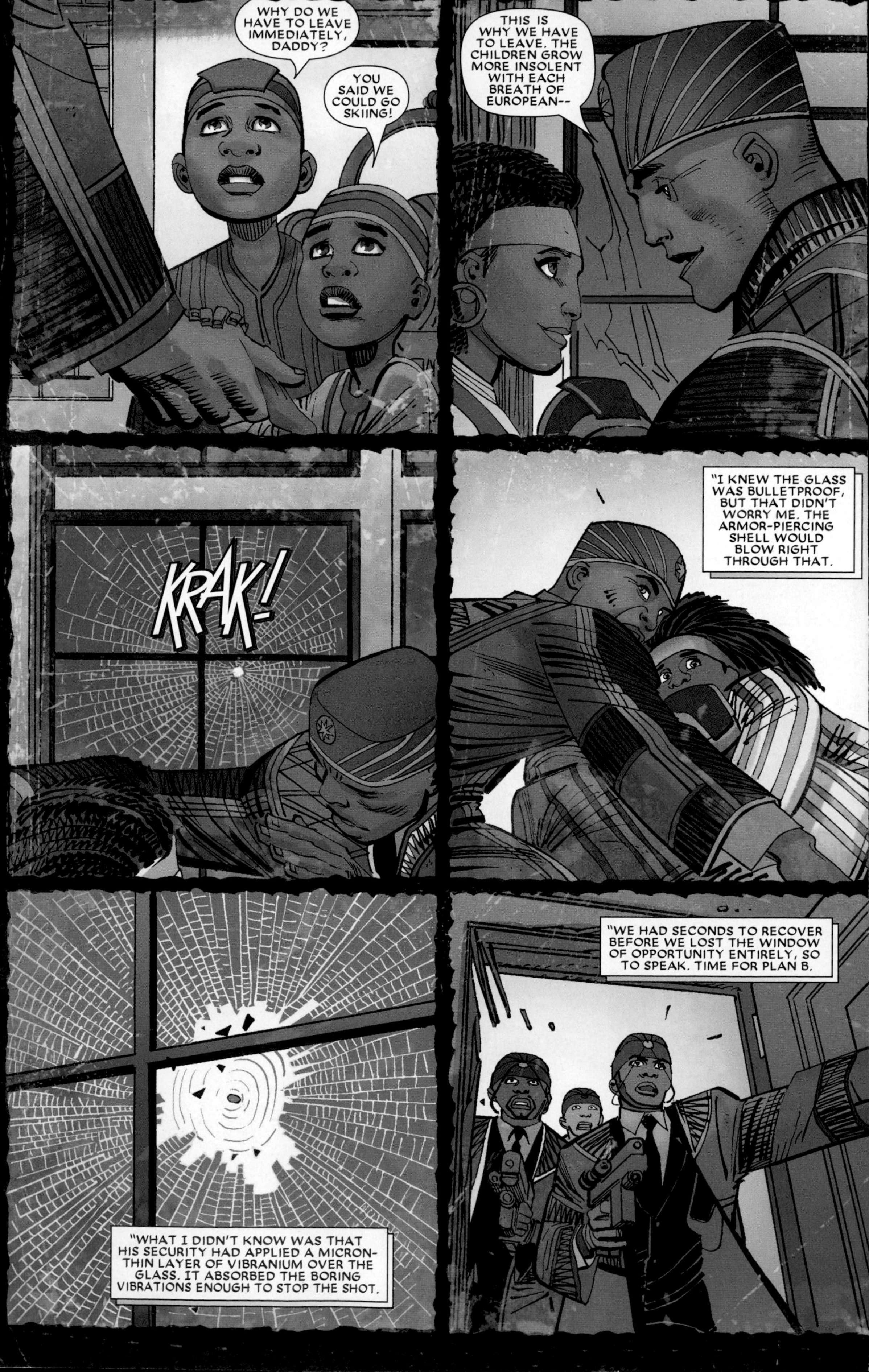
WHY DO WE HAVE TO LEAVE IMMEDIATELY, DADDY?
YOU SAID WE COULD GO SKIING!
THIS IS WHY WE HAVE TO LEAVE. THE CHILDREN GROW MORE INSOLENT WITH EACH BREATH OF EUROPEAN--
KRAK!
"I KNEW THE GLASS WAS BULLETPROOF, BUT THAT DIDN'T WORRY ME. THE ARMOR-PIERCING SHELL WOULD BLOW RIGHT THROUGH THAT.
"WHAT I DIDN'T KNOW WAS THAT HIS SECURITY HAD APPLIED A MICRON-THIN LAYER OF VIBRANIUM OVER THE GLASS. IT ABSORBED THE BORING VIBRATIONS ENOUGH TO STOP THE SHOT.
"WE HAD SECONDS TO RECOVER BEFORE WE LOST THE WINDOW OF OPPORTUNITY ENTIRELY, SO TO SPEAK. TIME FOR PLAN B.

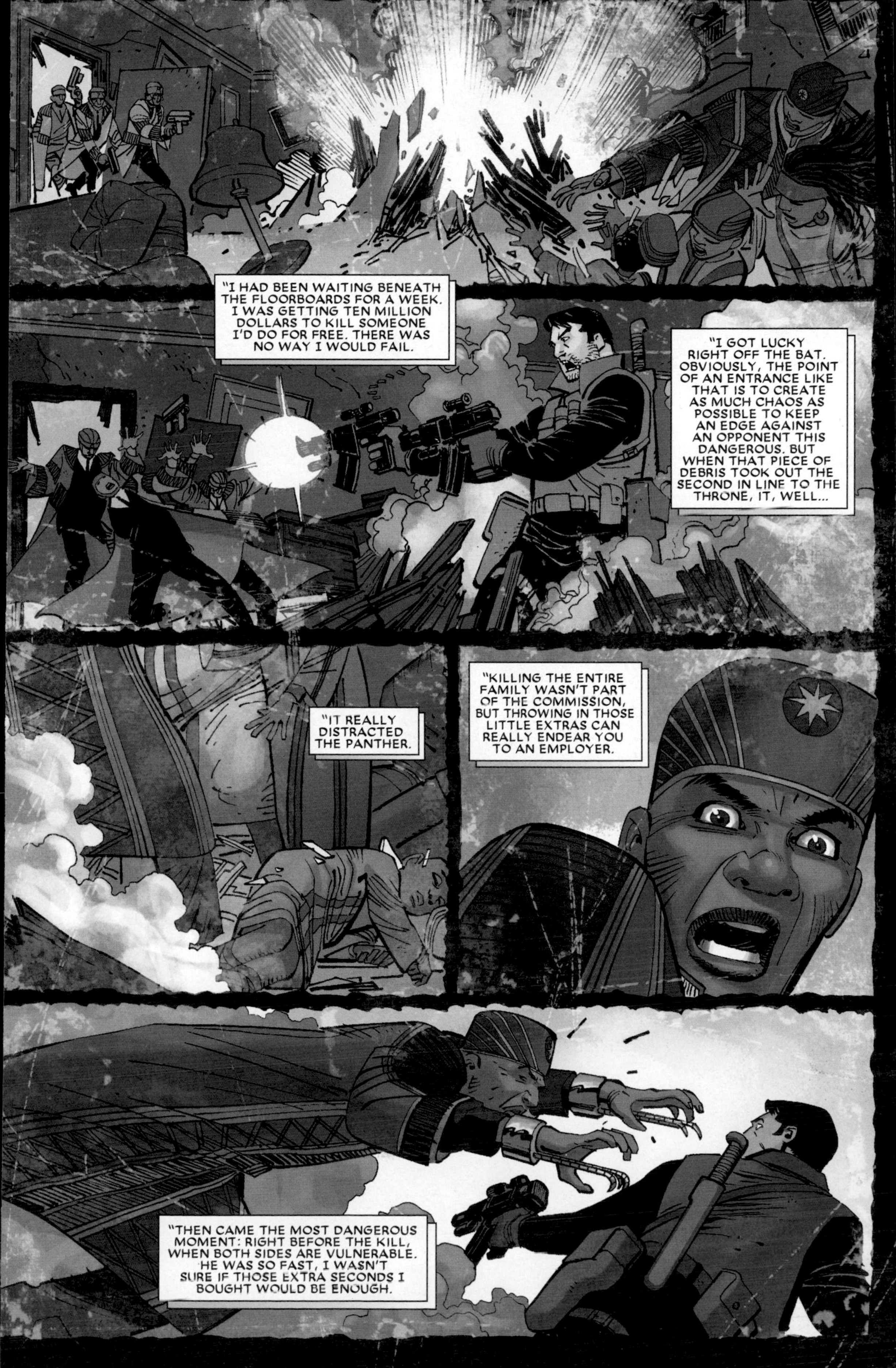
"I HAD BEEN WAITING BENEATH THE FLOORBOARDS FOR A WEEK. I WAS GETTING TEN MILLION DOLLARS TO KILL SOMEONE I'D DO FOR FREE. THERE WAS NO WAY I WOULD FAIL.
"I GOT LUCKY RIGHT OFF THE BAT. OBVIOUSLY, THE POINT OF AN ENTRANCE LIKE THAT IS TO CREATE AS MUCH CHAOS AS POSSIBLE TO KEEP AN EDGE AGAINST AN OPPONENT THIS DANGEROUS. BUT WHEN THAT PIECE OF DEBRIS TOOK OUT THE SECOND IN LINE TO THE THRONE, IT, WELL...
"IT REALLY DISTRACTED THE PANTHER.
"KILLING THE ENTIRE FAMILY WASN'T PART OF THE COMMISSION, BUT THROWING IN THOSE LITTLE EXTRAS CAN REALLY ENDEAR YOU TO AN EMPLOYER.
"THEN CAME THE MOST DANGEROUS MOMENT: RIGHT BEFORE THE KILL, WHEN BOTH SIDES ARE VULNERABLE. HE WAS SO FAST, I WASN'T SURE IF THOSE EXTRA SECONDS I BOUGHT WOULD BE ENOUGH.

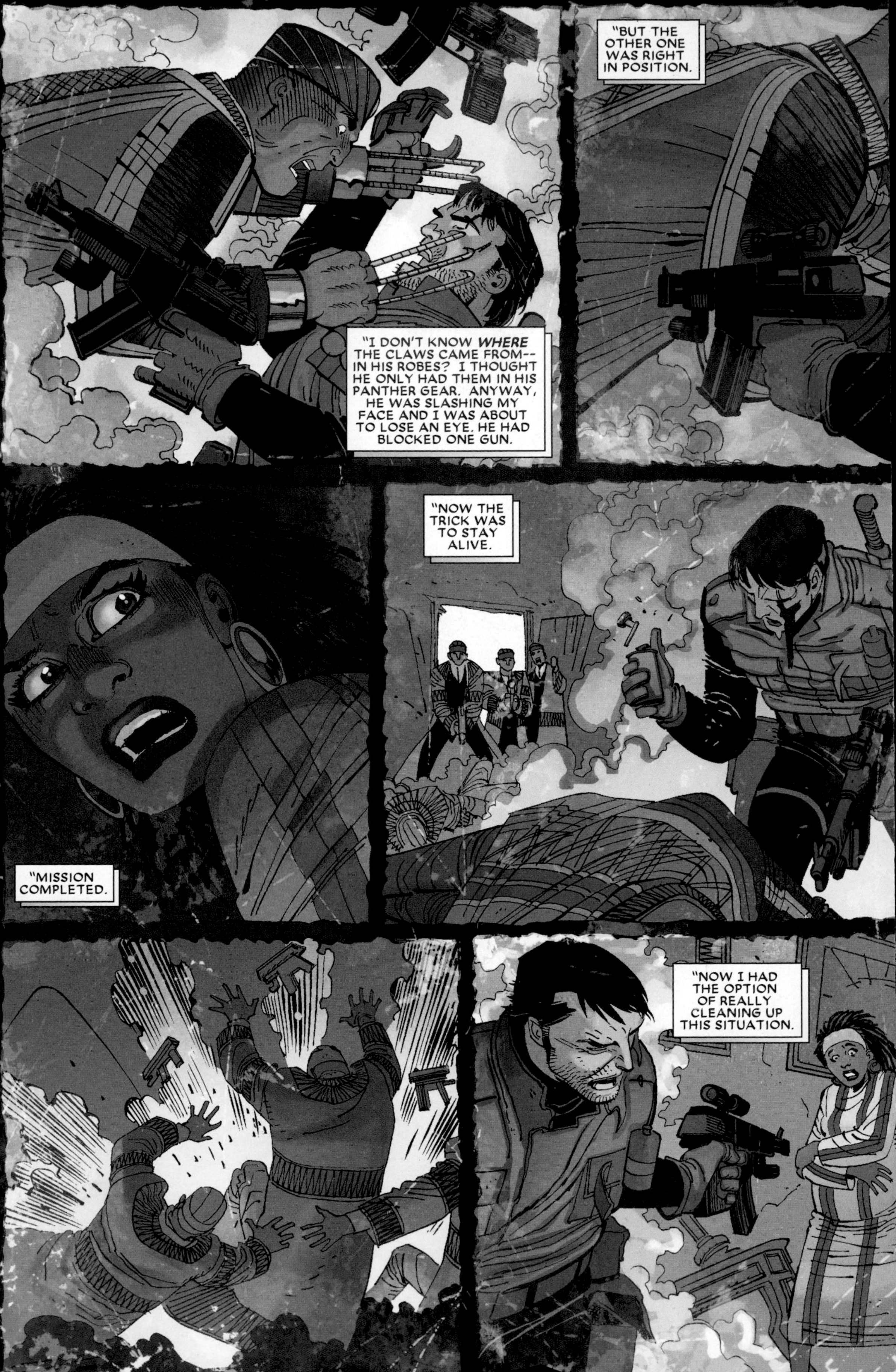
"I DON'T KNOW WHERE THE CLAWS CAME FROM--IN HIS ROBES? I THOUGHT HE ONLY HAD THEM IN HIS PANTHER GEAR. ANYWAY, HE WAS SLASHING MY FACE AND I WAS ABOUT TO LOSE AN EYE. HE HAD BLOCKED ONE GUN.
"BUT THE OTHER ONE WAS RIGHT IN POSITION.
"MISSION COMPLETED.
"NOW THE TRICK WAS TO STAY ALIVE.
"NOW I HAD THE OPTION OF REALLY CLEANING UP THIS SITUATION.

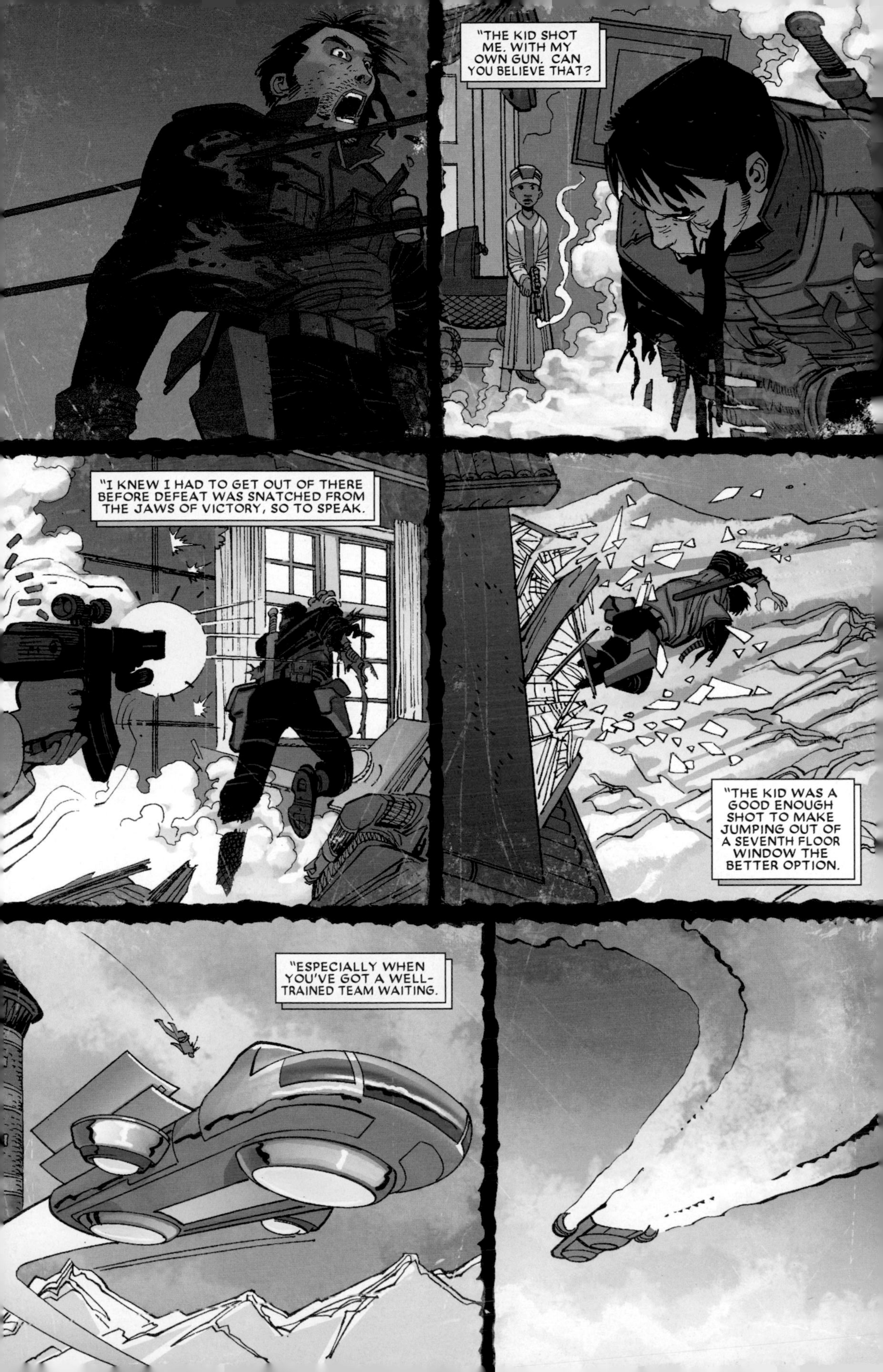
"THE KID SHOT ME. WITH MY OWN GUN. CAN YOU BELIEVE THAT?
"I KNEW I HAD TO GET OUT OF THERE BEFORE DEFEAT WAS SNATCHED FROM THE JAWS OF VICTORY, SO TO SPEAK.
"THE KID WAS A GOOD ENOUGH SHOT TO MAKE JUMPING OUT OF A SEVENTH FLOOR WINDOW THE BETTER OPTION.
"ESPECIALLY WHEN YOU'VE GOT A WELL-TRAINED TEAM WAITING.

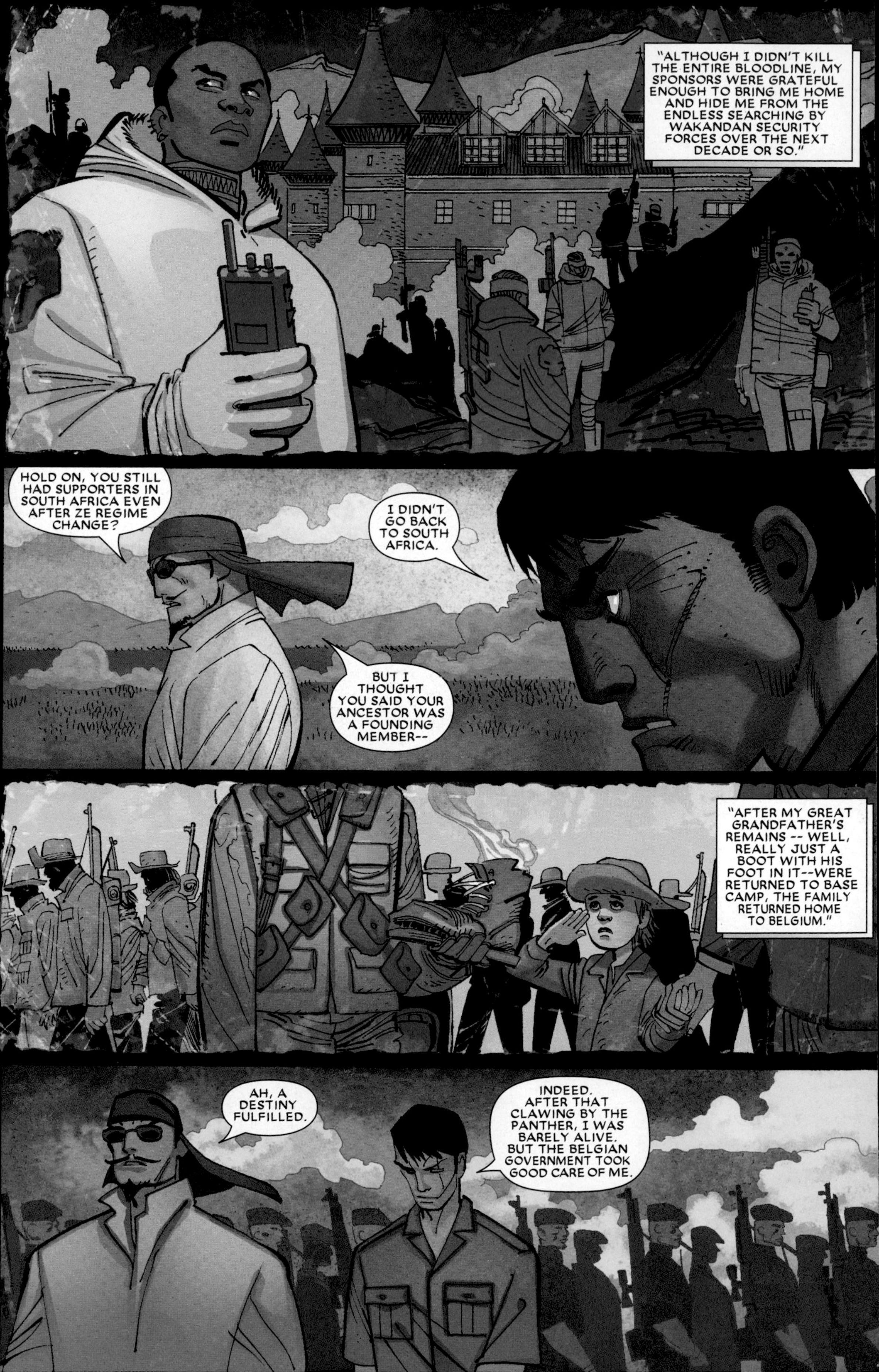
"ALTHOUGH I DIDN'T KILL THE ENTIRE BLOODLINE, MY SPONSORS WERE GRATEFUL ENOUGH TO BRING ME HOME AND HIDE ME FROM THE ENDLESS SEARCHING BY WAKANDAN SECURITY FORCES OVER THE NEXT DECADE OR SO."
HOLD ON, YOU STILL HAD SUPPORTERS IN SOUTH AFRICA EVEN AFTER ZE REGIME CHANGE?
I DIDN'T GO BACK TO SOUTH AFRICA.
BUT I THOUGHT YOU SAID YOUR ANCESTOR WAS A FOUNDING MEMBER--
"AFTER MY GREAT GRANDFATHER'S REMAINS -- WELL, REALLY JUST A BOOT WITH HIS FOOT IN IT--WERE RETURNED TO BASE CAMP, THE FAMILY RETURNED HOME TO BELGIUM."
AH, A DESTINY FULFILLED.
INDEED. AFTER THAT CLAWING BY THE PANTHER, I WAS BARELY ALIVE. BUT THE BELGIAN GOVERNMENT TOOK GOOD CARE OF ME.

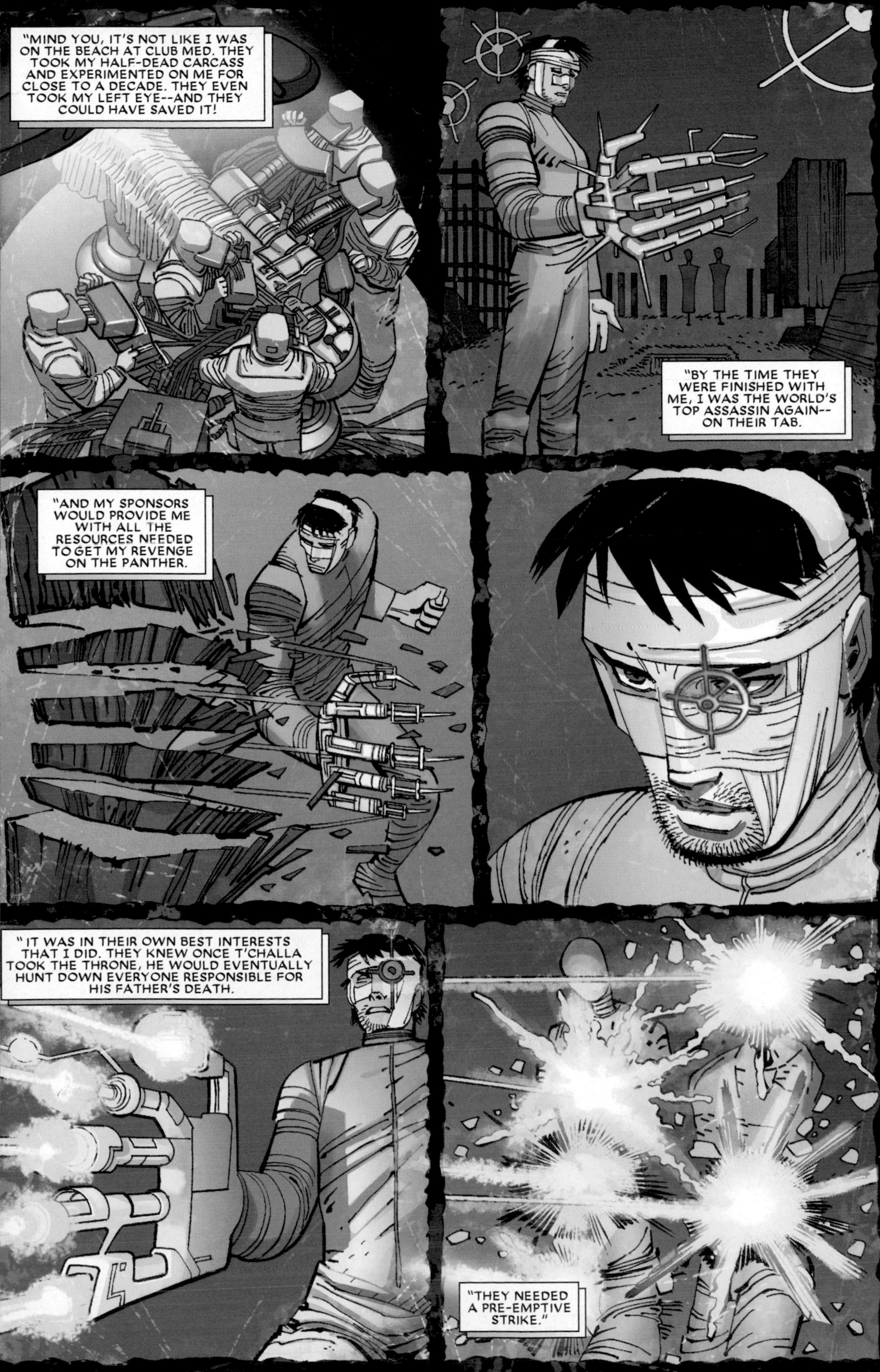
"MIND YOU, IT'S NOT LIKE I WAS ON THE BEACH AT CLUB MED. THEY TOOK MY HALF-DEAD CARCASS AND EXPERIMENTED ON ME FOR CLOSE TO A DECADE. THEY EVEN TOOK MY LEFT EYE--AND THEY COULD HAVE SAVED IT!
"BY THE TIME THEY WERE FINISHED WITH ME, I WAS THE WORLD'S TOP ASSASSIN AGAIN-- ON THEIR TAB.
"AND MY SPONSORS WOULD PROVIDE ME WITH ALL THE RESOURCES NEEDED TO GET MY REVENGE ON THE PANTHER.
"IT WAS IN THEIR OWN BEST INTERESTS THAT I DID. THEY KNEW ONCE T'CHALLA TOOK THE THRONE, HE WOULD EVENTUALLY HUNT DOWN EVERYONE RESPONSIBLE FOR HIS FATHER'S DEATH.
"THEY NEEDED A PRE-EMPTIVE STRIKE."

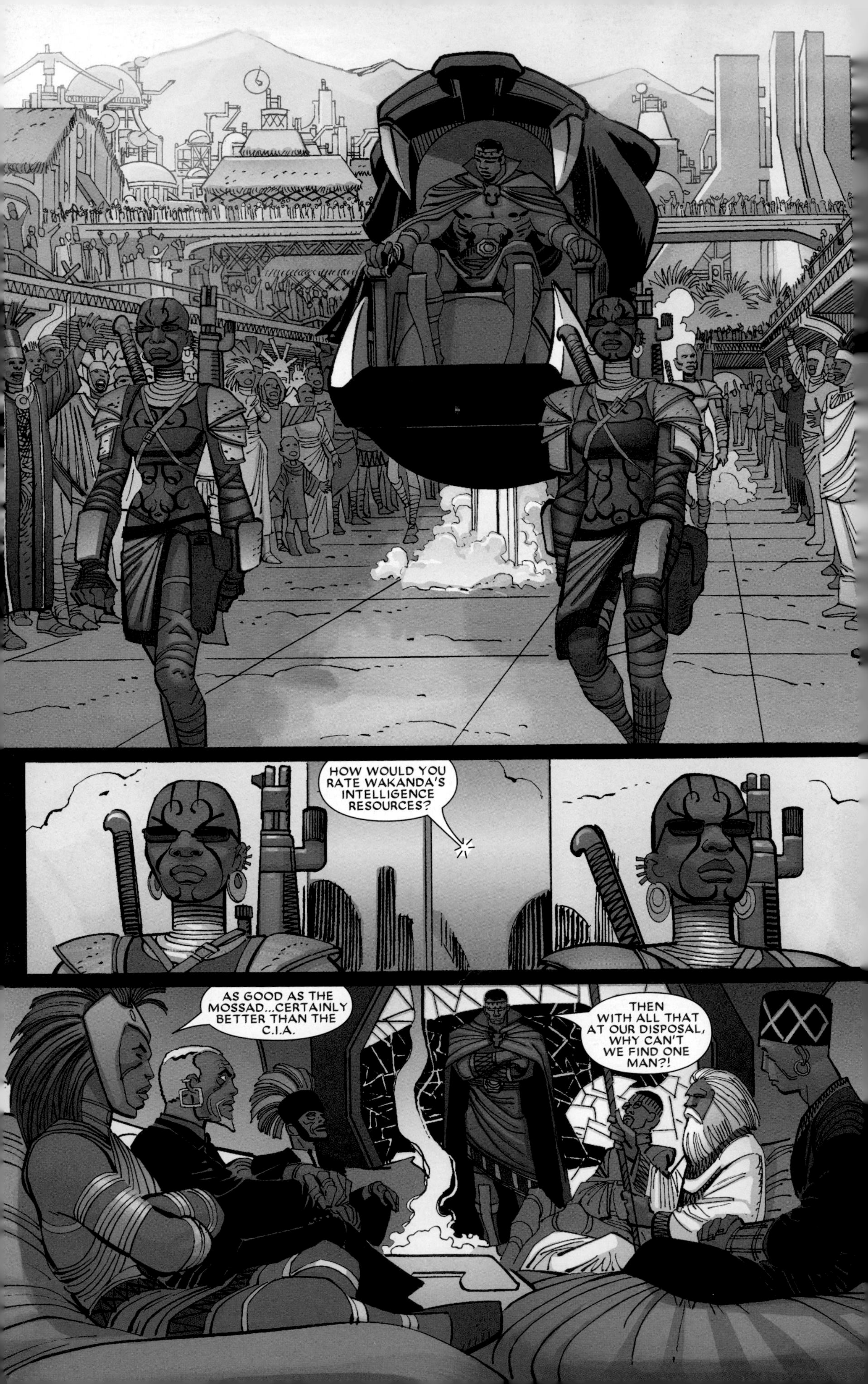
HOW WOULD YOU RATE WAKANDA'S INTELLIGENCE RESOURCES?
AS GOOD AS THE MOSSAD...CERTAINLY BETTER THAN THE C.I.A.
THEN WITH ALL THAT AT OUR DISPOSAL, WHY CAN'T WE FIND ONE MAN?!

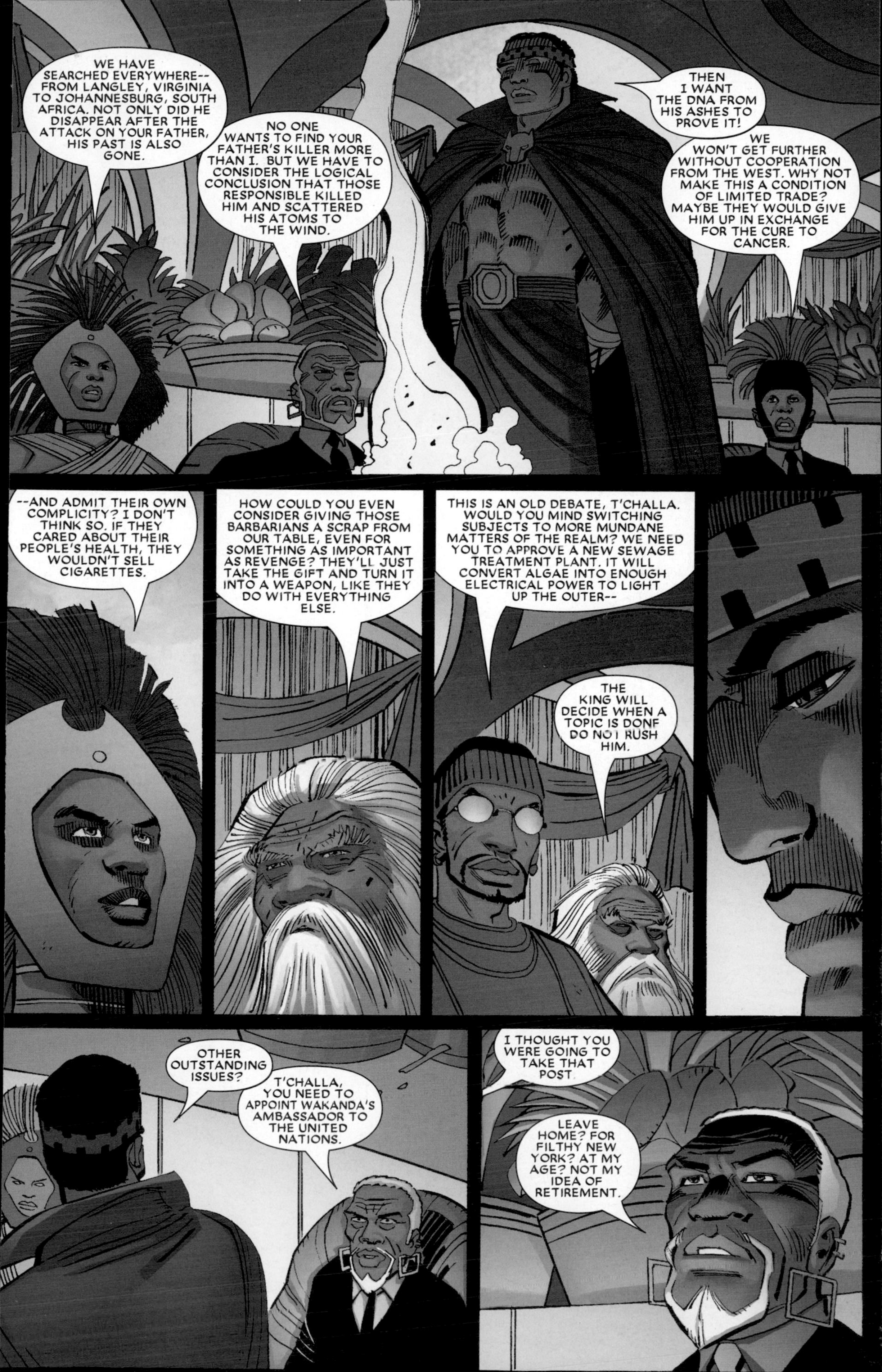
WE HAVE SEARCHED EVERYWHERE-- FROM LANGLEY, VIRGINIA TO JOHANNESBURG, SOUTH AFRICA. NOT ONLY DID HE DISAPPEAR AFTER THE ATTACK ON YOUR FATHER, HIS PAST IS ALSO GONE.
NO ONE WANTS TO FIND YOUR FATHER'S KILLER MORE THAN I. BUT WE HAVE TO CONSIDER THE LOGICAL CONCLUSION THAT THOSE RESPONSIBLE KILLED HIM AND SCATTERED HIS ATOMS TO THE WIND.
THEN I WANT THE DNA FROM HIS ASHES TO PROVE IT!
WE WON'T GET FURTHER WITHOUT COOPERATION FROM THE WEST. WHY NOT MAKE THIS A CONDITION OF LIMITED TRADE? MAYBE THEY WOULD GIVE HIM UP IN EXCHANGE FOR THE CURE TO CANCER.
--AND ADMIT THEIR OWN COMPLICITY? I DON'T THINK SO. IF THEY CARED ABOUT THEIR PEOPLE'S HEALTH, THEY WOULDN'T SELL CIGARETTES.
HOW COULD YOU EVEN CONSIDER GIVING THOSE BARBARIANS A SCRAP FROM OUR TABLE, EVEN FOR SOMETHING AS IMPORTANT AS REVENGE? THEY'LL JUST TAKE THE GIFT AND TURN IT INTO A WEAPON, LIKE THEY DO WITH EVERYTHING ELSE.
THIS IS AN OLD DEBATE, T'CHALLA. WOULD YOU MIND SWITCHING SUBJECTS TO MORE MUNDANE MATTERS OF THE REALM? WE NEED YOU TO APPROVE A NEW SEWAGE TREATMENT PLANT. IT WILL CONVERT ALGAE INTO ENOUGH ELECTRICAL POWER TO LIGHT UP THE OUTER--
THE KING WILL DECIDE WHEN A TOPIC IS DONE DO NOT RUSH HIM.
OTHER OUTSTANDING ISSUES?
T'CHALLA, YOU NEED TO APPOINT WAKANDA'S AMBASSADOR TO THE UNITED NATIONS.
I THOUGHT YOU WERE GOING TO TAKE THAT POST.
LEAVE HOME? FOR FILTHY NEW YORK? AT MY AGE? NOT MY IDEA OF RETIREMENT.

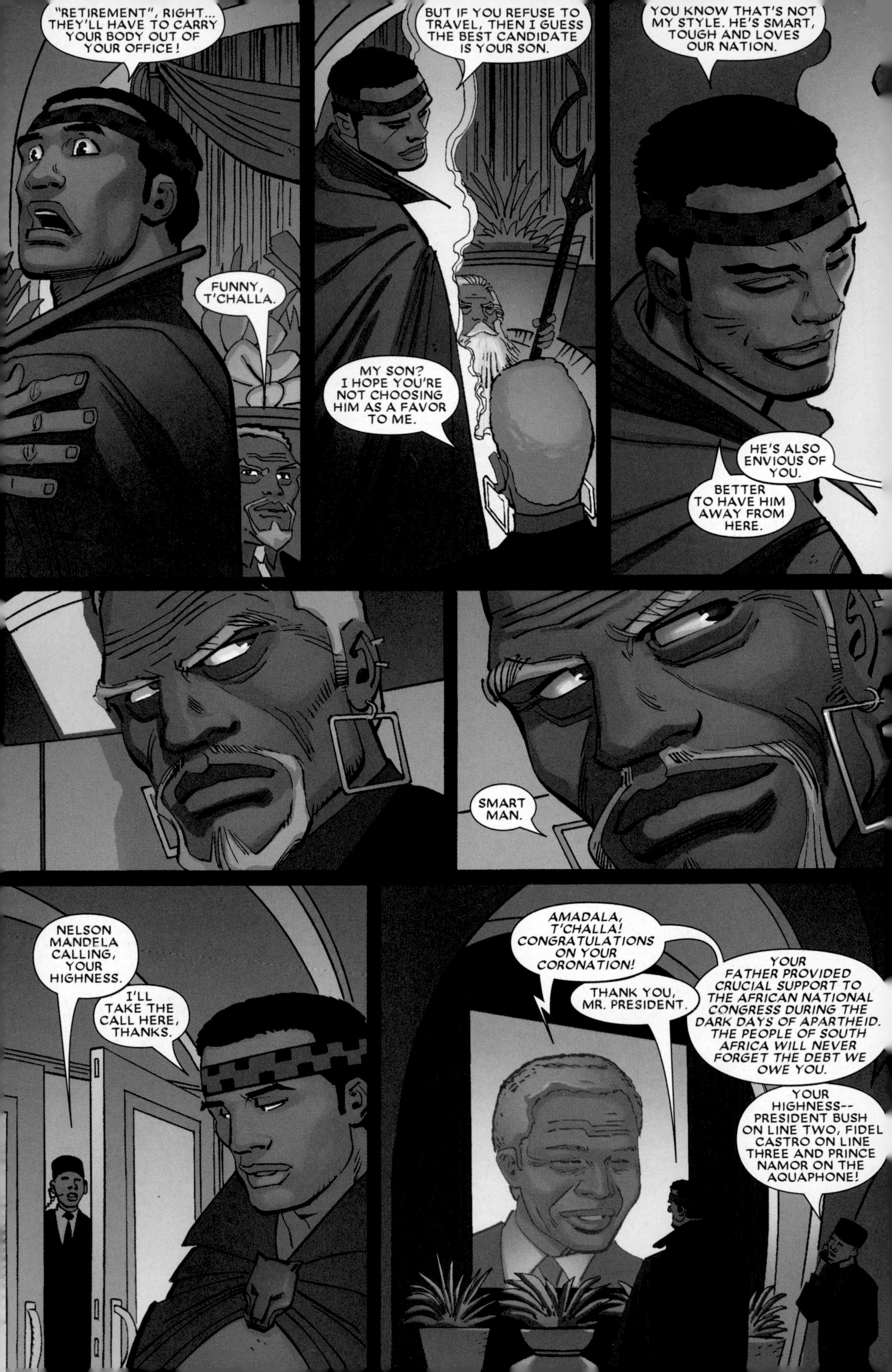
"RETIREMENT", RIGHT... THEY'LL HAVE TO CARRY YOUR BODY OUT OF YOUR OFFICE!
FUNNY, T'CHALLA.
BUT IF YOU REFUSE TO TRAVEL, THEN I GUESS THE BEST CANDIDATE IS YOUR SON.
MY SON? I HOPE YOU'RE NOT CHOOSING HIM AS A FAVOR TO ME.
YOU KNOW THAT'S NOT MY STYLE. HE'S SMART, TOUGH AND LOVES OUR NATION.
HE'S ALSO ENVIOUS OF YOU.
BETTER TO HAVE HIM AWAY FROM HERE.
SMART MAN.
NELSON MANDELA CALLING, YOUR HIGHNESS.
I'LL TAKE THE CALL HERE, THANKS.
AMADALA, T'CHALLA! CONGRATULATIONS ON YOUR CORONATION!
THANK YOU, MR. PRESIDENT.
YOUR FATHER PROVIDED CRUCIAL SUPPORT TO THE AFRICAN NATIONAL CONGRESS DURING THE DARK DAYS OF APARTHEID. THE PEOPLE OF SOUTH AFRICA WILL NEVER FORGET THE DEBT WE OWE YOU.
YOUR HIGHNESS-- PRESIDENT BUSH ON LINE TWO, FIDEL CASTRO ON LINE THREE AND PRINCE NAMOR ON THE AQUAPHONE!

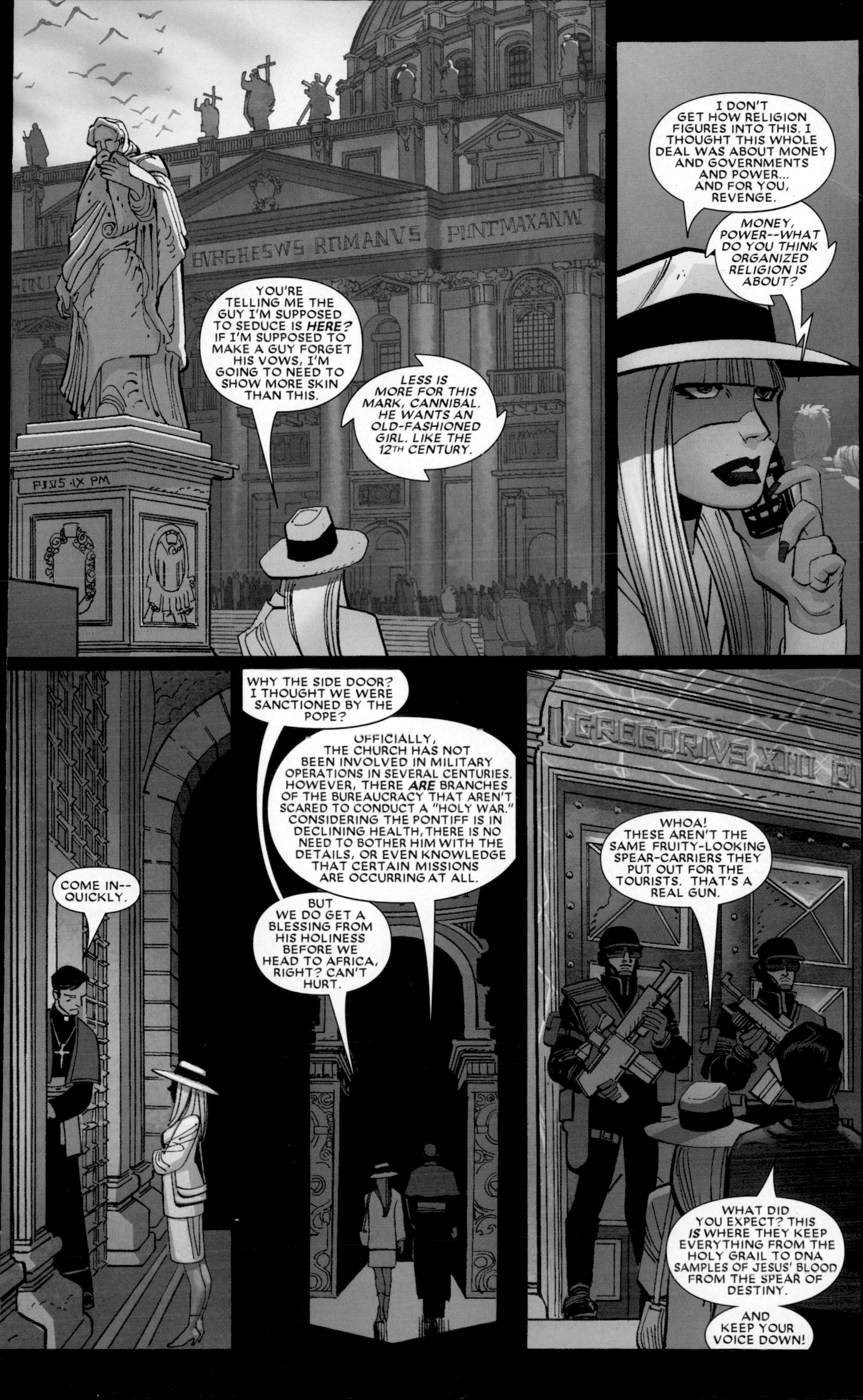
BVRGHESWS ROMANVS PINTMAXANW
PIVS IX PM
YOU'RE TELLING ME THE GUY I'M SUPPOSED TO SEDUCE IS *HERE?* IF I'M SUPPOSED TO MAKE A GUY FORGET HIS VOWS, I'M GOING TO NEED TO SHOW MORE SKIN THAN THIS.
LESS IS MORE FOR THIS MARK, CANNIBAL. HE WANTS AN OLD-FASHIONED GIRL. LIKE THE 12TH CENTURY.
I DON'T GET HOW RELIGION FIGURES INTO THIS. I THOUGHT THIS WHOLE DEAL WAS ABOUT MONEY AND GOVERNMENTS AND POWER... AND FOR YOU, REVENGE.
MONEY, POWER--WHAT DO YOU THINK ORGANIZED RELIGION IS ABOUT?
COME IN--QUICKLY.
WHY THE SIDE DOOR? I THOUGHT WE WERE SANCTIONED BY THE POPE?
OFFICIALLY, THE CHURCH HAS NOT BEEN INVOLVED IN MILITARY OPERATIONS IN SEVERAL CENTURIES. HOWEVER, THERE *ARE* BRANCHES OF THE BUREAUCRACY THAT AREN'T SCARED TO CONDUCT A "HOLY WAR." CONSIDERING THE PONTIFF IS IN DECLINING HEALTH, THERE IS NO NEED TO BOTHER HIM WITH THE DETAILS, OR EVEN KNOWLEDGE THAT CERTAIN MISSIONS ARE OCCURRING AT ALL.
BUT WE DO GET A BLESSING FROM HIS HOLINESS BEFORE WE HEAD TO AFRICA, RIGHT? CAN'T HURT.
GREGORIVS XIII PI
WHOA! THESE AREN'T THE SAME FRUITY-LOOKING SPEAR-CARRIERS THEY PUT OUT FOR THE TOURISTS. THAT'S A REAL GUN.
WHAT DID YOU EXPECT? THIS *IS* WHERE THEY KEEP EVERYTHING FROM THE HOLY GRAIL TO DNA SAMPLES OF JESUS' BLOOD FROM THE SPEAR OF DESTINY.
AND KEEP YOUR VOICE DOWN!

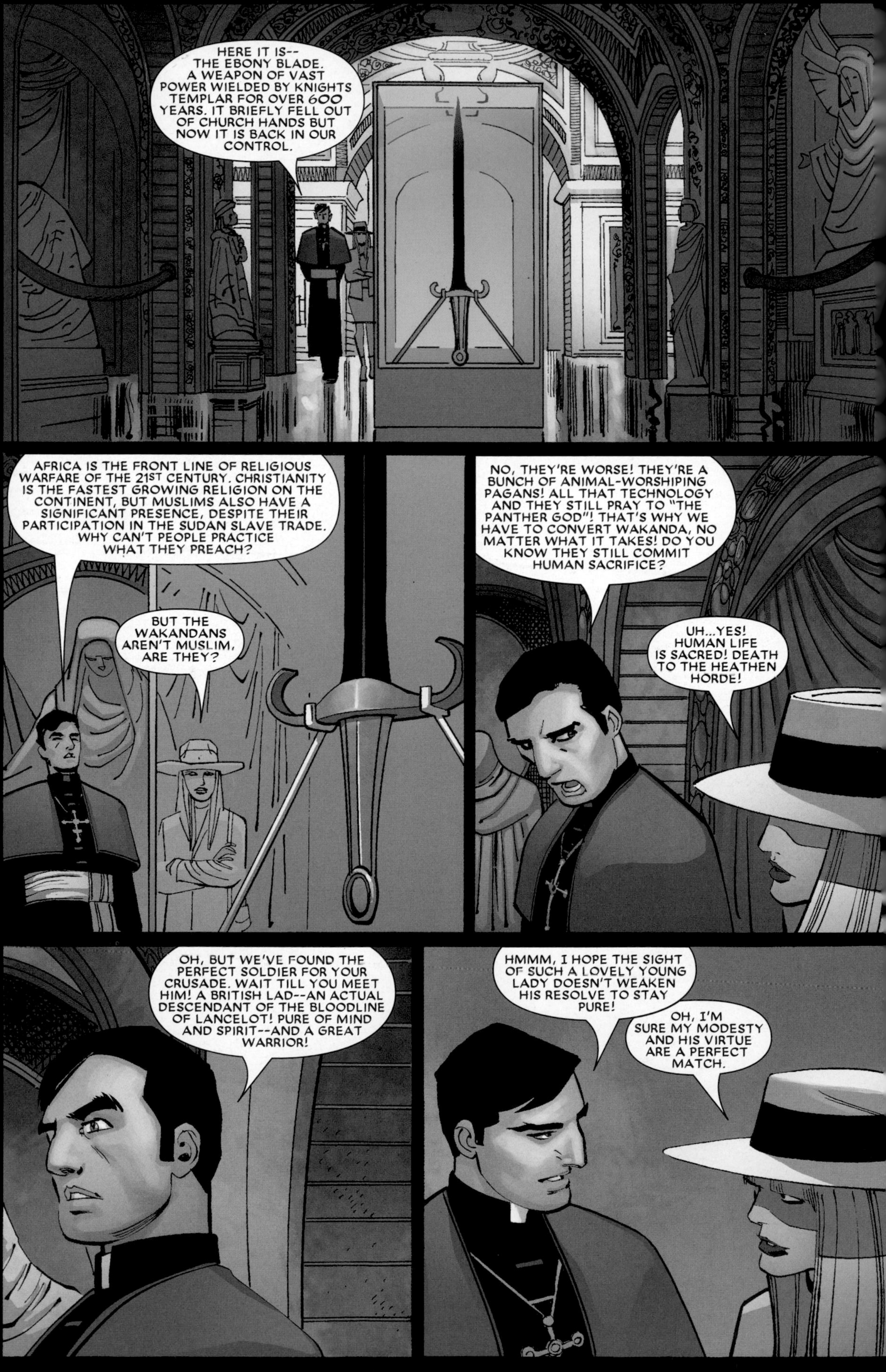

HERE IT IS-- THE EBONY BLADE. A WEAPON OF VAST POWER WIELDED BY KNIGHTS TEMPLAR FOR OVER 600 YEARS. IT BRIEFLY FELL OUT OF CHURCH HANDS BUT NOW IT IS BACK IN OUR CONTROL.
AFRICA IS THE FRONT LINE OF RELIGIOUS WARFARE OF THE 21ST CENTURY. CHRISTIANITY IS THE FASTEST GROWING RELIGION ON THE CONTINENT, BUT MUSLIMS ALSO HAVE A SIGNIFICANT PRESENCE, DESPITE THEIR PARTICIPATION IN THE SUDAN SLAVE TRADE. WHY CAN'T PEOPLE PRACTICE WHAT THEY PREACH?
BUT THE WAKANDANS AREN'T MUSLIM, ARE THEY?
NO, THEY'RE WORSE! THEY'RE A BUNCH OF ANIMAL-WORSHIPING PAGANS! ALL THAT TECHNOLOGY AND THEY STILL PRAY TO "THE PANTHER GOD"! THAT'S WHY WE HAVE TO CONVERT WAKANDA, NO MATTER WHAT IT TAKES! DO YOU KNOW THEY STILL COMMIT HUMAN SACRIFICE?
UH...YES! HUMAN LIFE IS SACRED! DEATH TO THE HEATHEN HORDE!
OH, BUT WE'VE FOUND THE PERFECT SOLDIER FOR YOUR CRUSADE. WAIT TILL YOU MEET HIM! A BRITISH LAD--AN ACTUAL DESCENDANT OF THE BLOODLINE OF LANCELOT! PURE OF MIND AND SPIRIT--AND A GREAT WARRIOR!
HMMM, I HOPE THE SIGHT OF SUCH A LOVELY YOUNG LADY DOESN'T WEAKEN HIS RESOLVE TO STAY PURE!
OH, I'M SURE MY MODESTY AND HIS VIRTUE ARE A PERFECT MATCH.

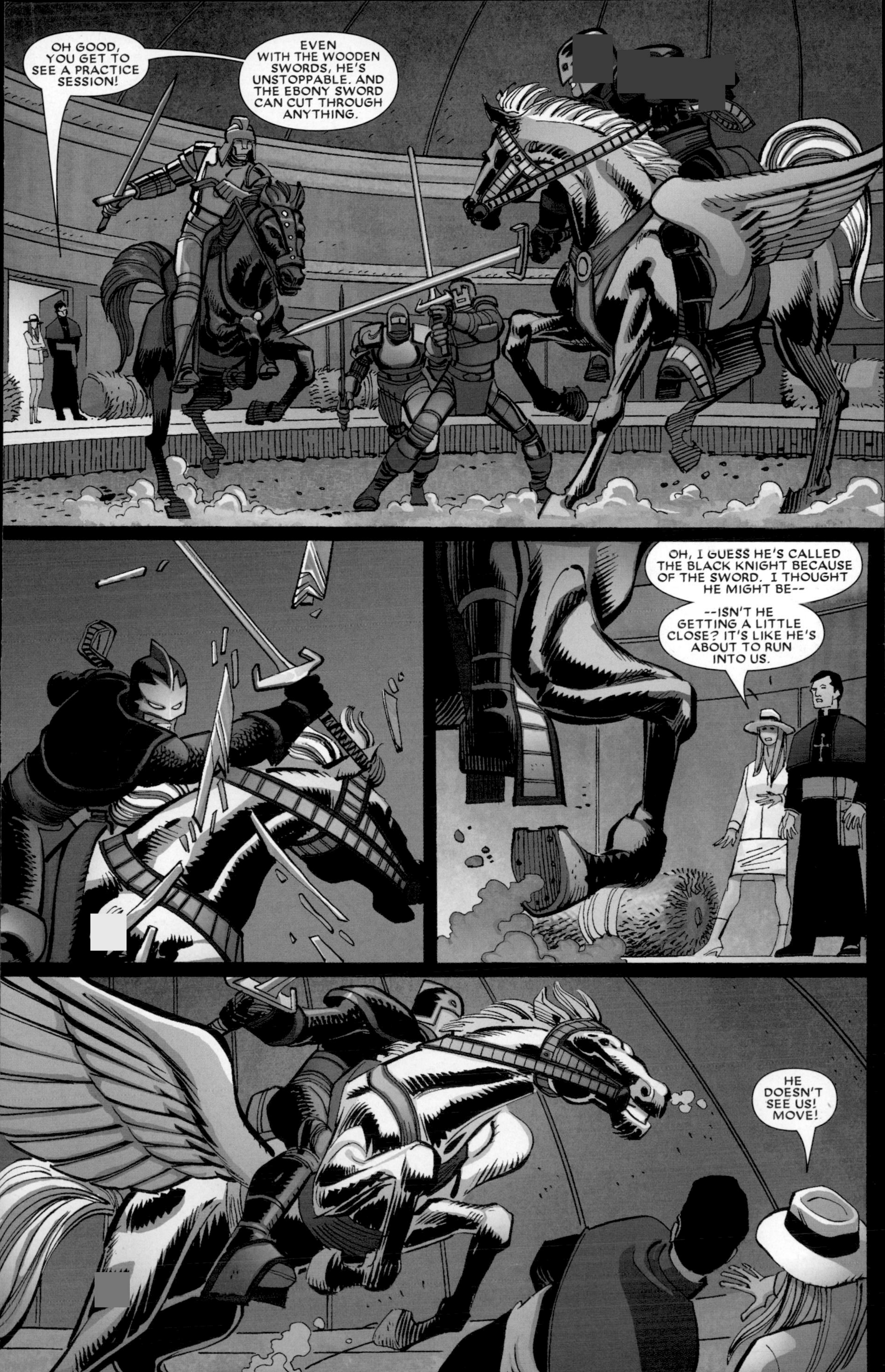
OH GOOD, YOU GET TO SEE A PRACTICE SESSION!
EVEN WITH THE WOODEN SWORDS, HE'S UNSTOPPABLE. AND THE EBONY SWORD CAN CUT THROUGH ANYTHING.
OH, I GUESS HE'S CALLED THE BLACK KNIGHT BECAUSE OF THE SWORD. I THOUGHT HE MIGHT BE--
--ISN'T HE GETTING A LITTLE CLOSE? IT'S LIKE HE'S ABOUT TO RUN INTO US.
HE DOESN'T SEE US! MOVE!

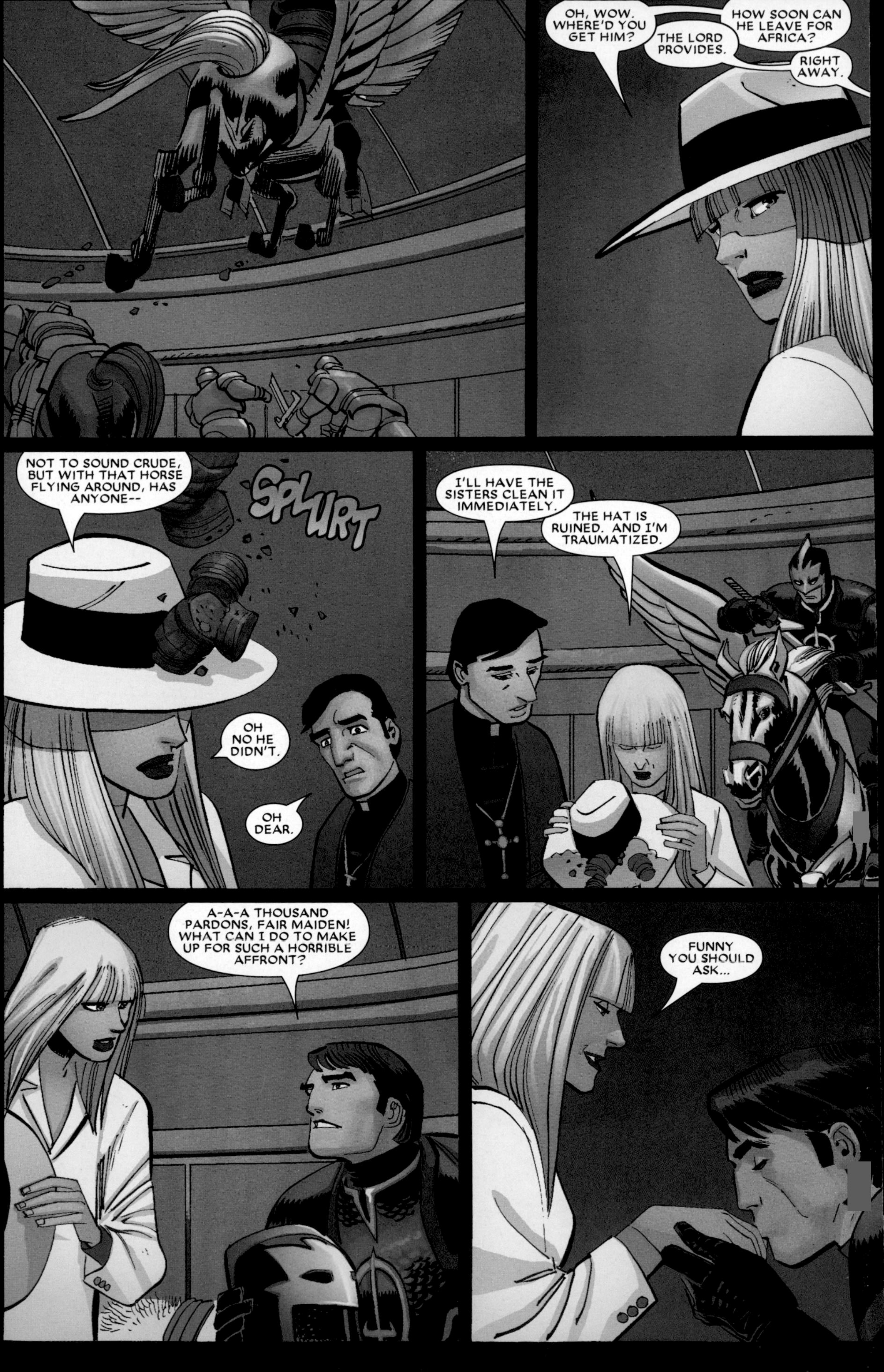
OH, WOW. WHERE'D YOU GET HIM?
THE LORD PROVIDES.
HOW SOON CAN HE LEAVE FOR AFRICA?
RIGHT AWAY.
NOT TO SOUND CRUDE, BUT WITH THAT HORSE FLYING AROUND, HAS ANYONE--
SPLURT
OH NO HE DIDN'T.
OH DEAR.
I'LL HAVE THE SISTERS CLEAN IT IMMEDIATELY.
THE HAT IS RUINED. AND I'M TRAUMATIZED.
A-A-A THOUSAND PARDONS, FAIR MAIDEN! WHAT CAN I DO TO MAKE UP FOR SUCH A HORRIBLE AFFRONT?
FUNNY YOU SHOULD ASK...

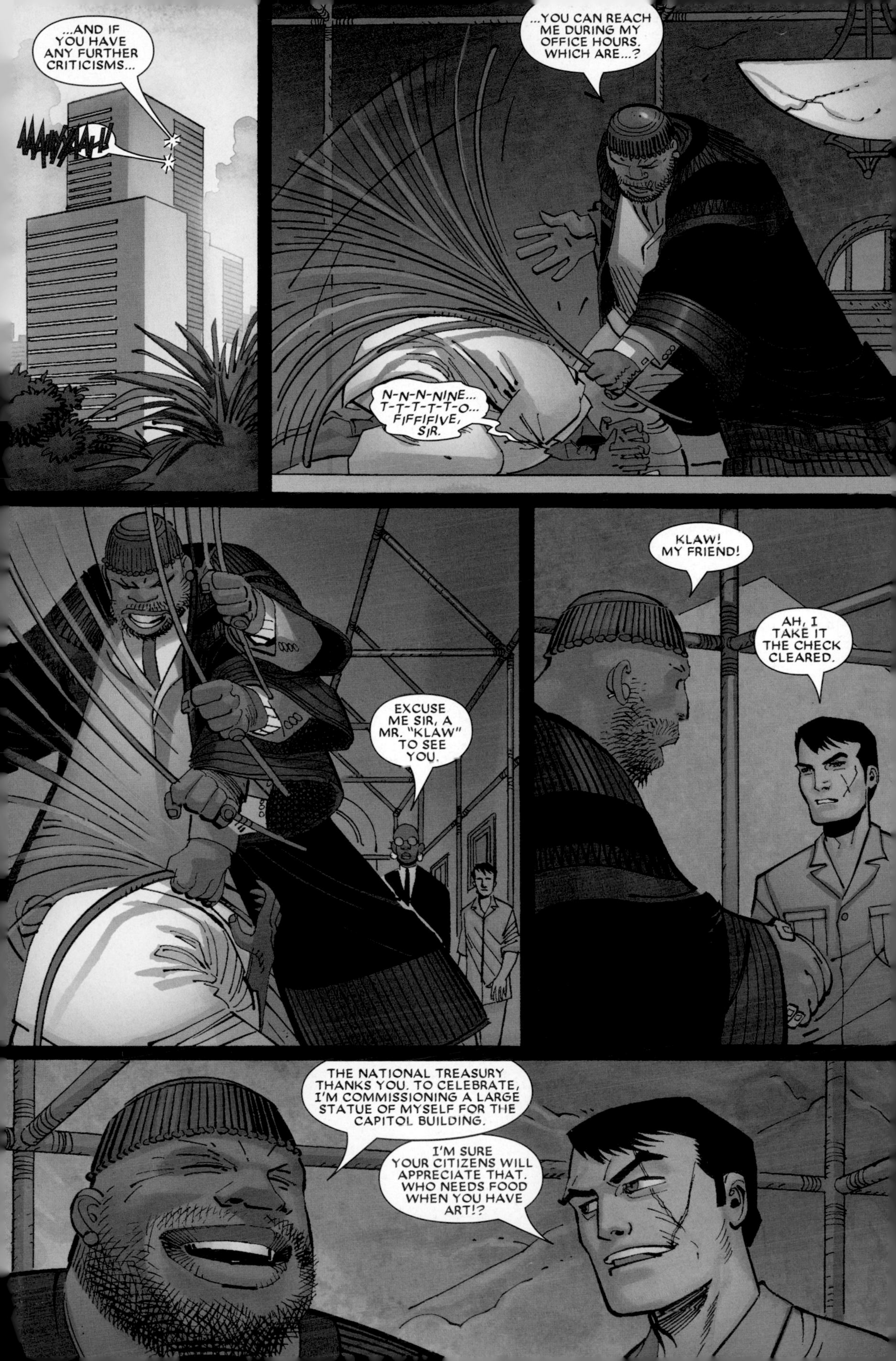
...AND IF YOU HAVE ANY FURTHER CRITICISMS...
...YOU CAN REACH ME DURING MY OFFICE HOURS. WHICH ARE...?
N-N-N-NINE... T-T-T-T-T-O... FIFFIFIVE, SIR.
EXCUSE ME SIR, A MR. "KLAW" TO SEE YOU.
KLAW! MY FRIEND!
AH, I TAKE IT THE CHECK CLEARED.
THE NATIONAL TREASURY THANKS YOU. TO CELEBRATE, I'M COMMISSIONING A LARGE STATUE OF MYSELF FOR THE CAPITOL BUILDING.
I'M SURE YOUR CITIZENS WILL APPRECIATE THAT. WHO NEEDS FOOD WHEN YOU HAVE ART!?

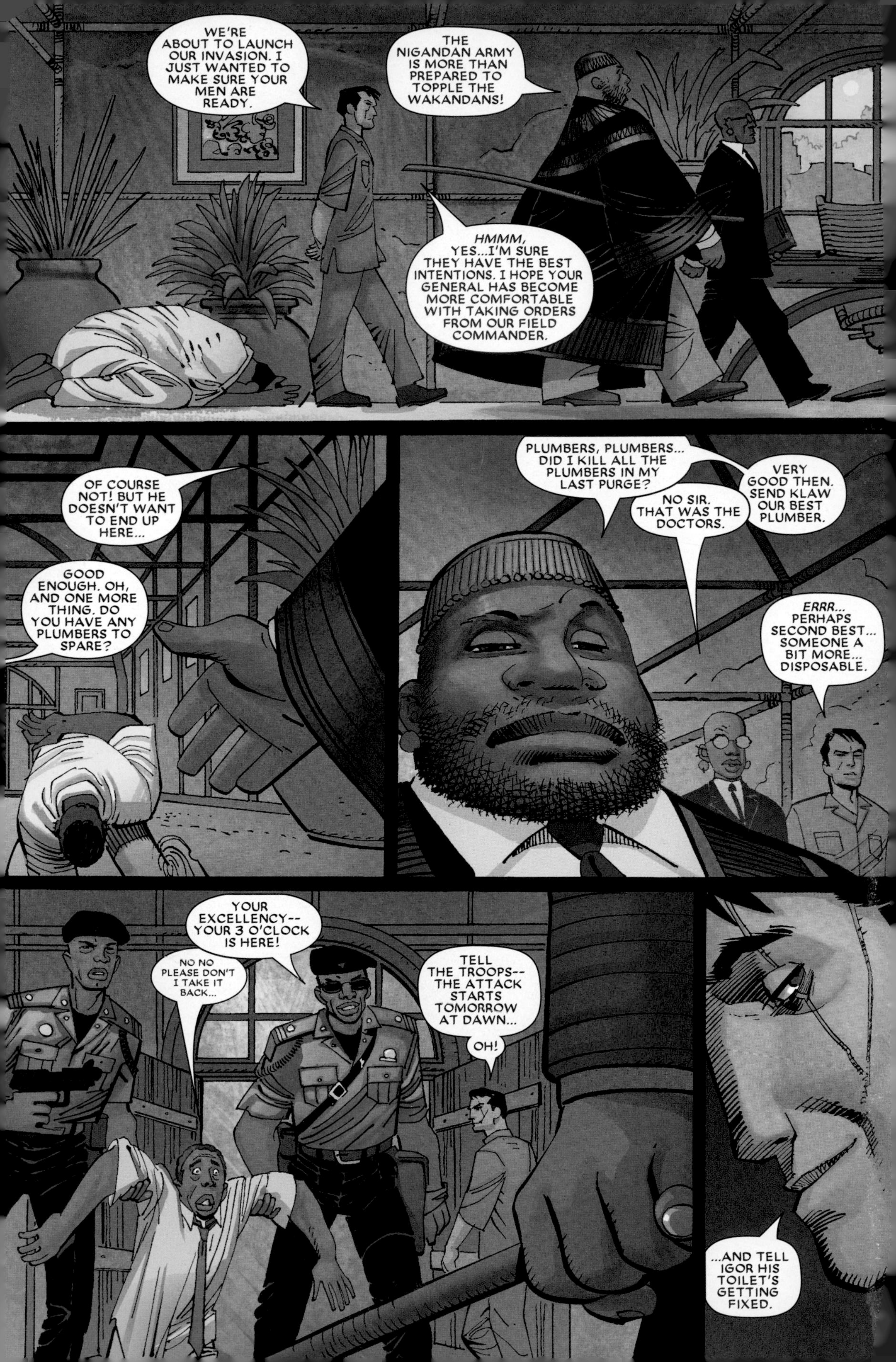
WE'RE ABOUT TO LAUNCH OUR INVASION. I JUST WANTED TO MAKE SURE YOUR MEN ARE READY.
THE NIGANDAN ARMY IS MORE THAN PREPARED TO TOPPLE THE WAKANDANS!
HMMM, YES...I'M SURE THEY HAVE THE BEST INTENTIONS. I HOPE YOUR GENERAL HAS BECOME MORE COMFORTABLE WITH TAKING ORDERS FROM OUR FIELD COMMANDER.
OF COURSE NOT! BUT HE DOESN'T WANT TO END UP HERE...
GOOD ENOUGH. OH, AND ONE MORE THING. DO YOU HAVE ANY PLUMBERS TO SPARE?
PLUMBERS, PLUMBERS... DID I KILL ALL THE PLUMBERS IN MY LAST PURGE?
NO SIR. THAT WAS THE DOCTORS.
VERY GOOD THEN. SEND KLAW OUR BEST PLUMBER.
ERRR... PERHAPS SECOND BEST... SOMEONE A BIT MORE... DISPOSABLE.
YOUR EXCELLENCY-- YOUR 3 O'CLOCK IS HERE!
NO NO PLEASE DON'T I TAKE IT BACK...
TELL THE TROOPS-- THE ATTACK STARTS TOMORROW AT DAWN...
OH!
...AND TELL IGOR HIS TOILET'S GETTING FIXED.

4

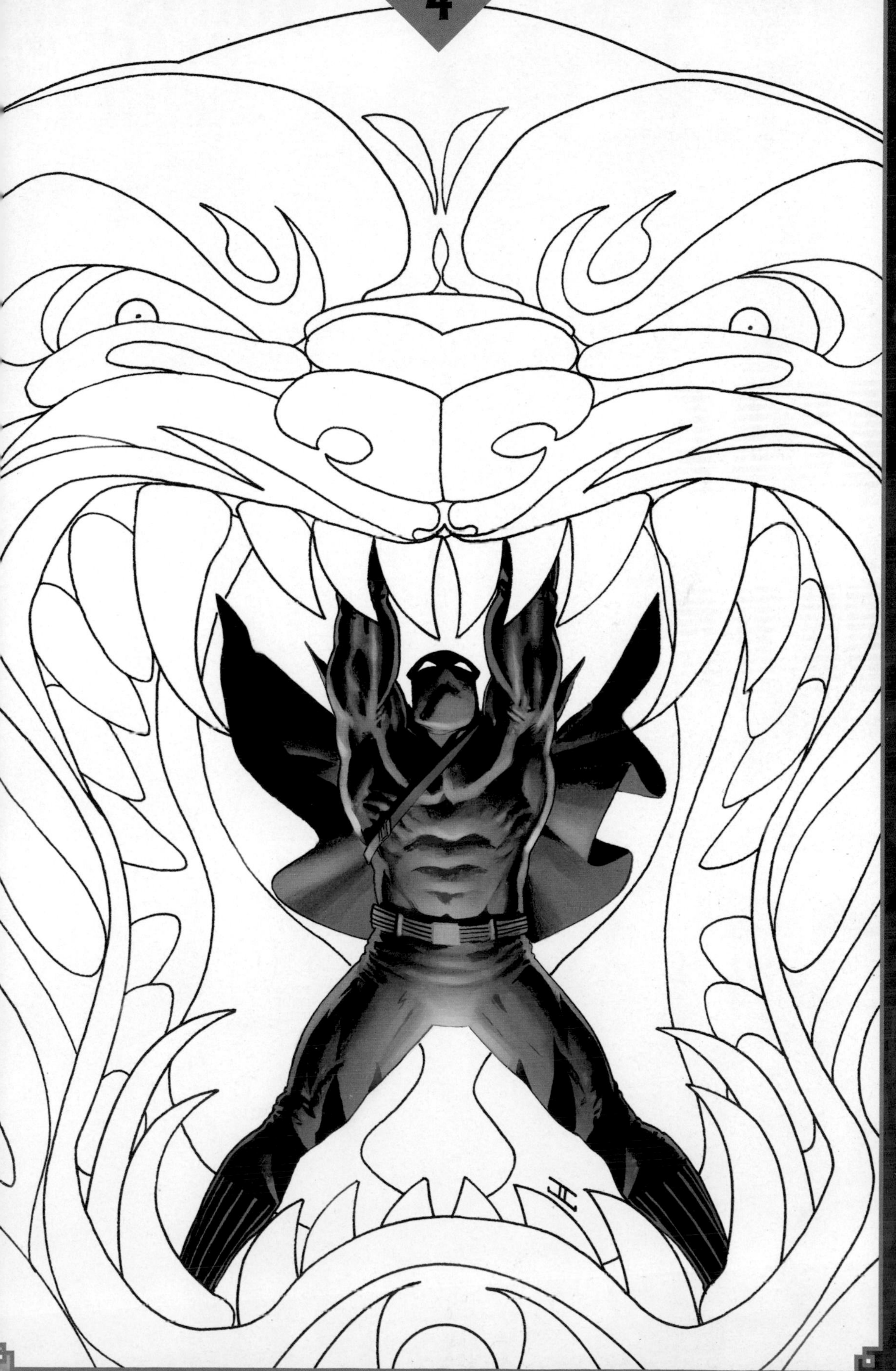

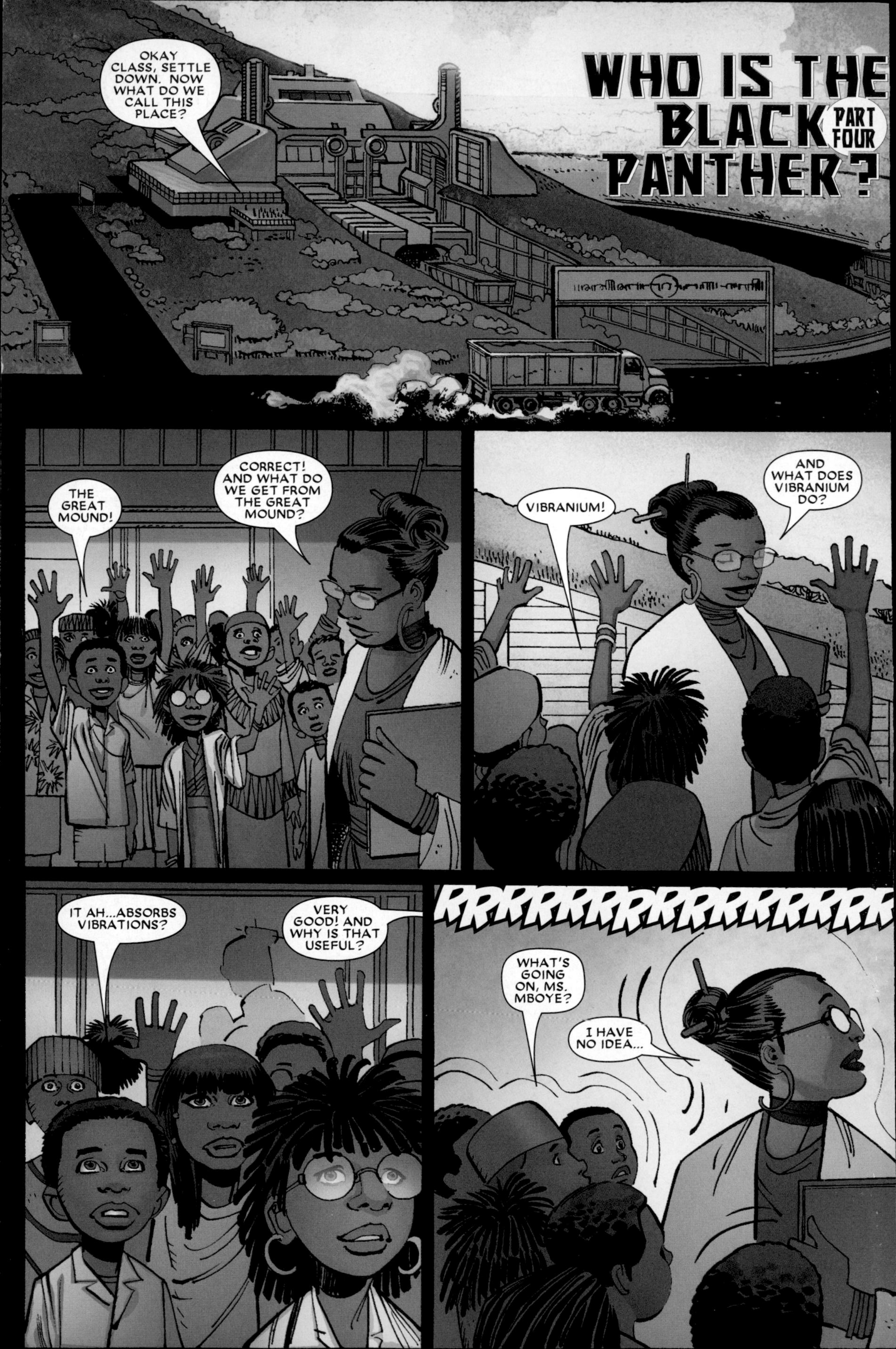

WHO IS THE BLACK PANTHER? PART FOUR
OKAY CLASS, SETTLE DOWN. NOW WHAT DO WE CALL THIS PLACE?
THE GREAT MOUND!
CORRECT! AND WHAT DO WE GET FROM THE GREAT MOUND?
VIBRANIUM!
AND WHAT DOES VIBRANIUM DO?
IT AH...ABSORBS VIBRATIONS?
VERY GOOD! AND WHY IS THAT USEFUL?
RRRRRRRRRRRRRRRRRRR
WHAT'S GOING ON, MS. MBOYE?
I HAVE NO IDEA...

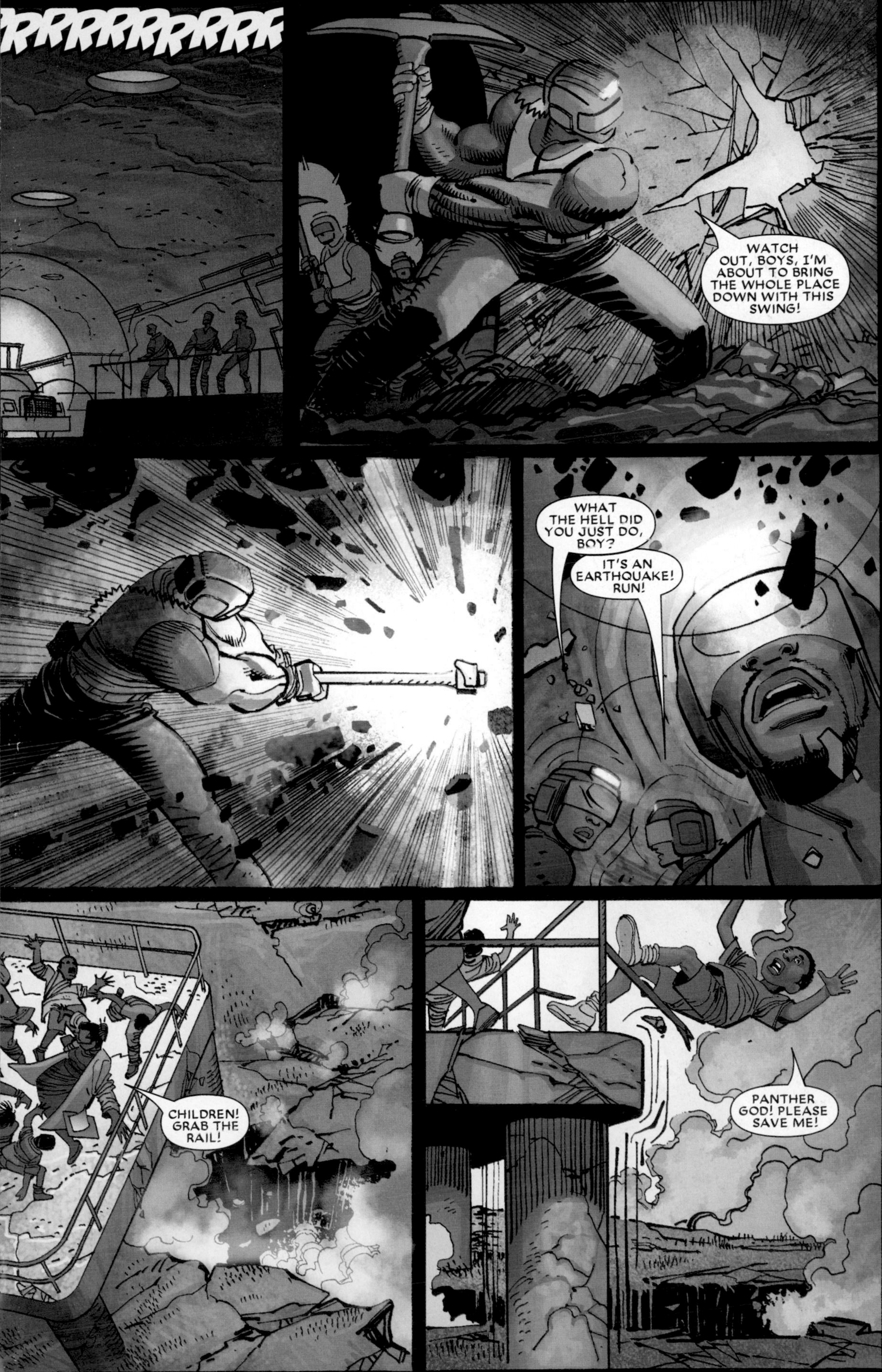
RRRRRRRRRRRR
WATCH OUT, BOYS, I'M ABOUT TO BRING THE WHOLE PLACE DOWN WITH THIS SWING!
WHAT THE HELL DID YOU JUST DO, BOY?
IT'S AN EARTHQUAKE! RUN!
CHILDREN! GRAB THE RAIL!
PANTHER GOD! PLEASE SAVE ME!

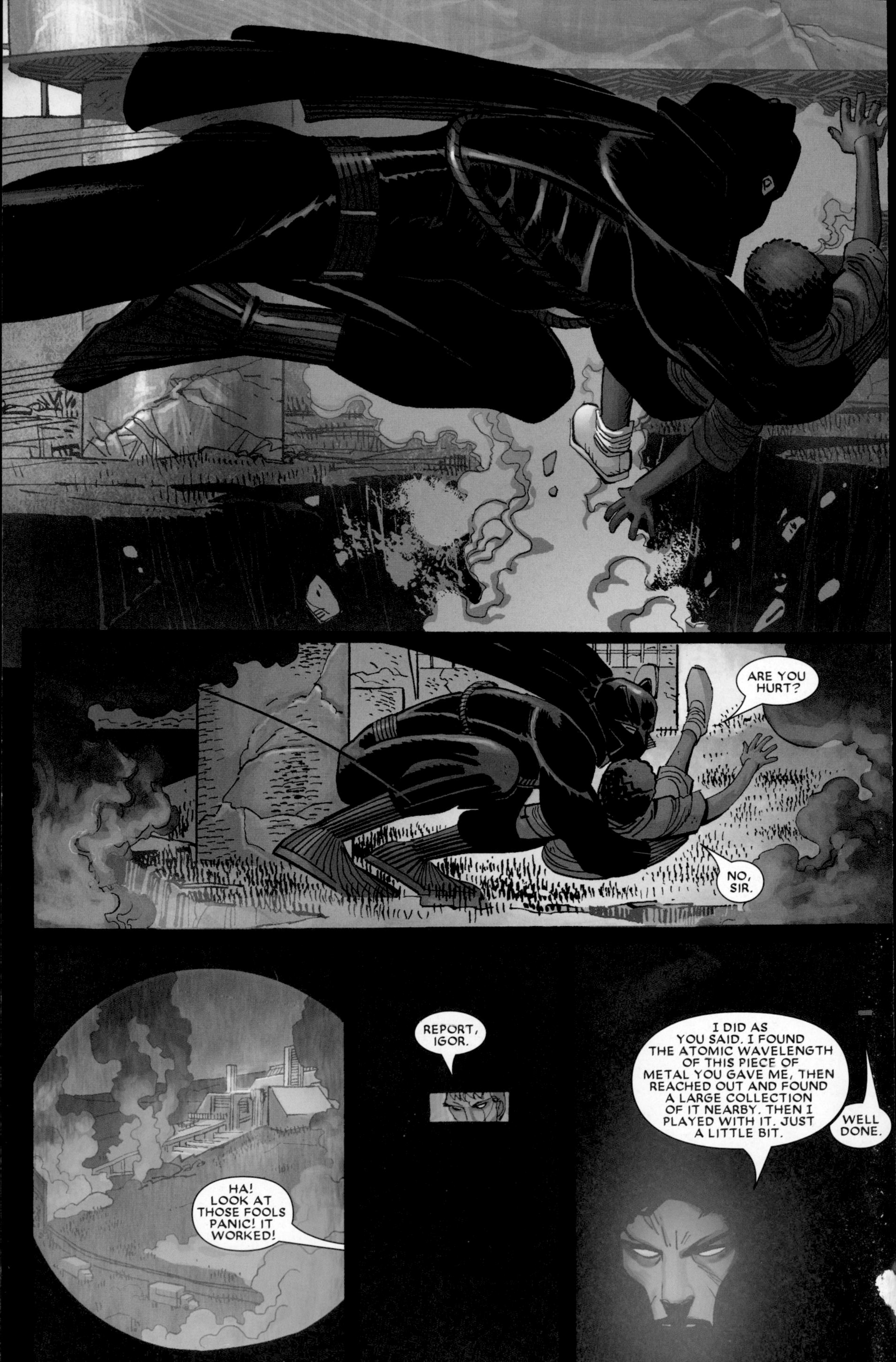
ARE YOU HURT?
NO, SIR.
HA! LOOK AT THOSE FOOLS PANIC! IT WORKED!
REPORT, IGOR.
I DID AS YOU SAID. I FOUND THE ATOMIC WAVELENGTH OF THIS PIECE OF METAL YOU GAVE ME, THEN REACHED OUT AND FOUND A LARGE COLLECTION OF IT NEARBY. THEN I PLAYED WITH IT. JUST A LITTLE BIT.
WELL DONE.

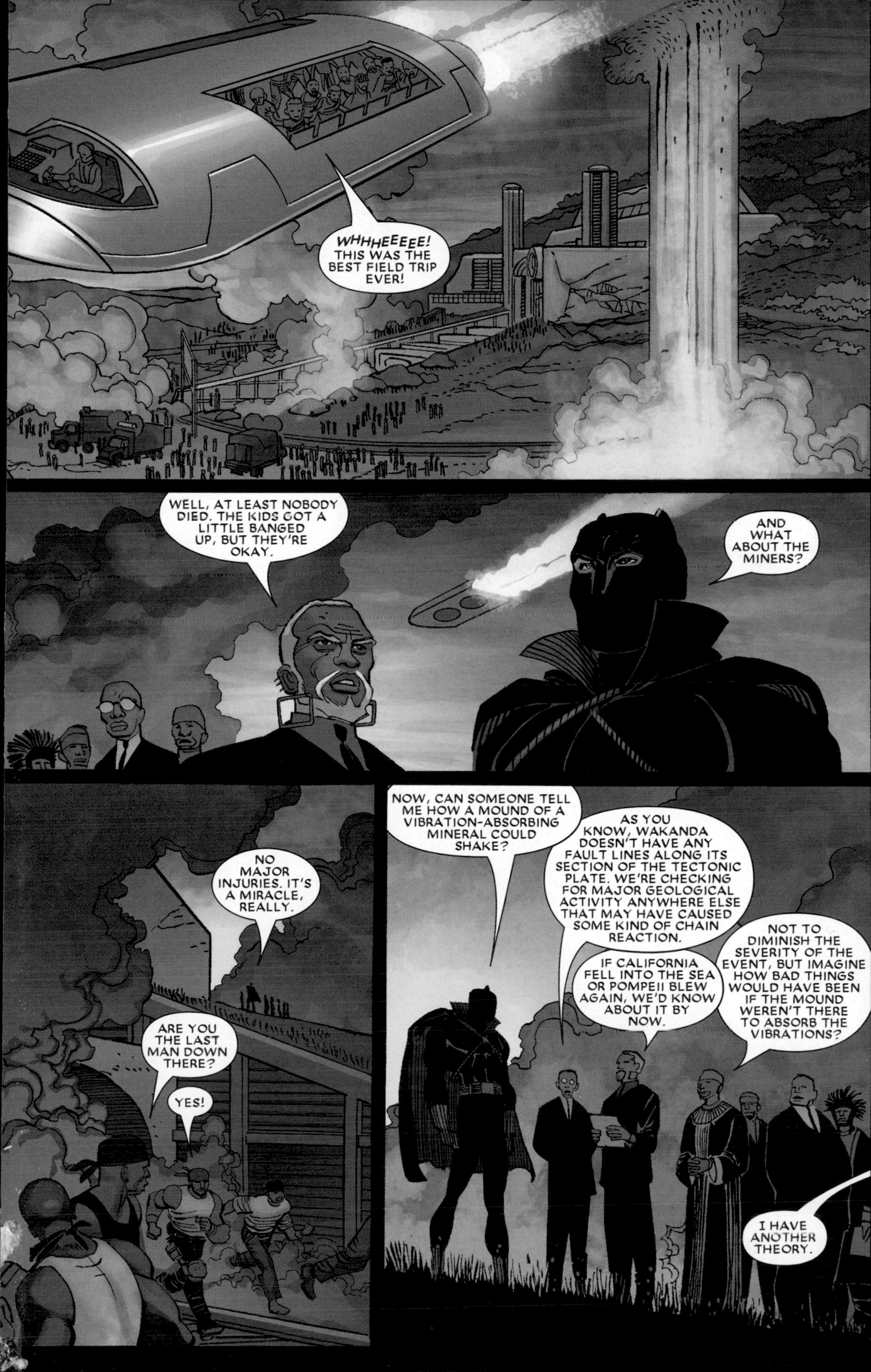
WHHHEEEEE! THIS WAS THE BEST FIELD TRIP EVER!
WELL, AT LEAST NOBODY DIED. THE KIDS GOT A LITTLE BANGED UP, BUT THEY'RE OKAY.
AND WHAT ABOUT THE MINERS?
NO MAJOR INJURIES. IT'S A MIRACLE, REALLY.
ARE YOU THE LAST MAN DOWN THERE?
YES!
NOW, CAN SOMEONE TELL ME HOW A MOUND OF A VIBRATION-ABSORBING MINERAL COULD SHAKE?
AS YOU KNOW, WAKANDA DOESN'T HAVE ANY FAULT LINES ALONG ITS SECTION OF THE TECTONIC PLATE. WE'RE CHECKING FOR MAJOR GEOLOGICAL ACTIVITY ANYWHERE ELSE THAT MAY HAVE CAUSED SOME KIND OF CHAIN REACTION.
IF CALIFORNIA FELL INTO THE SEA OR POMPEII BLEW AGAIN, WE'D KNOW ABOUT IT BY NOW.
NOT TO DIMINISH THE SEVERITY OF THE EVENT, BUT IMAGINE HOW BAD THINGS WOULD HAVE BEEN IF THE MOUND WEREN'T THERE TO ABSORB THE VIBRATIONS?
I HAVE ANOTHER THEORY.

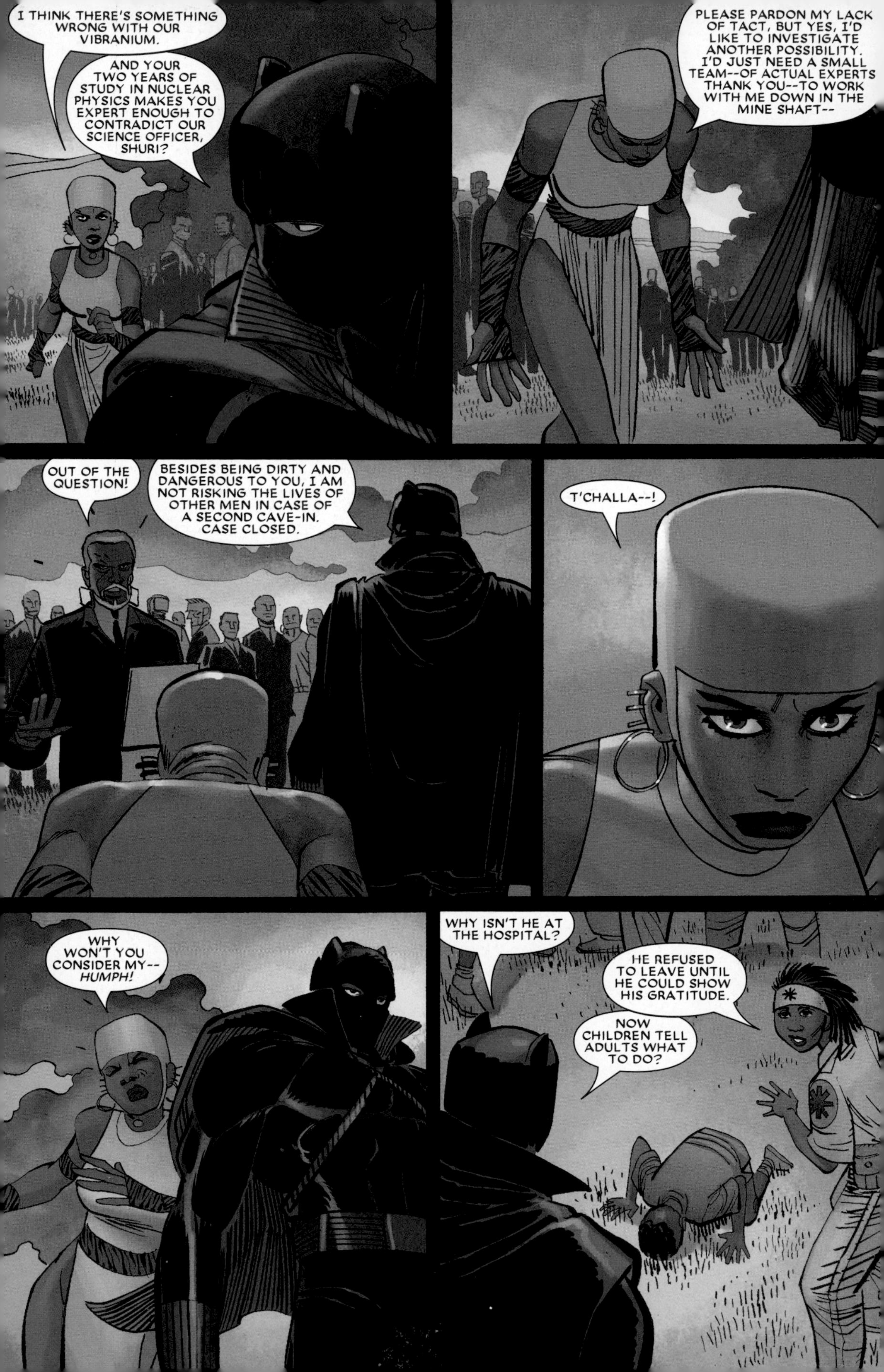
I THINK THERE'S SOMETHING WRONG WITH OUR VIBRANIUM.
AND YOUR TWO YEARS OF STUDY IN NUCLEAR PHYSICS MAKES YOU EXPERT ENOUGH TO CONTRADICT OUR SCIENCE OFFICER, SHURI?
PLEASE PARDON MY LACK OF TACT, BUT YES, I'D LIKE TO INVESTIGATE ANOTHER POSSIBILITY. I'D JUST NEED A SMALL TEAM--OF ACTUAL EXPERTS THANK YOU--TO WORK WITH ME DOWN IN THE MINE SHAFT--
OUT OF THE QUESTION!
BESIDES BEING DIRTY AND DANGEROUS TO YOU, I AM NOT RISKING THE LIVES OF OTHER MEN IN CASE OF A SECOND CAVE-IN. CASE CLOSED.
T'CHALLA--!
WHY WON'T YOU CONSIDER MY-- *HUMPH!*
WHY ISN'T HE AT THE HOSPITAL?
HE REFUSED TO LEAVE UNTIL HE COULD SHOW HIS GRATITUDE.
NOW CHILDREN TELL ADULTS WHAT TO DO?

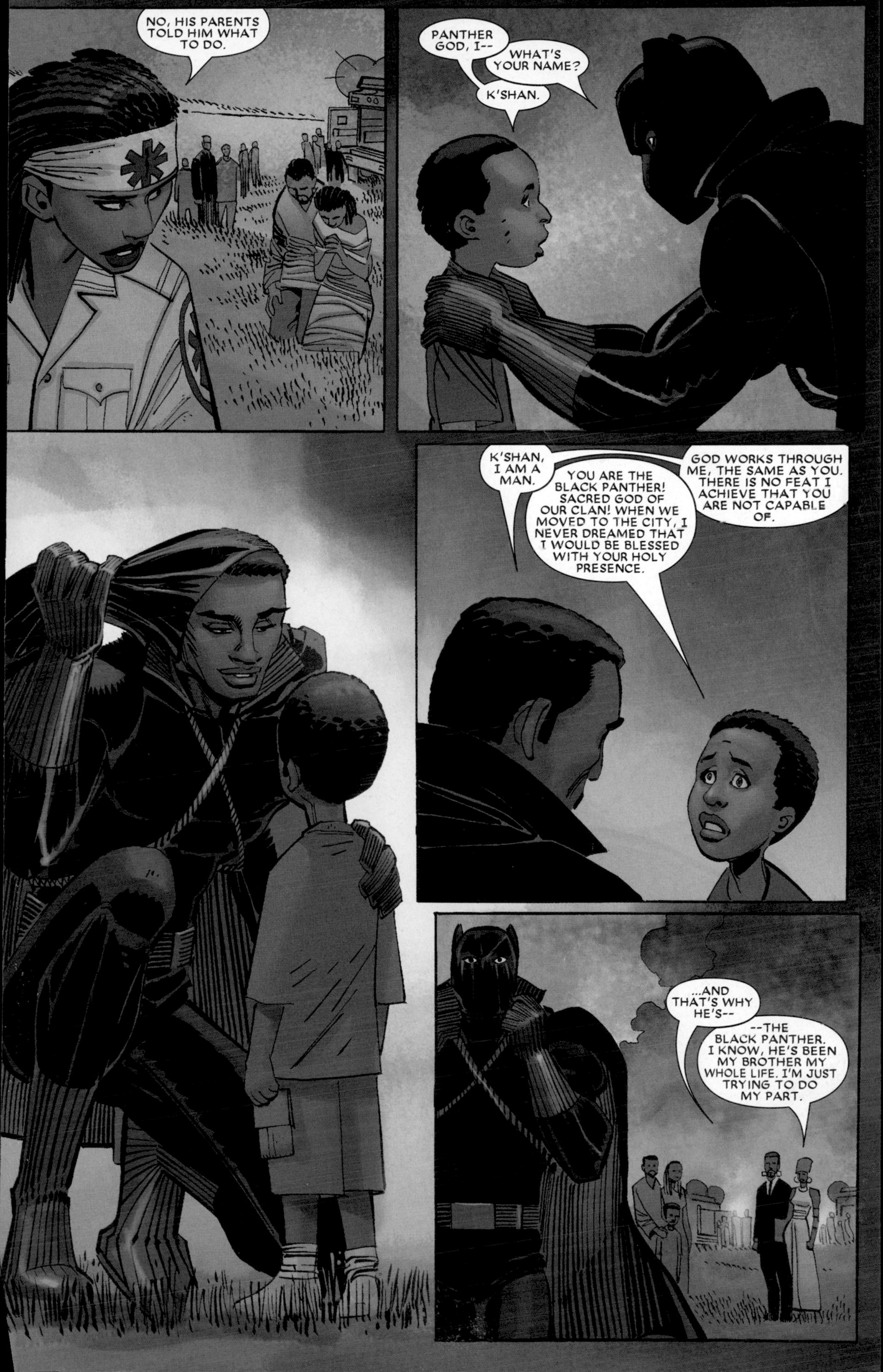
NO, HIS PARENTS TOLD HIM WHAT TO DO.
PANTHER GOD, I--
WHAT'S YOUR NAME?
K'SHAN.
K'SHAN, I AM A MAN.
YOU ARE THE BLACK PANTHER! SACRED GOD OF OUR CLAN! WHEN WE MOVED TO THE CITY, I NEVER DREAMED THAT I WOULD BE BLESSED WITH YOUR HOLY PRESENCE.
GOD WORKS THROUGH ME, THE SAME AS YOU. THERE IS NO FEAT I ACHIEVE THAT YOU ARE NOT CAPABLE OF.
...AND THAT'S WHY HE'S--
--THE BLACK PANTHER. I KNOW, HE'S BEEN MY BROTHER MY WHOLE LIFE. I'M JUST TRYING TO DO MY PART.

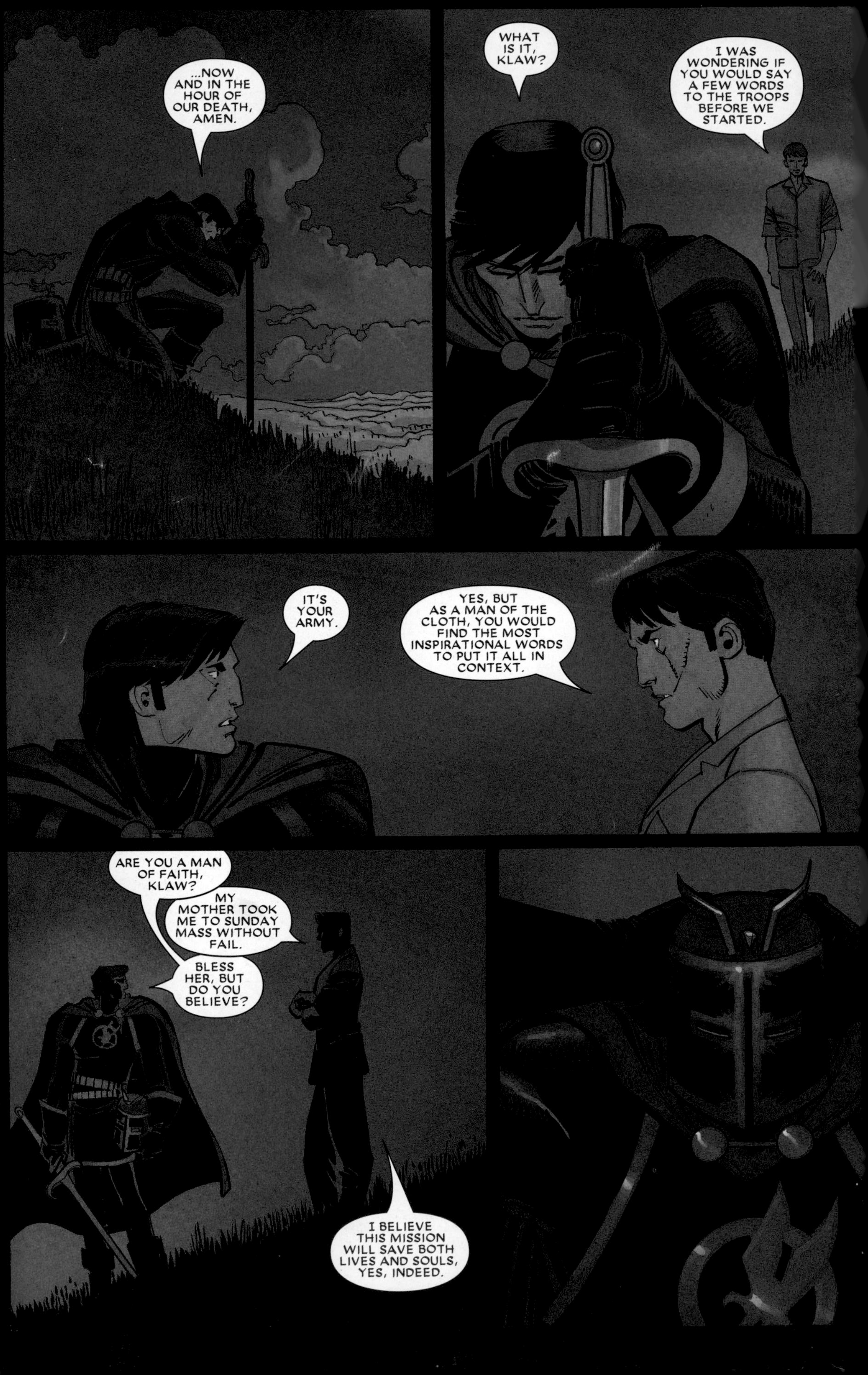
...NOW AND IN THE HOUR OF OUR DEATH, AMEN.
WHAT IS IT, KLAW?
I WAS WONDERING IF YOU WOULD SAY A FEW WORDS TO THE TROOPS BEFORE WE STARTED.
IT'S YOUR ARMY.
YES, BUT AS A MAN OF THE CLOTH, YOU WOULD FIND THE MOST INSPIRATIONAL WORDS TO PUT IT ALL IN CONTEXT.
ARE YOU A MAN OF FAITH, KLAW?
MY MOTHER TOOK ME TO SUNDAY MASS WITHOUT FAIL.
BLESS HER, BUT DO YOU BELIEVE?
I BELIEVE THIS MISSION WILL SAVE BOTH LIVES AND SOULS, YES, INDEED.

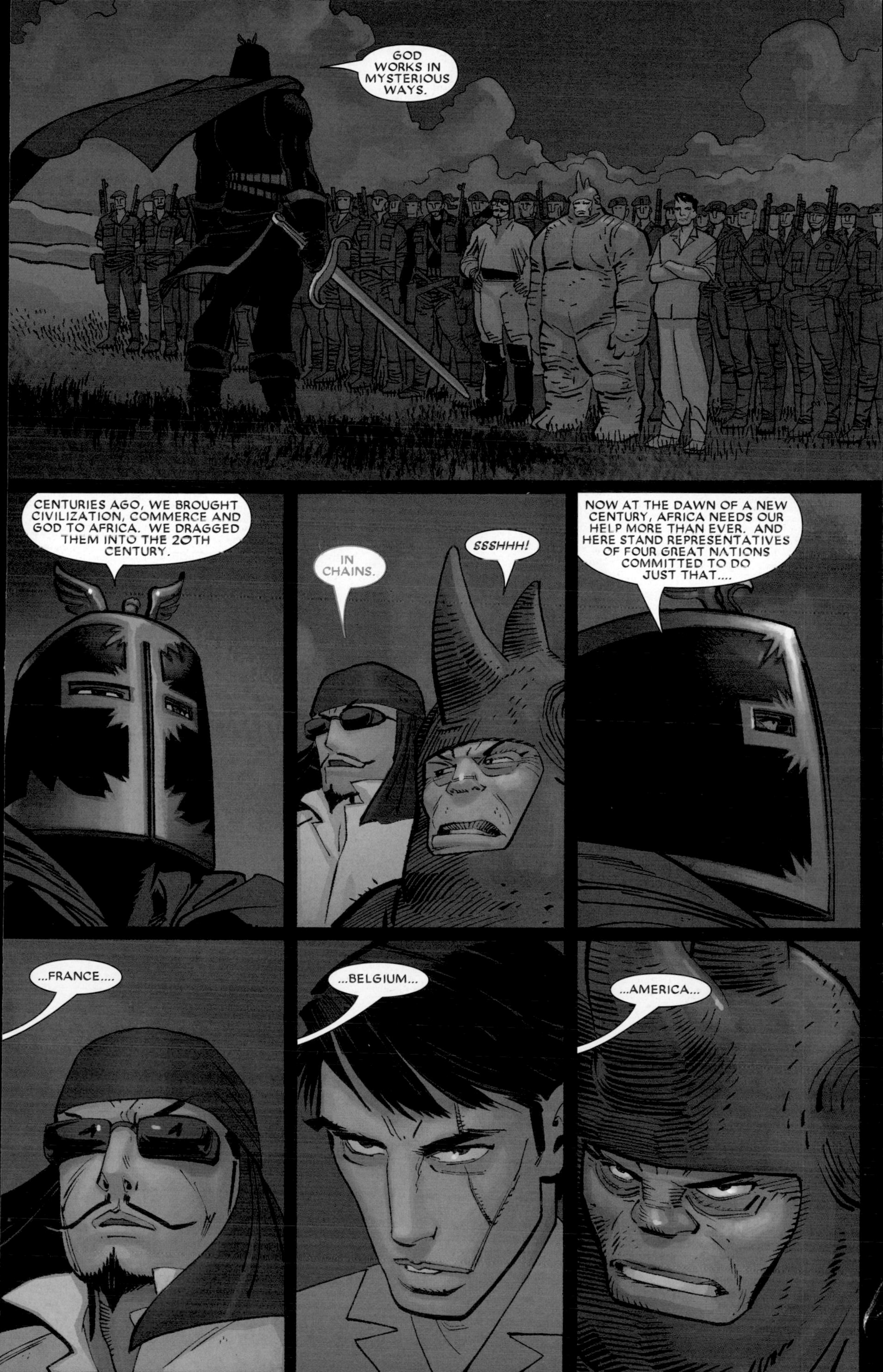
GOD WORKS IN MYSTERIOUS WAYS.
CENTURIES AGO, WE BROUGHT CIVILIZATION, COMMERCE AND GOD TO AFRICA. WE DRAGGED THEM INTO THE 20TH CENTURY.
IN CHAINS.
SSSHHH!
NOW AT THE DAWN OF A NEW CENTURY, AFRICA NEEDS OUR HELP MORE THAN EVER. AND HERE STAND REPRESENTATIVES OF FOUR GREAT NATIONS COMMITTED TO DO JUST THAT....
...FRANCE....
...BELGIUM...
...AMERICA...

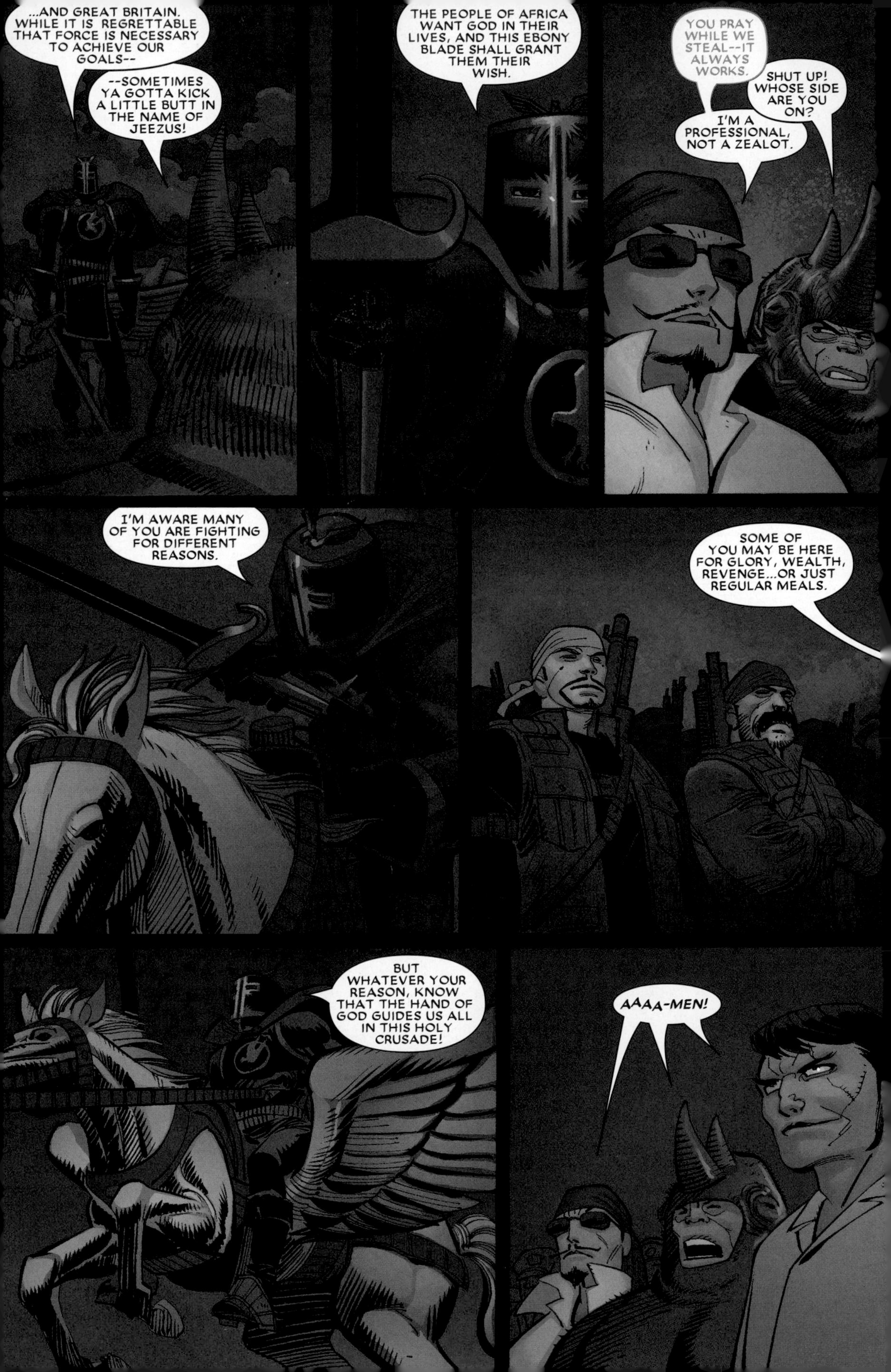
...AND GREAT BRITAIN. WHILE IT IS REGRETTABLE THAT FORCE IS NECESSARY TO ACHIEVE OUR GOALS--
--SOMETIMES YA GOTTA KICK A LITTLE BUTT IN THE NAME OF JEEZUS!
THE PEOPLE OF AFRICA WANT GOD IN THEIR LIVES, AND THIS EBONY BLADE SHALL GRANT THEM THEIR WISH.
YOU PRAY WHILE WE STEAL--IT ALWAYS WORKS.
SHUT UP! WHOSE SIDE ARE YOU ON?
I'M A PROFESSIONAL, NOT A ZEALOT.
I'M AWARE MANY OF YOU ARE FIGHTING FOR DIFFERENT REASONS.
SOME OF YOU MAY BE HERE FOR GLORY, WEALTH, REVENGE...OR JUST REGULAR MEALS.
BUT WHATEVER YOUR REASON, KNOW THAT THE HAND OF GOD GUIDES US ALL IN THIS HOLY CRUSADE!
AAAA-MEN!

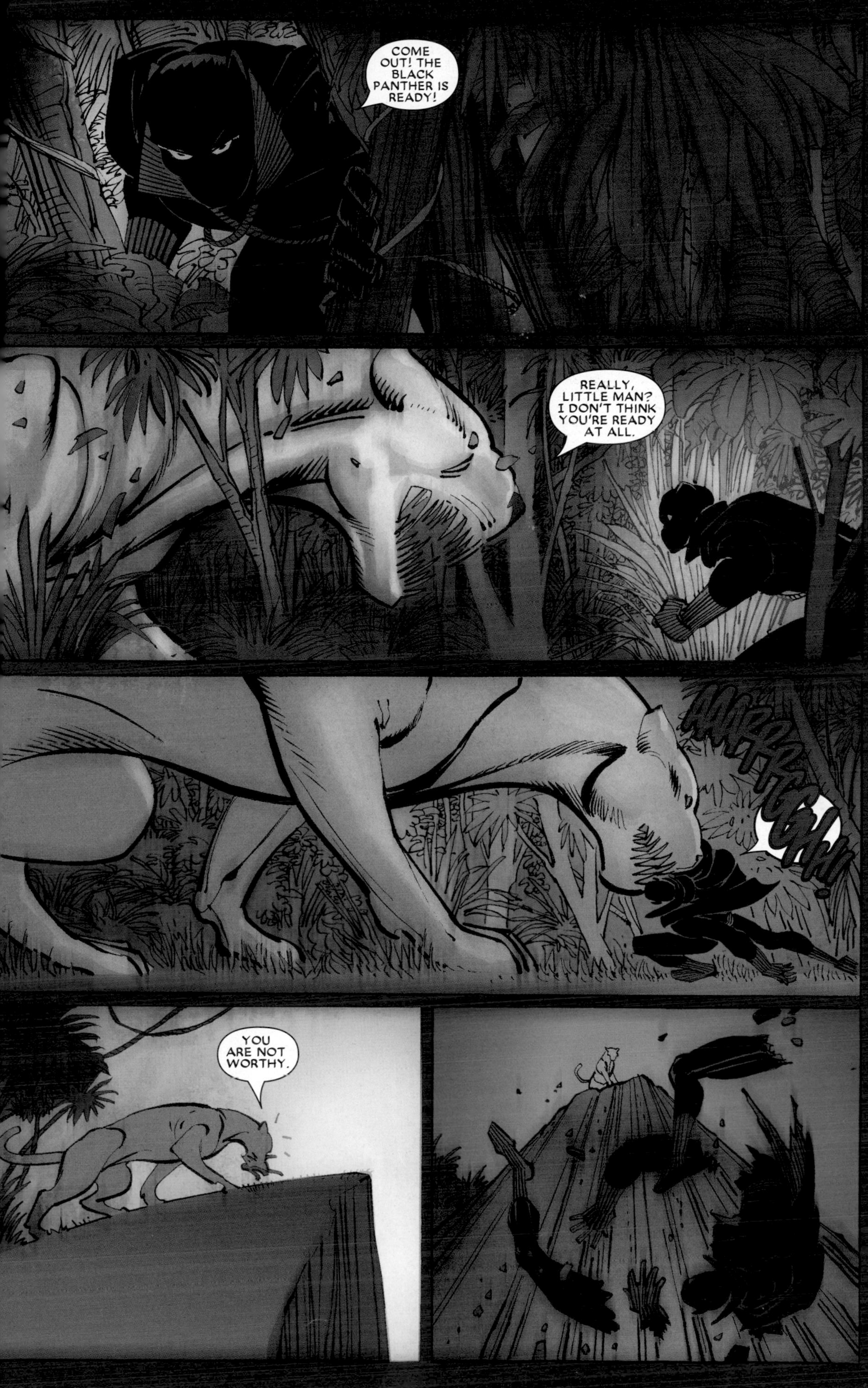
COME OUT! THE BLACK PANTHER IS READY!
REALLY, LITTLE MAN? I DON'T THINK YOU'RE READY AT ALL.
AAARRGGHH!
YOU ARE NOT WORTHY.

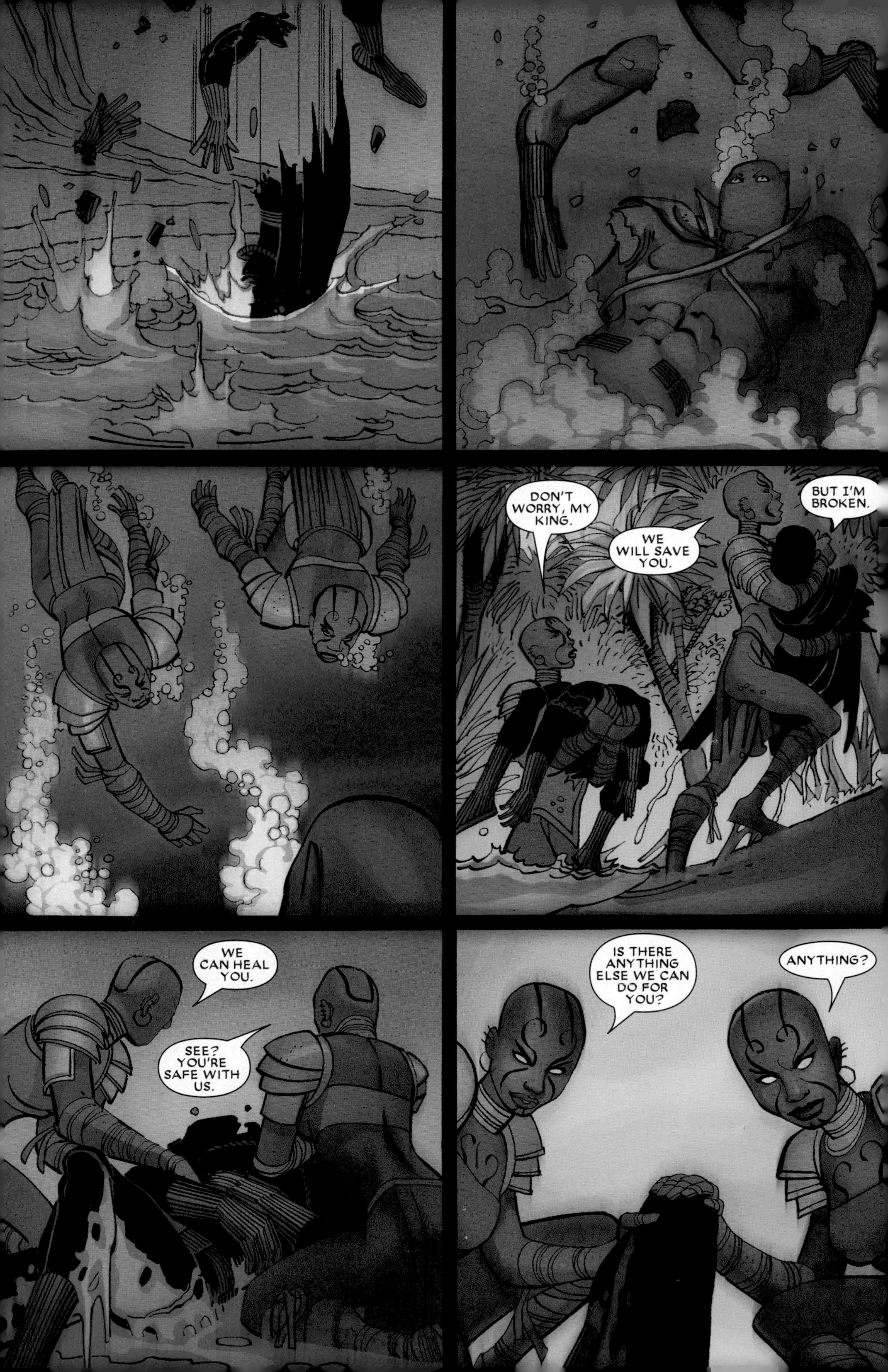
DON'T WORRY, MY KING.
WE WILL SAVE YOU.
BUT I'M BROKEN.
WE CAN HEAL YOU.
SEE? YOU'RE SAFE WITH US.
IS THERE ANYTHING ELSE WE CAN DO FOR YOU?
ANYTHING?

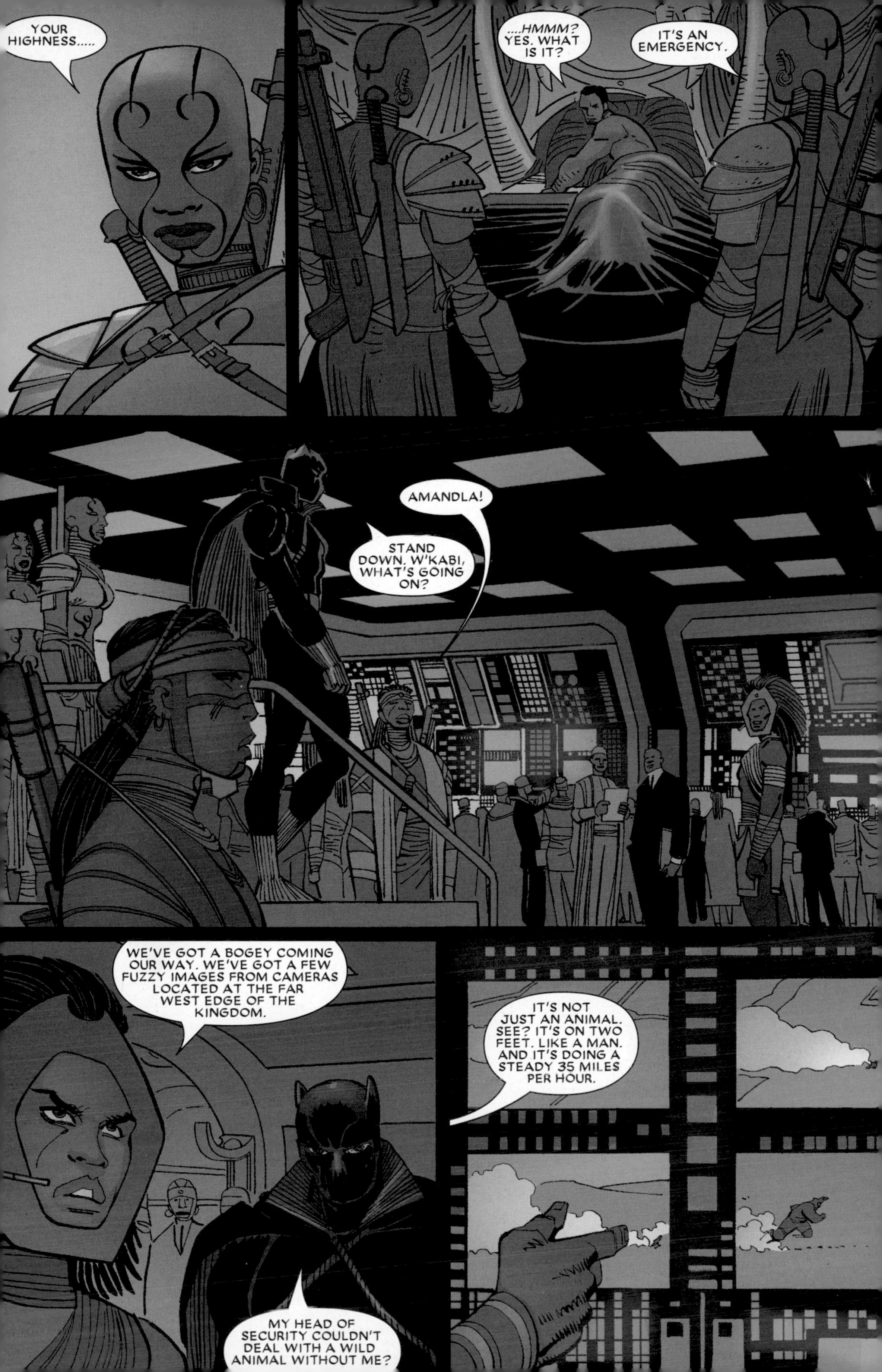
YOUR HIGHNESS.....
....HMMM? YES. WHAT IS IT?
IT'S AN EMERGENCY.
AMANDLA!
STAND DOWN, W'KABI, WHAT'S GOING ON?
WE'VE GOT A BOGEY COMING OUR WAY. WE'VE GOT A FEW FUZZY IMAGES FROM CAMERAS LOCATED AT THE FAR WEST EDGE OF THE KINGDOM.
MY HEAD OF SECURITY COULDN'T DEAL WITH A WILD ANIMAL WITHOUT ME?
IT'S NOT JUST AN ANIMAL. SEE? IT'S ON TWO FEET. LIKE A MAN. AND IT'S DOING A STEADY 35 MILES PER HOUR.

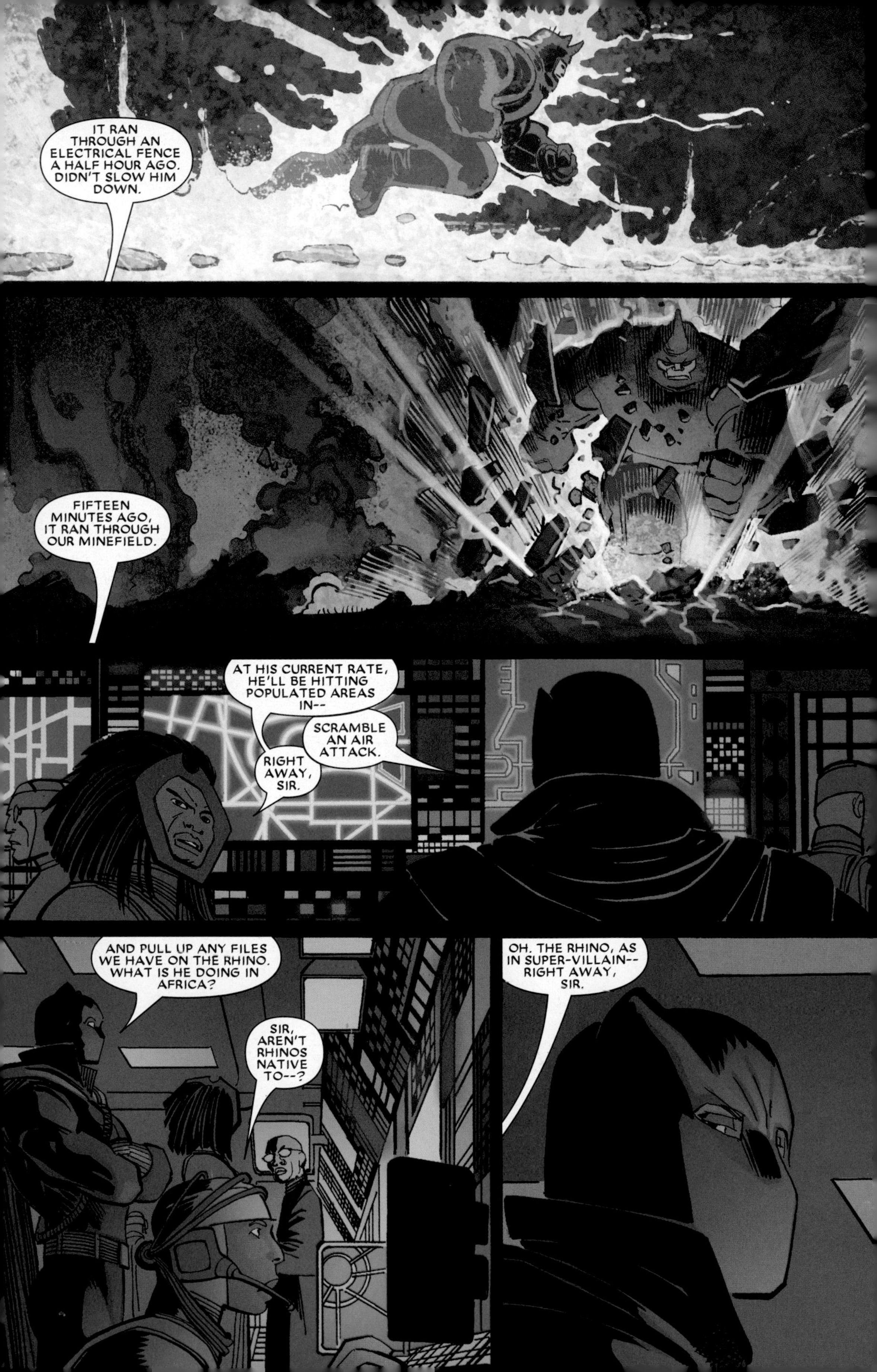
IT RAN THROUGH AN ELECTRICAL FENCE A HALF HOUR AGO. DIDN'T SLOW HIM DOWN.
FIFTEEN MINUTES AGO, IT RAN THROUGH OUR MINEFIELD.
AT HIS CURRENT RATE, HE'LL BE HITTING POPULATED AREAS IN--
SCRAMBLE AN AIR ATTACK.
RIGHT AWAY, SIR.
AND PULL UP ANY FILES WE HAVE ON THE RHINO. WHAT IS HE DOING IN AFRICA?
SIR, AREN'T RHINOS NATIVE TO--?
OH. THE RHINO, AS IN SUPER-VILLAIN-- RIGHT AWAY, SIR.

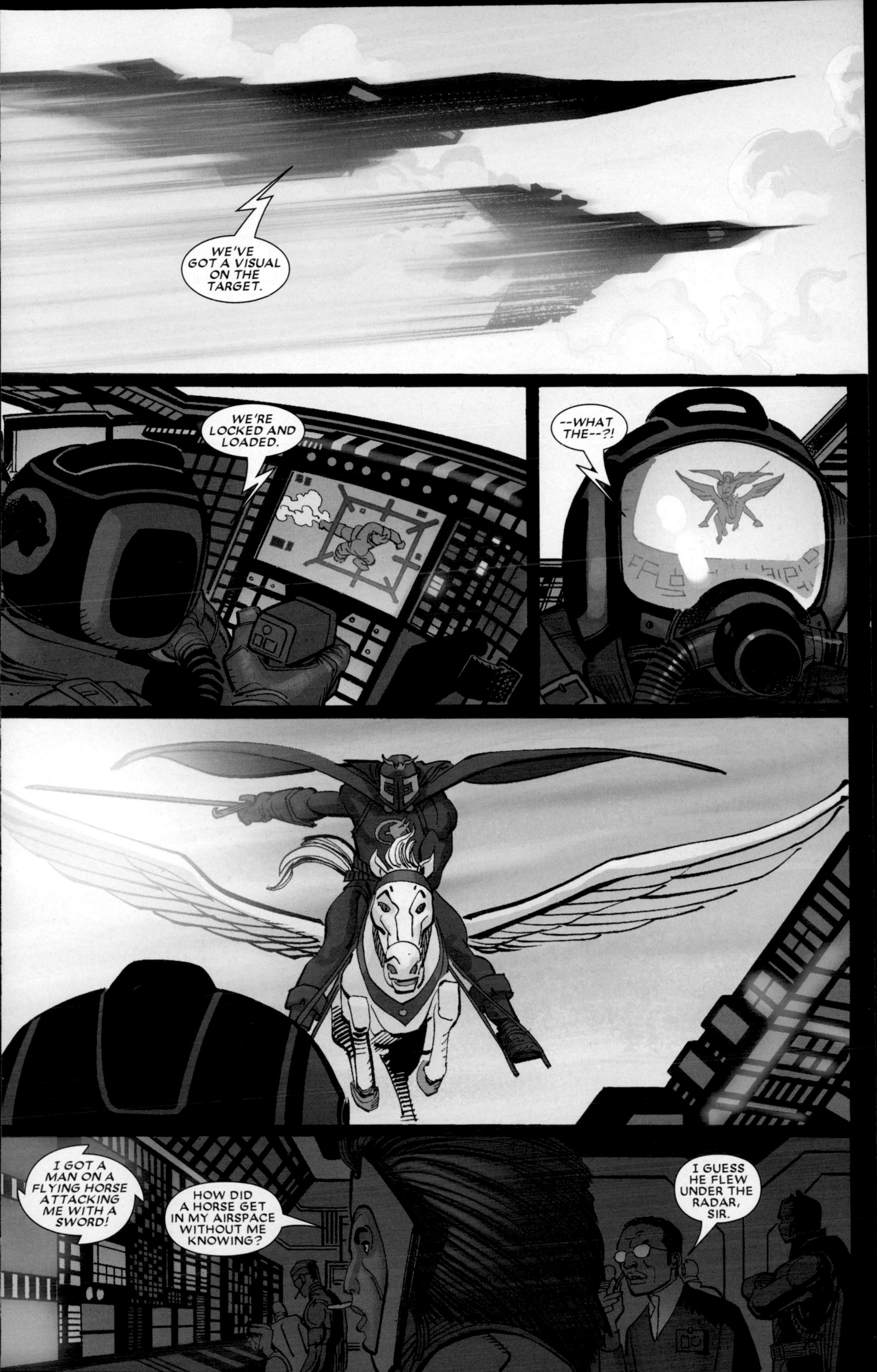
WE'VE GOT A VISUAL ON THE TARGET.
WE'RE LOCKED AND LOADED.
--WHAT THE--?!
I GOT A MAN ON A FLYING HORSE ATTACKING ME WITH A SWORD!
HOW DID A HORSE GET IN MY AIRSPACE WITHOUT ME KNOWING?
I GUESS HE FLEW UNDER THE RADAR, SIR.

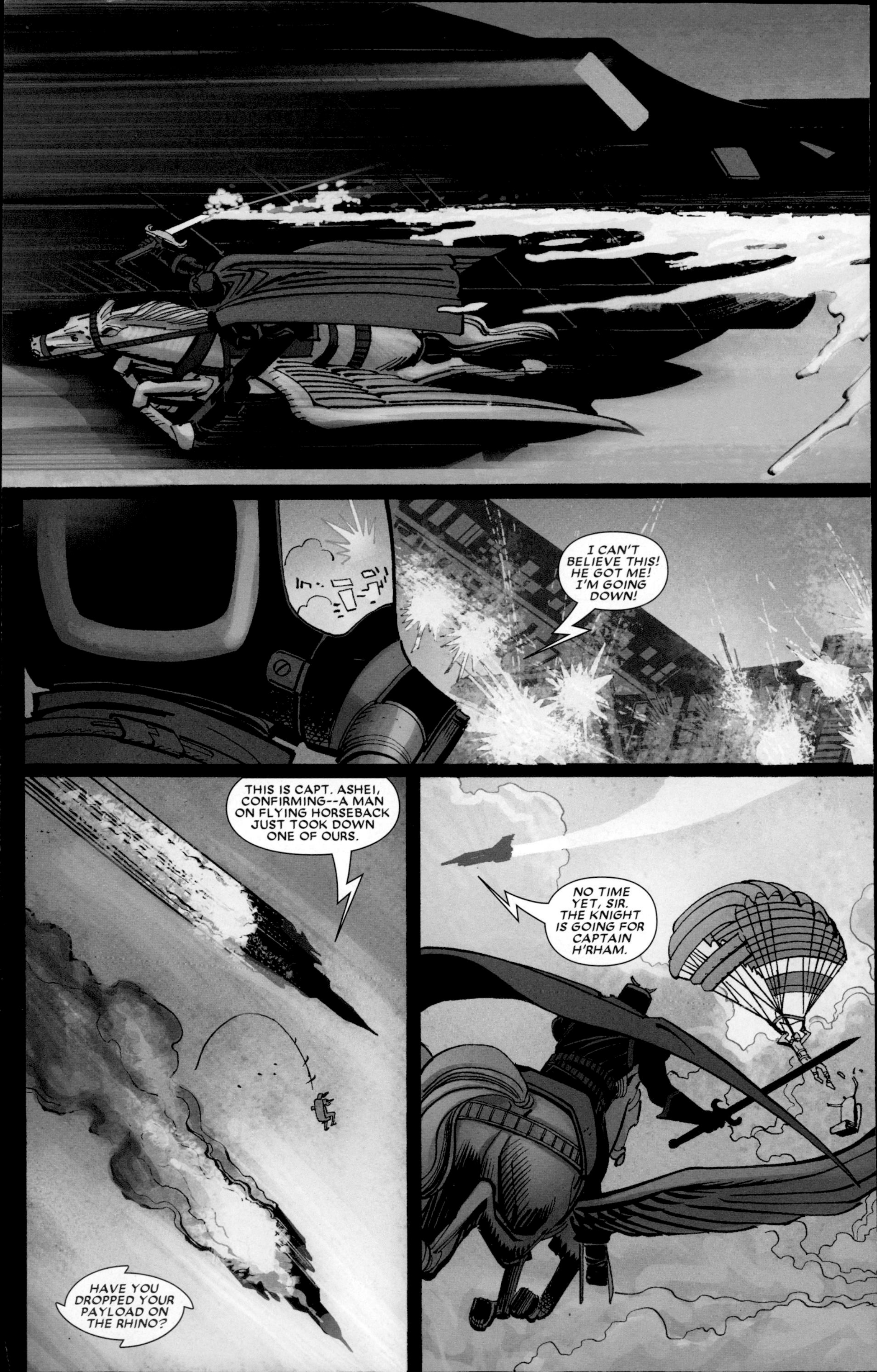
I CAN'T BELIEVE THIS! HE GOT ME! I'M GOING DOWN!
THIS IS CAPT. ASHEI, CONFIRMING--A MAN ON FLYING HORSEBACK JUST TOOK DOWN ONE OF OURS.
HAVE YOU DROPPED YOUR PAYLOAD ON THE RHINO?
NO TIME YET, SIR. THE KNIGHT IS GOING FOR CAPTAIN H'RHAM.

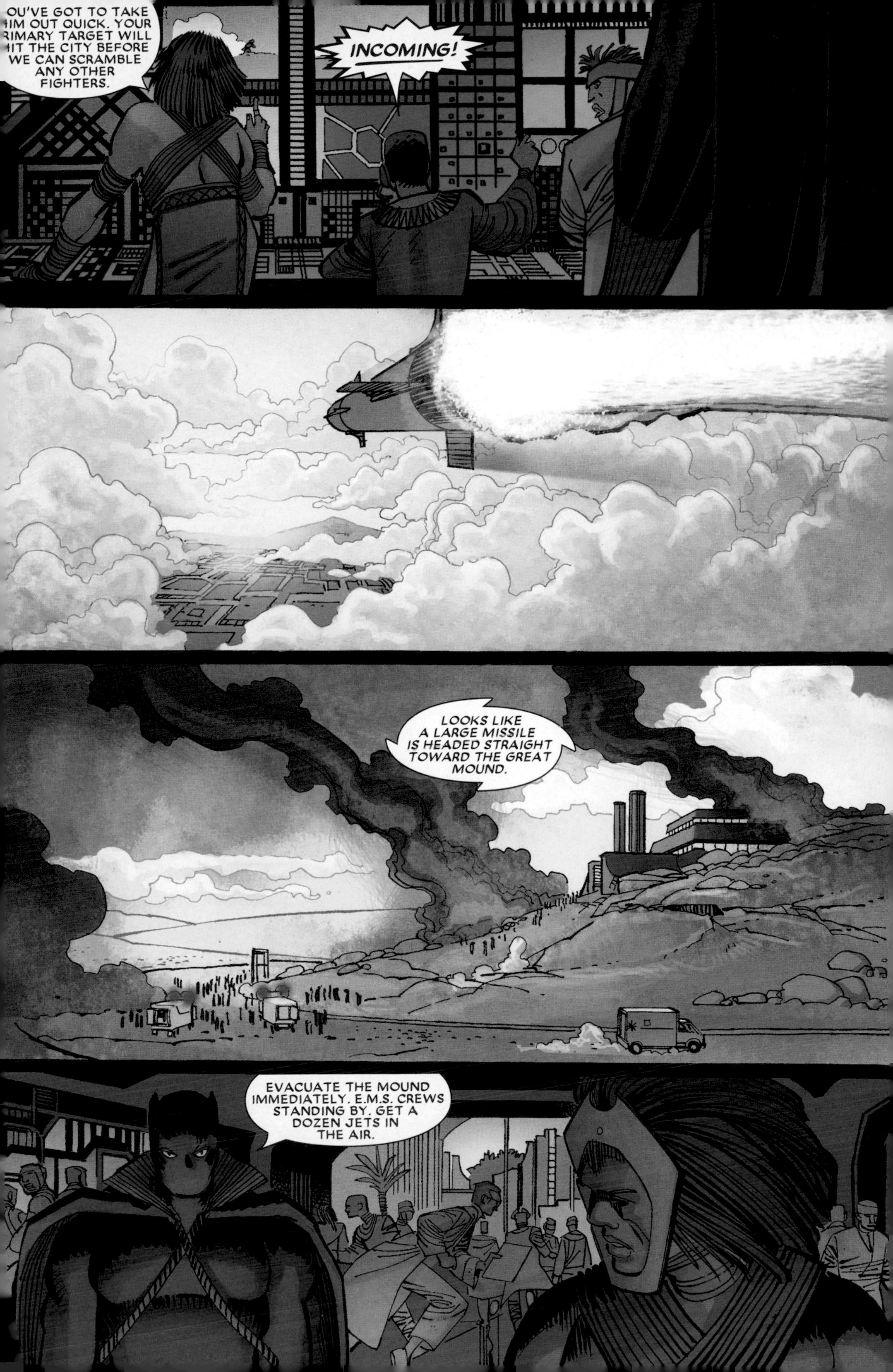
OU'VE GOT TO TAKE
IM OUT QUICK. YOUR
RIMARY TARGET WILL
IT THE CITY BEFORE
WE CAN SCRAMBLE
ANY OTHER
FIGHTERS.
INCOMING!
LOOKS LIKE A LARGE MISSILE IS HEADED STRAIGHT TOWARD THE GREAT MOUND.
EVACUATE THE MOUND IMMEDIATELY. E.M.S. CREWS STANDING BY. GET A DOZEN JETS IN THE AIR.

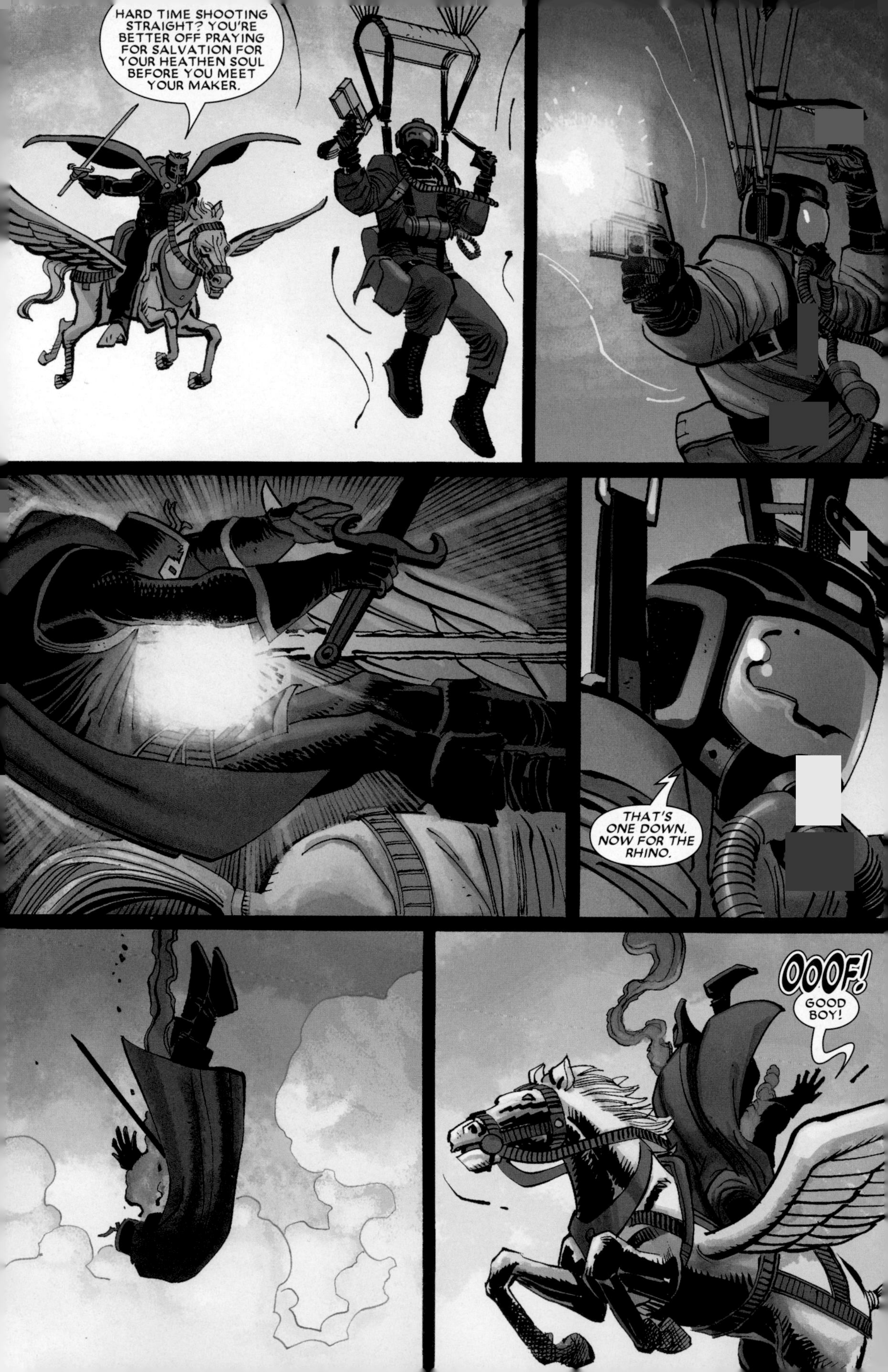
HARD TIME SHOOTING STRAIGHT? YOU'RE BETTER OFF PRAYING FOR SALVATION FOR YOUR HEATHEN SOUL BEFORE YOU MEET YOUR MAKER.
THAT'S ONE DOWN. NOW FOR THE RHINO.
OOOF!
GOOD BOY!

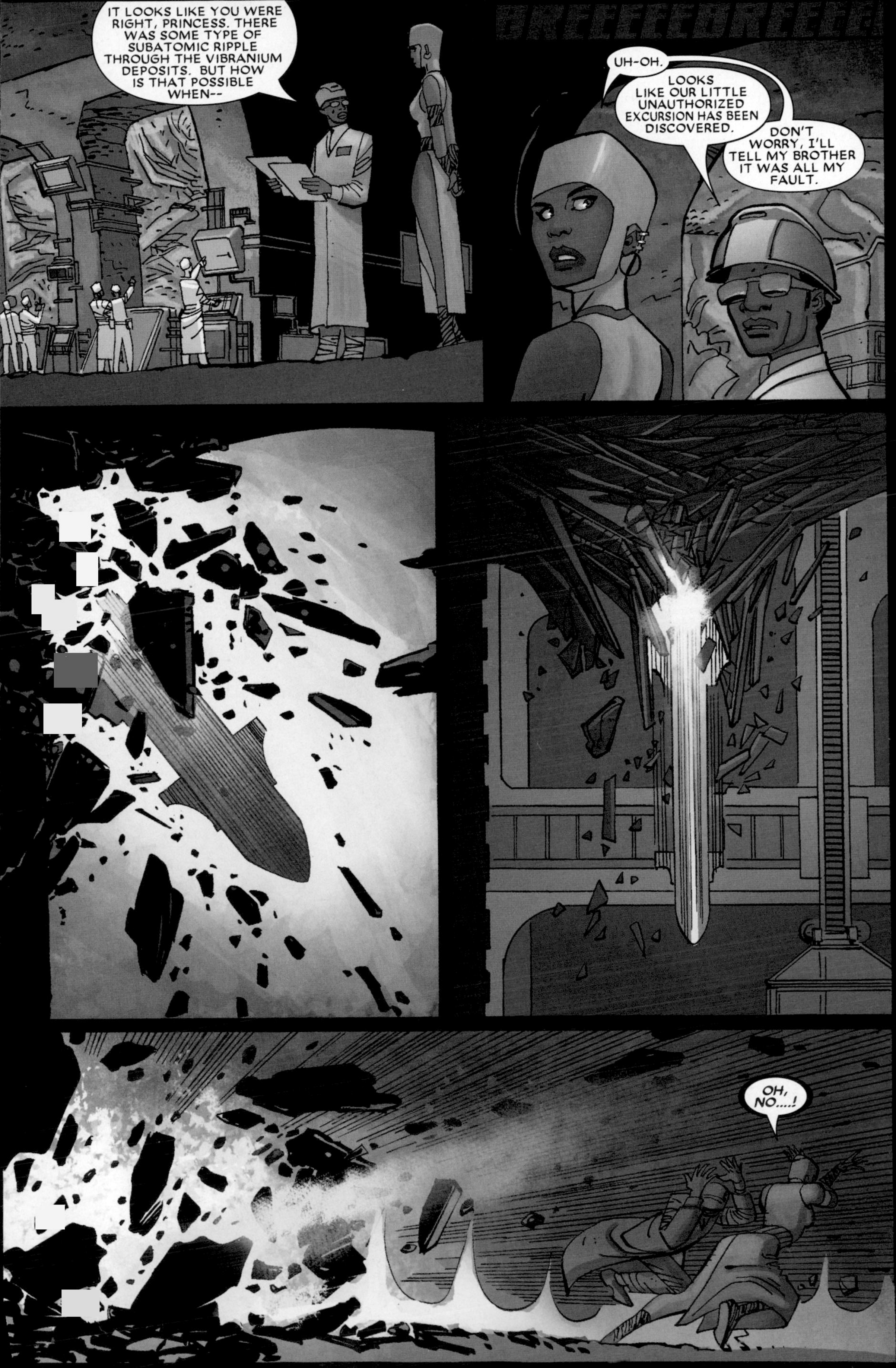
IT LOOKS LIKE YOU WERE RIGHT, PRINCESS. THERE WAS SOME TYPE OF SUBATOMIC RIPPLE THROUGH THE VIBRANIUM DEPOSITS. BUT HOW IS THAT POSSIBLE WHEN--
UH-OH.
LOOKS LIKE OUR LITTLE UNAUTHORIZED EXCURSION HAS BEEN DISCOVERED.
DON'T WORRY, I'LL TELL MY BROTHER IT WAS ALL MY FAULT.
OH, NO....!

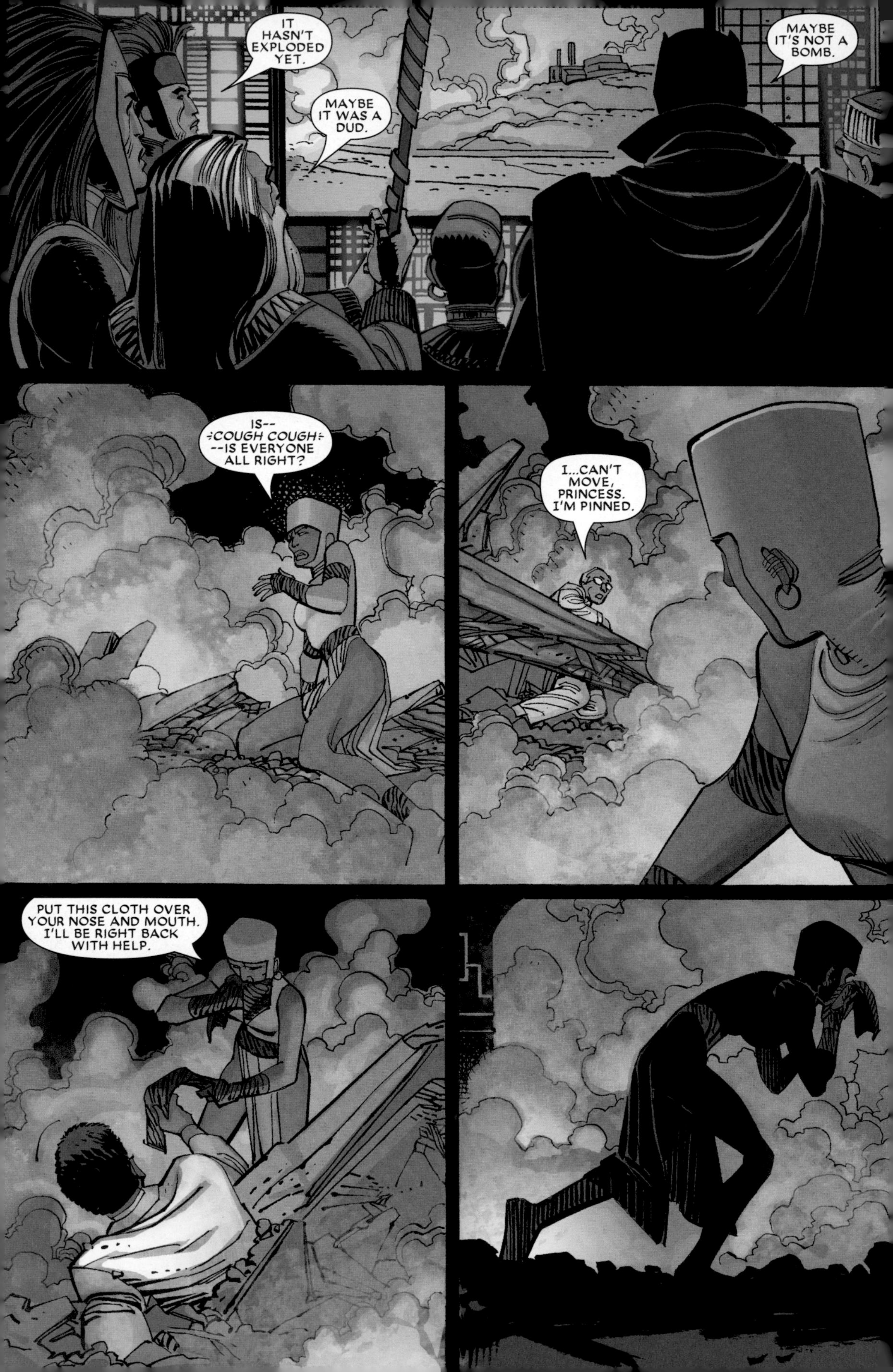
IT HASN'T EXPLODED YET.
MAYBE IT WAS A DUD.
MAYBE IT'S NOT A BOMB.
IS-- -COUGH COUGH- --IS EVERYONE ALL RIGHT?
I...CAN'T MOVE, PRINCESS. I'M PINNED.
PUT THIS CLOTH OVER YOUR NOSE AND MOUTH. I'LL BE RIGHT BACK WITH HELP.

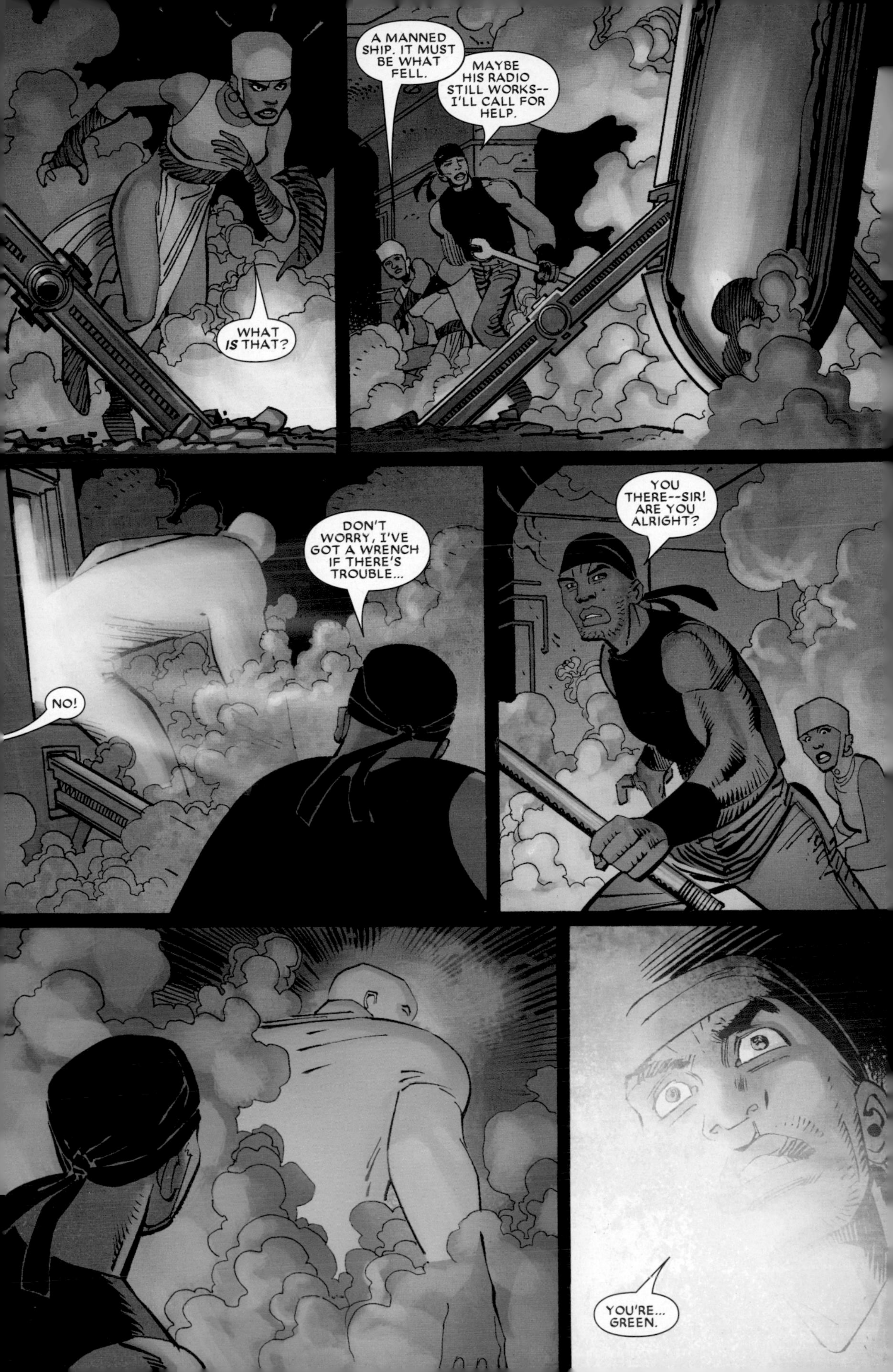
WHAT IS THAT?
A MANNED SHIP. IT MUST BE WHAT FELL.
MAYBE HIS RADIO STILL WORKS-- I'LL CALL FOR HELP.
NO!
DON'T WORRY, I'VE GOT A WRENCH IF THERE'S TROUBLE...
YOU THERE--SIR! ARE YOU ALRIGHT?
YOU'RE... GREEN.

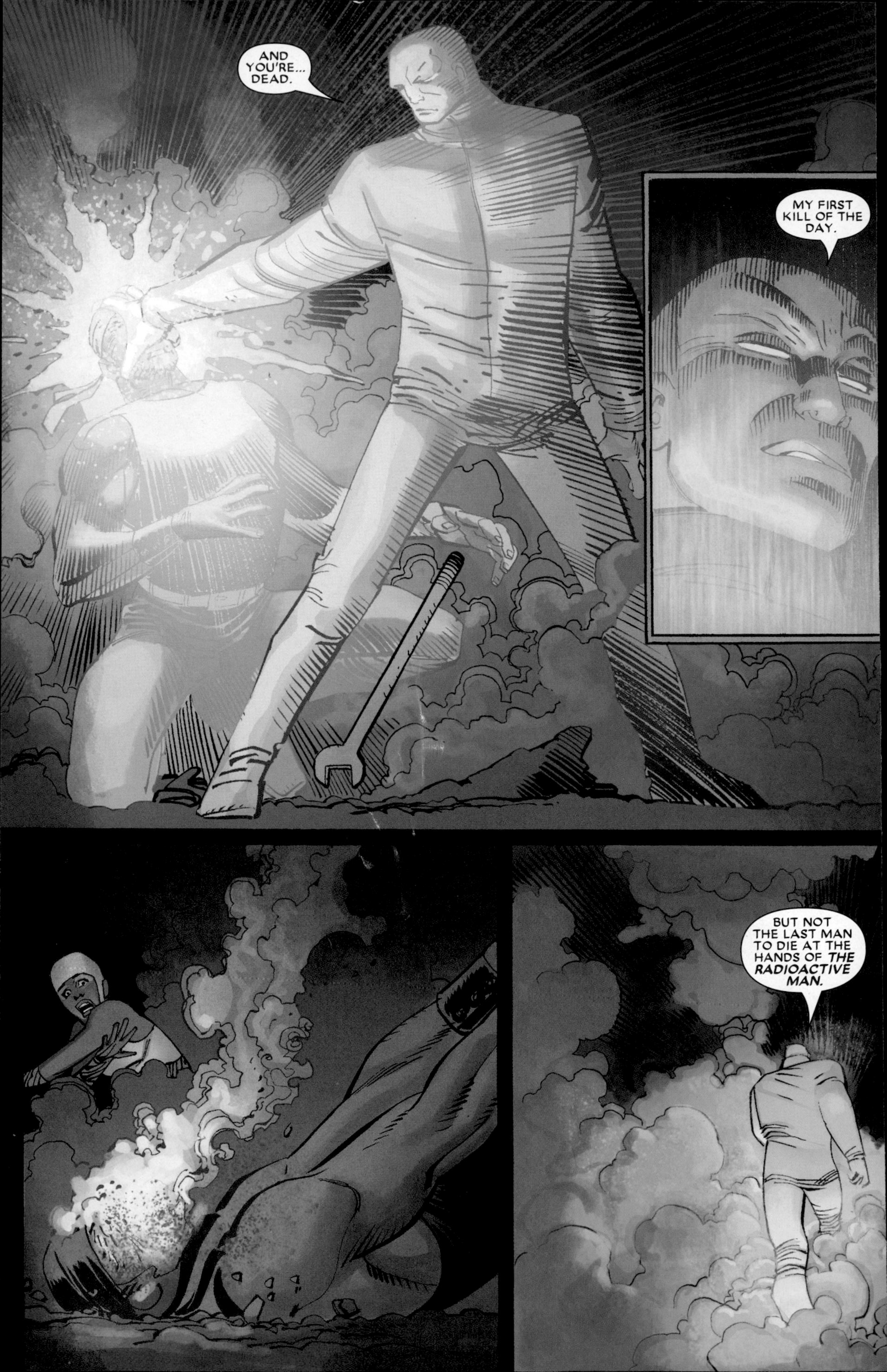
AND YOU'RE... DEAD.
MY FIRST KILL OF THE DAY.
BUT NOT THE LAST MAN TO DIE AT THE HANDS OF *THE RADIOACTIVE MAN.*

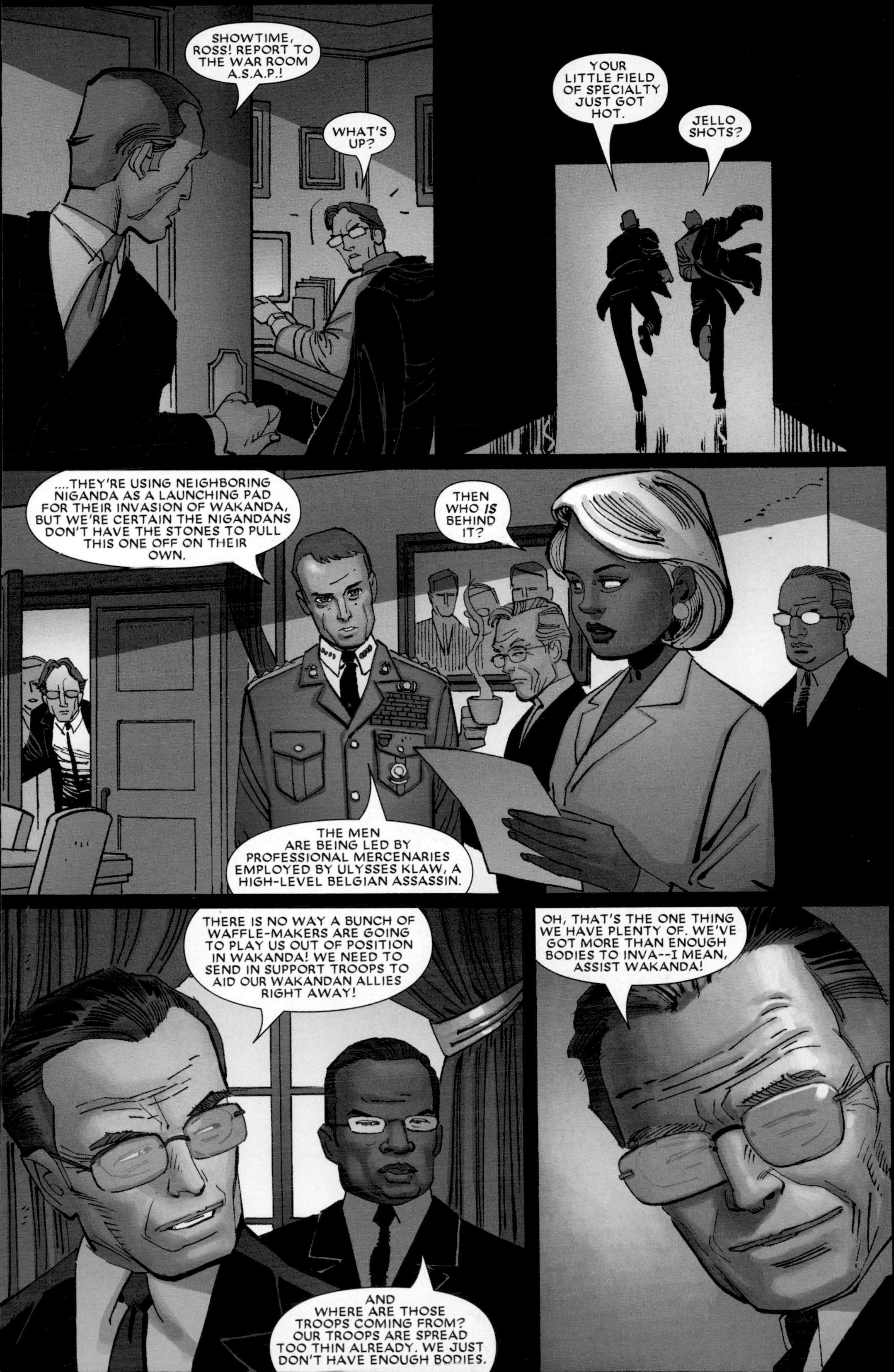
SHOWTIME, ROSS! REPORT TO THE WAR ROOM A.S.A.P.!
WHAT'S UP?
YOUR LITTLE FIELD OF SPECIALTY JUST GOT HOT.
JELLO SHOTS?
....THEY'RE USING NEIGHBORING NIGANDA AS A LAUNCHING PAD FOR THEIR INVASION OF WAKANDA, BUT WE'RE CERTAIN THE NIGANDANS DON'T HAVE THE STONES TO PULL THIS ONE OFF ON THEIR OWN.
THEN WHO *IS* BEHIND IT?
THE MEN ARE BEING LED BY PROFESSIONAL MERCENARIES EMPLOYED BY ULYSSES KLAW, A HIGH-LEVEL BELGIAN ASSASSIN.
THERE IS NO WAY A BUNCH OF WAFFLE-MAKERS ARE GOING TO PLAY US OUT OF POSITION IN WAKANDA! WE NEED TO SEND IN SUPPORT TROOPS TO AID OUR WAKANDAN ALLIES RIGHT AWAY!
AND WHERE ARE THOSE TROOPS COMING FROM? OUR TROOPS ARE SPREAD TOO THIN ALREADY. WE JUST DON'T HAVE ENOUGH BODIES.
OH, THAT'S THE ONE THING WE HAVE PLENTY OF. WE'VE GOT MORE THAN ENOUGH BODIES TO INVA--I MEAN, ASSIST WAKANDA!

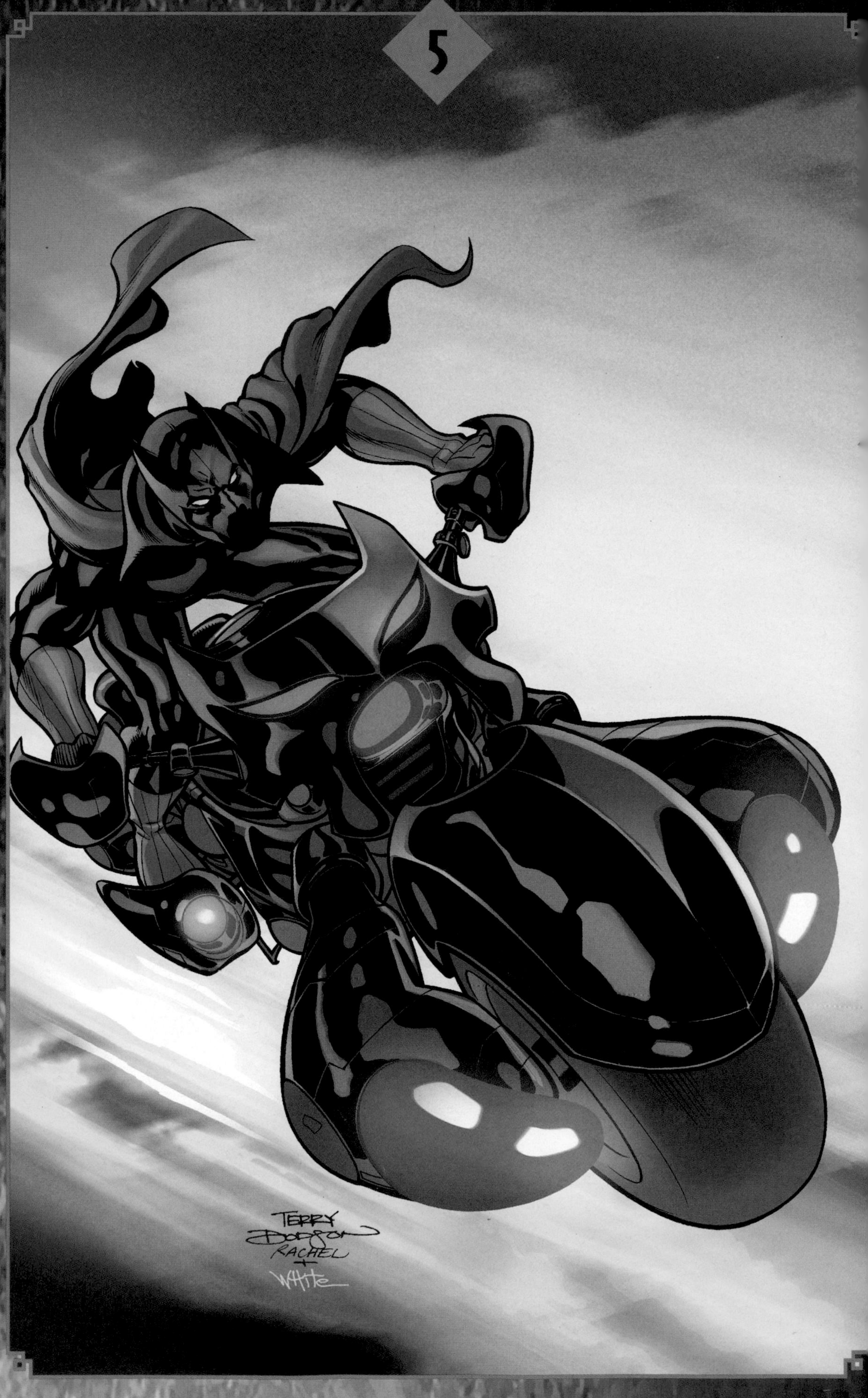
5
TERRY
DODSON
RACHEL
+
WHITE

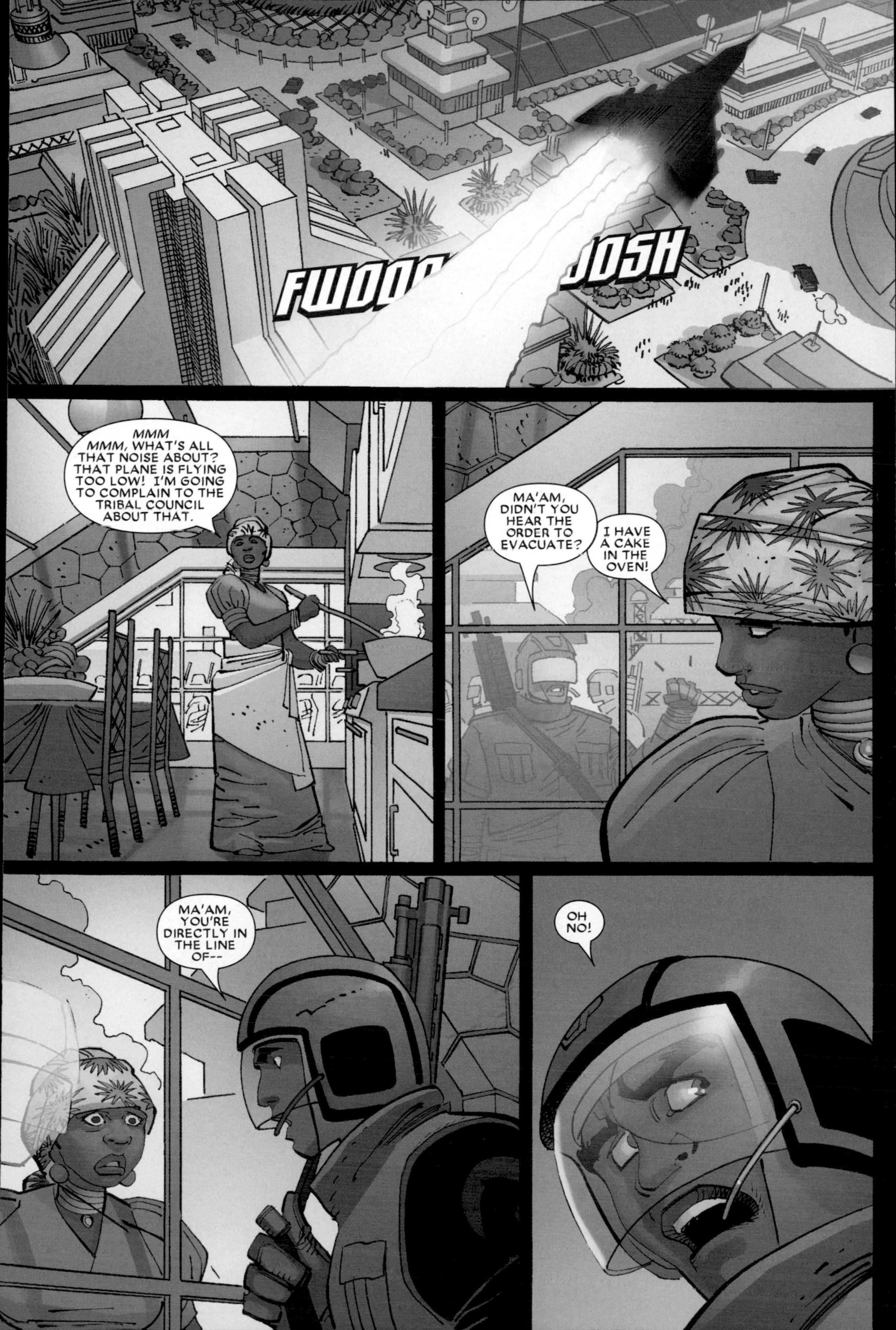
FWOOO
JOSH
MMM MMM, WHAT'S ALL THAT NOISE ABOUT? THAT PLANE IS FLYING TOO LOW! I'M GOING TO COMPLAIN TO THE TRIBAL COUNCIL ABOUT THAT.
MA'AM, DIDN'T YOU HEAR THE ORDER TO EVACUATE?
I HAVE A CAKE IN THE OVEN!
MA'AM, YOU'RE DIRECTLY IN THE LINE OF--
OH NO!

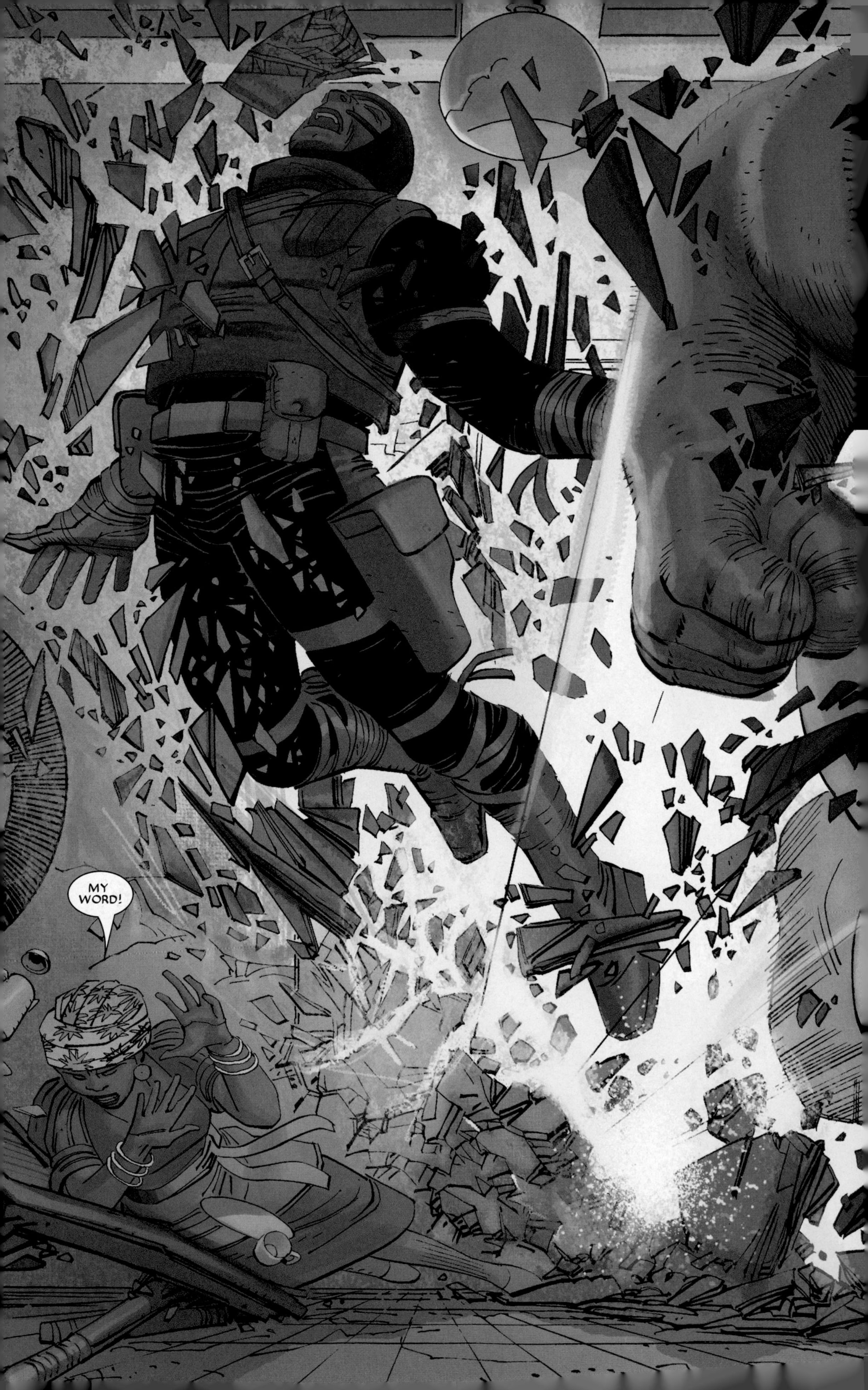
MY WORD!

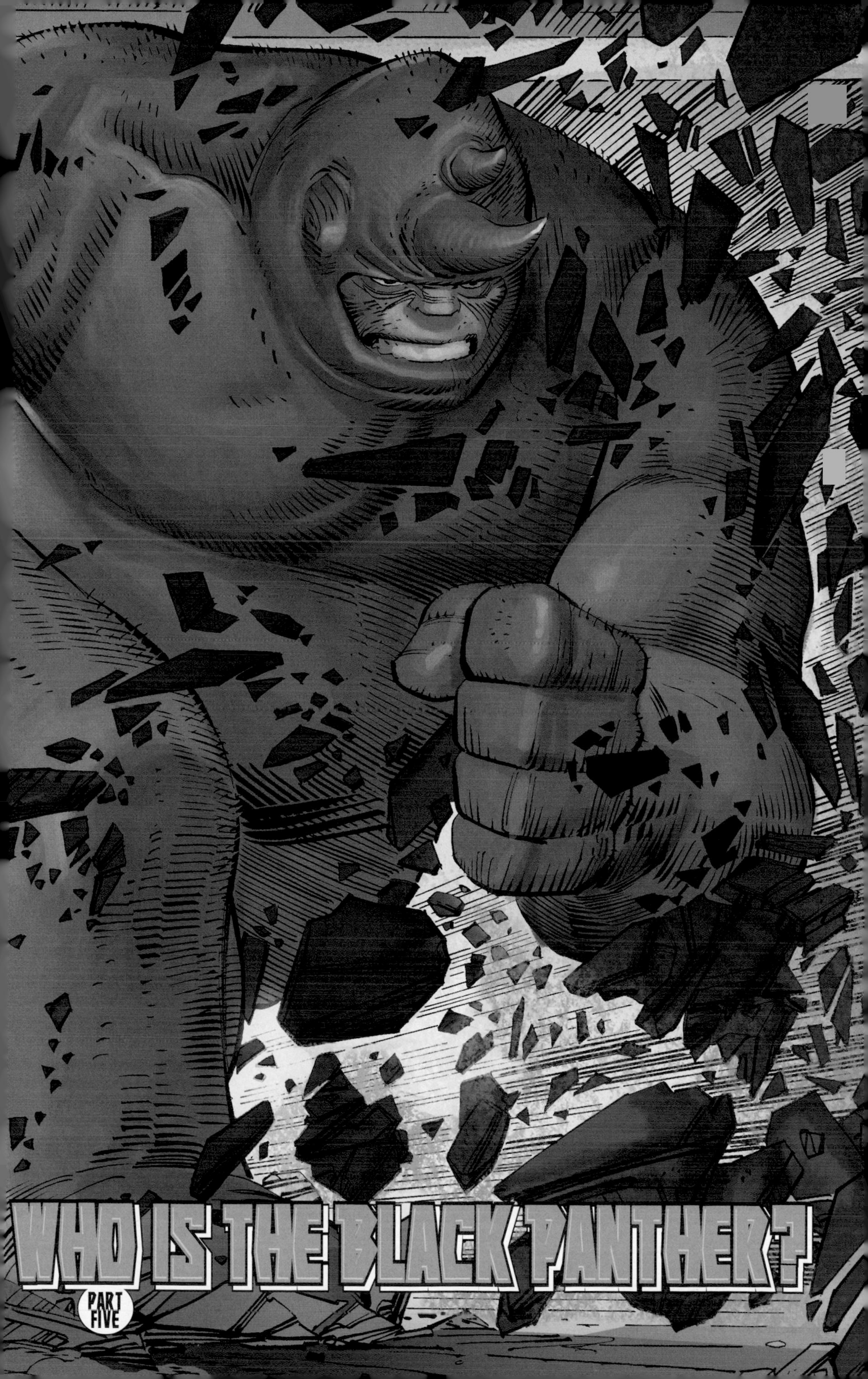
WHO IS THE BLACK PANTHER?
PART FIVE

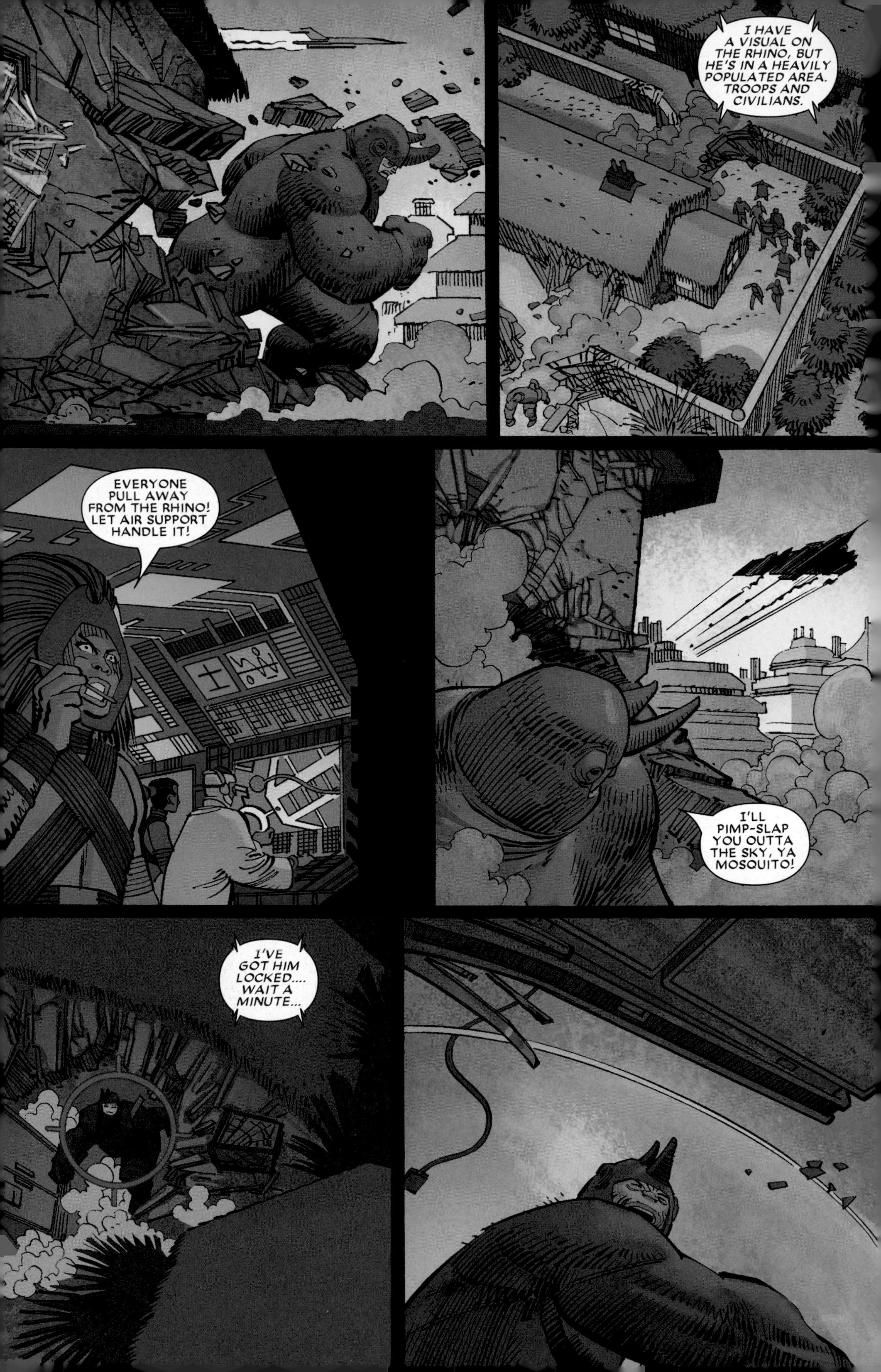
I HAVE A VISUAL ON THE RHINO, BUT HE'S IN A HEAVILY POPULATED AREA. TROOPS AND CIVILIANS.
EVERYONE PULL AWAY FROM THE RHINO! LET AIR SUPPORT HANDLE IT!
I'LL PIMP-SLAP YOU OUTTA THE SKY, YA MOSQUITO!
I'VE GOT HIM LOCKED.... WAIT A MINUTE...

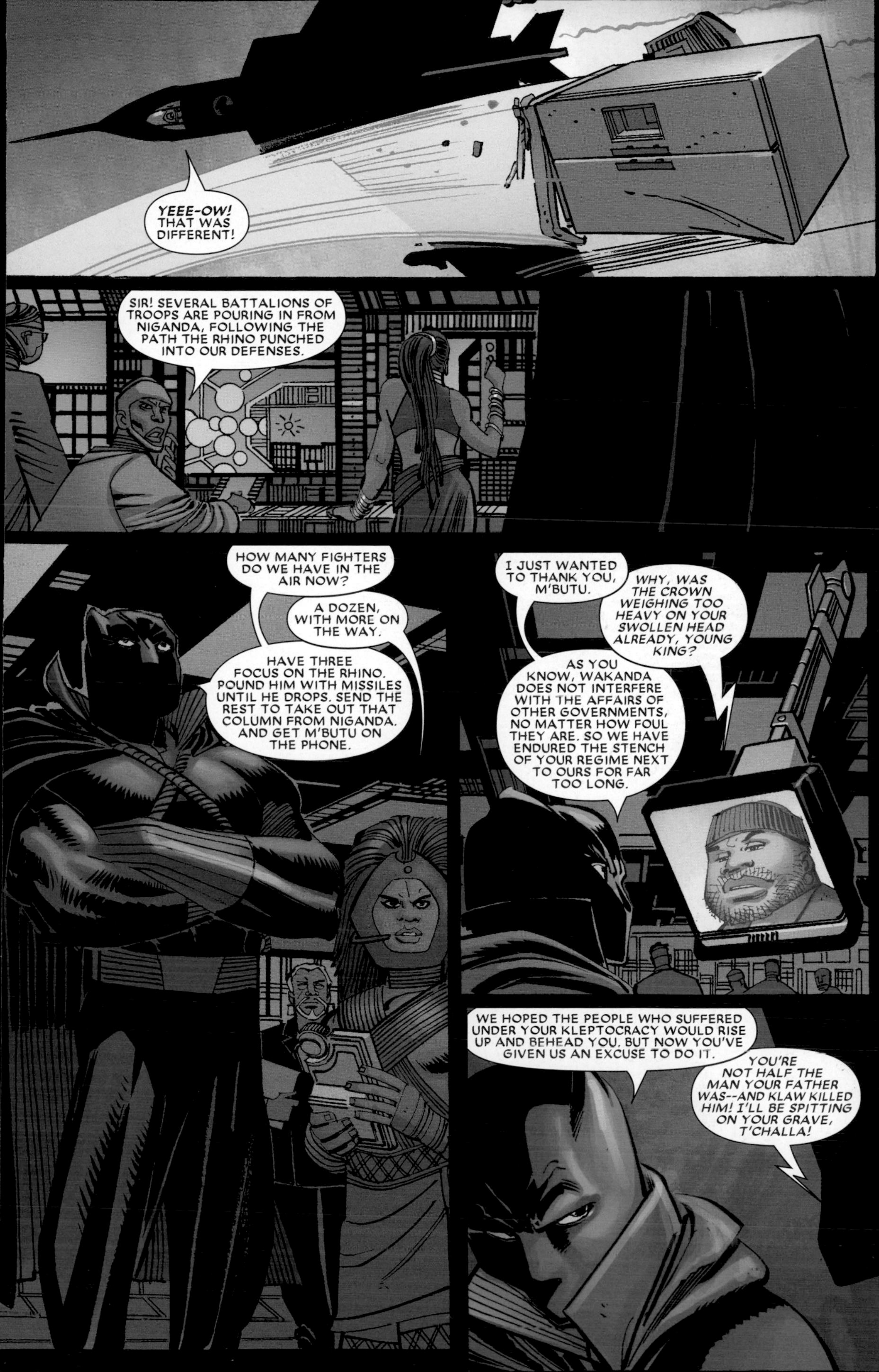
YEEE-OW! THAT WAS DIFFERENT!
SIR! SEVERAL BATTALIONS OF TROOPS ARE POURING IN FROM NIGANDA, FOLLOWING THE PATH THE RHINO PUNCHED INTO OUR DEFENSES.
HOW MANY FIGHTERS DO WE HAVE IN THE AIR NOW?
A DOZEN, WITH MORE ON THE WAY.
HAVE THREE FOCUS ON THE RHINO. POUND HIM WITH MISSILES UNTIL HE DROPS. SEND THE REST TO TAKE OUT THAT COLUMN FROM NIGANDA. AND GET M'BUTU ON THE PHONE.
I JUST WANTED TO THANK YOU, M'BUTU.
WHY, WAS THE CROWN WEIGHING TOO HEAVY ON YOUR SWOLLEN HEAD ALREADY, YOUNG KING?
AS YOU KNOW, WAKANDA DOES NOT INTERFERE WITH THE AFFAIRS OF OTHER GOVERNMENTS, NO MATTER HOW FOUL THEY ARE. SO WE HAVE ENDURED THE STENCH OF YOUR REGIME NEXT TO OURS FOR FAR TOO LONG.
WE HOPED THE PEOPLE WHO SUFFERED UNDER YOUR KLEPTOCRACY WOULD RISE UP AND BEHEAD YOU. BUT NOW YOU'VE GIVEN US AN EXCUSE TO DO IT.
YOU'RE NOT HALF THE MAN YOUR FATHER WAS--AND KLAW KILLED HIM! I'LL BE SPITTING ON YOUR GRAVE, T'CHALLA!

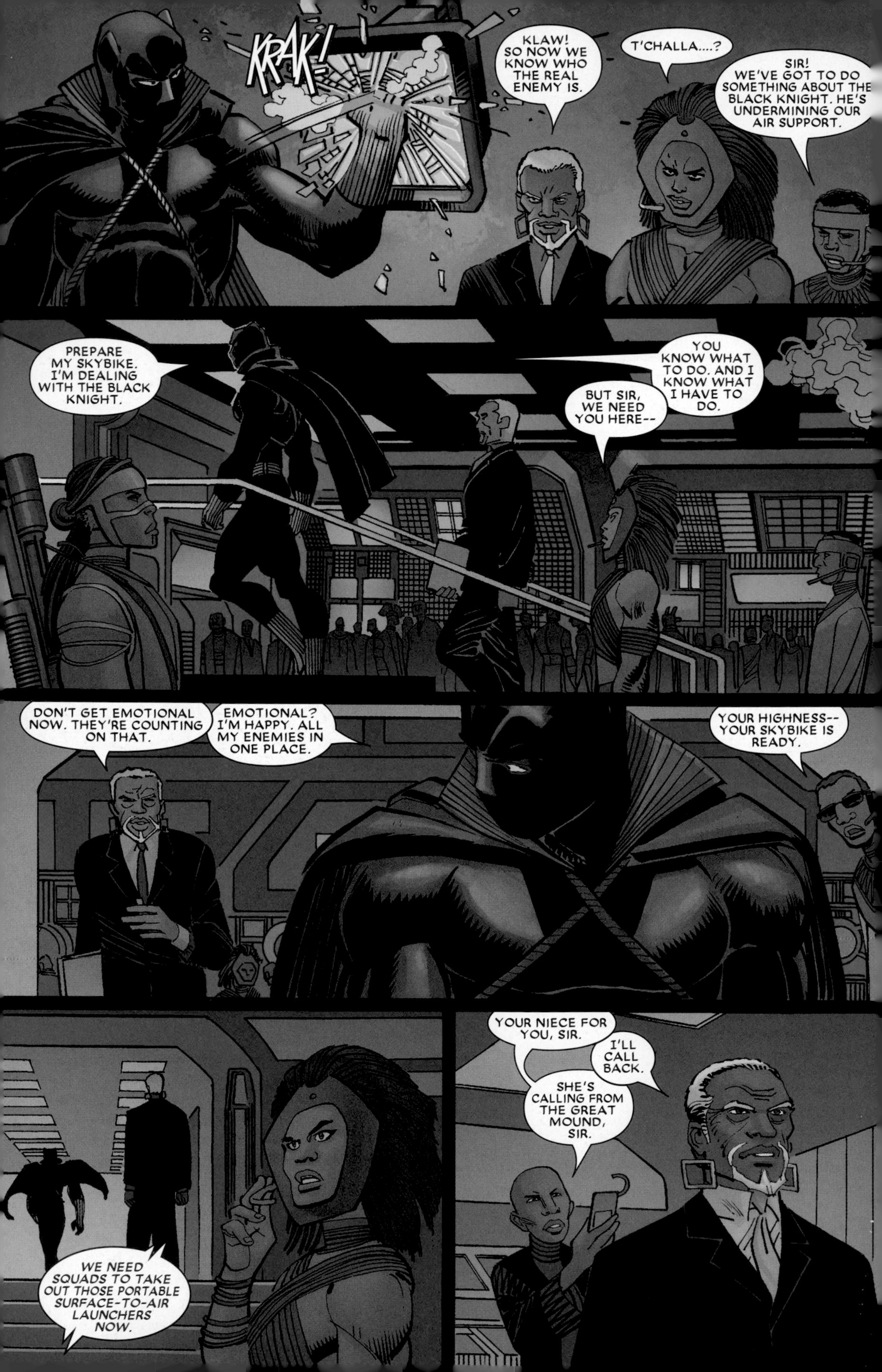
KRAK!
KLAW! SO NOW WE KNOW WHO THE REAL ENEMY IS.
T'CHALLA....?
SIR! WE'VE GOT TO DO SOMETHING ABOUT THE BLACK KNIGHT. HE'S UNDERMINING OUR AIR SUPPORT.
PREPARE MY SKYBIKE. I'M DEALING WITH THE BLACK KNIGHT.
BUT SIR, WE NEED YOU HERE--
YOU KNOW WHAT TO DO. AND I KNOW WHAT I HAVE TO DO.
DON'T GET EMOTIONAL NOW. THEY'RE COUNTING ON THAT.
EMOTIONAL? I'M HAPPY. ALL MY ENEMIES IN ONE PLACE.
YOUR HIGHNESS-- YOUR SKYBIKE IS READY.
WE NEED SQUADS TO TAKE OUT THOSE PORTABLE SURFACE-TO-AIR LAUNCHERS NOW.
YOUR NIECE FOR YOU, SIR.
I'LL CALL BACK.
SHE'S CALLING FROM THE GREAT MOUND, SIR.

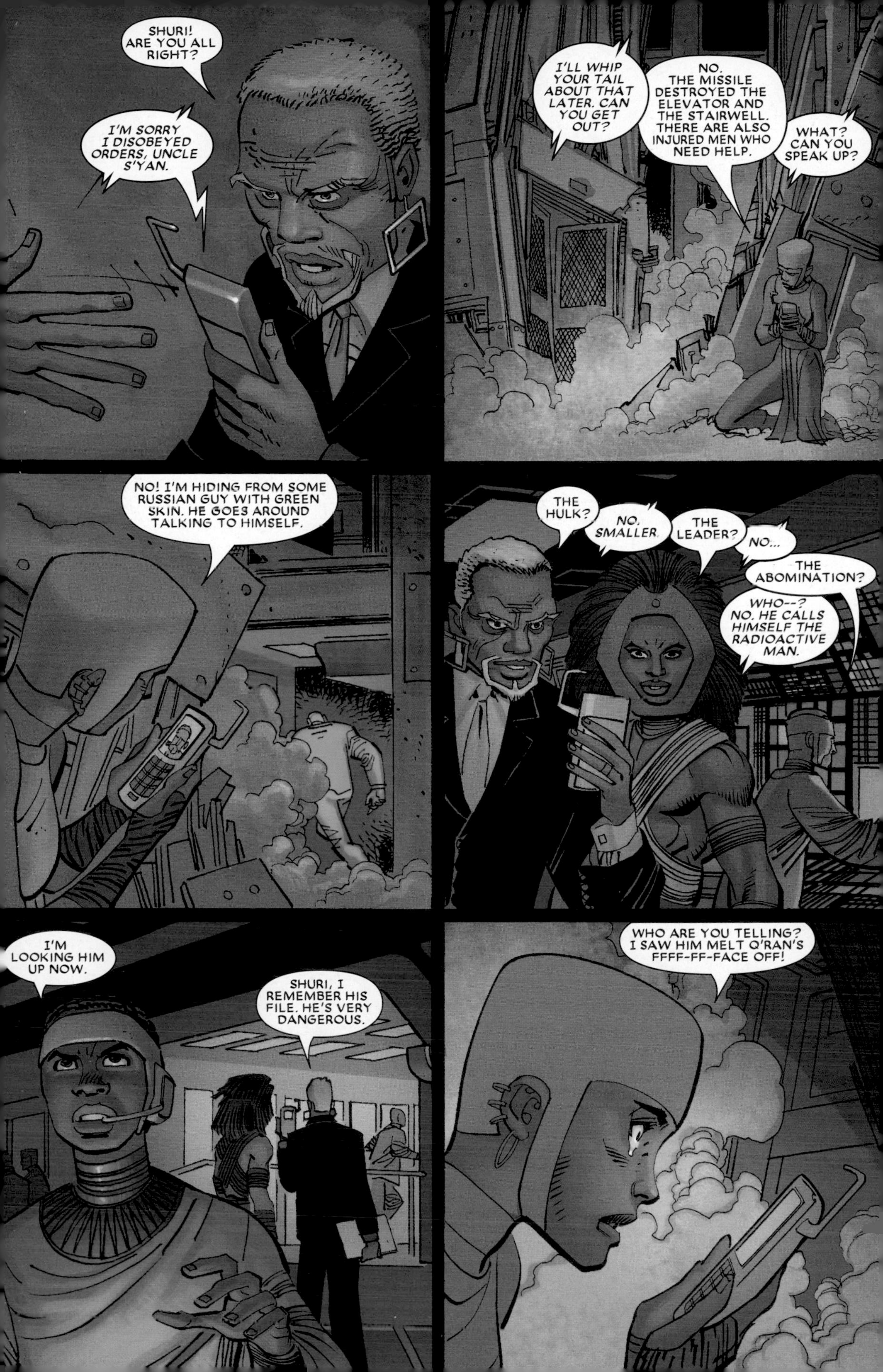
SHURI! ARE YOU ALL RIGHT?
I'M SORRY I DISOBEYED ORDERS, UNCLE S'YAN.
I'LL WHIP YOUR TAIL ABOUT THAT LATER. CAN YOU GET OUT?
NO. THE MISSILE DESTROYED THE ELEVATOR AND THE STAIRWELL. THERE ARE ALSO INJURED MEN WHO NEED HELP.
WHAT? CAN YOU SPEAK UP?
NO! I'M HIDING FROM SOME RUSSIAN GUY WITH GREEN SKIN. HE GOES AROUND TALKING TO HIMSELF.
THE HULK?
NO. SMALLER.
THE LEADER?
NO...
THE ABOMINATION?
WHO--? NO. HE CALLS HIMSELF THE RADIOACTIVE MAN.
I'M LOOKING HIM UP NOW.
SHURI, I REMEMBER HIS FILE. HE'S VERY DANGEROUS.
WHO ARE YOU TELLING? I SAW HIM MELT Q'RAN'S FFFF-FF-FACE OFF!

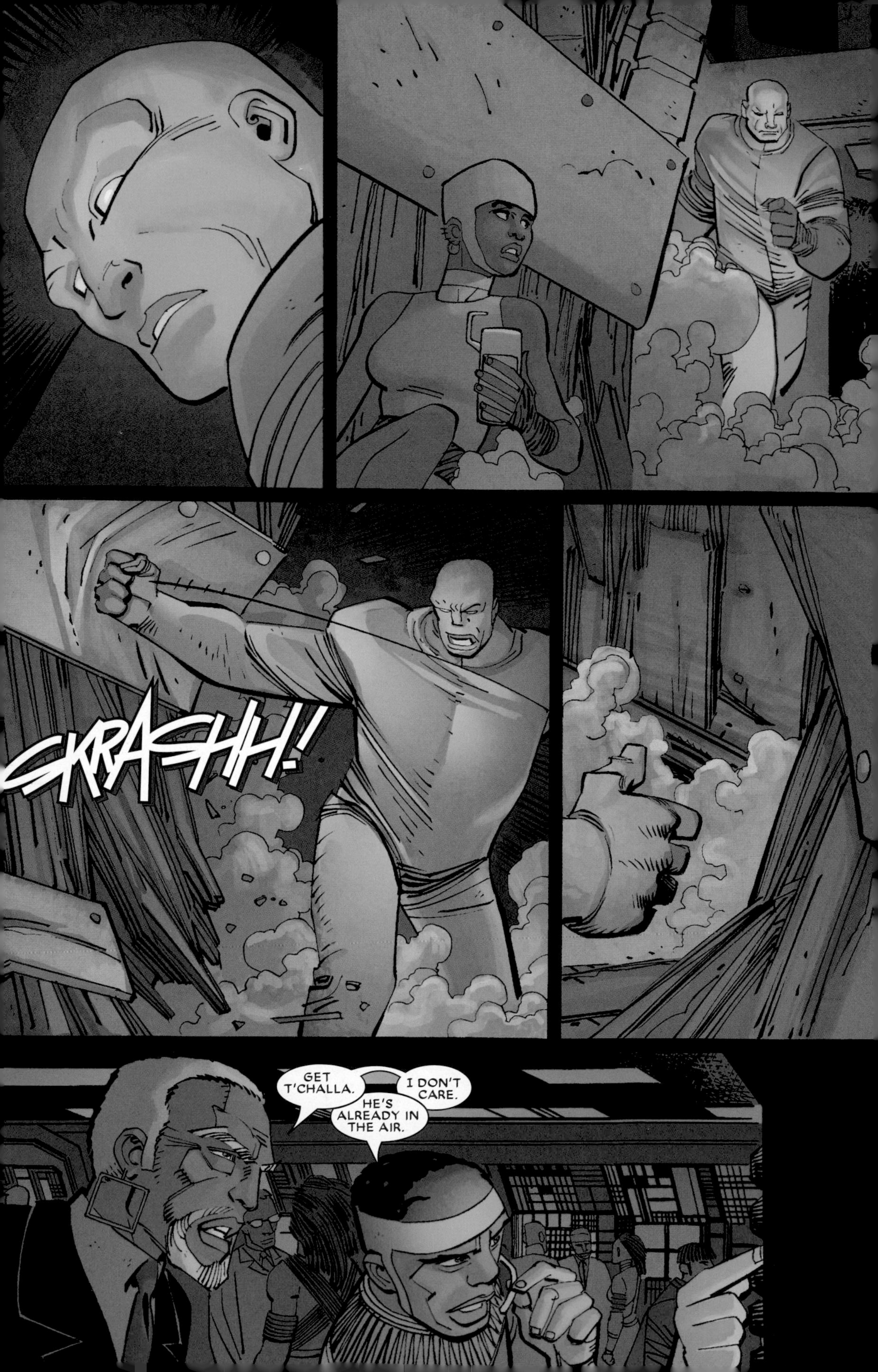
SKRASHH!
GET T'CHALLA.
HE'S ALREADY IN THE AIR.
I DON'T CARE.

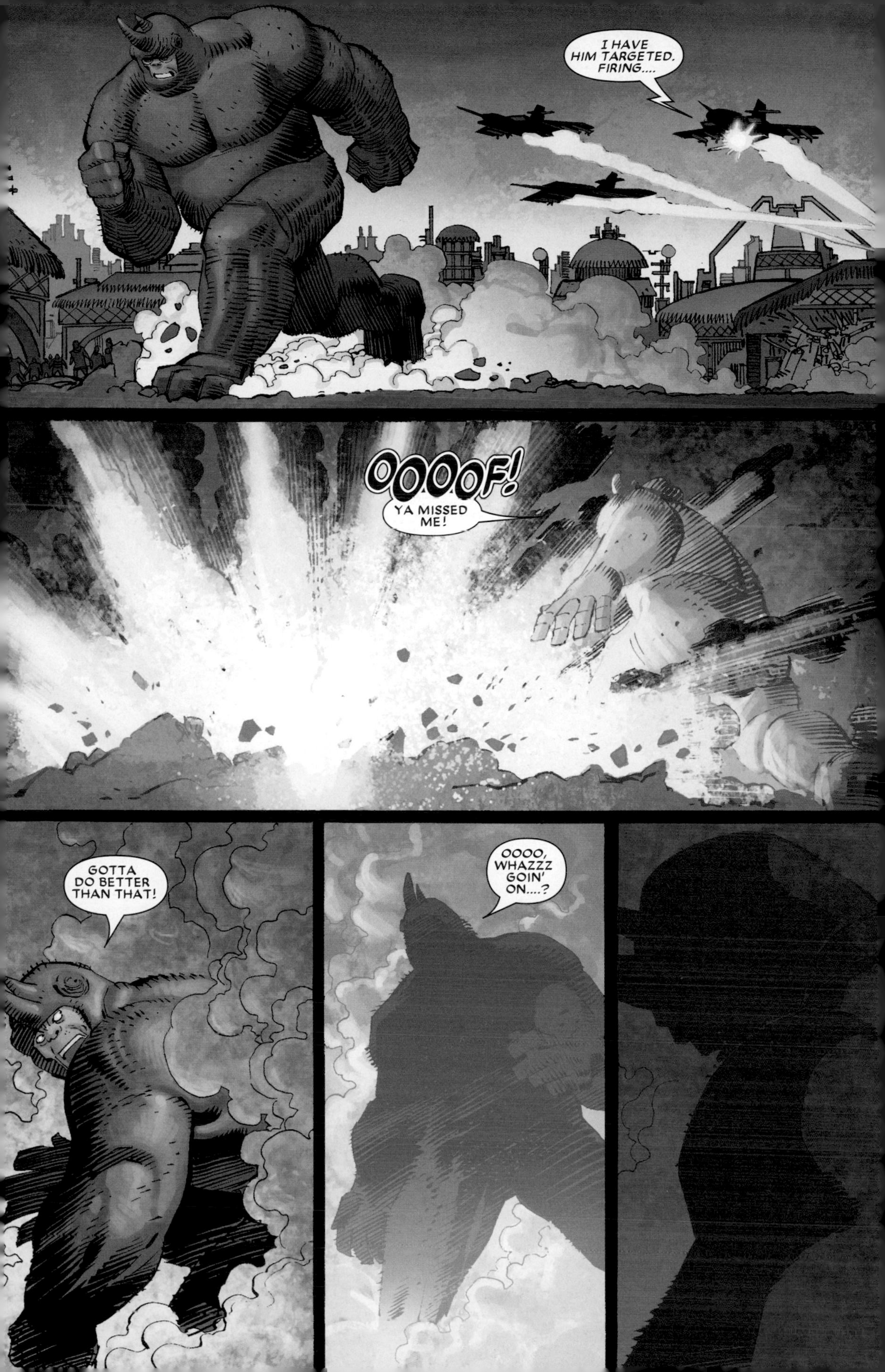
I HAVE HIM TARGETED. FIRING....
OOOOF!
YA MISSED ME!
GOTTA DO BETTER THAN THAT!
OOOO, WHAZZZ GOIN' ON....?

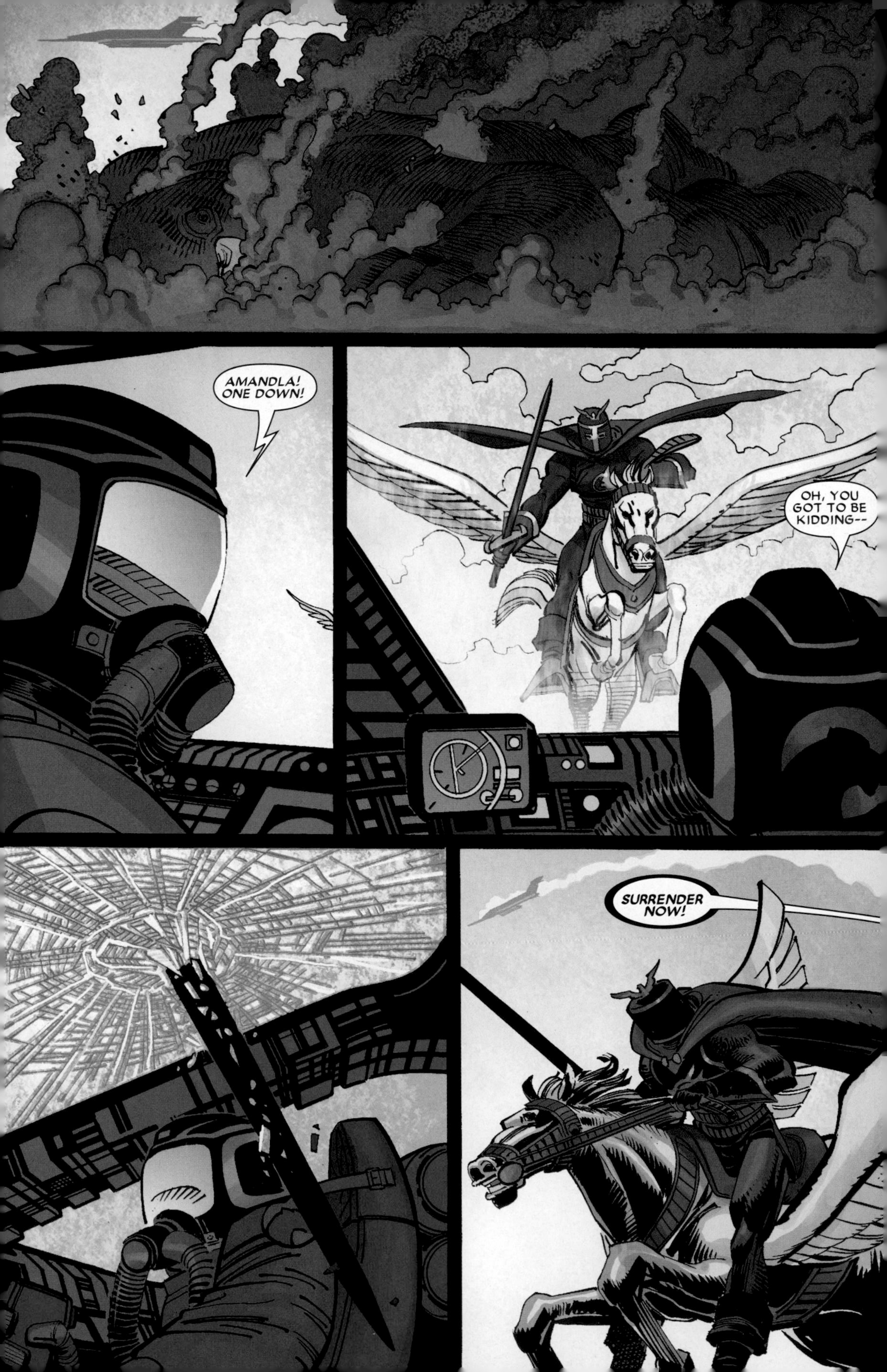
AMANDLA! ONE DOWN!
OH, YOU GOT TO BE KIDDING--
SURRENDER NOW!

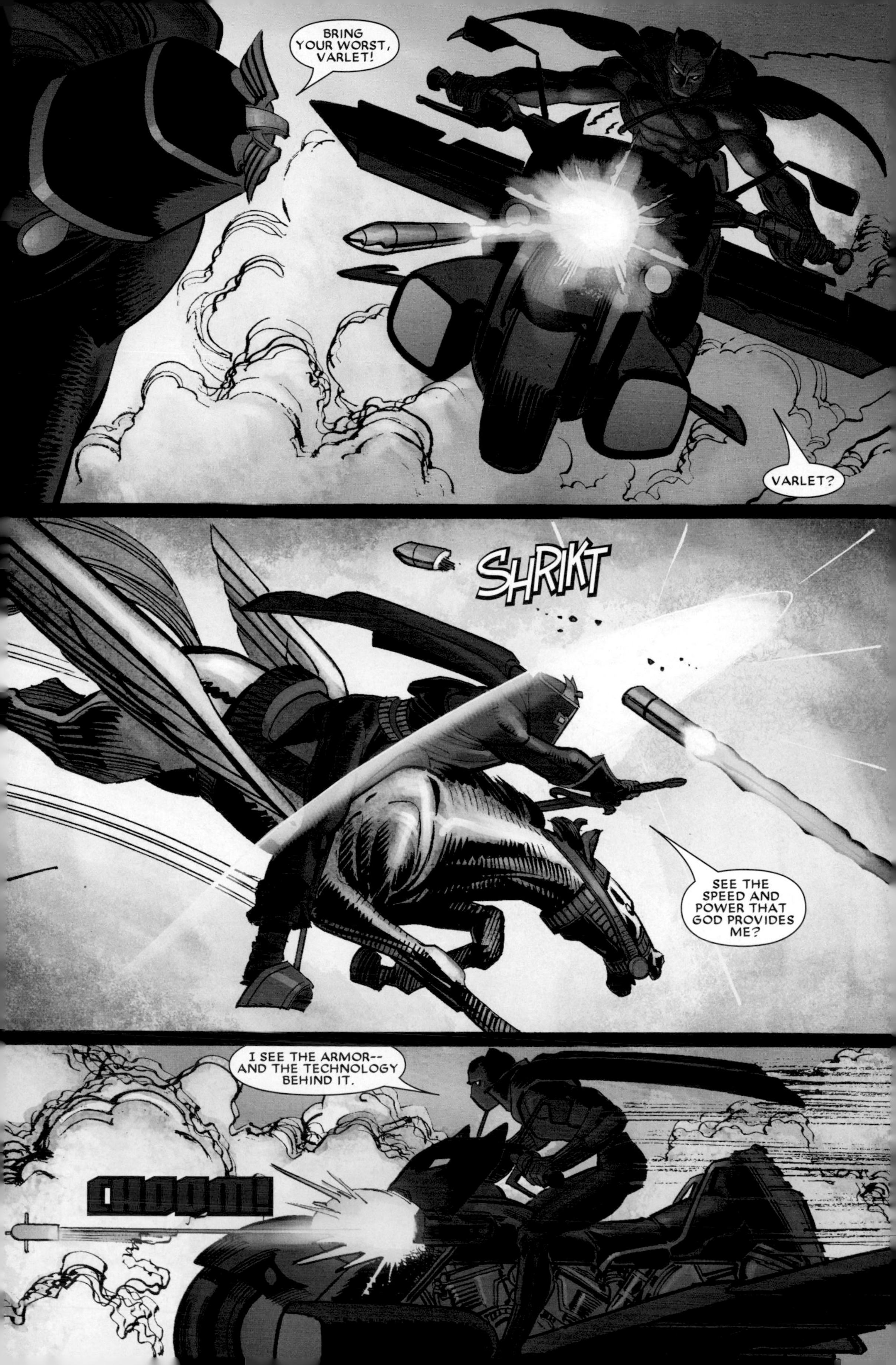
BRING YOUR WORST, VARLET!
VARLET?
SHRIKT
SEE THE SPEED AND POWER THAT GOD PROVIDES ME?
I SEE THE ARMOR-- AND THE TECHNOLOGY BEHIND IT.

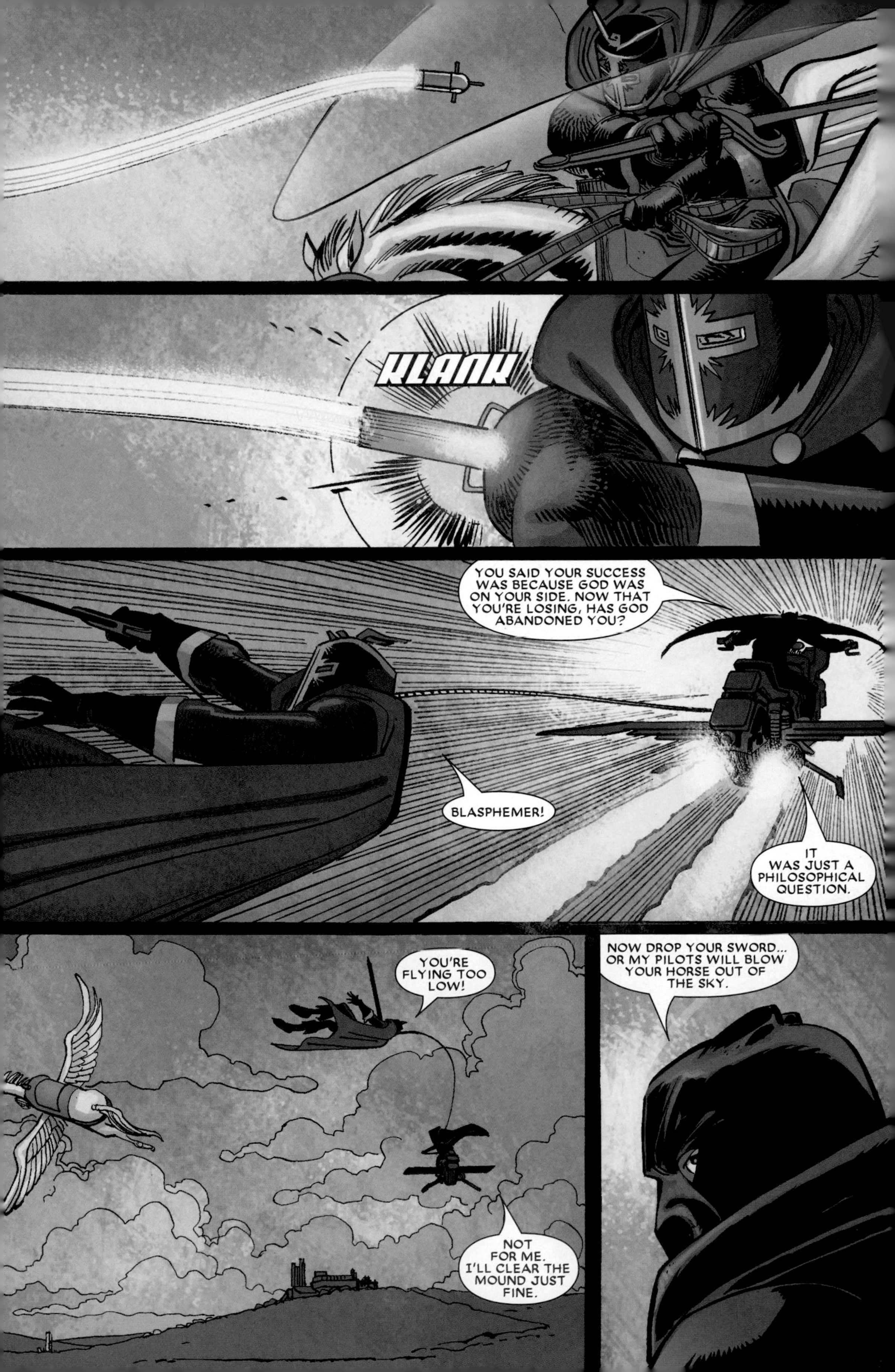
KLANK
YOU SAID YOUR SUCCESS WAS BECAUSE GOD WAS ON YOUR SIDE. NOW THAT YOU'RE LOSING, HAS GOD ABANDONED YOU?
BLASPHEMER!
IT WAS JUST A PHILOSOPHICAL QUESTION.
YOU'RE FLYING TOO LOW!
NOT FOR ME. I'LL CLEAR THE MOUND JUST FINE.
NOW DROP YOUR SWORD... OR MY PILOTS WILL BLOW YOUR HORSE OUT OF THE SKY.

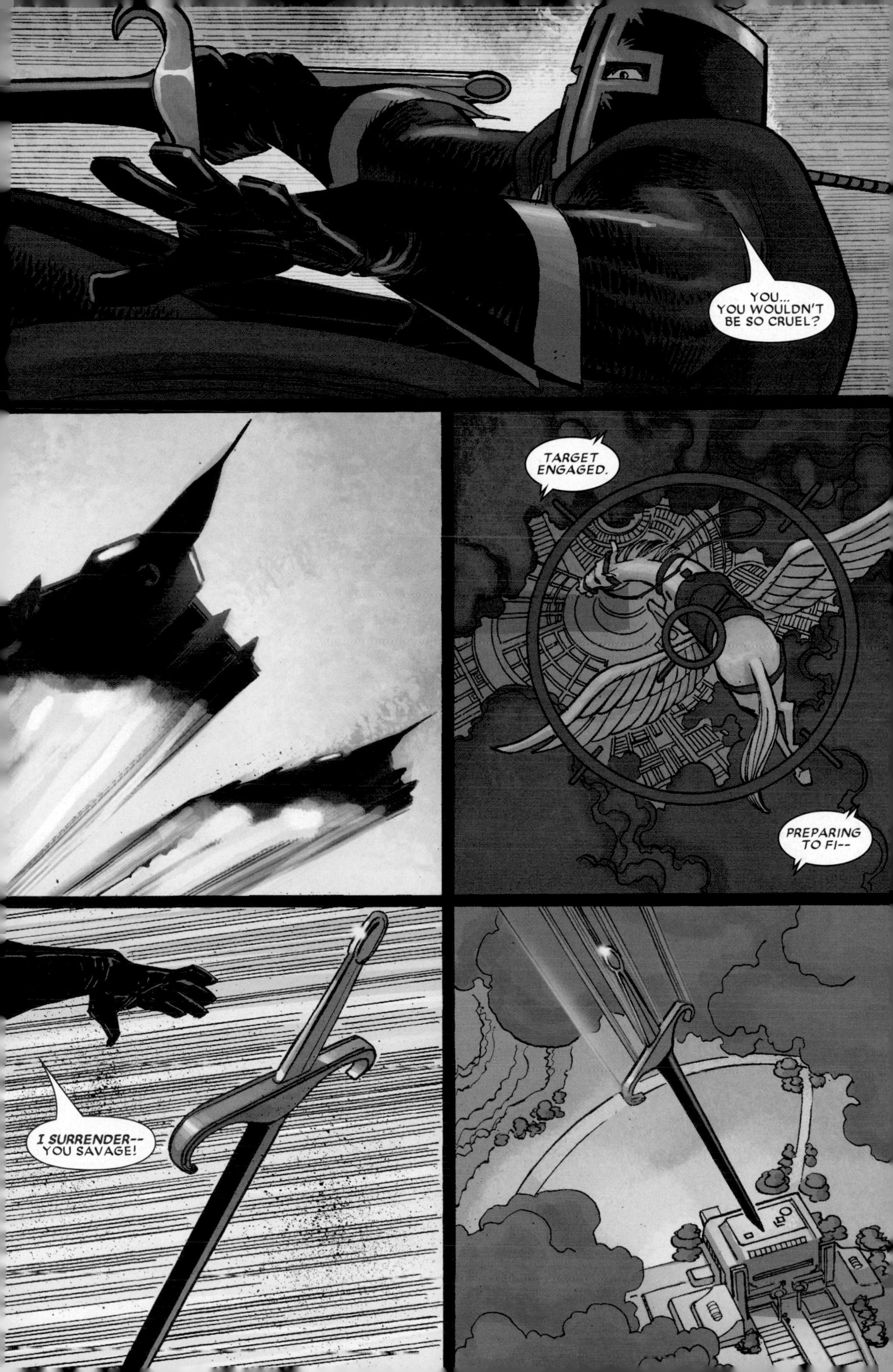
YOU... YOU WOULDN'T BE SO CRUEL?
TARGET ENGAGED.
PREPARING TO FI--
I SURRENDER-- YOU SAVAGE!

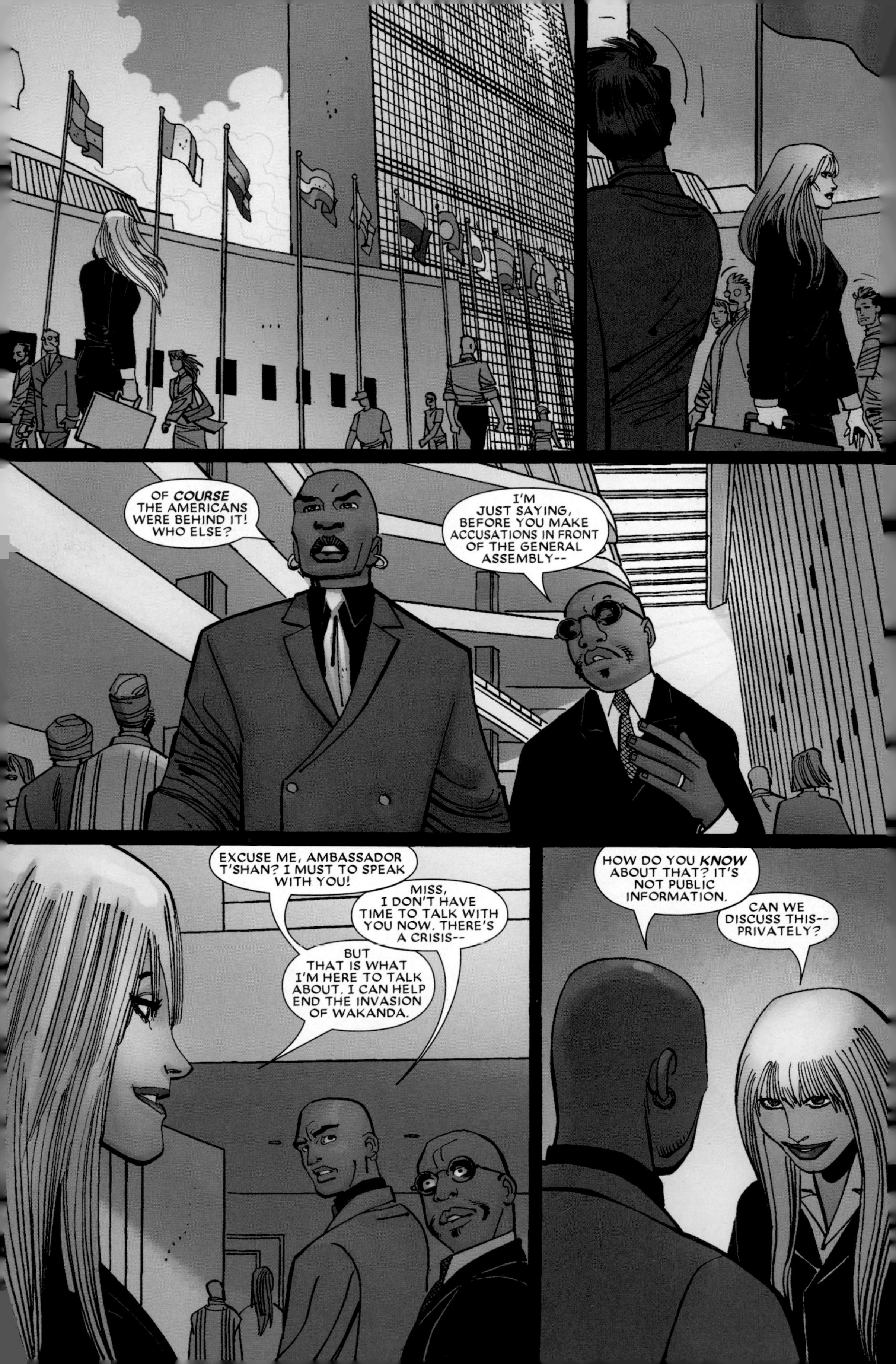

OF COURSE THE AMERICANS WERE BEHIND IT! WHO ELSE?
I'M JUST SAYING, BEFORE YOU MAKE ACCUSATIONS IN FRONT OF THE GENERAL ASSEMBLY--
EXCUSE ME, AMBASSADOR T'SHAN? I MUST TO SPEAK WITH YOU!
MISS, I DON'T HAVE TIME TO TALK WITH YOU NOW. THERE'S A CRISIS--
BUT THAT IS WHAT I'M HERE TO TALK ABOUT. I CAN HELP END THE INVASION OF WAKANDA.
HOW DO YOU KNOW ABOUT THAT? IT'S NOT PUBLIC INFORMATION.
CAN WE DISCUSS THIS-- PRIVATELY?

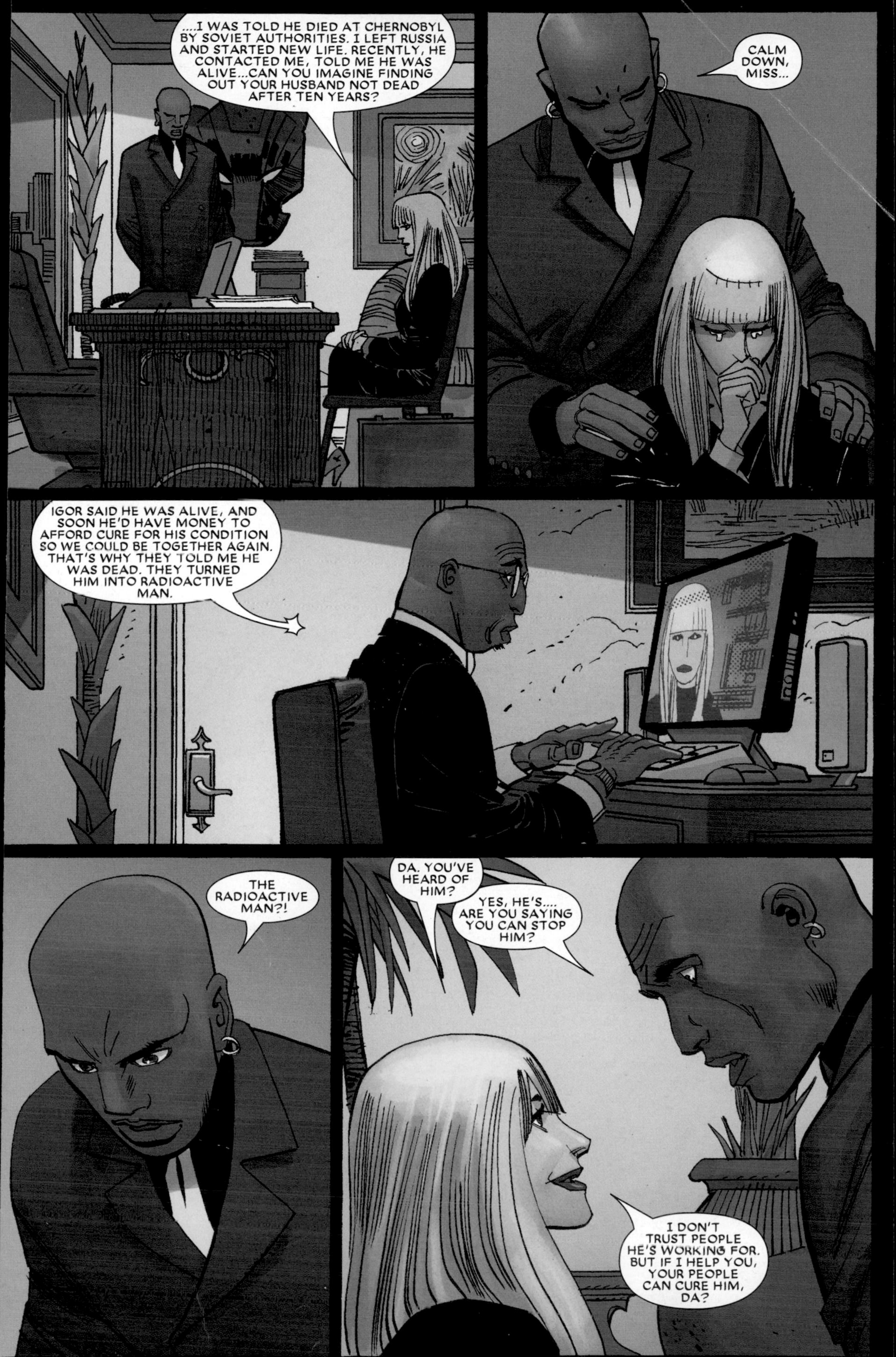
....I WAS TOLD HE DIED AT CHERNOBYL BY SOVIET AUTHORITIES. I LEFT RUSSIA AND STARTED NEW LIFE. RECENTLY, HE CONTACTED ME, TOLD ME HE WAS ALIVE...CAN YOU IMAGINE FINDING OUT YOUR HUSBAND NOT DEAD AFTER TEN YEARS?
CALM DOWN, MISS...
IGOR SAID HE WAS ALIVE, AND SOON HE'D HAVE MONEY TO AFFORD CURE FOR HIS CONDITION SO WE COULD BE TOGETHER AGAIN. THAT'S WHY THEY TOLD ME HE WAS DEAD. THEY TURNED HIM INTO RADIOACTIVE MAN.
THE RADIOACTIVE MAN?!
DA. YOU'VE HEARD OF HIM?
YES, HE'S.... ARE YOU SAYING YOU CAN STOP HIM?
I DON'T TRUST PEOPLE HE'S WORKING FOR. BUT IF I HELP YOU, YOUR PEOPLE CAN CURE HIM, DA?

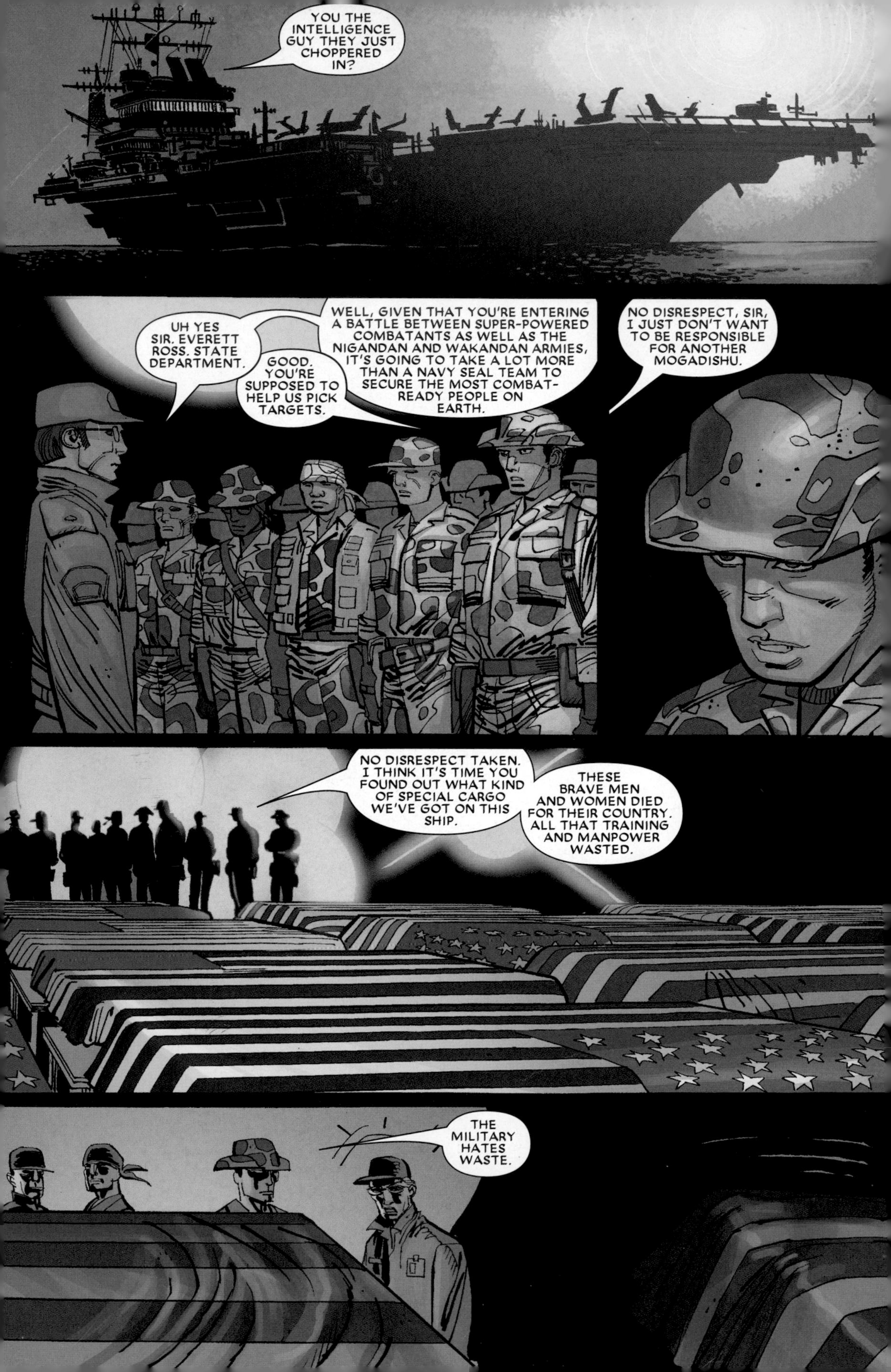
YOU THE INTELLIGENCE GUY THEY JUST CHOPPERED IN?
UH YES SIR. EVERETT ROSS. STATE DEPARTMENT.
GOOD. YOU'RE SUPPOSED TO HELP US PICK TARGETS.
WELL, GIVEN THAT YOU'RE ENTERING A BATTLE BETWEEN SUPER-POWERED COMBATANTS AS WELL AS THE NIGANDAN AND WAKANDAN ARMIES, IT'S GOING TO TAKE A LOT MORE THAN A NAVY SEAL TEAM TO SECURE THE MOST COMBAT-READY PEOPLE ON EARTH.
NO DISRESPECT, SIR, I JUST DON'T WANT TO BE RESPONSIBLE FOR ANOTHER MOGADISHU.
NO DISRESPECT TAKEN. I THINK IT'S TIME YOU FOUND OUT WHAT KIND OF SPECIAL CARGO WE'VE GOT ON THIS SHIP.
THESE BRAVE MEN AND WOMEN DIED FOR THEIR COUNTRY. ALL THAT TRAINING AND MANPOWER WASTED.
THE MILITARY HATES WASTE.

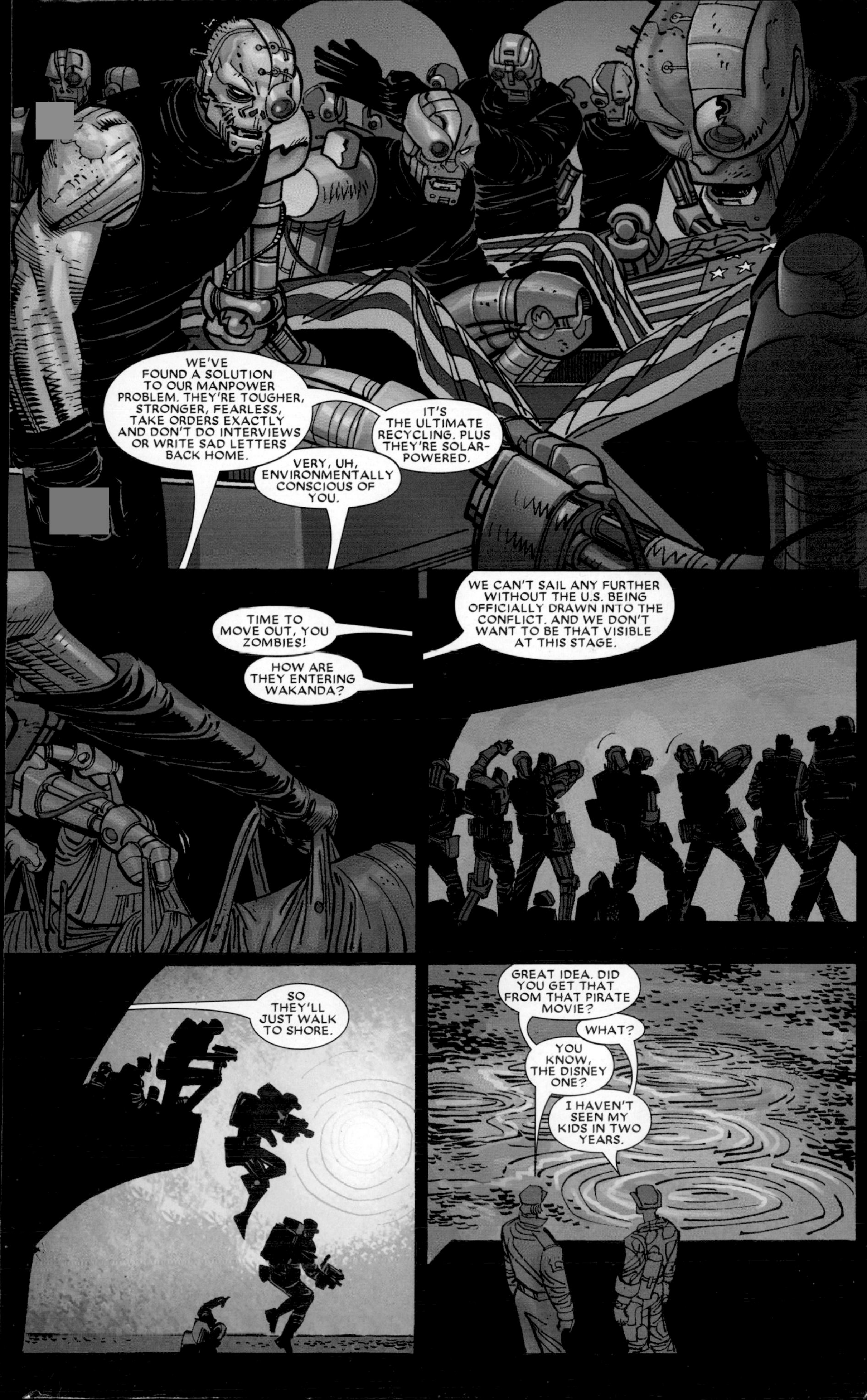

WE'VE FOUND A SOLUTION TO OUR MANPOWER PROBLEM. THEY'RE TOUGHER, STRONGER, FEARLESS, TAKE ORDERS EXACTLY AND DON'T DO INTERVIEWS OR WRITE SAD LETTERS BACK HOME.
IT'S THE ULTIMATE RECYCLING. PLUS THEY'RE SOLAR-POWERED.
VERY, UH, ENVIRONMENTALLY CONSCIOUS OF YOU.
TIME TO MOVE OUT, YOU ZOMBIES!
HOW ARE THEY ENTERING WAKANDA?
WE CAN'T SAIL ANY FURTHER WITHOUT THE U.S. BEING OFFICIALLY DRAWN INTO THE CONFLICT. AND WE DON'T WANT TO BE THAT VISIBLE AT THIS STAGE.
SO THEY'LL JUST WALK TO SHORE.
GREAT IDEA. DID YOU GET THAT FROM THAT PIRATE MOVIE?
WHAT?
YOU KNOW, THE DISNEY ONE?
I HAVEN'T SEEN MY KIDS IN TWO YEARS.

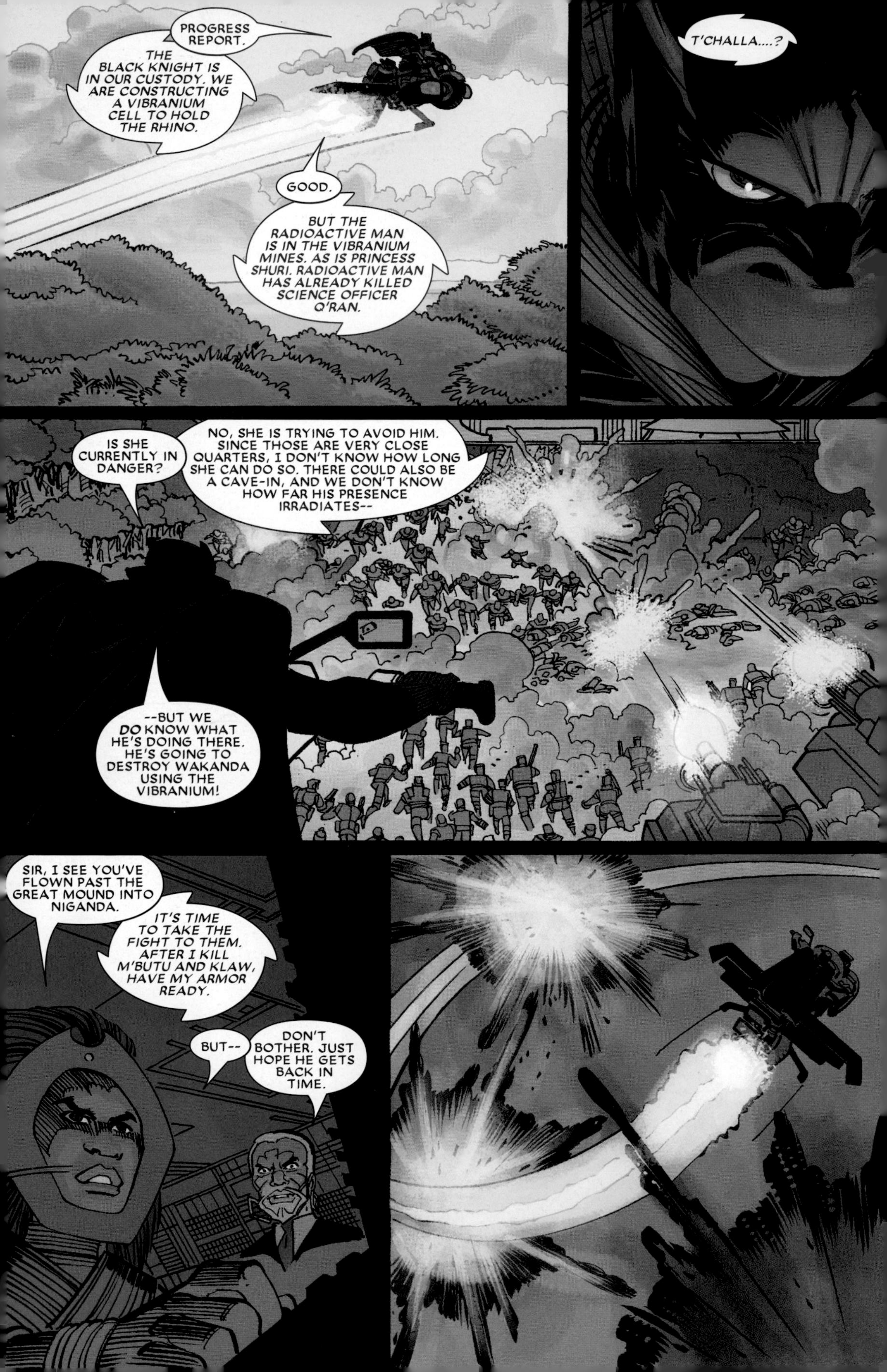

PROGRESS REPORT.
THE BLACK KNIGHT IS IN OUR CUSTODY. WE ARE CONSTRUCTING A VIBRANIUM CELL TO HOLD THE RHINO.
GOOD.
BUT THE RADIOACTIVE MAN IS IN THE VIBRANIUM MINES. AS IS PRINCESS SHURI. RADIOACTIVE MAN HAS ALREADY KILLED SCIENCE OFFICER Q'RAN.
T'CHALLA....?
IS SHE CURRENTLY IN DANGER?
NO, SHE IS TRYING TO AVOID HIM. SINCE THOSE ARE VERY CLOSE QUARTERS, I DON'T KNOW HOW LONG SHE CAN DO SO. THERE COULD ALSO BE A CAVE-IN, AND WE DON'T KNOW HOW FAR HIS PRESENCE IRRADIATES--
--BUT WE DO KNOW WHAT HE'S DOING THERE. HE'S GOING TO DESTROY WAKANDA USING THE VIBRANIUM!
SIR, I SEE YOU'VE FLOWN PAST THE GREAT MOUND INTO NIGANDA.
IT'S TIME TO TAKE THE FIGHT TO THEM. AFTER I KILL M'BUTU AND KLAW, HAVE MY ARMOR READY.
BUT--
DON'T BOTHER. JUST HOPE HE GETS BACK IN TIME.

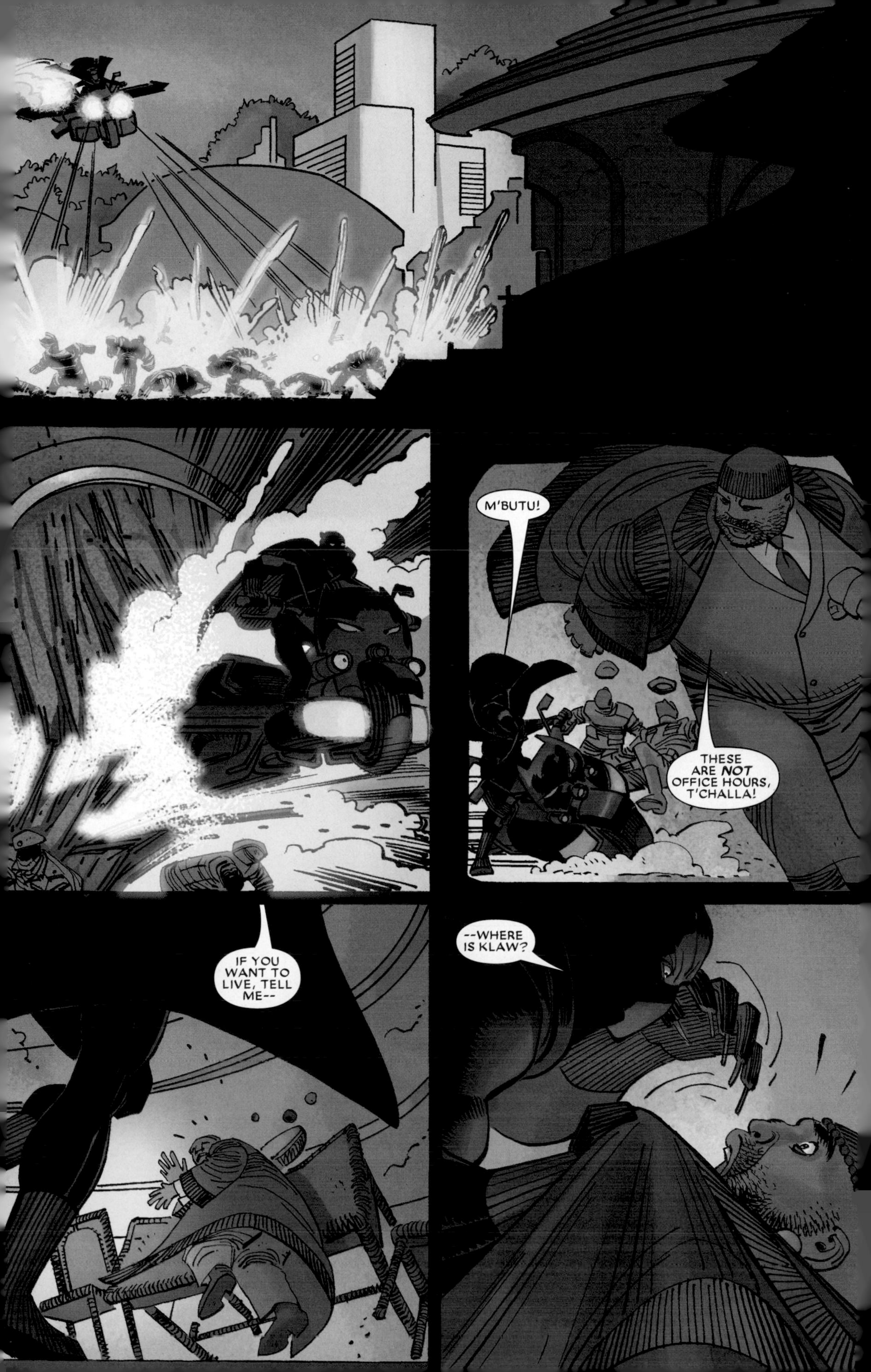
M'BUTU!
THESE ARE NOT OFFICE HOURS, T'CHALLA!
IF YOU WANT TO LIVE, TELL ME--
--WHERE IS KLAW?

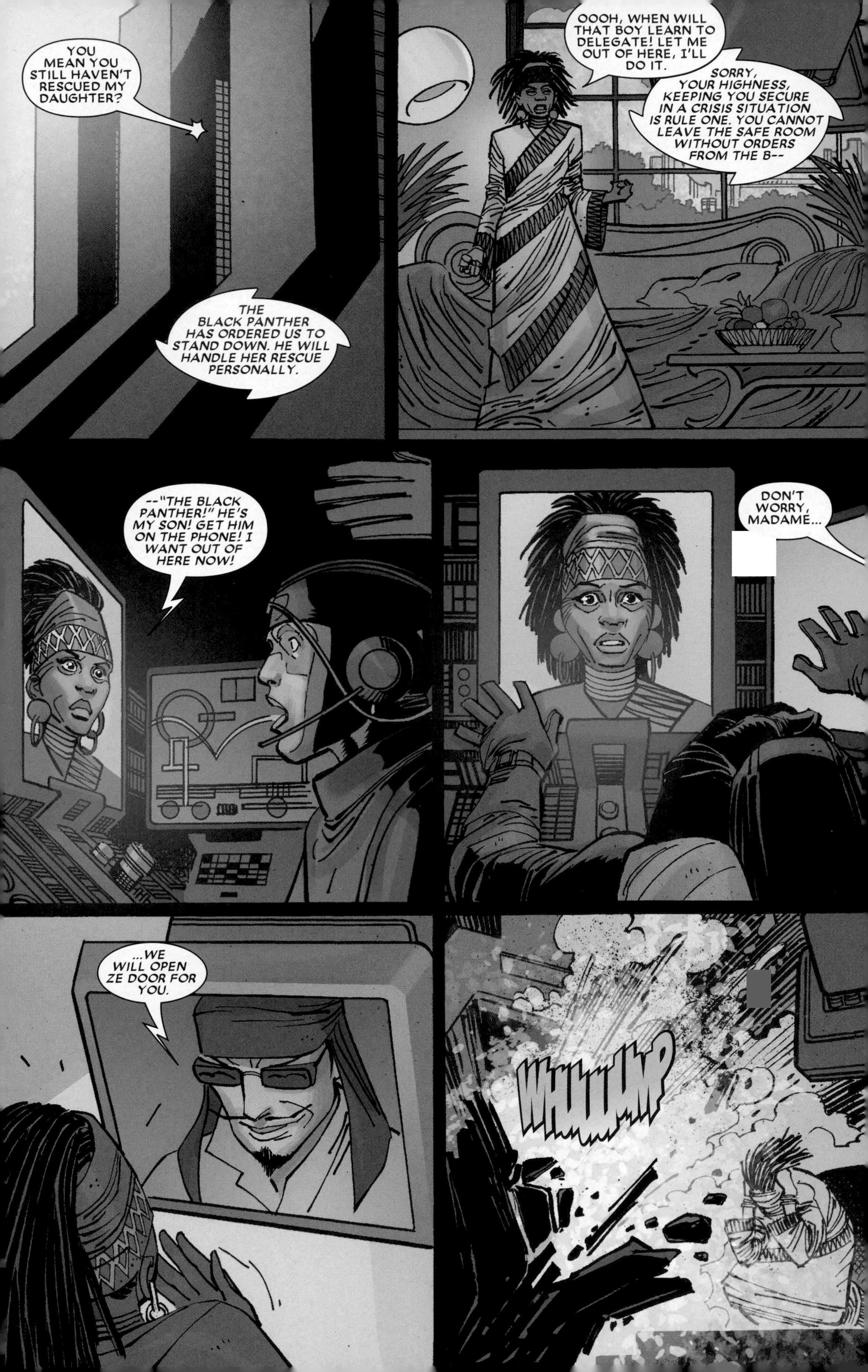
YOU MEAN YOU STILL HAVEN'T RESCUED MY DAUGHTER?
THE BLACK PANTHER HAS ORDERED US TO STAND DOWN. HE WILL HANDLE HER RESCUE PERSONALLY.
OOOH, WHEN WILL THAT BOY LEARN TO DELEGATE! LET ME OUT OF HERE, I'LL DO IT.
SORRY, YOUR HIGHNESS, KEEPING YOU SECURE IN A CRISIS SITUATION IS RULE ONE. YOU CANNOT LEAVE THE SAFE ROOM WITHOUT ORDERS FROM THE B--
--"THE BLACK PANTHER!" HE'S MY SON! GET HIM ON THE PHONE! I WANT OUT OF HERE NOW!
DON'T WORRY, MADAME...
...WE WILL OPEN ZE DOOR FOR YOU.
WHUUMP

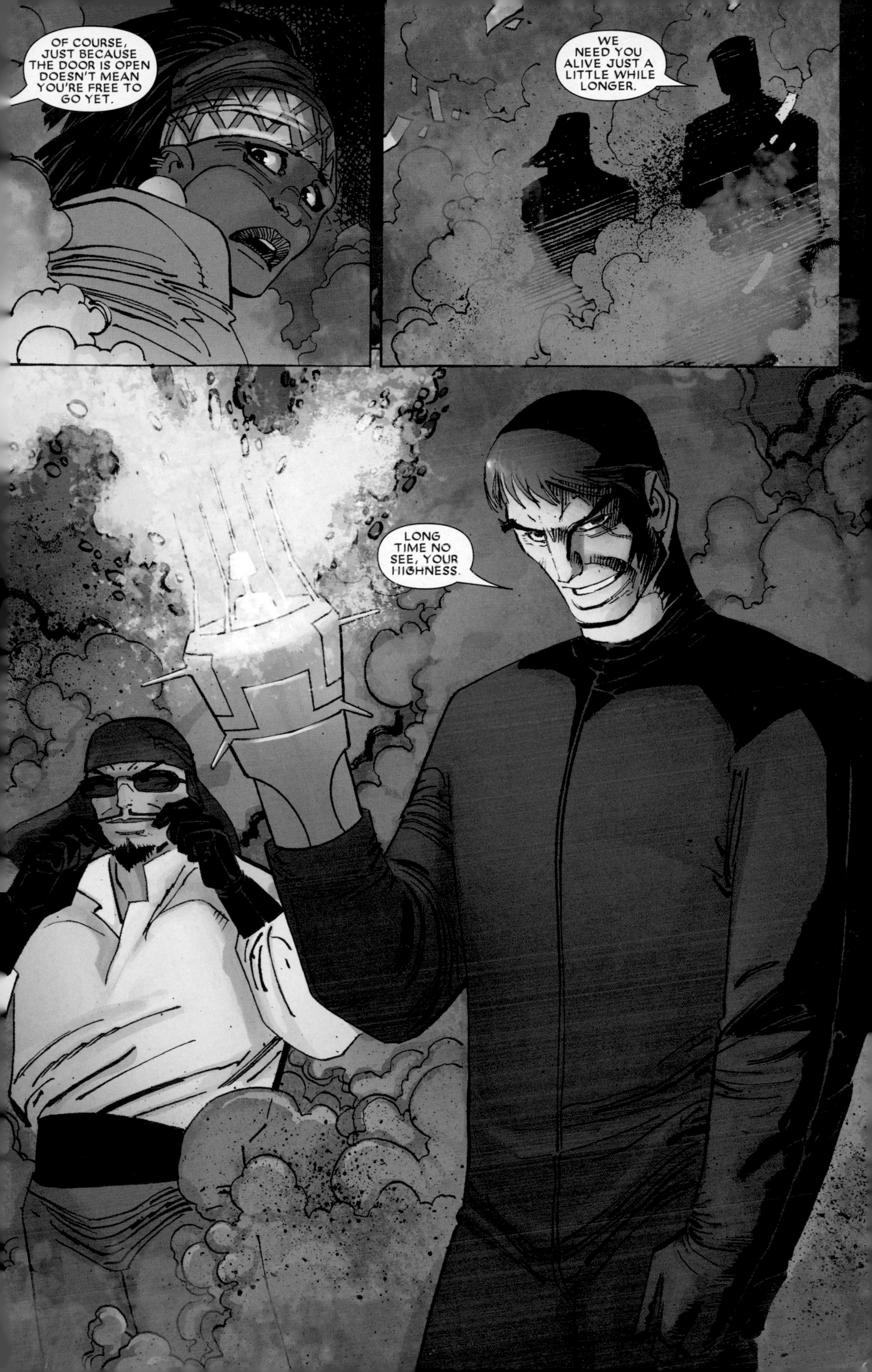
OF COURSE, JUST BECAUSE THE DOOR IS OPEN DOESN'T MEAN YOU'RE FREE TO GO YET.
WE NEED YOU ALIVE JUST A LITTLE WHILE LONGER.
LONG TIME NO SEE, YOUR HIGHNESS.

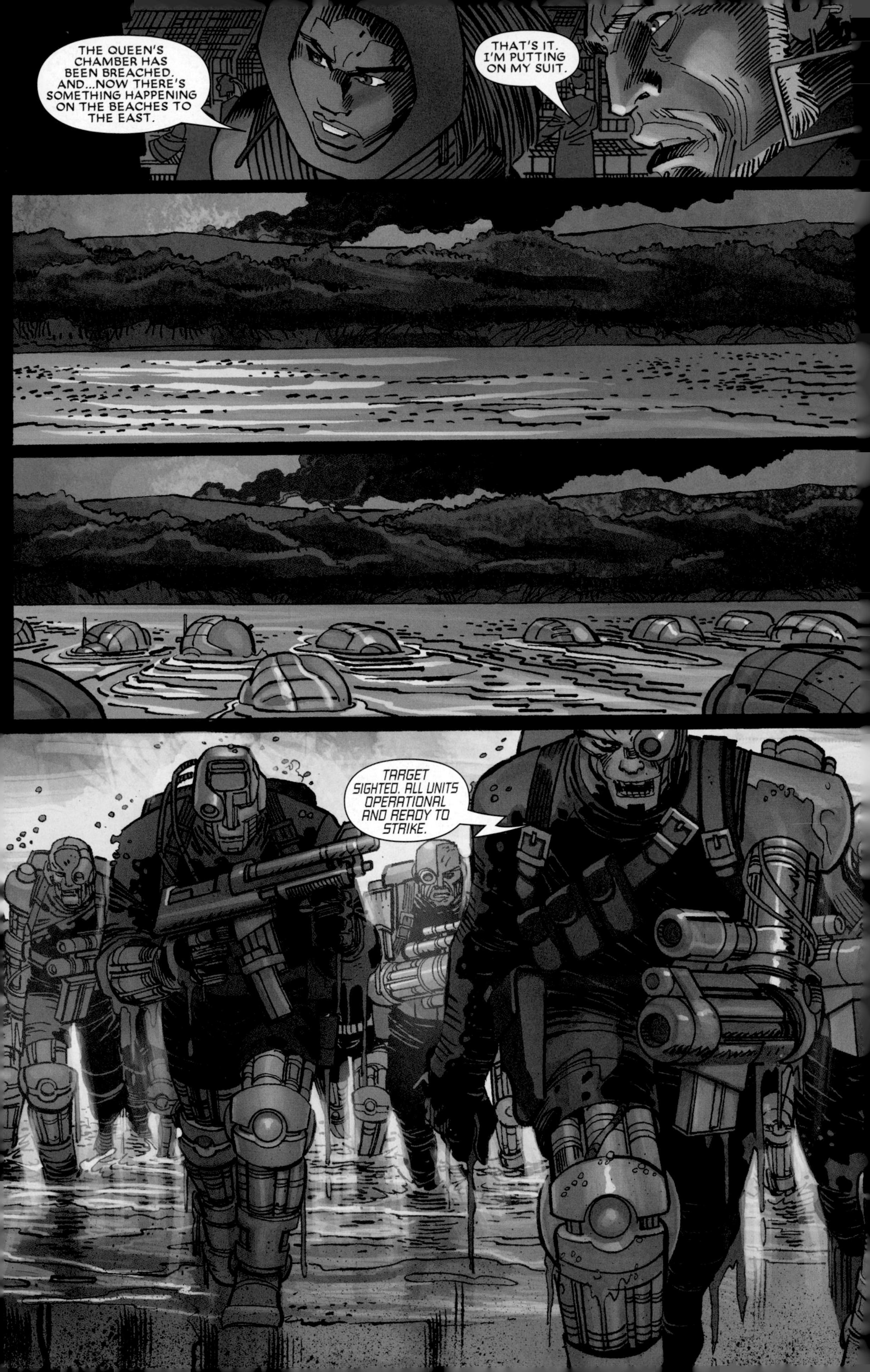
THE QUEEN'S CHAMBER HAS BEEN BREACHED. AND...NOW THERE'S SOMETHING HAPPENING ON THE BEACHES TO THE EAST.
THAT'S IT. I'M PUTTING ON MY SUIT.
TARGET SIGHTED. ALL UNITS OPERATIONAL AND READY TO STRIKE.

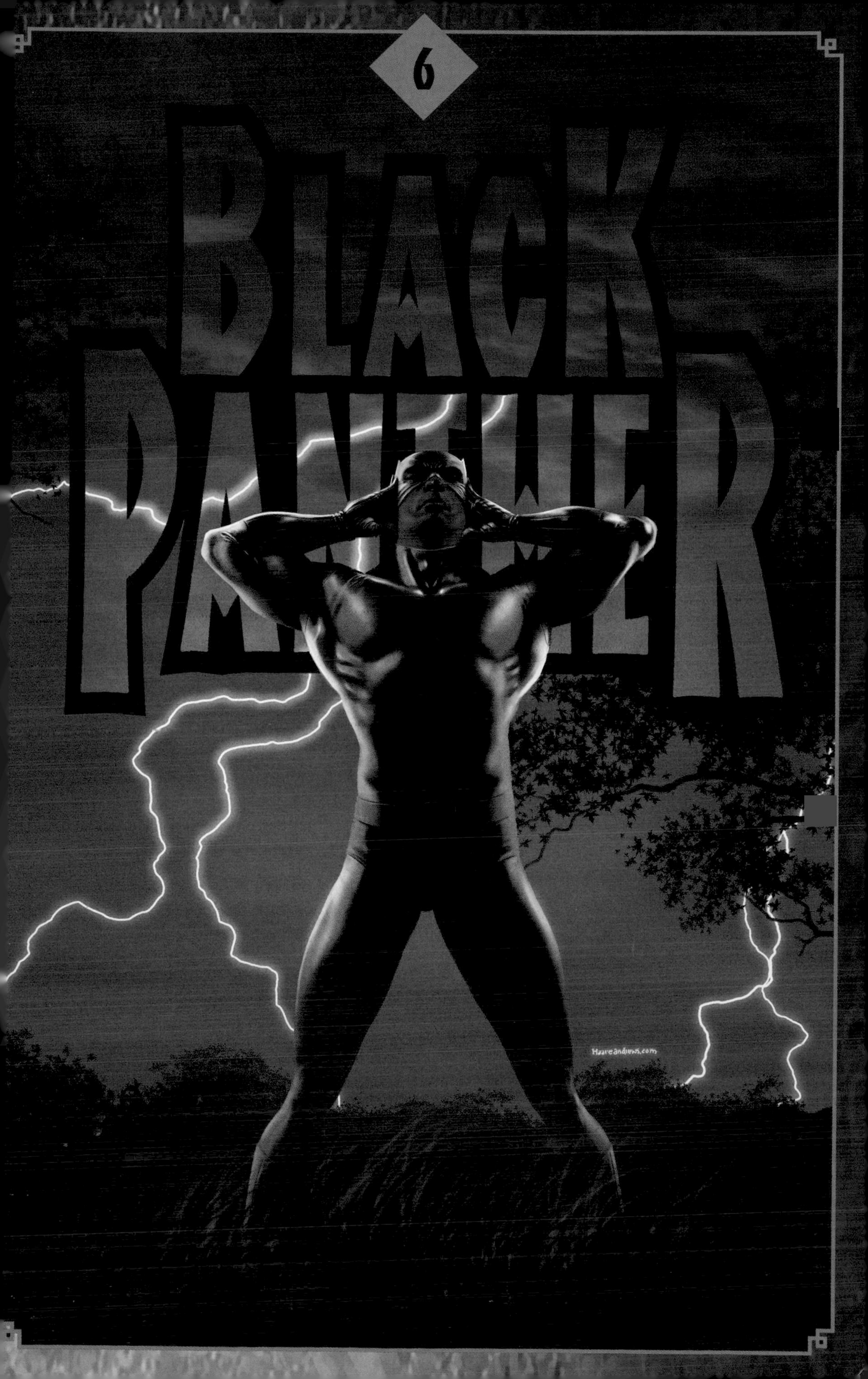
6
BLACK PANTHER
Mikeandrews.com

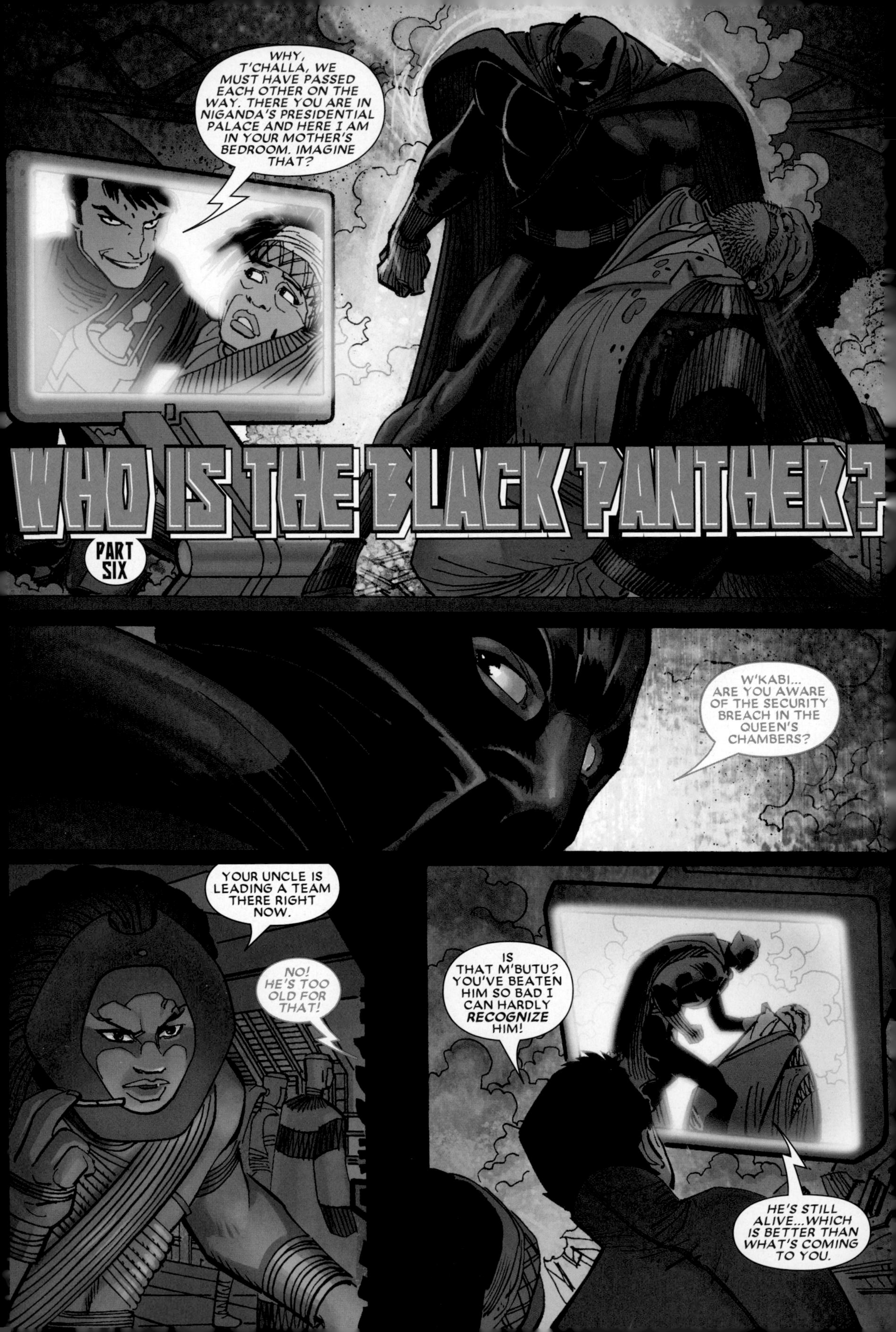
WHY, T'CHALLA, WE MUST HAVE PASSED EACH OTHER ON THE WAY. THERE YOU ARE IN NIGANDA'S PRESIDENTIAL PALACE AND HERE I AM IN YOUR MOTHER'S BEDROOM. IMAGINE THAT?
WHO IS THE BLACK PANTHER?
PART SIX
W'KABI... ARE YOU AWARE OF THE SECURITY BREACH IN THE QUEEN'S CHAMBERS?
YOUR UNCLE IS LEADING A TEAM THERE RIGHT NOW.
NO! HE'S TOO OLD FOR THAT!
IS THAT M'BUTU? YOU'VE BEATEN HIM SO BAD I CAN HARDLY RECOGNIZE HIM!
HE'S STILL ALIVE...WHICH IS BETTER THAN WHAT'S COMING TO YOU.

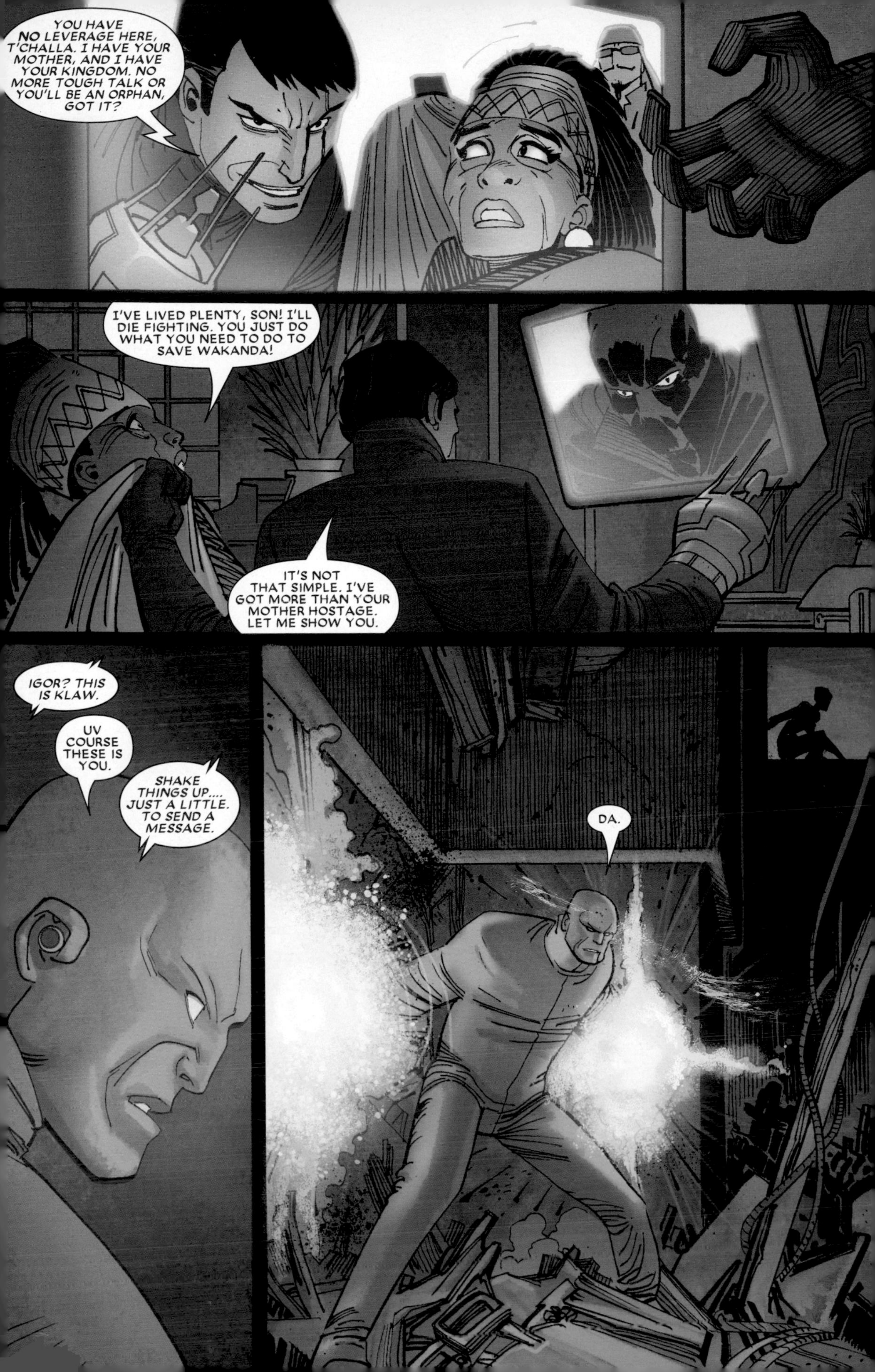
YOU HAVE NO LEVERAGE HERE, T'CHALLA. I HAVE YOUR MOTHER, AND I HAVE YOUR KINGDOM. NO MORE TOUGH TALK OR YOU'LL BE AN ORPHAN, GOT IT?
I'VE LIVED PLENTY, SON! I'LL DIE FIGHTING. YOU JUST DO WHAT YOU NEED TO DO TO SAVE WAKANDA!
IT'S NOT THAT SIMPLE. I'VE GOT MORE THAN YOUR MOTHER HOSTAGE. LET ME SHOW YOU.
IGOR? THIS IS KLAW.
UV COURSE THESE IS YOU.
SHAKE THINGS UP.... JUST A LITTLE. TO SEND A MESSAGE.
DA.

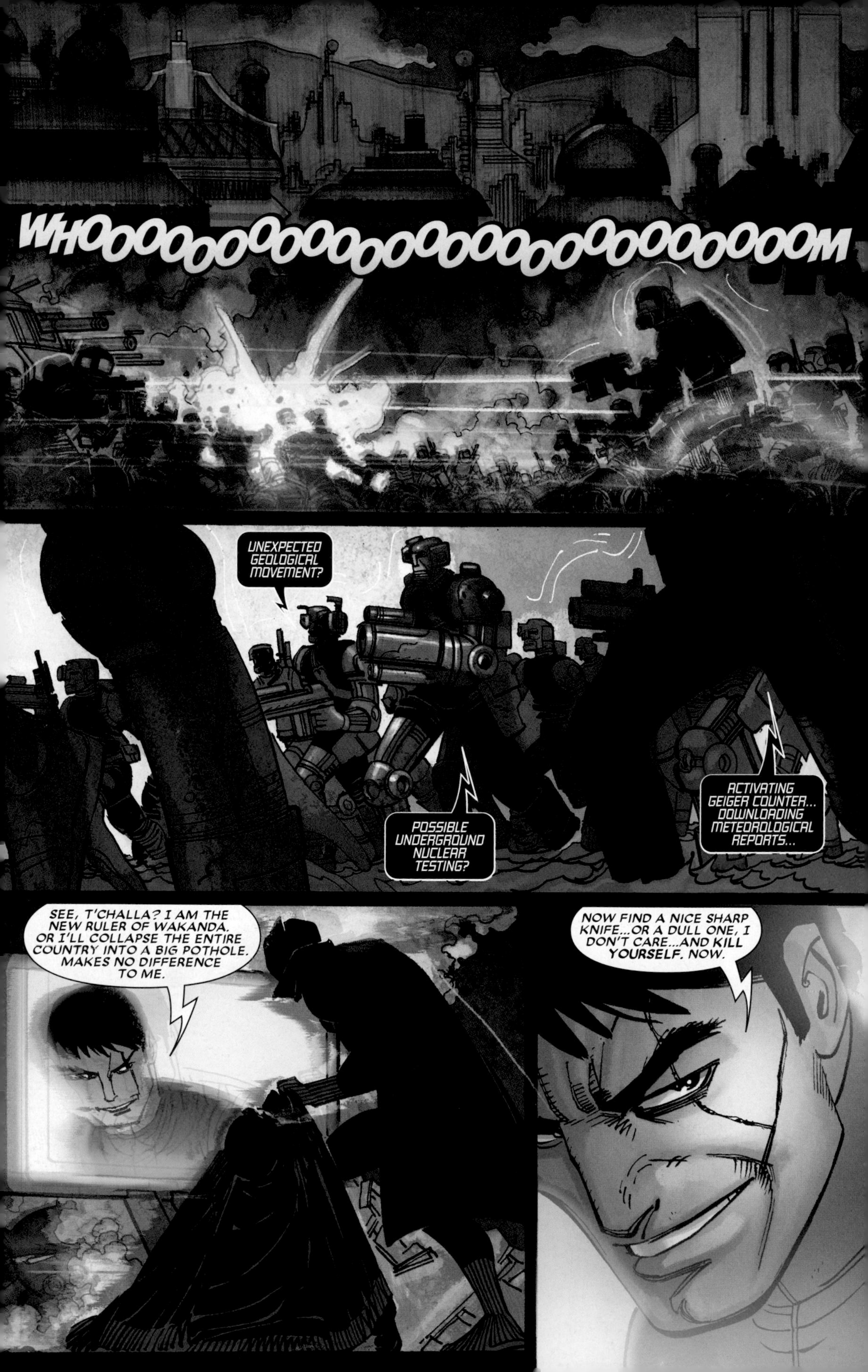
WHOOOOOOOOOOOOOOOOOOOOOOOOOOOM
UNEXPECTED GEOLOGICAL MOVEMENT?
POSSIBLE UNDERGROUND NUCLEAR TESTING?
ACTIVATING GEIGER COUNTER... DOWNLOADING METEOROLOGICAL REPORTS...
SEE, T'CHALLA? I AM THE NEW RULER OF WAKANDA. OR I'LL COLLAPSE THE ENTIRE COUNTRY INTO A BIG POTHOLE. MAKES NO DIFFERENCE TO ME.
NOW FIND A NICE SHARP KNIFE...OR A DULL ONE, I DON'T CARE...AND KILL YOURSELF. NOW.

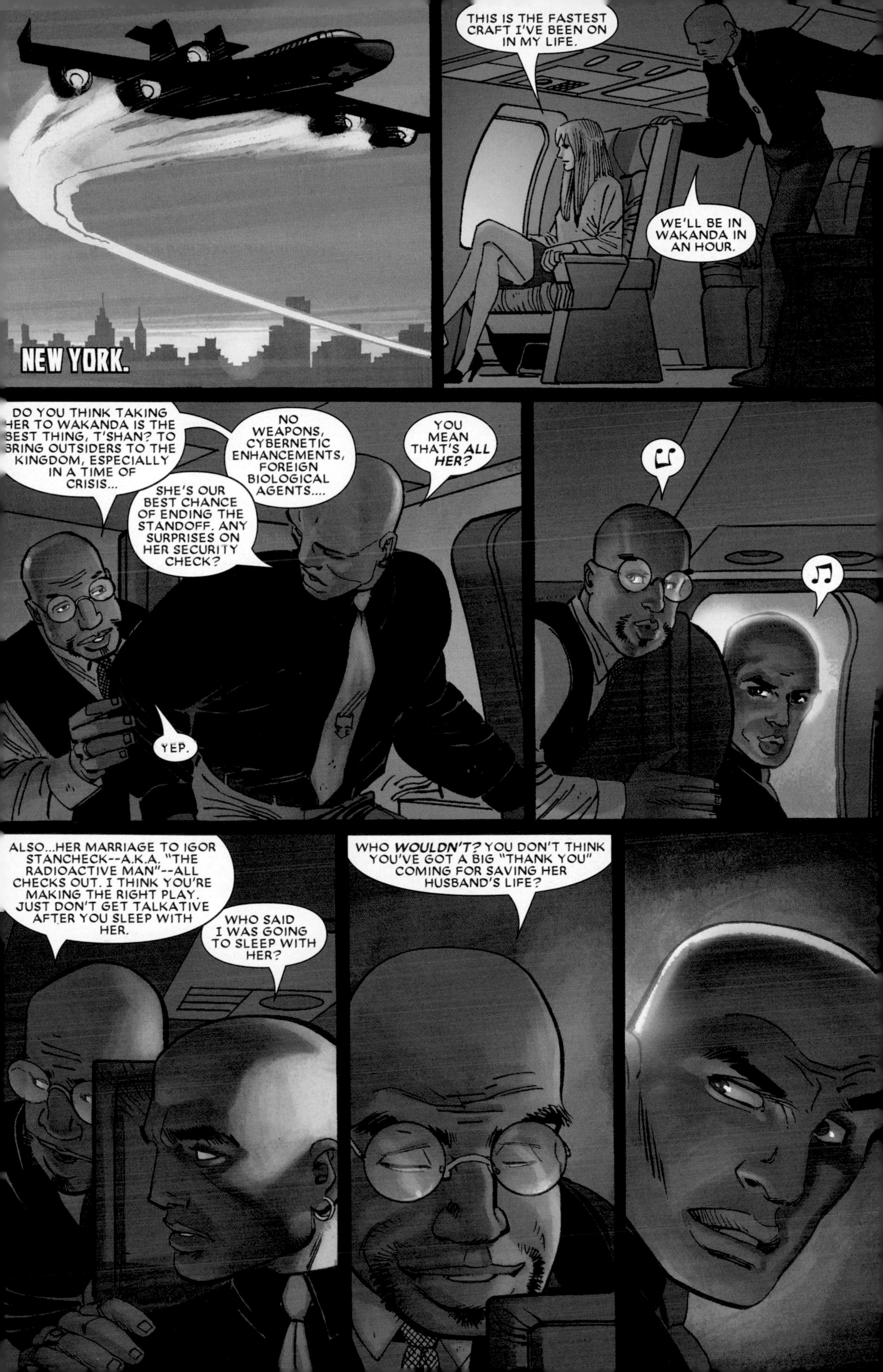
NEW YORK.
THIS IS THE FASTEST CRAFT I'VE BEEN ON IN MY LIFE.
WE'LL BE IN WAKANDA IN AN HOUR.
DO YOU THINK TAKING HER TO WAKANDA IS THE BEST THING, T'SHAN? TO BRING OUTSIDERS TO THE KINGDOM, ESPECIALLY IN A TIME OF CRISIS...
SHE'S OUR BEST CHANCE OF ENDING THE STANDOFF. ANY SURPRISES ON HER SECURITY CHECK?
YEP.
NO WEAPONS, CYBERNETIC ENHANCEMENTS, FOREIGN BIOLOGICAL AGENTS....
YOU MEAN THAT'S ALL HER?
♫
ALSO...HER MARRIAGE TO IGOR STANCHECK--A.K.A. "THE RADIOACTIVE MAN"--ALL CHECKS OUT. I THINK YOU'RE MAKING THE RIGHT PLAY. JUST DON'T GET TALKATIVE AFTER YOU SLEEP WITH HER.
WHO SAID I WAS GOING TO SLEEP WITH HER?
WHO WOULDN'T? YOU DON'T THINK YOU'VE GOT A BIG "THANK YOU" COMING FOR SAVING HER HUSBAND'S LIFE?

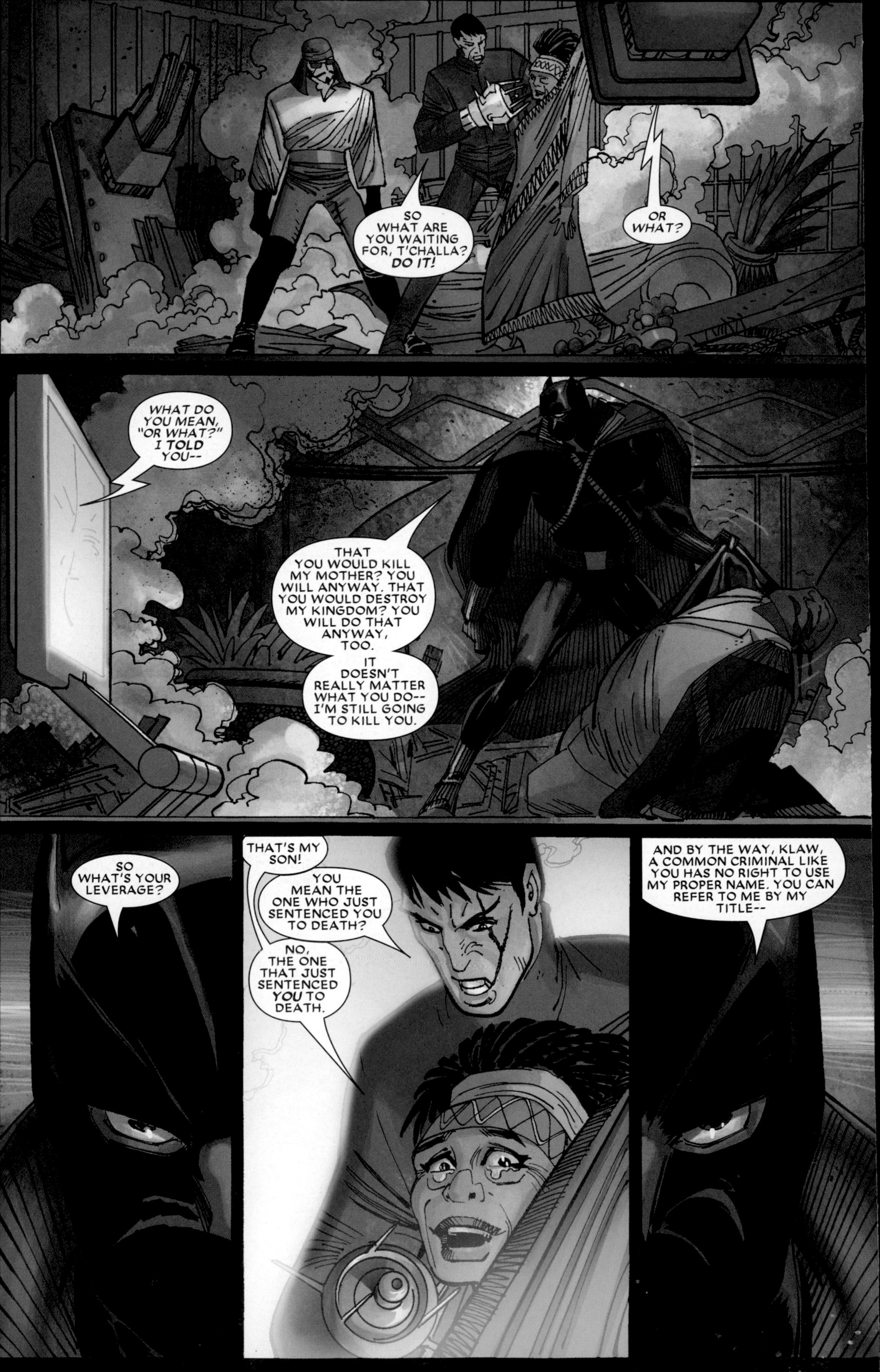
SO WHAT ARE YOU WAITING FOR, T'CHALLA? DO IT!
OR WHAT?
WHAT DO YOU MEAN, "OR WHAT?" I TOLD YOU--
THAT YOU WOULD KILL MY MOTHER? YOU WILL ANYWAY. THAT YOU WOULD DESTROY MY KINGDOM? YOU WILL DO THAT ANYWAY, TOO.
IT DOESN'T REALLY MATTER WHAT YOU DO-- I'M STILL GOING TO KILL YOU.
SO WHAT'S YOUR LEVERAGE?
THAT'S MY SON!
YOU MEAN THE ONE WHO JUST SENTENCED YOU TO DEATH?
NO, THE ONE THAT JUST SENTENCED YOU TO DEATH.
AND BY THE WAY, KLAW, A COMMON CRIMINAL LIKE YOU HAS NO RIGHT TO USE MY PROPER NAME. YOU CAN REFER TO ME BY MY TITLE--

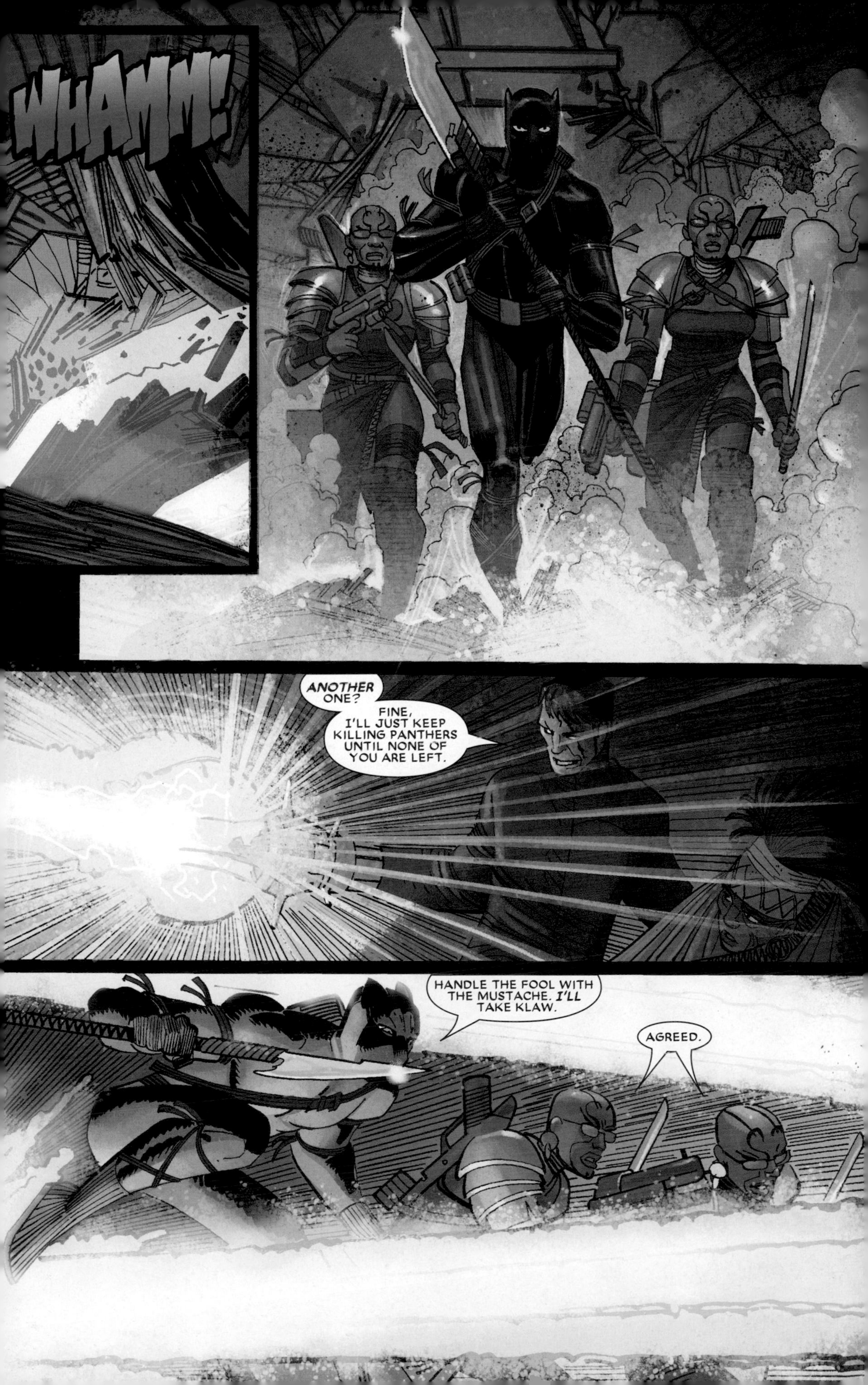
WHAMM!
ANOTHER ONE?
FINE, I'LL JUST KEEP KILLING PANTHERS UNTIL NONE OF YOU ARE LEFT.
HANDLE THE FOOL WITH THE MUSTACHE. I'LL TAKE KLAW.
AGREED.

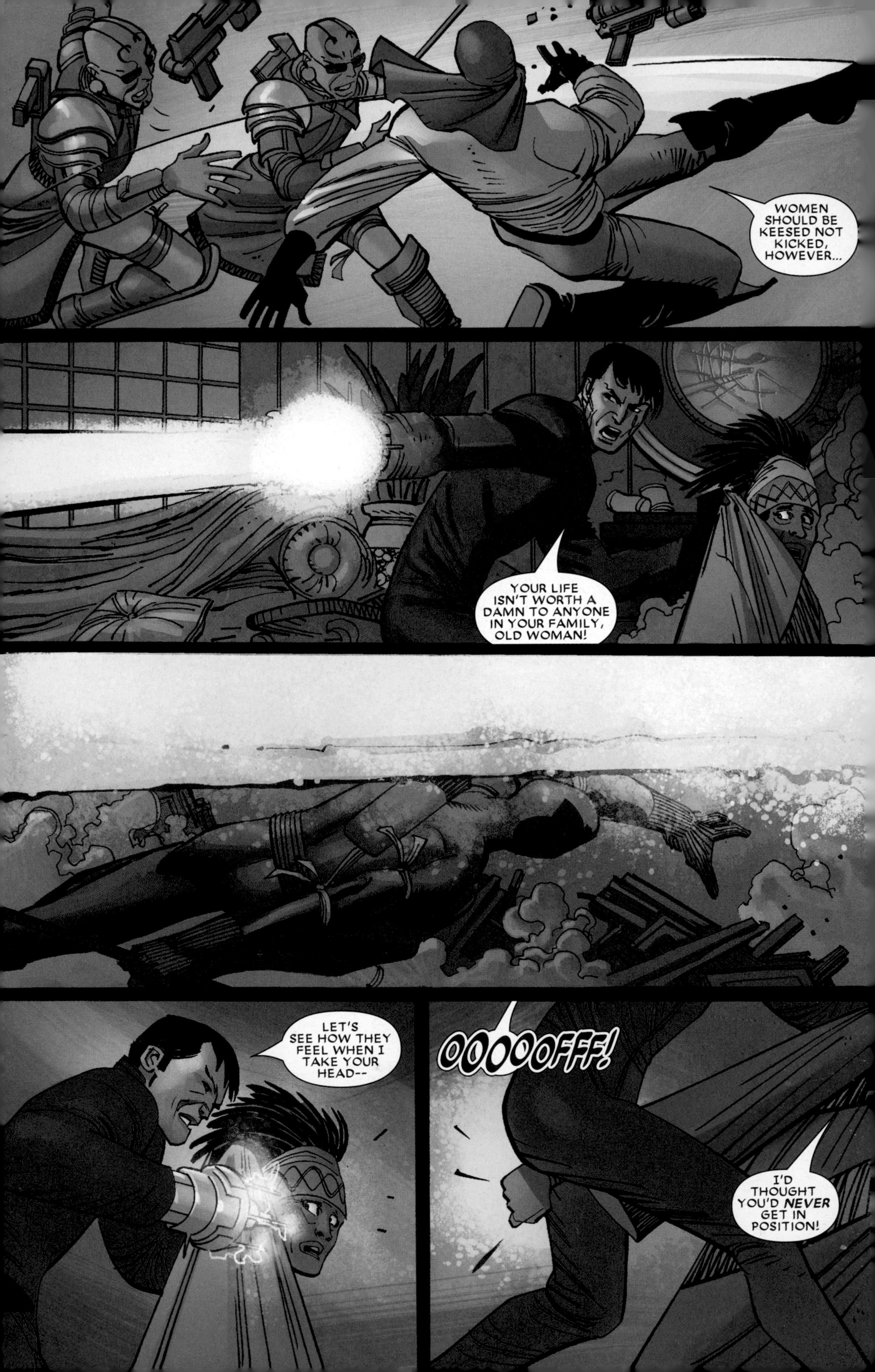
WOMEN SHOULD BE KEESED NOT KICKED, HOWEVER...
YOUR LIFE ISN'T WORTH A DAMN TO ANYONE IN YOUR FAMILY, OLD WOMAN!
LET'S SEE HOW THEY FEEL WHEN I TAKE YOUR HEAD--
OOOOOFFF!
I'D THOUGHT YOU'D NEVER GET IN POSITION!

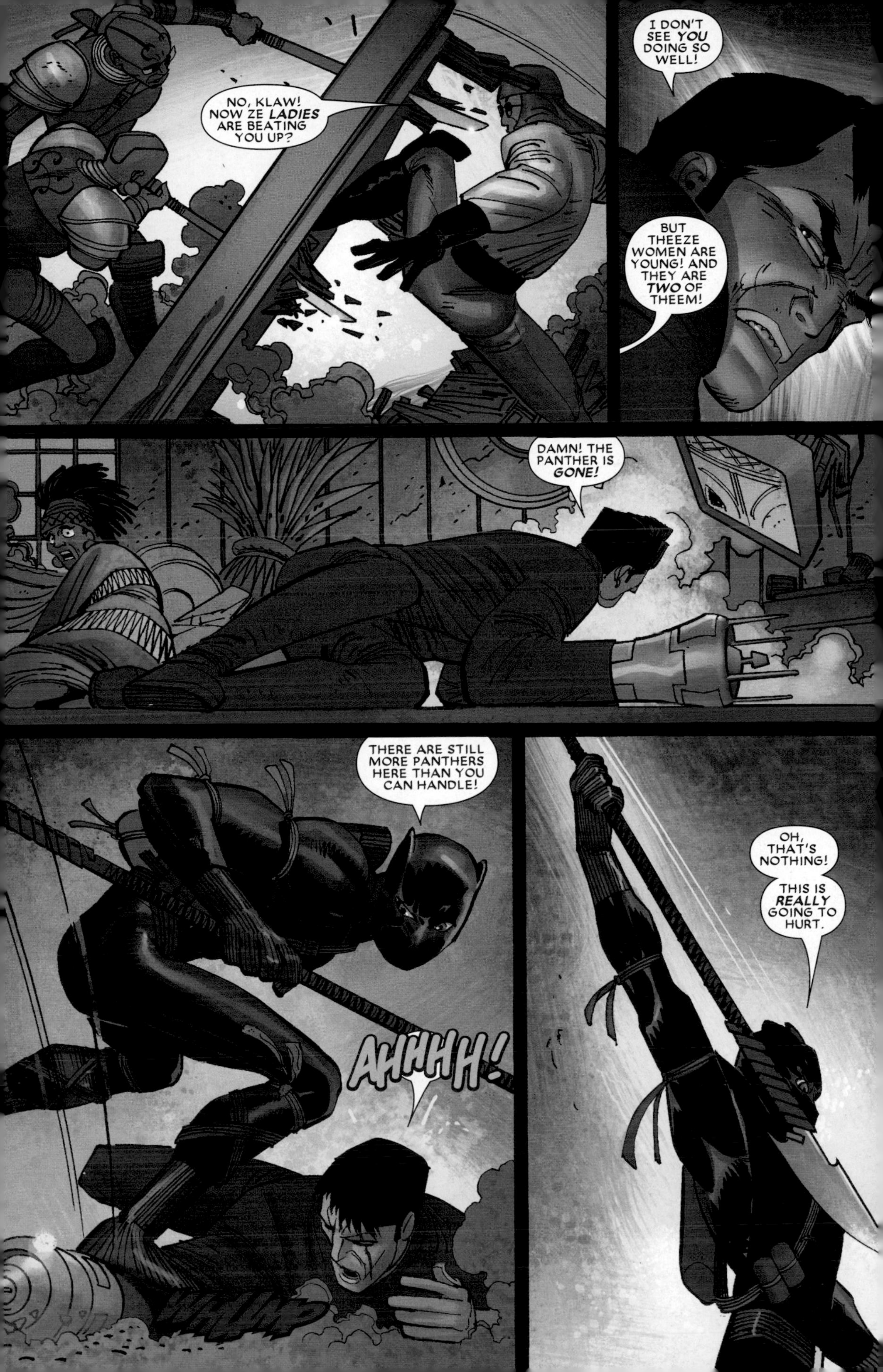
NO, KLAW! NOW ZE LADIES ARE BEATING YOU UP?
I DON'T SEE YOU DOING SO WELL!
BUT THEEZE WOMEN ARE YOUNG! AND THEY ARE TWO OF THEEM!
DAMN! THE PANTHER IS GONE!
THERE ARE STILL MORE PANTHERS HERE THAN YOU CAN HANDLE!
AHHHH!
OH, THAT'S NOTHING!
THIS IS REALLY GOING TO HURT.

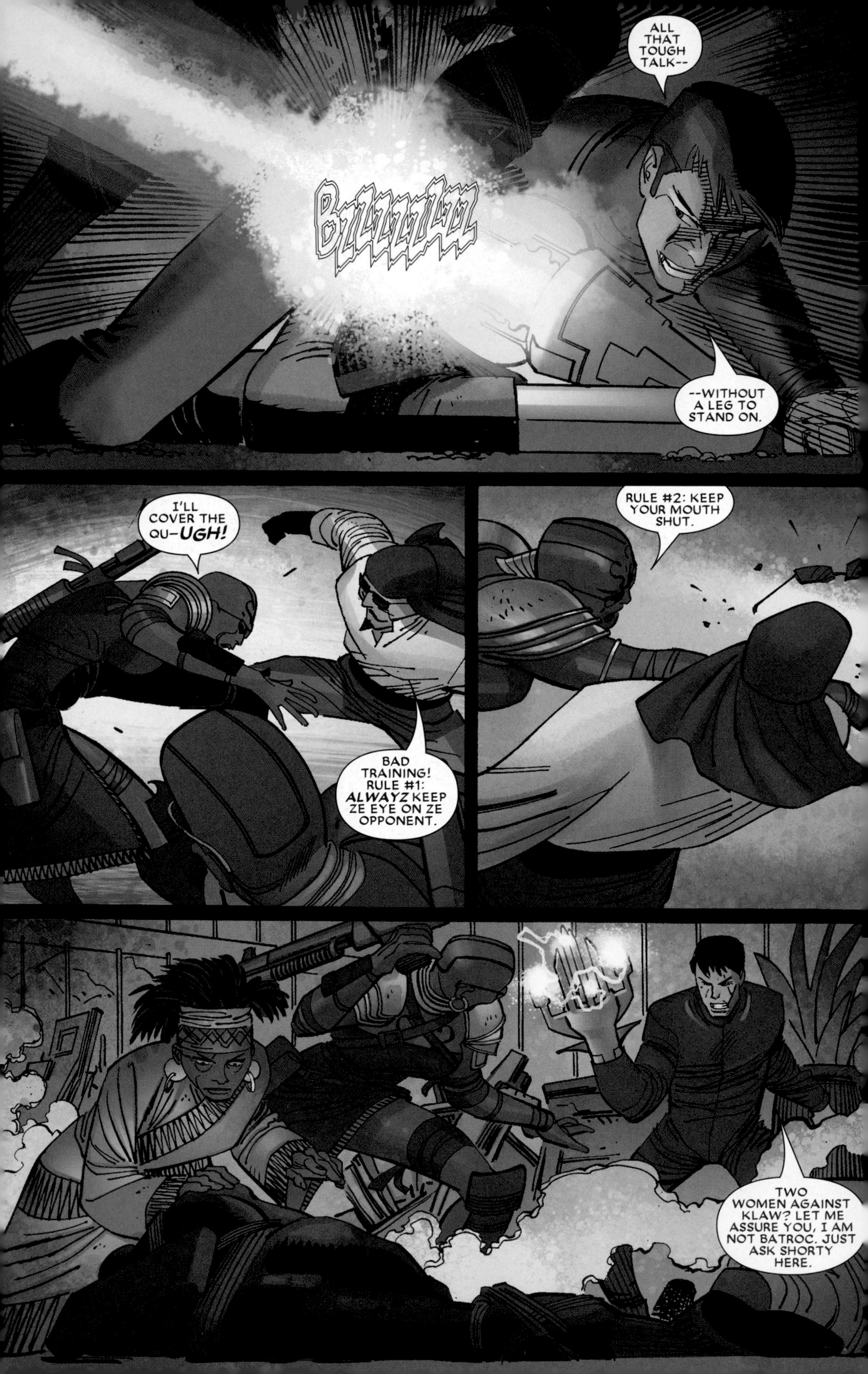
ALL THAT TOUGH TALK--
BZZZZZZZZ
--WITHOUT A LEG TO STAND ON.
I'LL COVER THE QU-UGH!
BAD TRAINING! RULE #1: ALWAYZ KEEP ZE EYE ON ZE OPPONENT.
RULE #2: KEEP YOUR MOUTH SHUT.
TWO WOMEN AGAINST KLAW? LET ME ASSURE YOU, I AM NOT BATROC. JUST ASK SHORTY HERE.

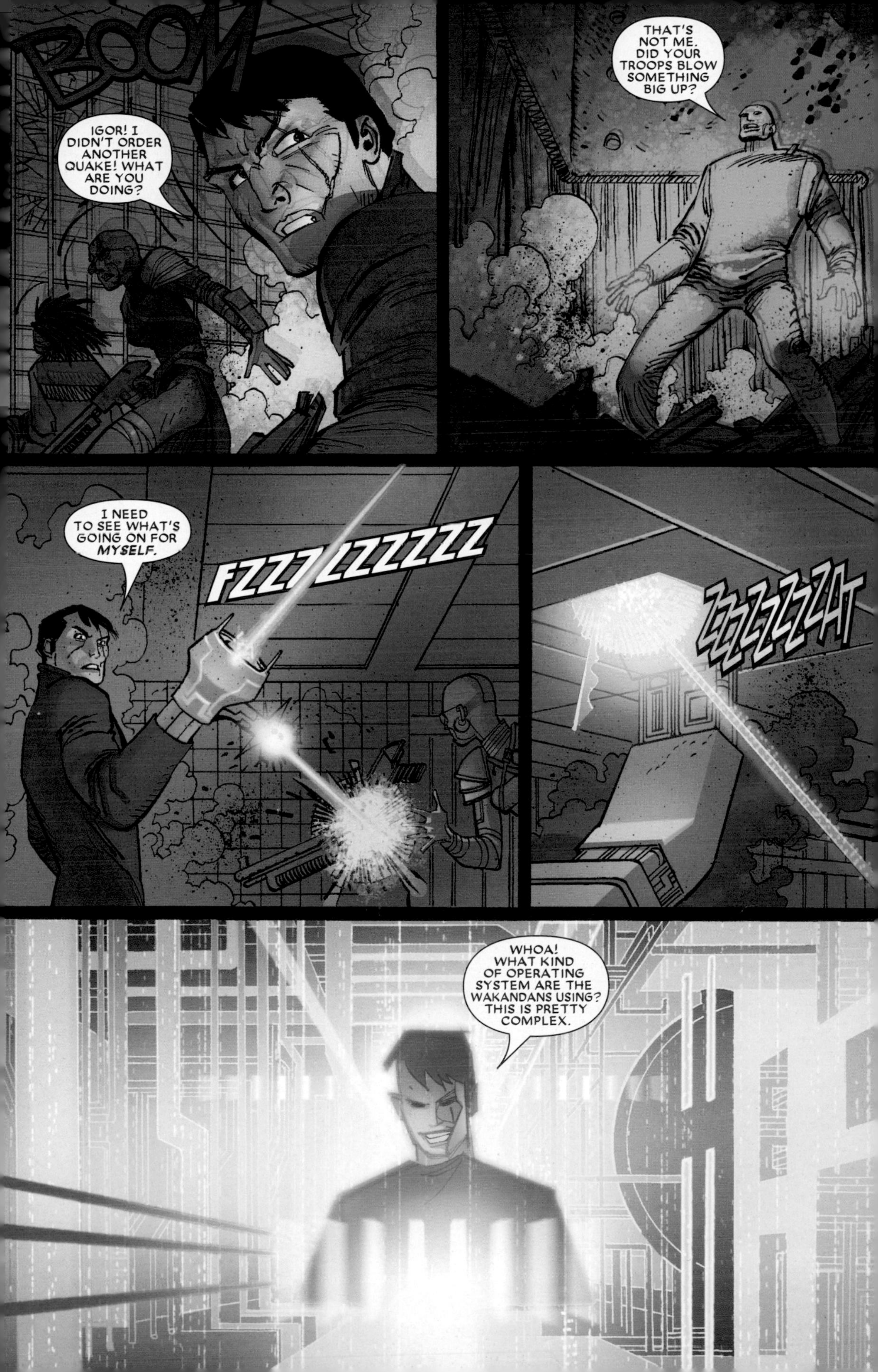
BOOM
IGOR! I DIDN'T ORDER ANOTHER QUAKE! WHAT ARE YOU DOING?
THAT'S NOT ME. DID YOUR TROOPS BLOW SOMETHING BIG UP?
I NEED TO SEE WHAT'S GOING ON FOR *MYSELF.*
FZZZZZZZZZ
ZZZZZZZZAT
WHOA! WHAT KIND OF OPERATING SYSTEM ARE THE WAKANDANS USING? THIS IS PRETTY COMPLEX.

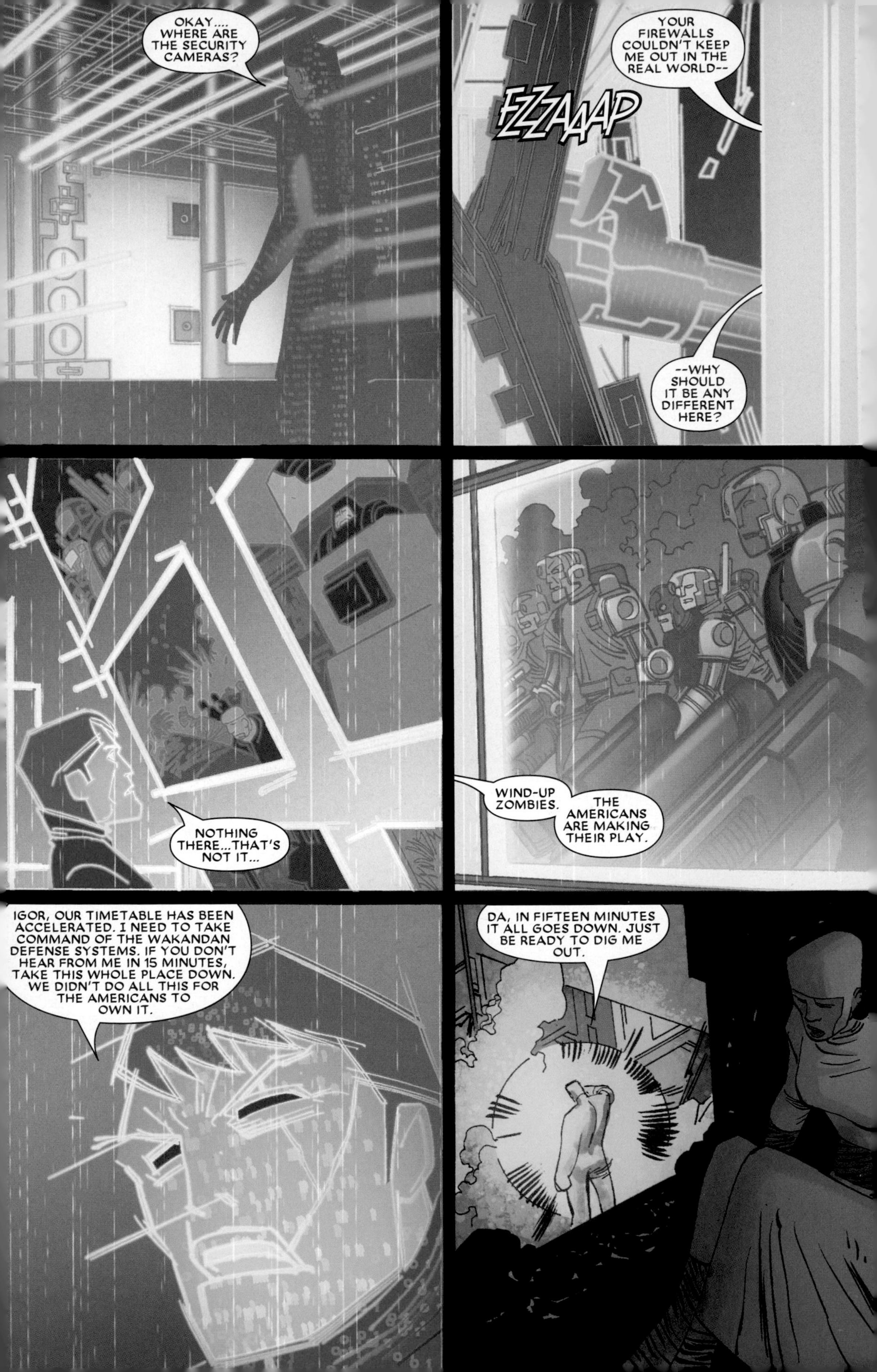
OKAY.... WHERE ARE THE SECURITY CAMERAS?
YOUR FIREWALLS COULDN'T KEEP ME OUT IN THE REAL WORLD--
FZZZAAAP
--WHY SHOULD IT BE ANY DIFFERENT HERE?
NOTHING THERE...THAT'S NOT IT...
WIND-UP ZOMBIES.
THE AMERICANS ARE MAKING THEIR PLAY.
IGOR, OUR TIMETABLE HAS BEEN ACCELERATED. I NEED TO TAKE COMMAND OF THE WAKANDAN DEFENSE SYSTEMS. IF YOU DON'T HEAR FROM ME IN 15 MINUTES, TAKE THIS WHOLE PLACE DOWN. WE DIDN'T DO ALL THIS FOR THE AMERICANS TO OWN IT.
DA, IN FIFTEEN MINUTES IT ALL GOES DOWN. JUST BE READY TO DIG ME OUT.

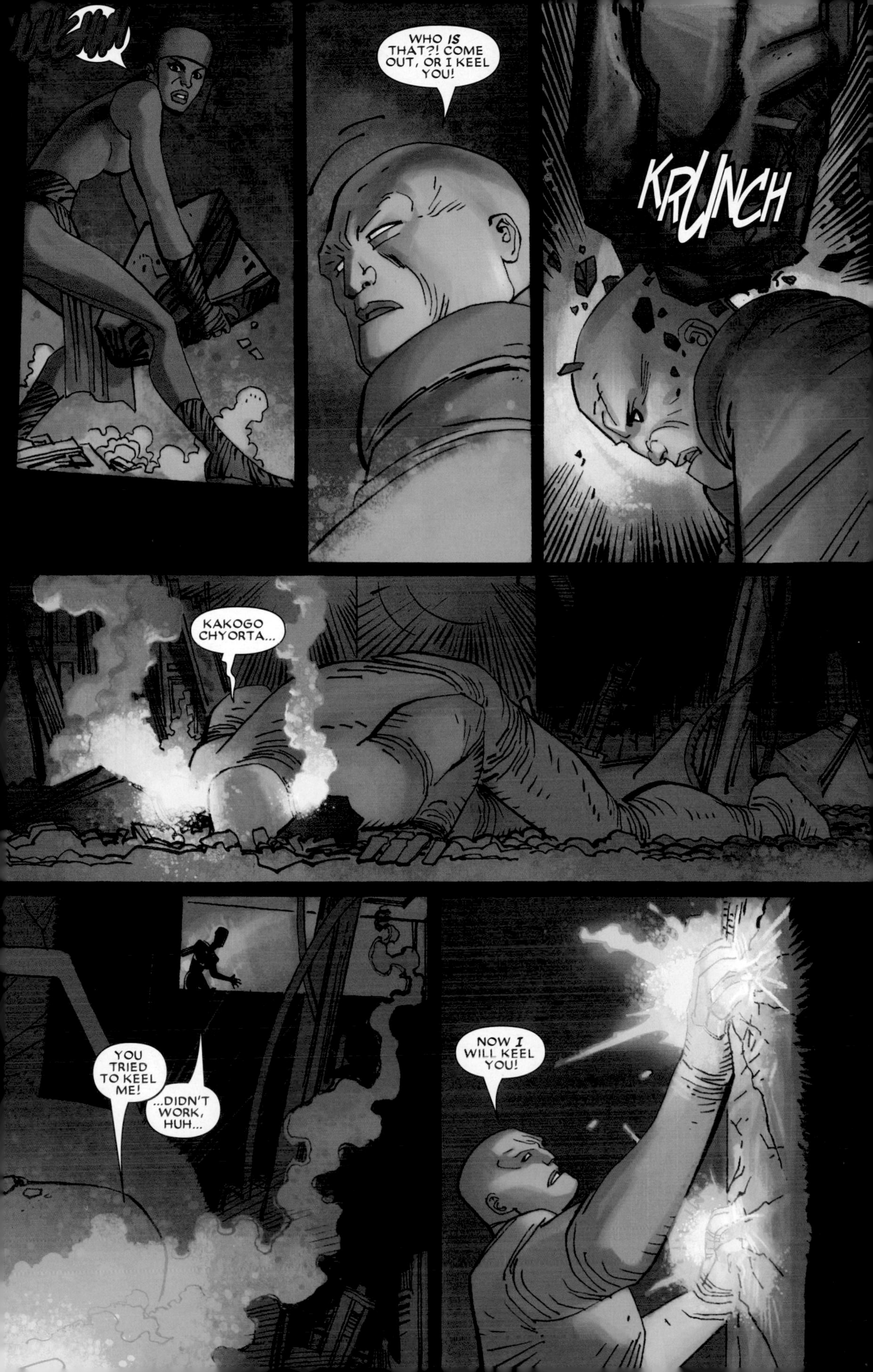
WHO IS THAT?! COME OUT, OR I KEEL YOU!
KRUNCH
KAKOGO CHYORTA...
YOU TRIED TO KEEL ME!
...DIDN'T WORK, HUH...
NOW I WILL KEEL YOU!

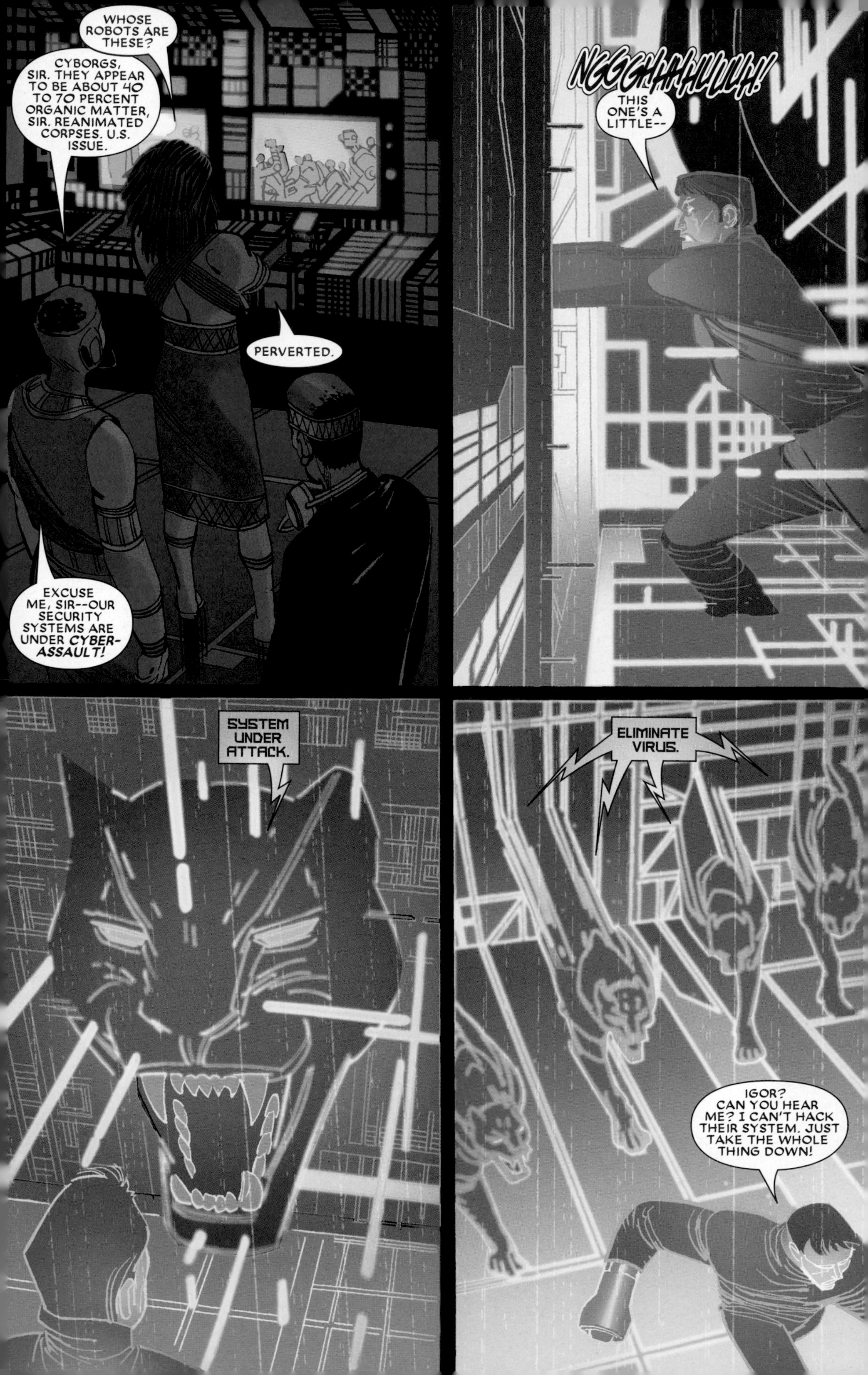
WHOSE ROBOTS ARE THESE?
CYBORGS, SIR. THEY APPEAR TO BE ABOUT 40 TO 70 PERCENT ORGANIC MATTER, SIR. REANIMATED CORPSES. U.S. ISSUE.
PERVERTED.
EXCUSE ME, SIR--OUR SECURITY SYSTEMS ARE UNDER CYBER-ASSAULT!
NGGGHAAHUUUH!
THIS ONE'S A LITTLE--
SYSTEM UNDER ATTACK.
ELIMINATE VIRUS.
IGOR? CAN YOU HEAR ME? I CAN'T HACK THEIR SYSTEM. JUST TAKE THE WHOLE THING DOWN!

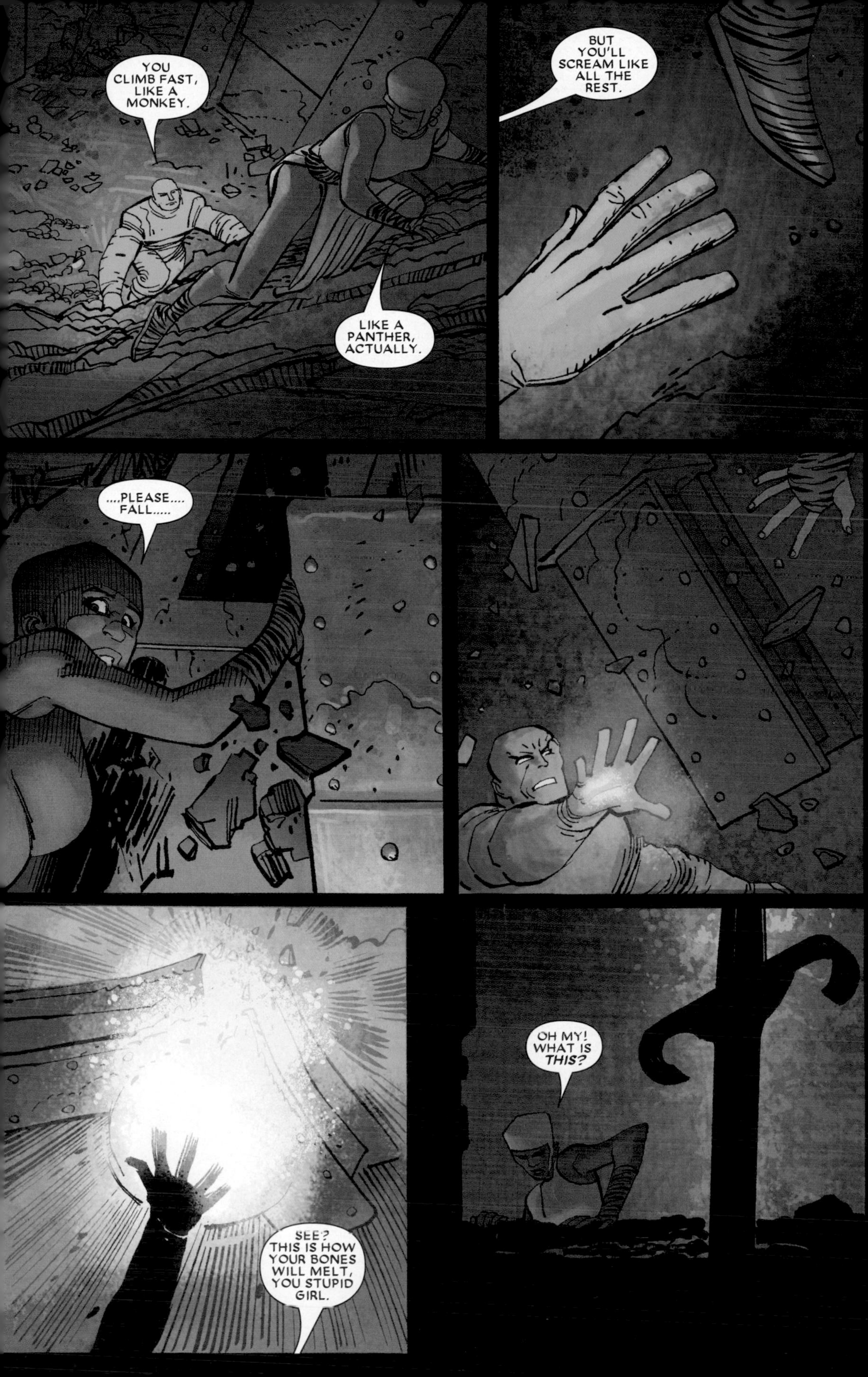
YOU CLIMB FAST, LIKE A MONKEY.
LIKE A PANTHER, ACTUALLY.
BUT YOU'LL SCREAM LIKE ALL THE REST.
....PLEASE.... FALL.....
SEE? THIS IS HOW YOUR BONES WILL MELT, YOU STUPID GIRL.
OH MY! WHAT IS *THIS?*

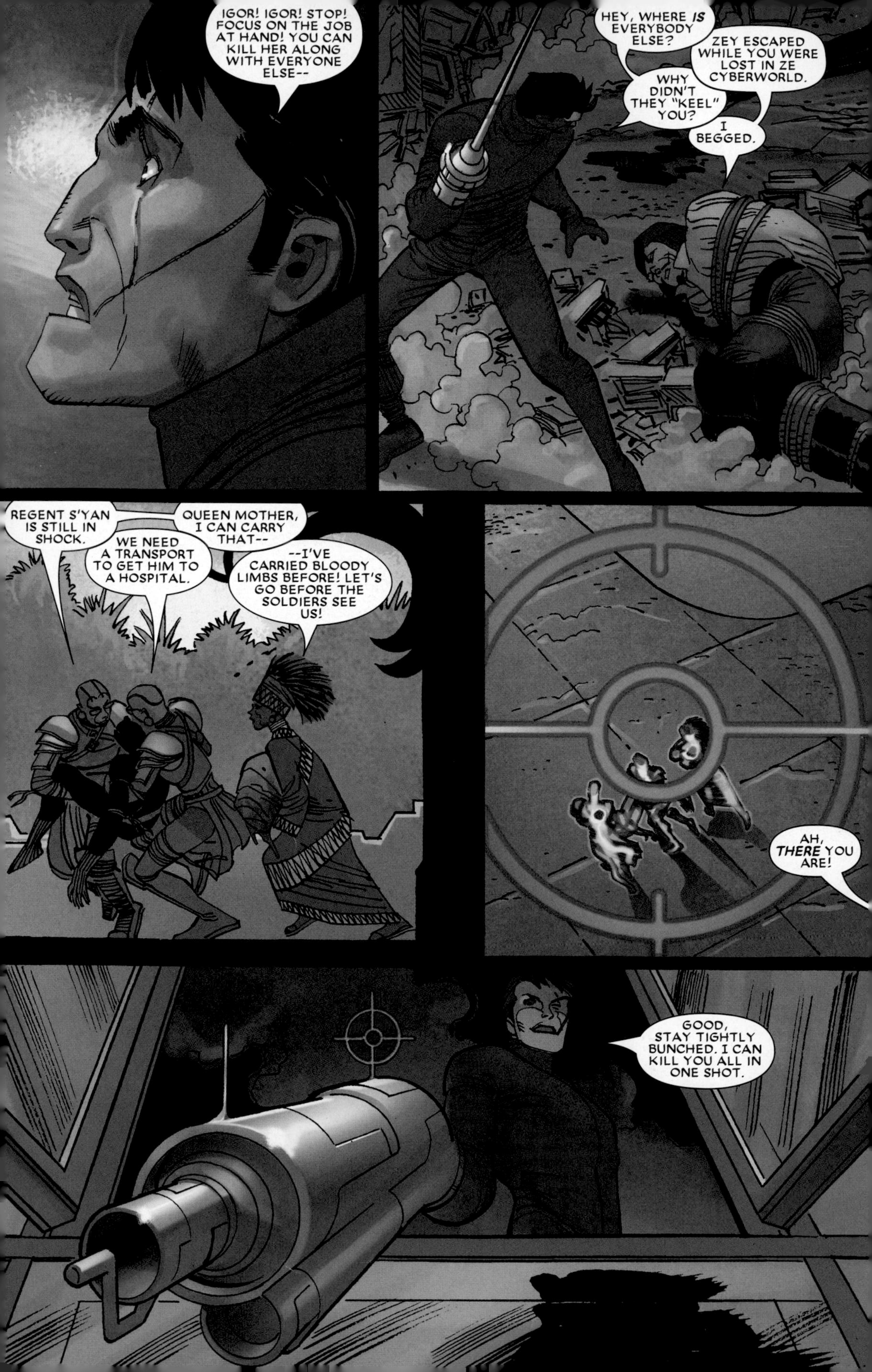
IGOR! IGOR! STOP! FOCUS ON THE JOB AT HAND! YOU CAN KILL HER ALONG WITH EVERYONE ELSE--
HEY, WHERE *IS* EVERYBODY ELSE?
ZEY ESCAPED WHILE YOU WERE LOST IN ZE CYBERWORLD.
WHY DIDN'T THEY "KEEL" YOU?
I BEGGED.
REGENT S'YAN IS STILL IN SHOCK.
WE NEED A TRANSPORT TO GET HIM TO A HOSPITAL.
QUEEN MOTHER, I CAN CARRY THAT--
--I'VE CARRIED BLOODY LIMBS BEFORE! LET'S GO BEFORE THE SOLDIERS SEE US!
AH, ***THERE*** YOU ARE!
GOOD, STAY TIGHTLY BUNCHED. I CAN KILL YOU ALL IN ONE SHOT.

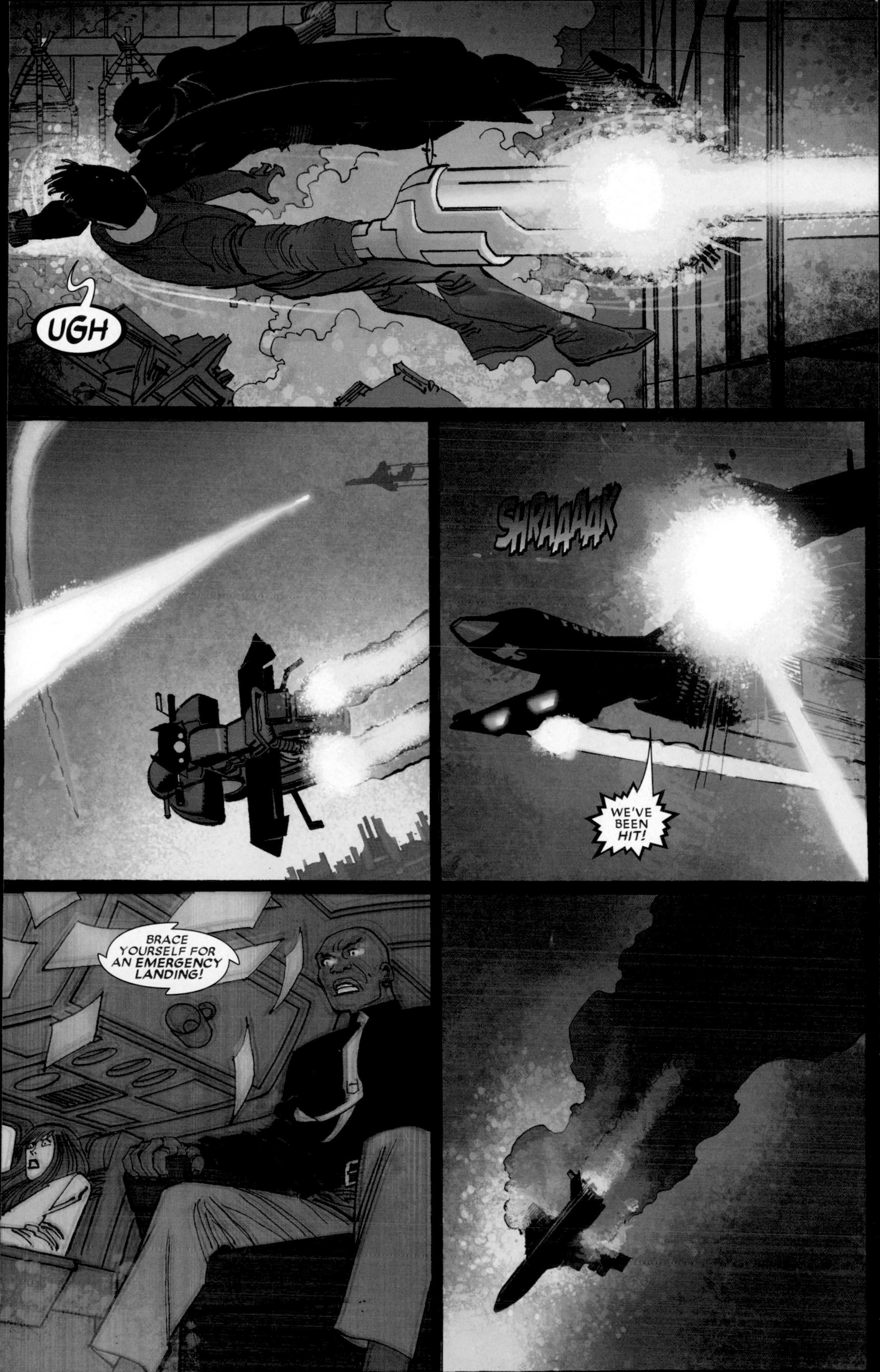
UGH
SHRAAAAK
WE'VE BEEN HIT!
BRACE YOURSELF FOR AN EMERGENCY LANDING!

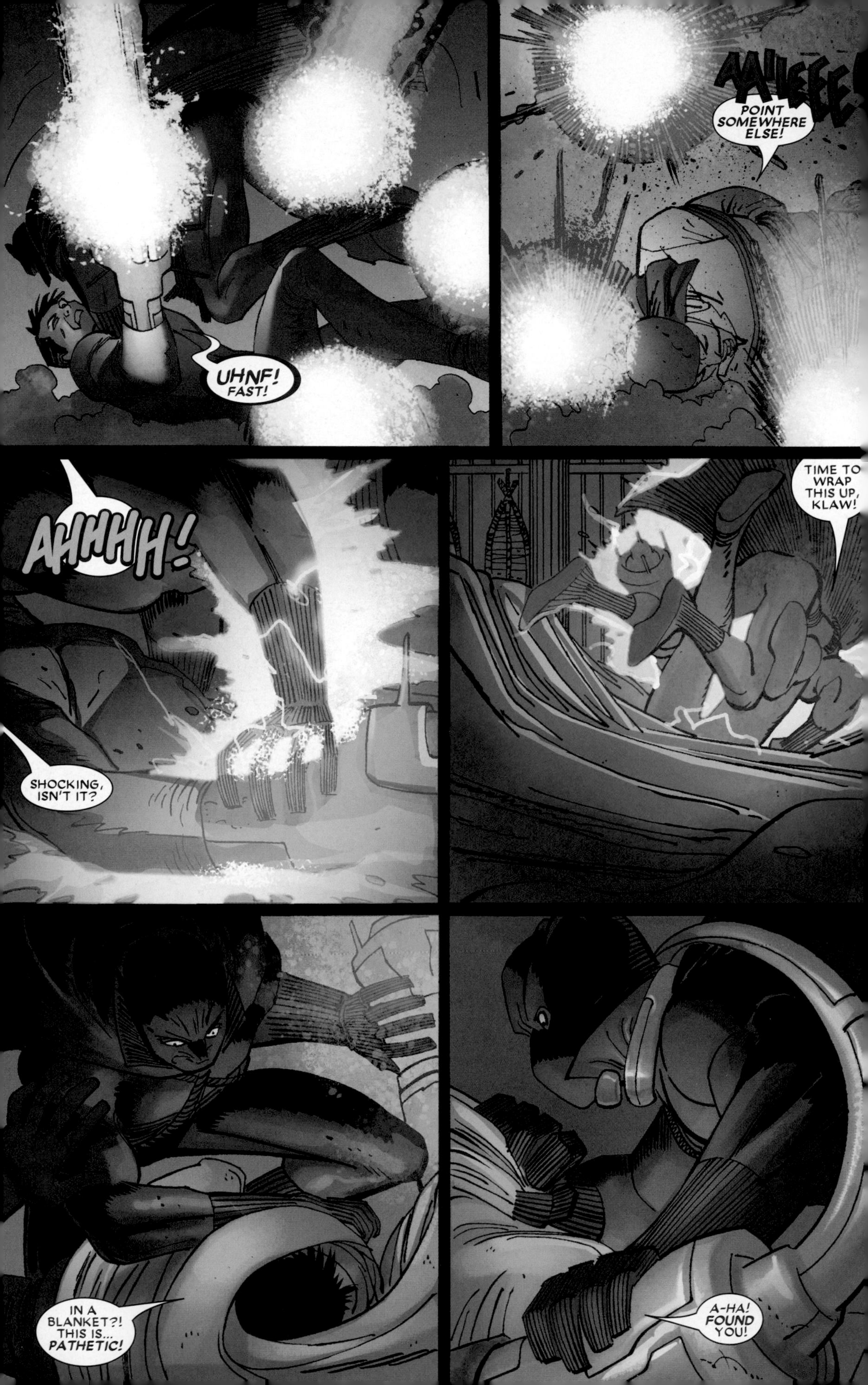
UHNF! FAST!
AAIIEEEE!
POINT SOMEWHERE ELSE!
AHHHHH!
SHOCKING, ISN'T IT?
TIME TO WRAP THIS UP, KLAW!
IN A BLANKET?! THIS IS... PATHETIC!
A-HA! FOUND YOU!

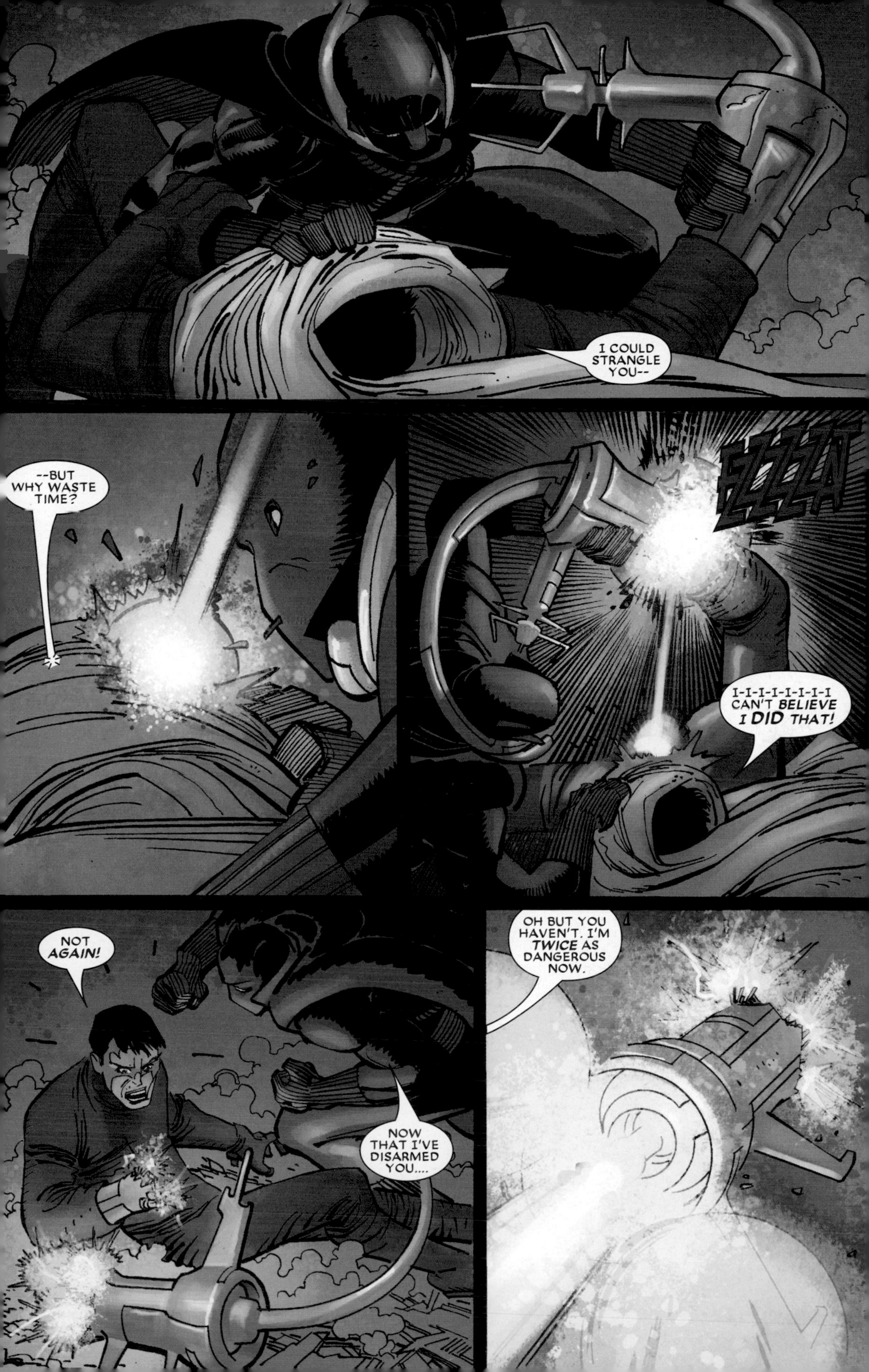
I COULD STRANGLE YOU--
--BUT WHY WASTE TIME?
FZZZZZAT
I-I-I-I-I-I-I-I CAN'T BELIEVE I DID THAT!
NOT AGAIN!
NOW THAT I'VE DISARMED YOU....
OH BUT YOU HAVEN'T. I'M TWICE AS DANGEROUS NOW.

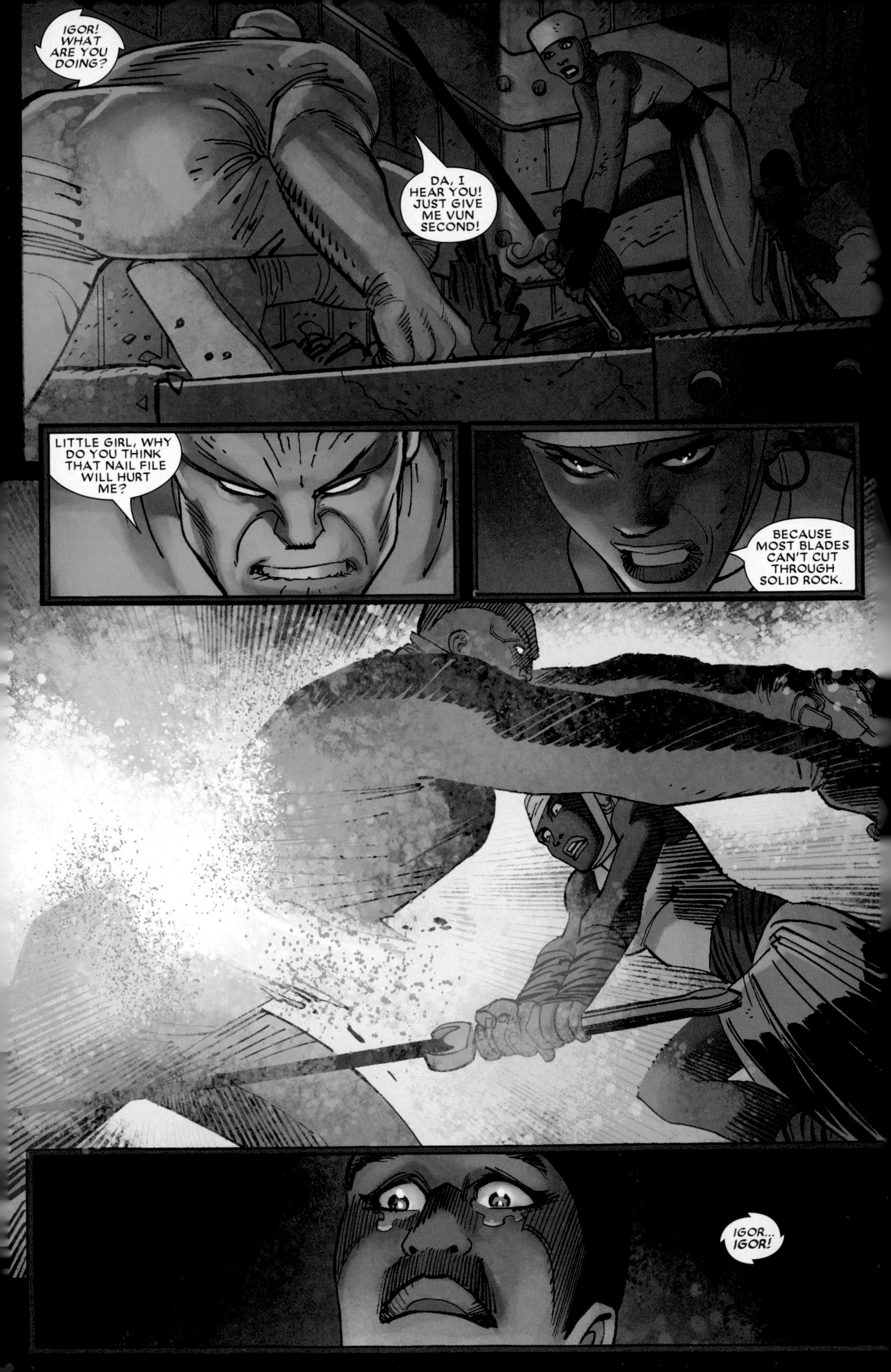
IGOR! WHAT ARE YOU DOING?
DA, I HEAR YOU! JUST GIVE ME VUN SECOND!
LITTLE GIRL, WHY DO YOU THINK THAT NAIL FILE WILL HURT ME?
BECAUSE MOST BLADES CAN'T CUT THROUGH SOLID ROCK.
IGOR... IGOR!

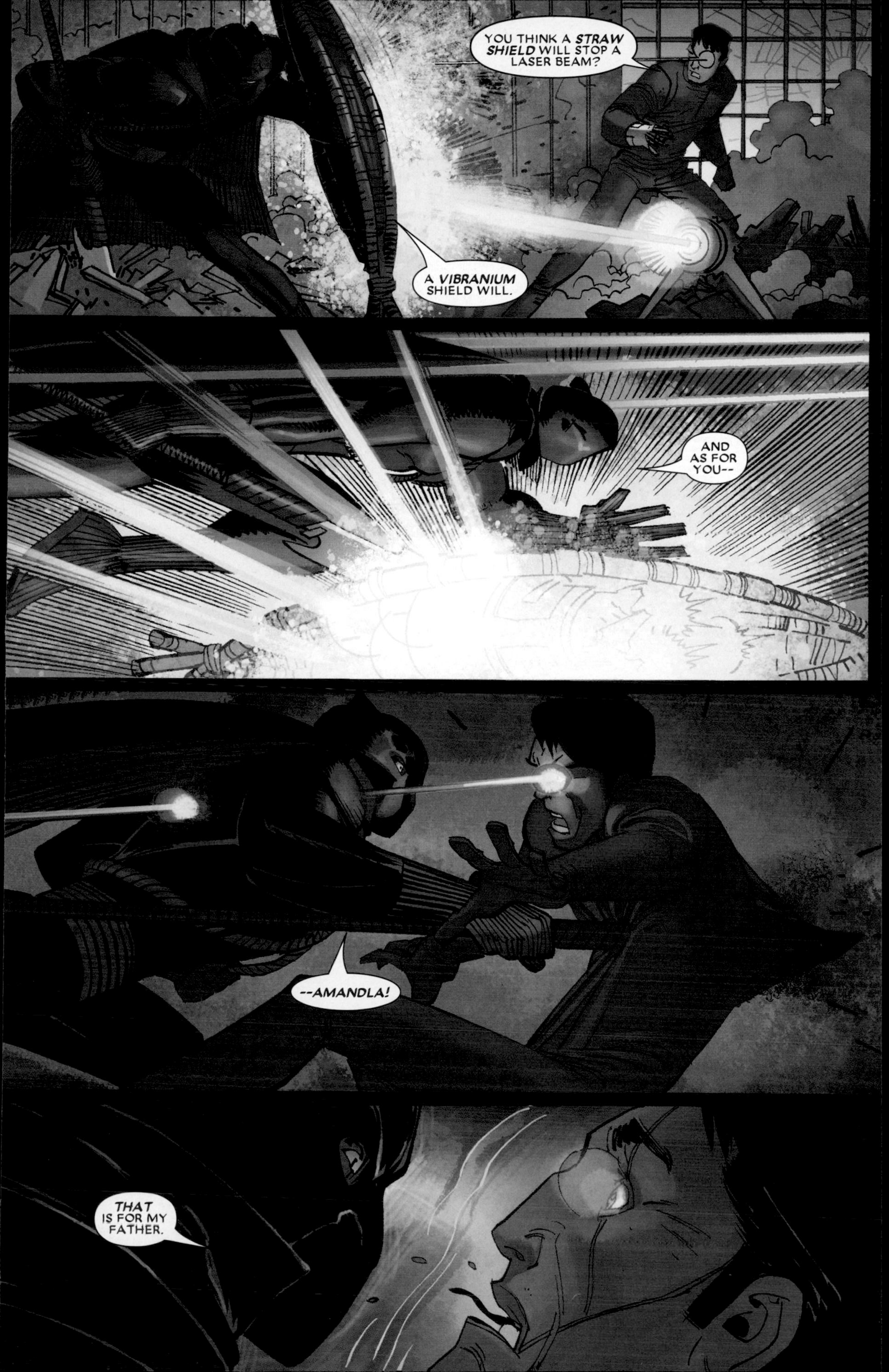
YOU THINK A STRAW SHIELD WILL STOP A LASER BEAM?
A VIBRANIUM SHIELD WILL.
AND AS FOR YOU--
--AMANDLA!
THAT IS FOR MY FATHER.

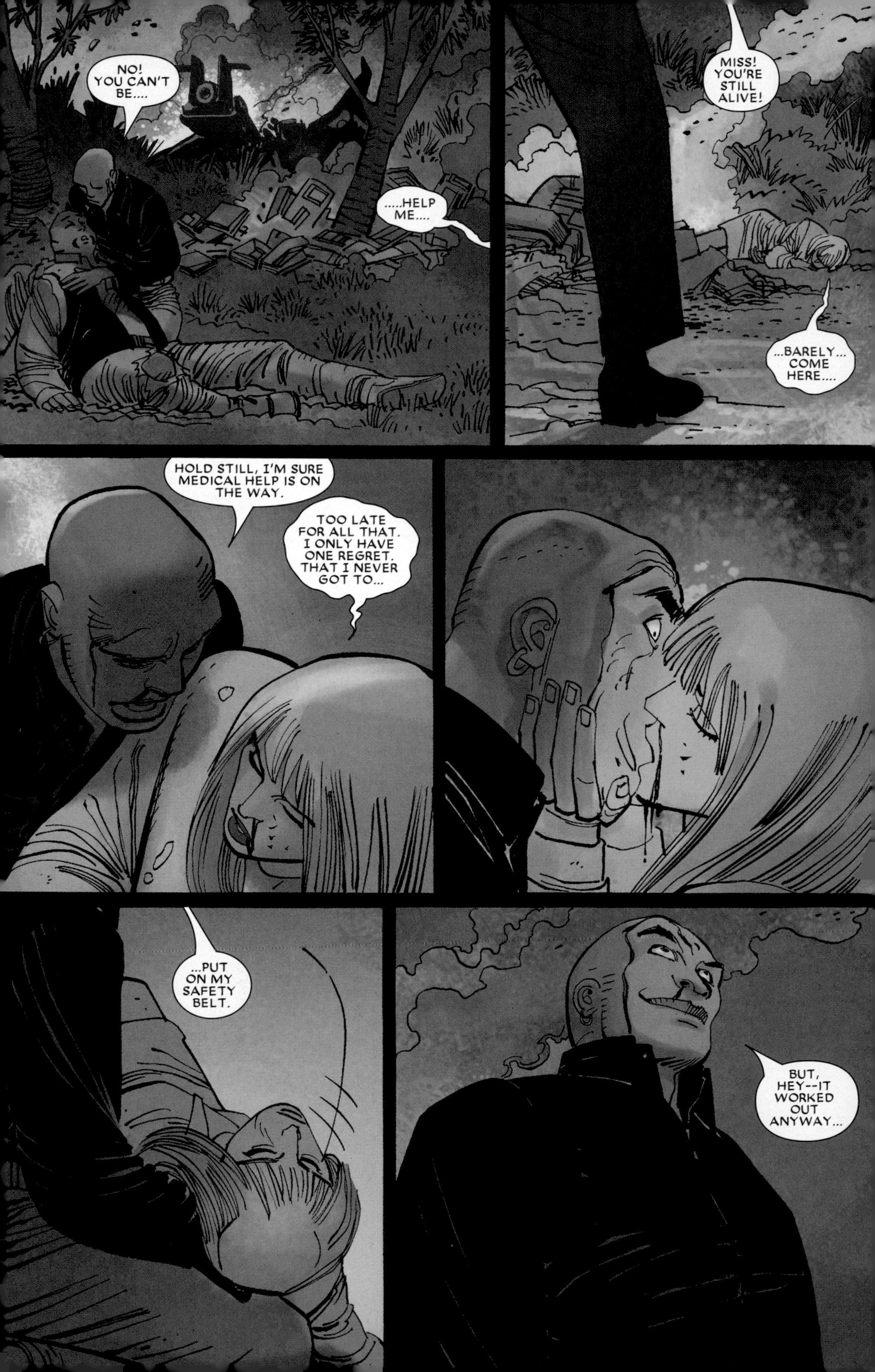
NO! YOU CAN'T BE....
.....HELP ME....
MISS! YOU'RE STILL ALIVE!
...BARELY... COME HERE....
HOLD STILL, I'M SURE MEDICAL HELP IS ON THE WAY.
TOO LATE FOR ALL THAT. I ONLY HAVE ONE REGRET. THAT I NEVER GOT TO...
...PUT ON MY SAFETY BELT.
BUT, HEY--IT WORKED OUT ANYWAY...

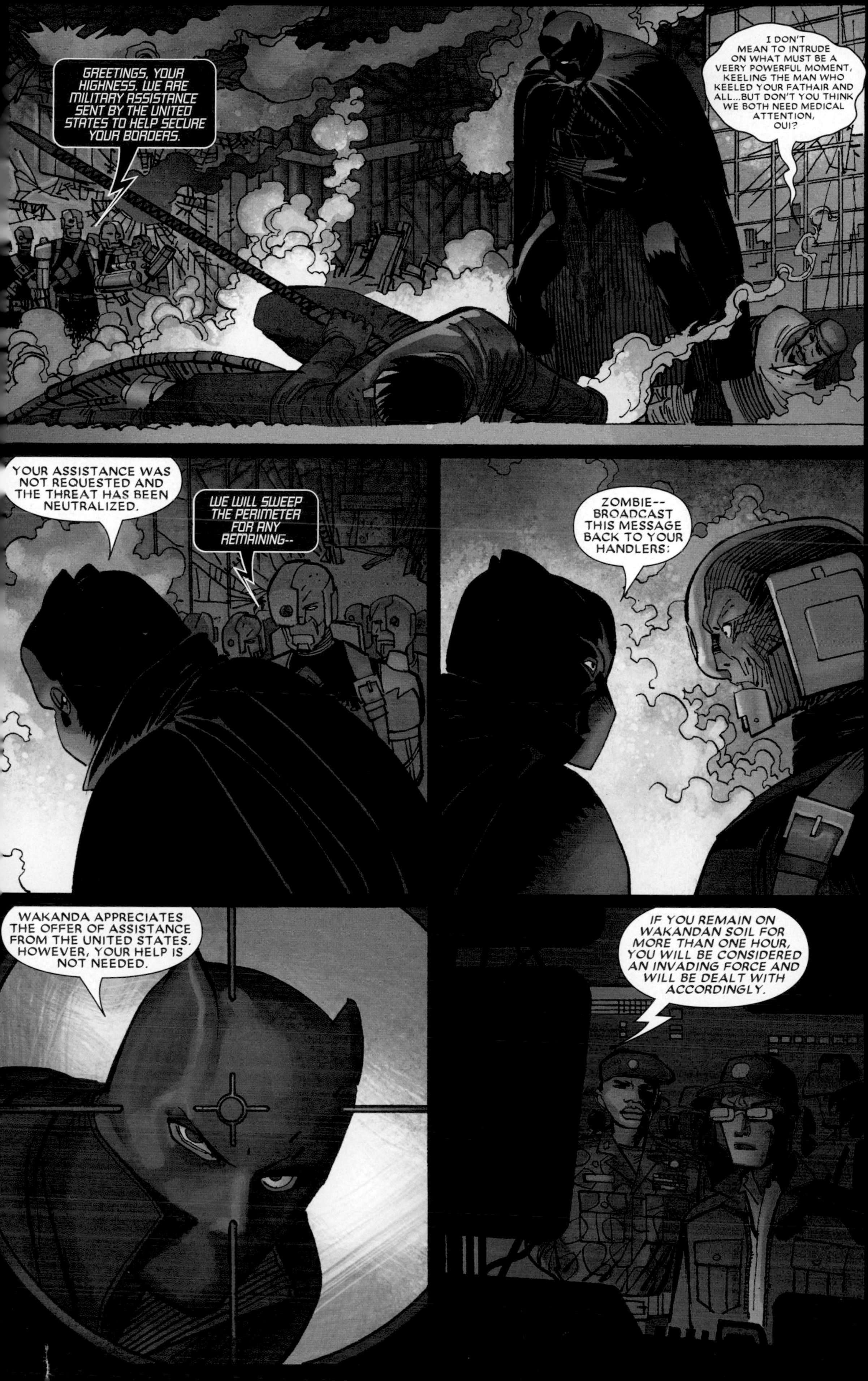
GREETINGS, YOUR HIGHNESS. WE ARE MILITARY ASSISTANCE SENT BY THE UNITED STATES TO HELP SECURE YOUR BORDERS.
I DON'T MEAN TO INTRUDE ON WHAT MUST BE A VEERY POWERFUL MOMENT, KEELING THE MAN WHO KEELED YOUR FATHAIR AND ALL...BUT DON'T YOU THINK WE BOTH NEED MEDICAL ATTENTION, OUI?
YOUR ASSISTANCE WAS NOT REQUESTED AND THE THREAT HAS BEEN NEUTRALIZED.
WE WILL SWEEP THE PERIMETER FOR ANY REMAINING--
ZOMBIE-- BROADCAST THIS MESSAGE BACK TO YOUR HANDLERS:
WAKANDA APPRECIATES THE OFFER OF ASSISTANCE FROM THE UNITED STATES. HOWEVER, YOUR HELP IS NOT NEEDED.
IF YOU REMAIN ON WAKANDAN SOIL FOR MORE THAN ONE HOUR, YOU WILL BE CONSIDERED AN INVADING FORCE AND WILL BE DEALT WITH ACCORDINGLY.

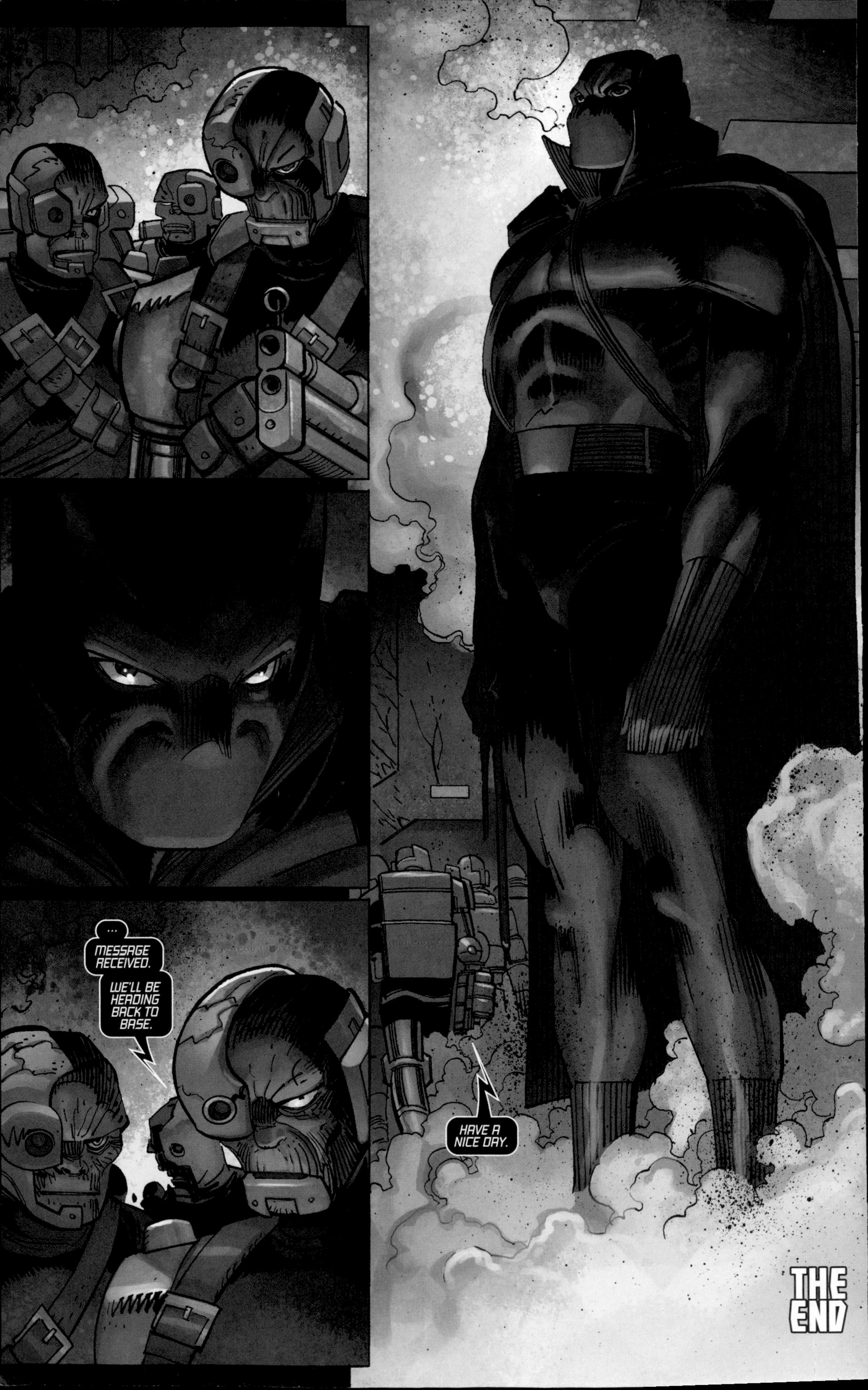
...
MESSAGE RECEIVED.
WE'LL BE HEADING BACK TO BASE.
HAVE A NICE DAY.
THE END

BLACK PANTHER #1 • VARIANT COVER

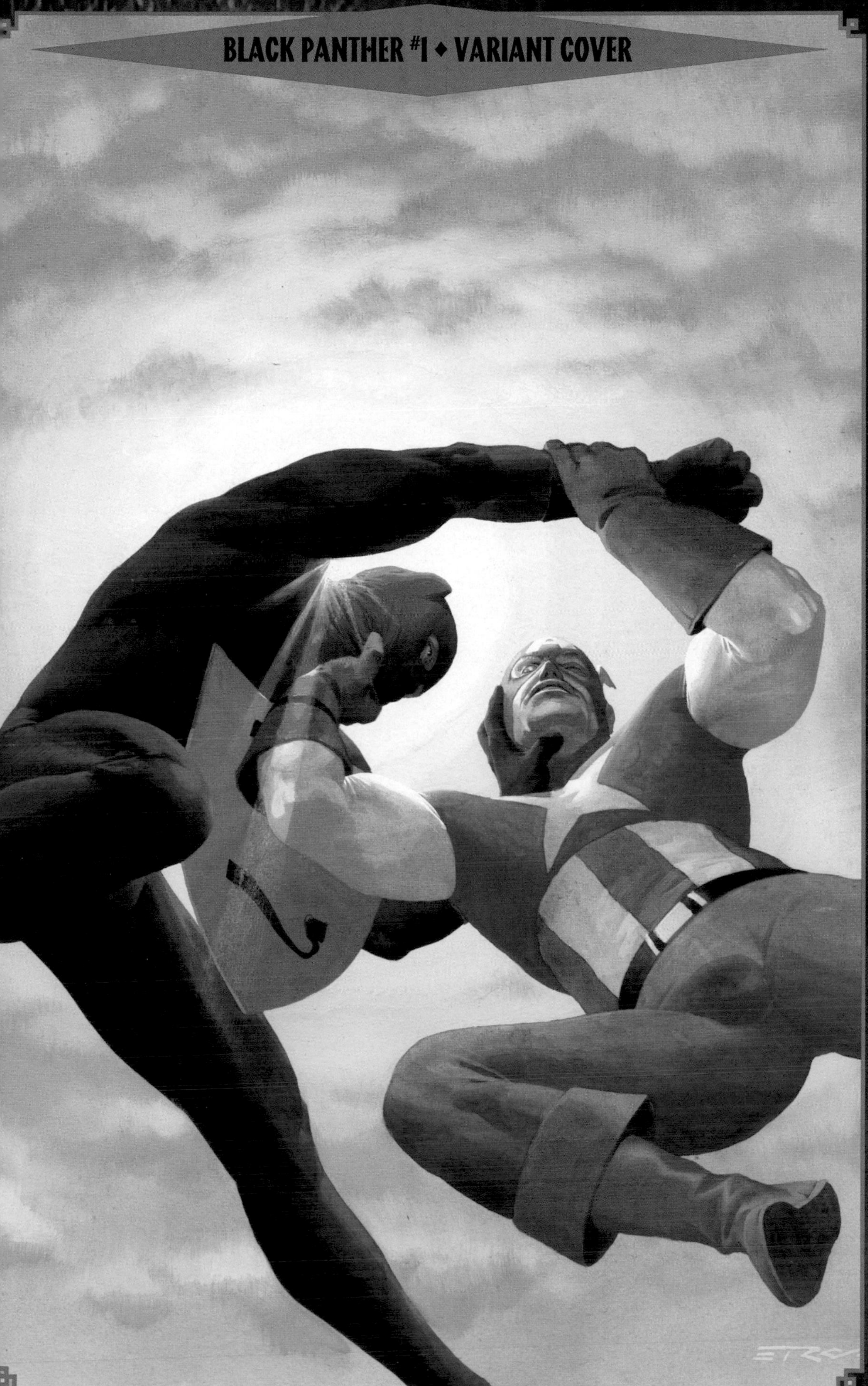

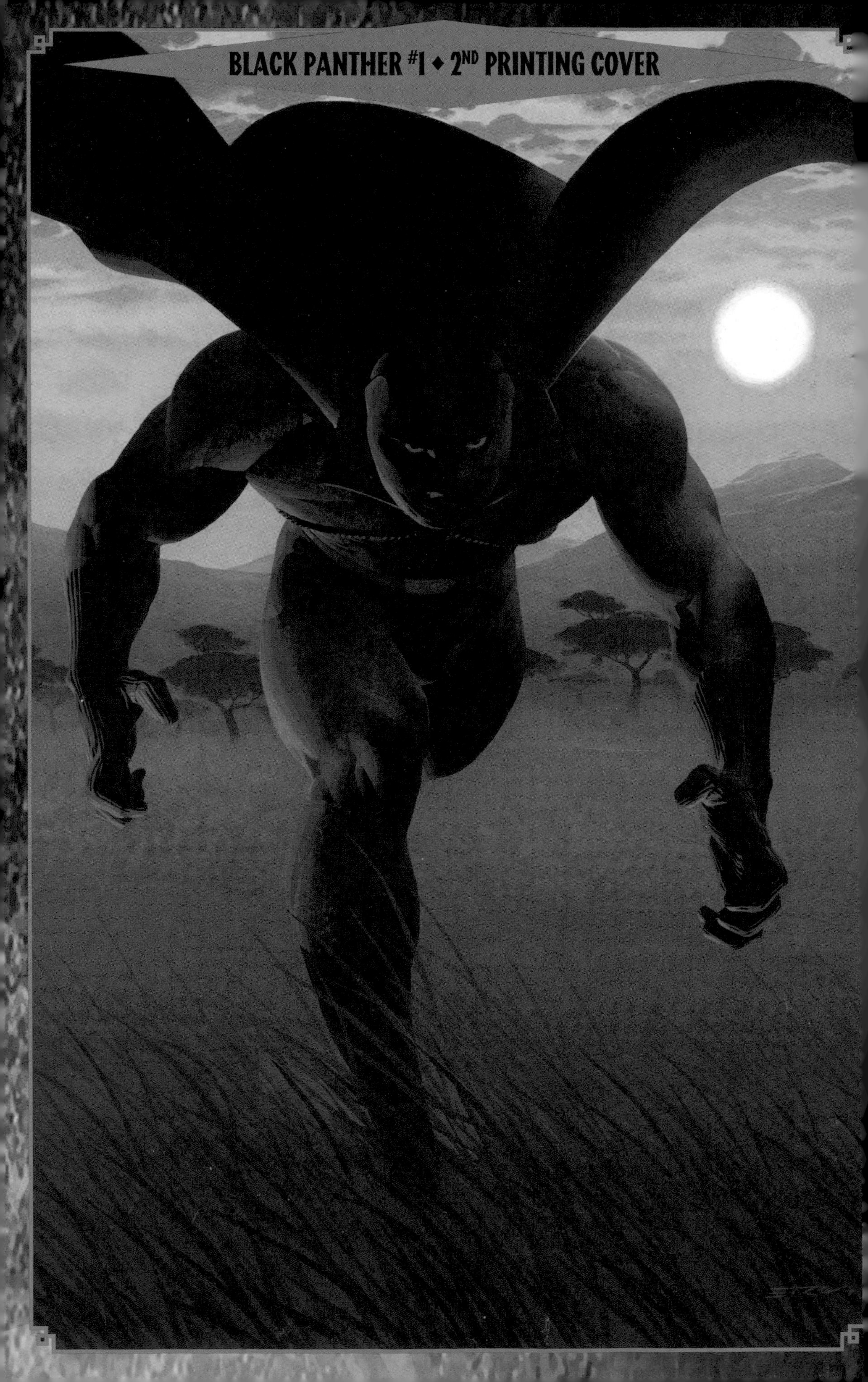
BLACK PANTHER #1 • 2ND PRINTING COVER

THE BLACK PANTHER
A HISTORICAL OVERVIEW AND A LOOK TO THE FUTURE.
BY REGINALD HUDLIN

When the Black Panther debuted in the '60s, he was so cool, so perfect a character in concept and execution it's hard to believe it was done by two white guys. But when the white guys in question were Stan Lee and Jack Kirby, then it makes sense. But to truly appreciate their achievement, it's worth putting it in context: No black super hero before or after the Black Panther is as cool as the Black Panther. Sure, others come close. Luke Cage is as brilliant a Marvel response to blaxploitation as Nick Fury, Agent of S.H.I.E.L.D. was to the James Bond/super spy trend. And the Milestone line of comics was wonderful and smart.

But the Black Panther is STILL The Man.

He's the king of his own country! He's rich! He's tough enough to defeat the Fantastic Four and Captain America! He's suave and sophisticated! He's got cool super-technology! And his name is...THE BLACK PANTHER. Just the name alone was so ahead of its time. (I wonder if the Black Panther Party in Oakland had gotten famous first, would Stan have used the name anyway? Well, he didn't change it, so double-kudos to him!)

The Panther's appearances in the Lee/Kirby issues of the FANTASTIC FOUR and CAPTAIN AMERICA were great, but nothing after that has been able to recapture the original magic. He never made much of an impression on me during any of his AVENGERS stints, and I never liked the McGregor-written series in JUNGLE ACTION. I even preferred the loopy but fun late Kirby series to McGregor's morose characters that endlessly droned on with overflowing captions with even more yakkety yakking. Enough already!

The Priest run on the PANTHER gave a much-needed shot in the arm to the character. His power level was restored to the point that the Panther had contingency plans to take on Galactus. Great! And he got two beautiful female bodyguards/concubines who can kick @$$. Great! He kicked it with fellow regents Namor and Doom. Great! He joined the Avengers to spy on them? The best idea yet!

The question is, how do we take the character to the next level?

Let's start by defining who he IS.

The Black Panther is the Black Captain America. He's the embodiment of the ideals of a people. As Americans, we feel good when we read Captain America because he reminds us of the potential of how good America can be, if, of course, we have the convictions to live by the principles the country was founded on. As a black person, the Black Panther should represent the fulfillment of the potential of the Motherland.

For a long time, the Black American equivalent of that ideal was represented by Sidney Poitier, a man who maintained his dignity even in degrading situations. But since the '80s, that ideal has shifted. In the post-integration, post-Reagan era, the new ideal is Spike Lee or Sean "Puffy" Combs, the artist/businessman hero who profits from his own cultural integrity. In other words, the man who has it all — the money, the politics and the cool and style of black culture.

What those celebrities named, along with Malcolm X, Miles Davis and Muhammad Ali, all have in common, is the knowledge that the act of being a black man in white America is an inherent act of rebellion. They are WILLING to be bad@$$es.

That's what hip hop is all about. Being a bad@$$. Everyone wants to be a bad@$$. That's why white kids have always loved black music — whether it's jazz, rock and roll or hip hop, black music is the music of bad@$$es, and plugging into that culture makes a suburban white kid feel like a bad@$$, too. And for a generation of white kids who have grown up without an "Elvis" — a white interpreter of black culture — their appreciation of edgy street culture is shocking even to me.

I say all this because the harder the Panther is, the more appealing he is to both black AND white audiences.

All we've got to do is let the Panther be who he is set up to be. After all, he's a Wakandan. Wakandans are so bad@$$ THEY'VE NEVER BEEN CONQUERED.

This is important. There are some countries that are like doormats — everybody's kicked their @$$ at one point or another. But there are other peoples in the world — Vietnam comes to mind — that kick the @$$ of everyone who messes with them, superpower or not.

The Wakandans are such people. I figure every 50 years or so, somebody tries to make a move on them, and they have to prove the point to that generation of would-be conquerors:

DON'T EVEN TRY IT!

The independence of the Wakandan people has got to be galling to the rest of the world for a lot of reasons. First of all, the rest of Africa has been carved up like a Christmas turkey. England, Germany, France, Belgium, the United States, the Soviet Union, Islamic and Christian invaders...so many empires have taken large chunks of land and resources for their own. Even after the independence movements of the '60s, any leader that was too competent got killed (like, say, Patrice Lumumba). So the colonial powers still controlled their territories through greedy thugs like Bokassa and Mubutu.

Not only does Wakanda's independence block the total dominance of Africa by colonial powers, its cultural evolution has gone unchecked for centuries. They were ahead of us a thousand years ago. And no one has colonized them, burned their books, erased their language, or broken their spirits.

Unfettered by the yoke of colonization, they have created a hi-tech, ecologically sound paradise that makes the rest of the world seem primitive by comparison. If the right company got their hands on their gadgets, their medicines, their R&D, they would vault themselves a century ahead of their competitors.

But the Wakandans can't be bought out. This isn't a bunch of starving orphans pimped by dictators who'll sell out for a sizable contribution to their Swiss bank account. Wakandans are led by the Black Panthers, a warrior cult that serves as the religious, political and military head of the country. That tower in the center of the country is like a big middle finger to the rest of the world — literally. Their borders are tightly shut and they deal with the world on their own terms...or not at all.

The first scene of the book would be in the 10th century. Start on some neighboring tribe walking across the savannah looking for its next conquest. They roll on Wakanda. But the Wakandans kick their @$$, using man-sized beartraps, crossbows and other technology that even Europeans didn't have at the time.

Cut to the turn of the century. The Boers have just finished conquering South Africa and are now moving on Wakanda. They've got rifles, they've got gatling guns. But the Wakandans have a magnetic based weapon that causes the Boer weapons to backfire, maiming and killing half their troops. The Panthers then move in, leaving one man alive, as they usually do, to spread the word — DON'T EVEN THINK ABOUT IT.

We see Captain America getting his butt whipped by T'Chaka during World War Two. Yeah, they will whip anybody's butt.

Okay, let me stop. I'm starting on scenes and I haven't even given an overview yet.

The first six issues of the book will be a re-telling of the Panther's origin. That hasn't been done during this incarnation of the Panther, and is the best way to set the tone for the book.

It will be a version without the Fantastic Four, much like the Lee/Kirby SILVER SURFER graphic novel from the '70s, which retold his origin without the FF's involvement in the story.

The first six issues will essentially be my version of what the BLACK PANTHER MOVIE should be. But no matter what happens with the movie, or if the movie ever happens, there will be a TPB that people can pick up and see the character done right. No matter how horrible the Joel Schumacher BATMAN movies are, they cannot erase the greatness of THE DARK KNIGHT RETURNS or BATMAN: YEAR ONE. Hopefully, this book will do the same for T'Challa.

I know some people at Marvel feel the Panther's base being in Africa is a problem. It shouldn't be. The Panther should move back and forth between Wakanda and the rest of the world the same way Thor moves between Asgard and Earth. He's an INTERNATIONAL player who's equally at home at the Davos Conference in Switzerland, meeting with Colin Powell in D.C., kicking it in Harlem with Bill Clinton and Al Sharpton, and brokering deals off the coast of Cuba with Fidel Castro and Prince Namor.

A great hero is defined by his villains. The Panther doesn't have his equivalents to Dr. Doom, the Red Skull, or Magneto. Instead he's got a guy wearing a white gorilla fur. I don't even know that loser's name, but he will never be seen inside the pages of the book I write.

Since the first story arc will be his origin, the main villain will be Klaw...but not the Murderous Master of Sound that he was in the 1960s. No way. Our villain is a South African who was named after his ancestor, who was one of the Boers who led the abortive attempt to invade Wakanda a century ago. In an act of revenge for the murder of his great-grandfather, and as part of a conspiracy to overthrow Wakanda, Klaw murdered T'Chaka. As he was about to kill the rest of the royal family, T'Challa, T'Chaka's son, blows Klaw's hand off, LITERALLY disarming him.

Now Klaw is equipped with a cybernetic hand that can turn into any number of murderous devices. He's invading Wakanda again, with a small commando squad of superpowered killers, to kill T'Challa and take over Wakanda.

But he's not the only person with the bright idea to invade Wakanda. Is the Panther ready to wage war at home — on multiple fronts?

And will he be betrayed from within?

Okay, that's not a whole pitch, but it's a start. I won't get into the second story arc with Cage, Shang-Chi, Photon and Storm...but that's gonna be even better.

— Reginald Hudlin

BLACK PANTHER #1 COVER SKETCHES
BY JOHN ROMITA JR.

BLACK PANTHER #1 COVER
PENCILS BY JOHN ROMITA JR. / INKS BY KLAUS JANSON

Black Panther #2 Cover Sketches by Esad Ribic

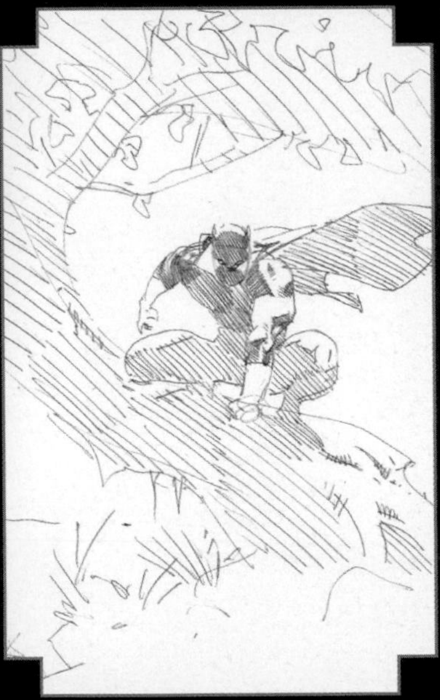
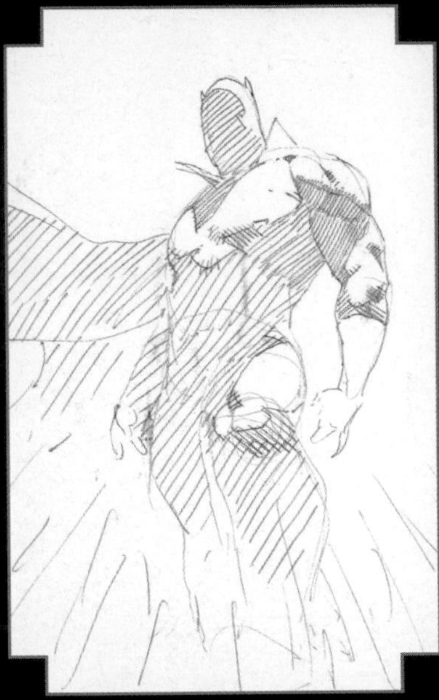
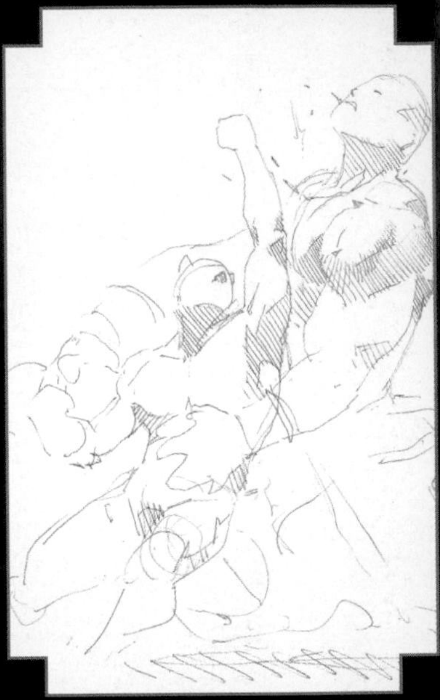

Black Panther #6 Cover Concepts by Kaare Andrews

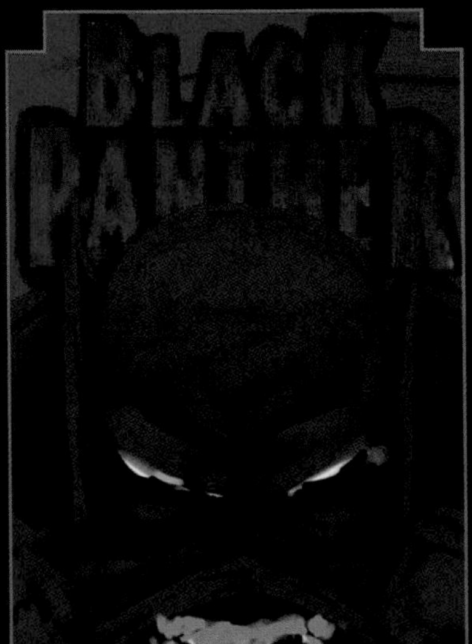
BLACK PANTHER
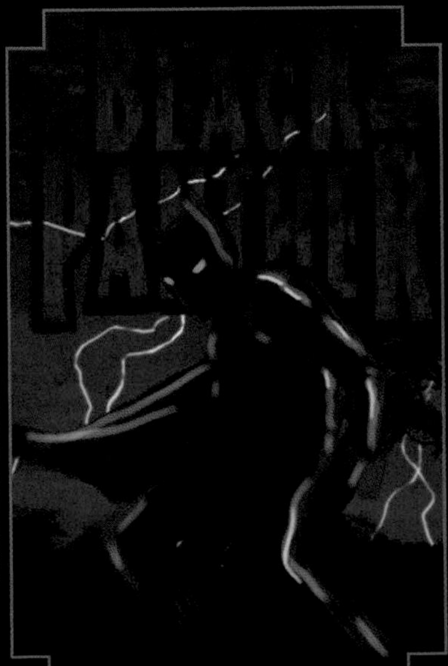
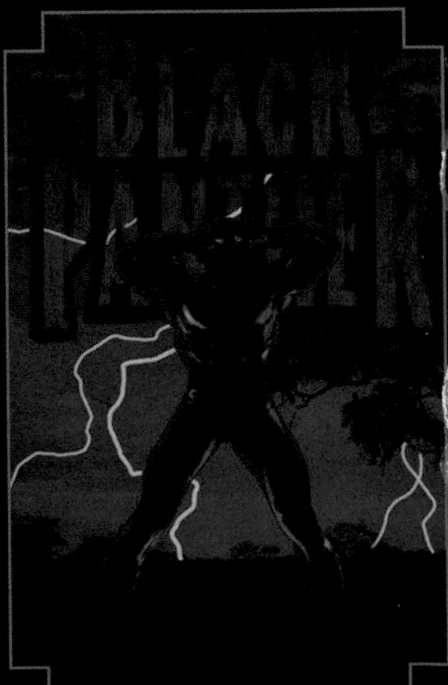